ANATOLIA

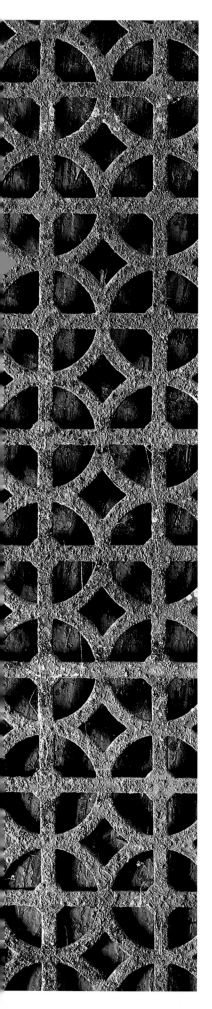
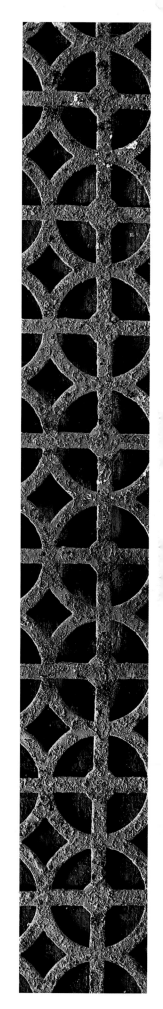

ADVENTURES IN TURKISH COOKING

ANATOLIA

SOMER SIVRIOĞLU
& DAVID DALE

MURDOCH BOOKS

View of Galata Tower and the Old City from
the rooftop bar at the Hotel Marmara, Istanbul.

CONTENTS

DEDICATION

This book has two inspirations: Musa Dağdeviren, who introduced regional Anatolian food to the world long before it was trendy; and Janni Kyritsis, great chef and great friend, who embodies the notion that generosity of spirit crosses all national boundaries.

One of the few surviving Istanbul street markets, in Kadıköy.

ABOUT THE AUTHORS

Somer Sivrioğlu grew up in Istanbul and moved to Sydney when he was twenty-five. He now runs Efendy restaurant in Balmain where he draws on a multitude of cultural influences to recreate the food traditions of his homeland.

David Dale is an Australian political journalist, commentator on popular culture and food and travel writer. His earlier books include *Soffritto: A Return to Italy*; *The Art of Pasta* (with Lucio Galletto); *Essential Places*; and *The Obsessive Traveller or Why I Don't Steal Towels from Great Hotels Anymore*.

Fans of Galatasaray football team gather in Istanbul's *meyhane* district, before losing 6–1 to Real Madrid.

DAVID'S PREFACE

For a while I was keen to call this book *The Garden of Eden*, but my sensible co-author talked me out of it.

The idea came up when we were flying east from Istanbul and I was studying a map of our destination—the town of Gaziantep near the Syrian border. I said to Somer: 'This river that's labelled Firat—is that the Euphrates?' He replied: 'Yes, that's the old name for it.'

In growing excitement, I asked: 'Is the Tigris also on this map?' Somer: 'Yes, just down there, it's called the Dicle [dizh-leh] nowadays.' Me: 'So actually we are headed for the Garden of Eden, where all the fruits and vegetables in the world originated, and where the forbidden apple was probably a fig?' Somer (eyes narrowed): 'Well, I suppose you could say that.'

One of the first things I learned about Somer Sivrioğlu (pronounced 'Sivriolu', with the 'g' silent, as in tagliatelle) is that he prefers science to superstition, and he's inclined to regard references to Adam and Eve with caution. I share his scepticism, but I love a good story, particularly when it's about food. I was charmed by the notion that Anatolian was the world's oldest cuisine.

We'd met three months earlier when a Greek friend took me to lunch at Somer's restaurant—Efendy, in the Sydney suburb of Balmain. The meal we ate shattered my stereotypes about Turkish food, and our conversation demonstrated that Somer was not only a great cook but also a great scholar.

Our Greek friend , Janni Kyritsis, was happy to concede that while Greek cooking had stagnated, Turkish cooking seemed still to be evolving. With a mischievous smile, Somer told us: 'Turkish is one of the three great cuisines of the world, but only Turks know this. The other two are French and Chinese, but the French got their cream sauces from our *yoğurt*, and the Chinese got their dumplings from our *manti*.'

It became apparent that Somer likes to make fun of his countrymen's tendency to claim ownership of every great cooking technique in the Western world, and to cling to absurd food myths that promote Turkish nationalism. He prefers to use the more ancient word Anatolia when talking about the geographical area that is now called Turkey, and to give credit to the many cultures that contributed to the region's food repertoire.

I asked Somer if he'd be interested in doing a book that would challenge old theories about Turkish cooking and create a few new ones; that would give readers a way to recreate classic dishes at home and also help them understand what they're eating when they visit Turkey.

We worked up a pitch to Sue Hines at Murdoch Books, and three months later were flying towards the Garden of Eden. The town of Gaziantep turned out to be very strange. For breakfast, they eat liver *kebaps* or chilli soup. They make the best baklava in the world, using the best pistachios. They proudly preserve a cooking style that has never needed to make compromises with tourism. Whether or not it was once paradise, it was the best possible place for me to begin my lessons in Anatolian culture.

Gaziantep has a tradition that inspired the way we approached this book. Whenever a family has to spend the day rolling the hundreds of tiny meatballs that go into a festive soup called *yuvalama*, they bring in a professional storyteller to keep the rollers from getting bored.

We decided to tell a tale with every recipe. Sometimes we would talk about the mythical origins of the dish or its ingredients, sometimes we would talk about Somer's first experience of the dish, and sometimes we would talk about its place in the rituals and fashions of ancient and modern Anatolia.

Working with Somer, I learned that Anatolian cooks take a pretty relaxed approach to their creations. They rarely use written recipes and, when they do, the instructions tend to be vague, as in 'measure with your eyes', 'add whatever it needs'; or else poetic, as in 'cut into bird's heads' (cubed), 'small as a rat's tooth' (finely chopped) or 'till the dough has the texture of an earlobe'. We've tried to avoid the vagueness but retain the relaxation. While breads and pastries need precise measures, most other recipes can be varied according to your taste—more chilli, less onion, more vegetables, less meat, as you fancy.

The stories and the recipes are told in Somer's voice. I hope you enjoy your conversation with him and share the joy I experienced in learning about an approach to life's greatest pleasure that is still evolving after 5000 years.

DAVID DALE

SOMER'S PREFACE

The 1970s was an eventful decade in Turkey, and not only because I was born then. In 1971, the military staged a coup for the second time (the first one being in 1960); left-wing students and right-wing militants supported by the government were at war with each other; and day and night curfews were in place.

I grew up knowing the difference in sound between a gunshot in the next street and a bomb in the next suburb. Even in the midst of civil war, my *babaanne* (grandma) retained her sense of hospitality. 'Do not close the door, Somer—our neighbours might think we want to keep them away', she would tell me every time I shut the door to the family apartment in Istanbul.

My grandad had bought the apartment building in the Kadıköy neighbourhood after selling his hotel and *hamam* (Turkish bath) in the rural town of Eskişehir. He'd moved the whole family to the multicultural suburb on the Anatolian side of the city, giving one flat to each of his children so the whole family could live near each other. The block felt like a village, with the hallways full of cooking smells floating from open doorways.

I was lucky to be a kid during that time in Turkish history. People still shared food with their neighbours; every store in your suburb knew your name; the butcher would keep all the high-protein offal for families with growing children; and kids from different ethnic backgrounds not only played together but also ate together in whatever house they happened to find themselves around supper time.

We had neighbours with Greek, Armenian and Sephardic Jewish backgrounds, and I was blessed to taste their everyday meals. In an era of curfews, suppression and terror, I felt strangely safe in the company of family, friends and neighbours.

In 1980, Turkey, moving towards a free-market economy, suffered another military coup. My parents separated and I was living in another suburb in another kind of apartment, with double locks on the door. I had more toys and fewer friends, and a lot less diversity in my diet. My friends and I queued for two hours in front of the first McDonald's when it opened in Turkey, so that we could have burgers and Coke.

My priorities began to change after I landed in Australia in 1995. I'd graduated in hospitality from a college in Turkey, and now I was doing my MBA in Sydney, discussing Organisational Behaviour during the day and washing dishes at night (and being told my pan-scrubbing skills were not up to scratch). Living close to Sydney's Chinatown, and eating every cuisine but my own, I re-learned the value of a multicultural society and its contribution to national happiness.

Fast forward to 2007 and I am married to my beautiful wife Aslı. Just after we have our second baby, we open our first restaurant, serving what I imagined to be 'modern Turkish cuisine'. My first menu included okra in truffle oil, crab *mantı* and Turkish-coffee crème brûlée.

Looking back, I think I was silly. I was trying to impress by using the trendy ingredients of the time. I wasn't being true to myself or my culture. My excuse for playing around with the recipes was that I thought I didn't have access to the kind of produce I could have found in Turkey, so it would be impossible to cook at the same quality.

My mind was opened by a visit from my culinary hero, Musa Dağdeviren, from the world-famous Çiya restaurant in Kadıköy. When I picked him up at the airport, I apologised that Australian ingredients would be limiting. He asked if there was a Chinatown in Sydney and soon he was showing me all the wild weeds, fruits, vegetables and greens he could use. I'd worked just next door to those markets and I'd never noticed. During that visit, Musa made the best 'Sumac salad' I'd ever eaten using a native Australian fruit called Davidson plum instead of sumac.

He showed me that Turkish cooking is less about particular ingredients and more about philosophy. It's about sitting at a table in a Black Sea village, sharing a plate of Armenian *topik*, Kurdish *kebap*, Jewish *boyoz* and Greek *tarama*, and washing down the meal with a glass of *rakı* or *ayran*. It's about the ways different cultures have taken advantage of the abundance of produce in the area now called Anatolia.

In Australia, I'm regarded as a Turkish chef with a modern presentation. In Turkey, I'm regarded as an Australian chef experimenting with some sort of Turkish 'fusion'. I think I'm simply doing what the peoples of Anatolia have done for millennia—getting the best out of local produce with techniques tested and proved by my ancestors.

My family and friends are a diverse bunch. We support different football teams, different religions, different politicians, and different sexual orientations. We come from different ethnicities. So we are just like Turkey. We argue a lot—as the peoples of Anatolia have done for thousands of years. But when we sit together around a table, we are united by one idea—we want to enjoy our food. My hope is that this book will do that for you too.

SOMER SIVRIOĞLU

The Kadıköy apartment block where Somer grew up: 'We had Greek, Armenian and Sephardic Jewish neighbours, and I was blessed to taste their meals'

ESSENTIALS

HISTORY, INGREDIENTS & TECHNIQUES

ESSENTIALS

We called this book *Anatolia* because that word best conveys the history and diversity of a land that only started using the term Türkiye (Land of the Turks) in the eleventh century, and only became the Turkish Republic in 1923. The word Anatolia is used to show that our book includes the delicious Arab, Armenian, Assyrian, Balkan, Greek, Jewish, Kurdish and Romany contributions to the way Turks eat.

Turkish people have a passion for eating well. While they're enjoying breakfast, they're planning dinner. They cook a lot at home, but everyone has a favourite *kebap* shop, a favourite lunch *lokanta*, a favourite source of baklava, and a favourite street stall for sobering up with stuffed intestines after a long night drinking *rakı* in a *meyhane*. There is no time of day when you can't get interesting food, so instead of dividing this book into conventional chapters such as starters, mains, desserts and party food, we've arranged the chapters in the form of a typical Turkish eating day.

A LITTLE HISTORY

The first use of the term Anatolia was in clay tablets written 4300 years ago in the cuneiform letters of Mesopotamia, so that suggested a timespan for this book. (We could have taken you back 11,000 years, because the world's first human settlement has been discovered at Göbekli Tepe, near the town of Şanlıurfa in southeastern Anatolia, but information on the cuisine of that period is scarce.)

The Hittites may not have been the first organised civilisation on earth (that title should probably go to the Sumerians), but they do seem to have been the first to use iron weapons; the first to make wine and cultivate olives, almonds and apricots; and were the speakers of a language that turned into most of the dialects of modern Europe.

The Hittite Empire was at its peak 3500 years ago, and Troy was a west-coast branch. The defeat of Troy about 3200 years ago (as reported by Homer) was part of a Greek conquest of Anatolia that was confirmed by Alexander the Great about 2300 years ago. About 2600 years ago, a Greek demigod named Byzas founded the city that came to be called Byzantion (Byzantium), then New Rome, then Constantinople, and finally Istanbul (which literally translates as 'into the city').

The Greek Empire was replaced by the Roman Empire around 2000 years ago and Constantinople became the imperial capital when Rome fell to barbarians in the fourth century.

The last vestiges of Roman-Christian rule were eliminated in the eleventh century by the invading Seljuks (an extended family of Muslims from the northeast, whose empire also included Persia). The Seljuks spoke a language called Turkic.

Western Anatolia got involved in various disputes with European crusaders passing through on their way to Jerusalem, but stayed in Seljuk control until the arrival, around 1300, of an army under the command of a military strategist named Osman in Turkish and known to English speakers as Ottoman. This commander gave his name to an empire that proceeded to invade lands we now call Greece, Hungary, Bulgaria, Iraq, Iran, Syria, Egypt, Libya, Tunisia and Algeria.

One of the obsessions of the Ottoman Turks was the art of food, and at the peak of their power (under Sultan Süleyman the Magnificent in the sixteenth century), the Topkapı Palace in Istanbul had 400 cooks using ingredients and techniques from all over the empire.

In the sixteenth century, Anatolia welcomed Jews and Muslims who were expelled from Spain and Portugal by Christian fundamentalists. They brought new approaches to the way ingredients could be combined.

Then, in the seventeenth century, Anatolia welcomed Spanish and Portuguese traders who brought strange and exciting ingredients from the New World—tomatoes, peppers and potatoes.

Ottoman rule collapsed during the First World War, and in 1923 a bunch of modernisers took

An Istanbul ferry crosses the Bosphorus from the
Asian side of the city to the European shore.

over. The first president of the Turkish republic was Mustafa Kemal Atatürk, a soldier who had defeated the Allied invaders at Gelibolu (Gallipoli) in 1915. He abolished the dominance of the Islamic clergy (known as 'the caliphate'), gave women the vote and created a secular democracy. As part of a treaty between the new nation and the Allies, Anatolians of Greek background were told to move to Greece while Muslims of Turkish background moved from Greece to Turkey.

So you can see why Anatolian food is likely to have a fair bit in common with the cooking of Greece, Syria, Egypt, Armenia, Italy, Spain, Iran and even Hungary, and why so much culinary mythology has developed over the past four millennia.

Myths make good stories, so in this book we're going to recount the myths and then try to analyse where they deviate from reality. We are not going to waste time with disputes about which ethnic, religious or national group 'owns' a particular dish.

The cooking in a particular area is dictated by the climate, the soil, the range of ingredients available, the survival techniques developed over the millennia and the cultural assumptions passed on by successive waves of settlers. It's perfectly possible for a dish to be simultaneously Turkish, Greek, Italian and Syrian, or to be none of the above if it appeared long before those names were on any map. When in doubt, our default position is to describe a dish as 'adapted from the Hittite'.

So how is a non-Turkish-speaking visitor going to tap into this historical, geographical and cultural abundance? In Istanbul most waiters speak enough English to respond to your enthusiastic request to try a range of local specialities and avoid the tourist clichés. Outside Istanbul and the coastal resort towns, two phrases might come in handy in a lunch *lokanta* or *meze* bar: '*Herşey* [hershay] *den az az ortaya lütfen*', which means 'Can I have a variety of small servings, please' (literally, 'Little little in the middle')

and '*Ben de şundan* [shundan] *alabilir miyim, lütfen*' ('Could I have those, please'), with which you should point to a dish on another table or on display on the counter.

After the recipes, we've provided a list of recommendations on eating places worth visiting in Istanbul and around the countryside. In the unlikely event you don't find great food in Turkey, cook from this book and discover how it should have tasted.

THE REGIONS

The geographers divide modern Turkey into seven regions, which vary greatly in their approach to cooking …

The Marmara region (main cities Bursa, Edirne and Istanbul) contained all the palaces from which the Ottoman sultans controlled their empire, so Turkey's wealth, industry and gourmet faddism are concentrated here. Istanbul, with its 20 million residents, is the heart of the nation (although the political capital is Ankara, 400 km/250 miles away). You can find excellent examples of every region's specialities without leaving Istanbul, because every successful regional restaurant dreams of opening a branch there (even at the risk of losing authenticity). In Istanbul, go for seafood, because the Marmara Sea supplies tasty fish. Edirne is known for its sautéed liver. Bursa is known for *Iskender kebap*.

The Mediterranean coast (main cities Antalya and Adana) grows most of Turkey's fruits and greens. Hatay is the most multicultural city in Turkey, with large communities of Arabs, Christians and Jews—which makes its cuisine fascinating. Antalya is nicknamed 'Antalsky' in the summer months, because of the invasion of Russian tourists. That's when serious foodies leave the coast and head for the mountains.

In the wild and windy Black Sea region (main cities Trabzon and Samsun) the obsessions are

hazelnuts, corn, salad greens and a fish called *hamsi* (somewhere between a sardine and an anchovy). There are alleged to be more than 200 recipes for it, including a *hamsi* jam.

Not surprisingly, the Aegean coast (main cities Izmir and Bodrum) is Greek-influenced. The Greek islands are so close that at night Turks in the Aegean region can see the headlights of cars driving around Kos, Lesbos, Chios and Samos. No wonder it was so easy for the Greeks to invade Troy. It's a wine-making area, more liberal than the rest of Turkey in its attitude to alcohol. The best food is found in its *meyhanes*, which do seafood specialities, and olive oil-braised greens and other vegetables.

Central Anatolia (main cities Ankara, Konya and Kayseri) is the agricultural heartland, growing most of the vegetables and grains. The restaurants tend to specialise in lamb, *börek* pastries and casseroles with bulgur. Konya was one of the first places settled by the nomadic Turkic people when they arrived in the eleventh century, and has become a culinary and cultural centre. The Armenian community in Kayseri made the region famous for beef *pastırma* and *sucuk* sausage. Butter is the main cooking medium here, not olive oil.

Eastern Anatolia (main cities Van, Kars and Malatya) borders Iran, Armenia, Azerbaijan and Georgia, and has a large Kurdish population. On its western side, the climate is ideal for growing apricots, figs and grapes that turn into powerful red wines. On the eastern side, the cattle, sheep and goats produce wonderful cheeses.

Southeastern Anatolia (main cities Gaziantep, Şanlıurfa and Mardin) has a cuisine influenced by neighbouring Syria and Iraq. It produces the world's best pistachios and thus the world's best baklava. The climate is harsh in winter and hot and dry in summer, so they've perfected drying, preserving and pickling techniques to keep their eaters happy all year. The famous *isot* chilli pepper and *çiğ köfte* (raw veal and bulgur wheat) come from Şanlıurfa.

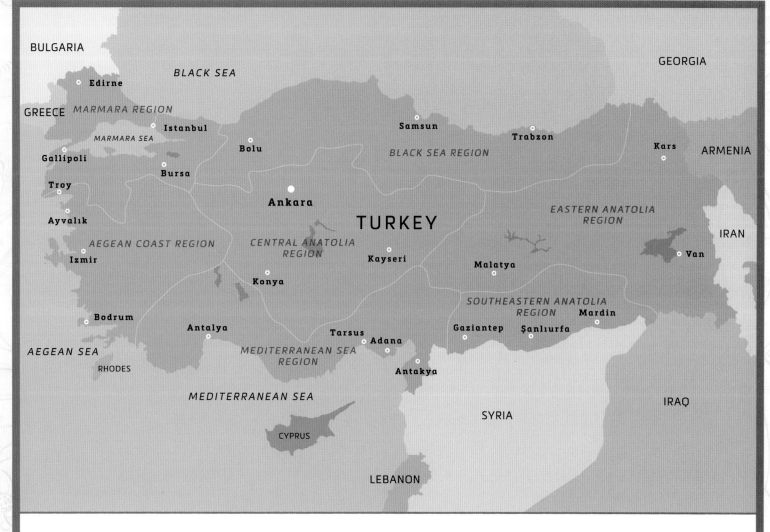

BULGARIA

BLACK SEA

GEORGIA

○ Edirne

GREECE *MARMARA REGION*

MARMARA SEA

Istanbul ○

Samsun ○

Trabzon ○

BLACK SEA REGION

Kars ○ ARMENIA

Bolu ○

Gallipoli

Bursa ○

Troy

Ankara ●

TURKEY

EASTERN ANATOLIA REGION

IRAN

Ayvalık

AEGEAN COAST REGION

CENTRAL ANATOLIA REGION

Kayseri ○

Malatya ○

Van ○

Izmir ○

Konya ○

SOUTHEASTERN ANATOLIA REGION

Mardin ○

Bodrum ○

Antalya ○

Tarsus

Gaziantep ○ **Şanlıurfa** ○

AEGEAN SEA

Adana ○

RHODES

MEDITERRANEAN SEA REGION

Antakya ○

MEDITERRANEAN SEA

IRAQ

SYRIA

CYPRUS

LEBANON

THE FOOD REGIONS OF TURKEY:

AEGEAN SEA: Olives, wines, salads, herbs, wild weeds and seafood
BLACK SEA: *Hamsi*, tea, corn, hazelnuts and pide bread
CENTRAL ANATOLIA: *Börek* pastries, beef *pastirma*, lamb casseroles and fruit molasses
EASTERN ANATOLIA: Cheeses, dried fruits, grains and lamb
MARMARA: *Mezes*, white wine, *rakı*, small fish and puddings
MEDITERRANEAN SEA: Large fish, salads, oranges, lemons and figs
SOUTHEASTERN ANATOLIA: *Kebaps*, bulgur wheat, baklava and peppers

THE FIFTEEN FAVOURITE INGREDIENTS

BREAD

Growing up in Istanbul, the only bread I knew was *ekmek*—a torpedo-shaped roll that was made every morning in a wood-fired stone oven by a bakery a few doors from my apartment. No Turks bake their own bread at home because the price of bread has been subsidised by the government since Ottoman times (when the sultans followed the Roman emperors' practice of pacifying the populace with 'bread and circuses').

Bread is subject to a multitude of laws specifying minimum size of loaf (250 g/9 oz), minimum flour type, maximum salt content (1.5 per cent) and hygiene for shops and delivery trucks (delivery truck needs to be washable), and can only use flour, yeast, salt and water.

Although my family was not religious, the holy month of Ramadan was an exciting time for me, because a new kind of bread appeared—a round and fluffy creation called pide, designed to be consumed hot as soon as the faithful break their fast at sunset. The cooks elaborated on the basic *ekmek* by putting *yoğurt* or molasses on top. I later discovered that if I visited southeastern Anatolia I could eat pide all year round because it's their standard form of bread. (Pide is not to be confused with pita, which is not a word used much in Turkey. The flatbread called pita by other cultures is called *lavaş* in Turkey.)

So if you go to the southeast of Turkey and ask for *ekmek*, you will get pide. If you ask for pide on the west coast, they will tell you 'It's not Ramadan yet'. In the Black Sea, if you ask for pide, they will ask you 'with cheese or lamb?' In Istanbul tourist restaurants they will serve you pide in the form of a balloon, made by throwing cardboard into the stone oven in the last few seconds of the baking process to create a sudden blast of heat that will make the bread puff up. Do not try this at home.

YOĞURT AND OTHER DAIRY

Being nomadic people, the Turkic groups who reached Anatolia in the eleventh century first drank horse milk. When they settled in one spot, they domesticated cows, sheep and goats, and found new flavour sensations.

Although I am sceptical about the Turkish habit of taking credit for all sorts of culinary creations, I think we are safe in saying those invaders gave *yoğurt* to the world (which is why I've used the Turkish spelling throughout this book). Turks are now the biggest consumers of plain *yoğurt* on the planet—our average consumption is 24 kg (over 50 lb) per person per year. We use it in or with just about everything.

For my grandma, *yoğurt* was as much a medicine as a food. A burnt hand got a *yoğurt* wrapping, a sunburn meant your whole back, neck and face were covered with it. If you got food poisoning, it settled your stomach. My grandma bought her *yoğurt* from a man who walked down her street at the same time every day carrying two pots suspended from a pole that went across his shoulders.

I like to say that I can offer four recipes in which the only ingredients are *yoğurt* and time— in its basic form as a sauce; thickened to become a dip (by hanging in a muslin cloth for three hours over a pot to catch the drips); thickened and sun-dried to become a cheese (hanging for twelve hours); and diluted to become a drink (which we call *ayran*—and okay, I must admit water is another ingredient, unless you got it from the pot under the bag in which you made the cheese).

To make your own *yoğurt*:

First buy a full-fat natural yoğurt (ideally pot-set). Boil 1 litre (35 fl oz/4 cups) of milk for 5 minutes and let it cool until you can keep your finger in it for 10 seconds. Stir 1 tablespoon of the commercial yoğurt through it and whisk with a fork to aerate. Cover the pot and leave it overnight in a warm place (in winter, wrap it in a blanket and keep it in the warmest part of the house). It should have turned to yoğurt within 8 hours, and then you can keep it in the fridge. You should eat it within 5 days, which won't be difficult if you're cooking Turkish recipes.

Butter is the main cooking medium in eastern Anatolia (on the west coast they follow the Greeks in preferring olive oil). Some of my recipes involve the use of clarified butter (ghee). If you want to make your own ghee:

Gözleme are a kind of pancake made popular by Yörük people who bring their food stalls from the mountains to coastal villages.

Nose to tail eating is common in Turkey, with two types of butcher shops: those that sell prime cuts and mince, and those that specialise in offal.

Melt butter over very low heat and when it starts to sizzle, pour it into a bowl and put it in the fridge. Next day, scrape the layer of fat off the top. The liquid at the bottom is ghee.

FETA AND OTHER CHEESES

A text published by the University of Kars (on Turkey's eastern border) identifies 193 types of cheese commonly used in Anatolia—twenty-three of them made in Kars. The favourite type is 'white', a variation on the Greek feta. Mostly it's made from cow's milk, but sometimes from sheep's or goat's or a mixture. It's an essential component of breakfast, while other cheeses start to appear later in the day.

Sheep were first domesticated in Anatolia around 10,000 years ago and, soon after that, the habit of storing milk in the stomachs of sheep produced the first cheese (because the milk reacted with the stomach enzymes, known as rennet).

The first written reference to cheese is in *The Iliad*, where Homer describes a wounded soldier being treated with a mixture of wine, barley and goat's cheese.

Next comes *kaşar*, a semi-hard yellow cheese often melted on toast. For the recipes in this book I've tried to suggest alternatives that might be available in deprived English-speaking countries, but when you're in Turkey, I urge you to try every regional artisanal cheese you can find, because the more unusual types are at risk of disappearing.

LAMB AND LESSER MEATS

Yes, we do eat chicken and beef (never pork), but I must admit that 80 per cent of the meat consumed in Turkey is lamb. We see it as a main meal, an ingredient in *kebaps*, and a flavouring for rice. We use every part of it, and in this book you'll find recipes for its head, liver and testicles. In 2012, somebody did a census and found that Turkey contained 8 million goats, 14 million cows and 28 million sheep.

Lamb was easily bred in the Anatolian climate, and became hallowed by religious ritual very early in our history. A common prayer goes: 'If you give me this, I will kill a sheep in your name and give it to the needy.'

Around 3000 years ago, so the holy texts tell us, the prophet Abraham sacrificed a sheep instead of his son after passing a test imposed by an angel sent from God. Many villages celebrate this in a religious holiday during which a lamb is tethered outside your house all day, then slaughtered, sliced and distributed to your neediest neighbours (you can only keep a third for yourself).

During the four-day religious festival called Kurban Bayramı, it's traditional for rich families to sacrifice a sheep and distribute it to the needy. In the past you'd go and select the animal yourself and watch it being slaughtered with appropriate prayer readings. Nowadays, busy people organise the whole thing online, and never see the sheep or its parts.

There are two varieties of lamb: those with a fatty tail and those with a thin tail. The fat-tailed sheep are highly prized by eastern Turks, who love the flavour of the tail fat, which melts at low temperatures. Some areas use tail fat the way the French use butter—to enrich a casserole. *Kebaps* are healthier because the fat drips off into the embers.

SEAFOOD

Turkey is girt by sea on three sides—the Black one at the top, the Aegean on the left and the Mediterranean on the bottom. The seafood varies hugely between regions, getting bigger the further south you go.

Turks don't feel the need for complex recipes for fish, and they don't bother much with fillets. The rule is grill the fish whole if large, and fry the fish whole if small, then serve with lemon and rocket (arugula). They get more imaginative with mussels, calamari, octopus, scallops and shrimps.

Everyone agrees the best fish come from Istanbul's Marmara Sea, which connects the Aegean with the Black, and the best month to eat it is September.

I grew up fishing in the Marmara with my father, who had his own boat and knew how the currents and the seasons affected the availability of the fish. Nowadays, fishing in that area is banned between April and early September, but once the ban is lifted, you will be astounded by the variety at the Kumkapı fish market, and you can eat wonderfully in restaurants along the Bosphorus (I've named a few of my favourites in the recommendations at the end of this book). The fish you should ask for is *lüfer*, which is usually translated as bluefish.

In this book I've tried to replace varieties unique to Turkey with similar fish available in English-speaking countries.

EGGPLANT AND OTHER VEGETABLES

Eggplants (aubergines) are even more common than lamb in Turkish recipes (usually disguised under poetic titles rather than their own name, *patlıcan*), so you might imagine we grew them first. But they seem to have been brought into Anatolia from India by Arab traders at least 3000 years ago. Per capita, Turks are the greatest consumers of eggplants in the world.

The best way to cook eggplant is to pierce the skin with a fork and put it directly over fire—either the embers of a barbecue or the gas flame of your stove. Be careful, though. Historians writing about Istanbul in the seventeenth century record frequent destruction of property due to 'eggplant fires', because householders would put them over flames and walk away, letting them drop onto the wooden floor.

You should stay nearby, turning the eggplant with tongs until the skin is blackened. Let it cool and drip in a colander for 10 minutes, then scrape out the flesh. If you're not going to eat it straight away, keep it in water into which you have squeezed half a lemon.

ÇOK. SULU
KOKULW
HARIKA
5. TL.

The handwritten sign says: Very juicy, wonderfully fragrant 5 Turkish lira.
Opposite: Somer and his father Güngör checking the daily catch at an Aegean village fish shop.

Our next most beloved ingredient is the tomato (*domates*)—which you're going to tell me should not be in this section because it is actually a fruit (but you'll never convince a Turk of this botanical detail). Its omnipresence is surprising since it only entered the Anatolian repertoire in the eighteenth century (imported from the Americas). Turkey is the fourth-biggest producer in the world, eating 11 million tonnes of tomatoes a year.

Every market across the land has tubs piled high with mounds of bright-red tomato paste (usually sitting next to a tub overflowing with even brighter peppers). We use it to boost the flavour of everything but fish (which works better with fresh tomato).

You can make your own tomato paste like this:

Slice 1 kg (2 lb 4 oz) of over-ripe tomatoes into quarters and let them rest for a day under a cloth. Then push them through a coarse sieve to get rid of the skins and most of the seeds. Wrap the pulp in a muslin cloth (cheesecloth) and put a weight on the parcel to squeeze the water out overnight.

Stir 1 tablespoon of olive oil and 1 teaspoon of rock salt through the pulp, and simmer for 1 hour, stirring regularly. Put the paste in clean jars, with some more olive oil at the top, and tightly seal the lids. You can keep the paste in the fridge, topping up with more olive oil each time you dig into it.

POMEGRANATE AND OTHER FRUITS

The pomegranate has been a symbol of opulent eating around the Mediterranean for thousands of years. A tradition going back to the Greek occupation of Anatolia is throwing a pomegranate into the doorway of your house on New Year's Eve to ensure abundance for the following year.

Turkey is the third-biggest pomegranate producer in the world, (after Iran and India). Turks call it a 'superfruit', believing it to contain an antioxidant that lowers cholesterol.

Every Turkish supermarket sells special-purpose pomegranate seeders and pomegranate juicers, but if you can't find these devices near you, don't despair. Cut the pomegranate in half, horizontally. Put one half face down over a bowl and tap gently all over the back. The seeds should pop out. Then you can crush them to make juice or use them to decorate dishes, savoury or sweet.

Turkish supermarkets also sell pomegranate molasses. To make your own:

Simmer the pomegranate juice in a heavy-based saucepan until it has reduced to a quarter its original volume. There's no need to add sugar.

You can use it in any dish where you might use balsamic vinegar or lemon. In my restaurant, I serve my bread with a saucer containing two tablespoons of olive oil and a teaspoon of pomegranate molasses. I also like to baste lamb in it, because it caramelises the exterior.

When I arrived in Sydney, I was delighted to learn that the Australian term for English people is pommie, supposedly because their faces quickly go the colour of my favourite fruit under the hot Australian sun.

The next most popular fruit in Turkey is the fig, which is at its best in autumn. It was apparently the first crop to be cultivated in the world—in southeastern Anatolia, of course, about 10,000 years ago. We use unripened figs in jams, fresh figs in salads, and dried figs in deserts and dolma stuffings.

Turkey supplies 80 per cent of the world's dried fruits, particularly apricots, dates and raisins. The Ottoman sultans embraced the Persian passion for combining dried fruits with stewed or roasted meats, as you'll see in our Dinner chapter.

PEPPERS

Before the appearance of chillies and peppers in the seventeenth century, the cooks in the Ottoman kitchens used huge quantities of ground black pepper to satisfy the jaded sultans' need for culinary kicks. In the sixteenth century, peppercorns were a major trading commodity, with 1 kg (2 lb 4 oz) costing as much as 35 kg (over 75 lb) of bulgur. Then the long red and green peppers and chillies arrived from the Americas, and the bottom dropped out of the black pepper market, because chilli proved to be a useful preservative as well as a flavour booster.

Heat preference varies hugely around Anatolia. In the southeastern culinary triangle of Şanlıurfa, Gaziantep and Maraş, spice is everything. They give chillies to children to chew on as an appetite stimulant. In villages near Şanlıurfa in late summer, you can see chillies laid out all over the flat roofs, then covered with sheets at night to 'sweat' them. The famous Maraş and *isot* chilli flakes are exported around the world, including to my restaurant in Sydney. Maraş is stronger, with an intense 'mouthburning' flavour. *Isot* (also known as Urfa pepper) is milder but longer lasting.

When I arrived in Australia, I was disappointed to find the peppers were much bigger, with thicker skins, than the ones I knew in Turkey. I have shifted to bullhorn peppers in some of my recipes, because they're closer to the taste and texture I knew in Turkey. Feel free to use whatever form you can find near you, but remember that smaller is better, especially if you are stuffing them.

BULGUR AND OTHER GRAINS

Wheat was first cultivated in eastern Anatolia about 10,000 years ago, and it's likely that before the grains were turned into flour for bread, they were stripped of their skins and boiled, to become a belly filler and a base for roasted meat or vegetables. Much later in history rice arrived from China, and the principle became: rice for the rich, bulgur for the poor. So the poor were better nourished.

In Turkey, bulgur is now sold in four grind classifications: extra fine (for kneading with raw meat in *çiğ köfte*); fine (for lentil *köfte*); coarse (for mixing into salads); and extra coarse (for

Drying red peppers for winter in Oğuzeli in southeastern Anatolia.

Pistachios and other nuts and pulses for sale at a village shop.

pilav, served with stews). To make an interesting bulgur pilav:

Sauté 1 finely chopped onion in butter for 5 minutes, then add 500 g (1 lb 2 oz) of bulgur and sauté for another 10 minutes. Add 750 ml (26 fl oz/3 cups) of water or chicken stock and simmer, covered, for another 10 minutes. Add a chopped tomato and/or a chopped capsicum (pepper) if you like. Decorate it with chopped flat-leaf (Italian) parsley, and serve it with a stew or kebaps or just with yoğurt as a dish in itself.

Another form of wheat, called freekeh, became trendy in Anatolia 4000 years ago and is now becoming trendy again in the English-speaking world. It is a green wheat that has been roasted (in southeastern Turkey they set fire to the wheat field to burn off the chaff and give the grains a smoky taste).

The name literally means 'rubbed', and of course it comes with a story: around 4000 years ago a bunch of Hittites harvested their wheat when it was unripe and stored it away in a wooden shed, which caught fire. When they recovered the stalks and rubbed off the blackened husks, they found the grains smelled and tasted delicious, and a fad was born.

Freekeh is easier to digest than bulgur, which can bloat you if you eat too much. A bowl of freekeh brings a beautiful aroma to the table, and makes an ideal base for a chicken stew or a healthy dose of fibre mixed into a salad.

RICE

In Ottoman times, rice (*pirinç*), initially imported from China, was a treat for the aristocrats. If you visited Istanbul's Topkapı Palace 500 years ago, you'd be offered three beautiful dishes—*dane-i-sarı* (yellow rice, made with saffron), *dane-i-yeşil* (green rice, made with spinach or fresh herbs), and *dane-i-kızıl* (red rice made with pomegranate or barberries). Nowadays, every class eats it, but more in Turkey's west than east.

There is much debate about how to get the best out of rice, but here's my preferred way to make an interesting rice pilav, learned from my mother-in-law:

Soak 200 g (7 oz/1 cup) of rice in 500 ml (17 fl oz/2 cups) of warm water and 1 tablespoon of salt for 1 hour. Rinse the rice and toss with 1 tablespoon of melted butter over medium heat for 2 minutes, then add 250 ml (9 fl oz/1 cup) of water (or chicken stock) and 1 grated tomato, and simmer, covered, for 15 minutes.

PASTRIES—YUFKA, FILO AND BÖREKS

Stuffing and baking pastries is a huge fad in Turkey, but it's rare for Turks to make the basic pastry at home, because so many shops sell sheets of *yufka* (for *böreks*) and filo (for baklava). The word *yufka* meant 'thin' in the old dialect, and that's exactly why you risk frustration if you try it at home.

But if you're game, this is what you need to do to make *yufka* sheets:

Mix 1 kg (2 lb 4 oz) of strong flour with 2 tablespoons of salt and 250 ml (9 fl oz/1 cup) of water. Knead for about 10 minutes until a flexible dough is formed. Divide the dough into ping-pong-ball-sized lumps. Covering your work surface, hands and a thin rolling pin with lots of flour to prevent sticking, roll and pull each ball out into a sheet about 50 cm (20 in) across. If you have a pasta machine, you could use that to start the rolling process, but you'll have to finish it by hand.

Now you need to partly cook the pastry. You'll need a large wok, which will become a device the Turks call a saç.

Scrub the wok clean, inside and out, and put the wok upside down over a lit burner on your stove. Drape a sheet of dough over the wok, and as soon as you see it start to bubble, put another sheet of pastry over it, and flip the pair over. Cook the bottom side of the second

sheet for 1 minute or so, then remove the pair (put them on a board next to you) and start again with another sheet. You're cooking every sheet on one side only, then adding its partner and flipping.

You can keep the partly cooked yufka sheets in the fridge for 3 days. When making böreks, always put the stuffing on the uncooked side.

The process for making filo is similar, except that the dough sometimes contains eggs, and must be rolled out even thinner than *yufka*—as thin as a page of this book, in fact.

In the recipes you're about to read, we'll show you how to make other forms of pastry (*gözleme, katmer, mille-feuille*), but we'll suggest buying commercial filo, as Turkish families do.

PISTACHIOS AND OTHER NUTS

Almonds and pistachios are the only two nuts mentioned in the ancient religious text that is accepted by Muslims, Jews and Christians (known as the Tevrat, the Torah or the Old Testament of the Bible). Both were first cultivated in Anatolia. Ground almonds became the basis for the favourite sauce of the early Ottoman sultans, and crushed pistachios became the basis for their favourite desert—baklava.

The world's best pistachios come from Gaziantep in southeastern Anatolia. That's been the case since at least the year 100, when the Roman emperor Trajan organised regular deliveries of pistachios from the village of Zeugma to Rome. They are expensive but versatile—the wild form makes an interesting form of coffee. Turkey is the third-largest producer in the world, but Iranian and Californian varieties are arguably of lesser quality. Gaziantep pistachios are harvested in midsummer, when they are small enough to be best for baklava.

Turkey produces 75 per cent of the world's hazelnuts, mostly in the Black Sea region. They are roasted for snacking or turned into oil for frying, paste as a breakfast spread, and meal for cakes.

CHICKPEAS AND OTHER PULSES

When you go out drinking of an evening anywhere in Turkey, you're likely to be given a bowl of what you think are salty nuts. They are more likely to be *leblebi* (toasted chickpeas), bought from nut shops that cook them all day in giant *leblebi* roasters. Chickpeas, now used to bulk out countless casseroles, were first cultivated in Anatolia more than 8000 years ago. In the fifteenth century, a vizier working for the sultan in the Topkapı Palace became famous for surprising his guests by hiding a golden chickpea in one of the dishes in every banquet.

The next most popular pulse is lentils. The green variety is produced in central Anatolia and used whole in sautés. It's known as the poor man's beef, because of its high iron content. The softer red variety is produced in the southeast and used in soups or as a paste in *köfte*.

Turks also use dried beans a lot—in particular the small white ones the Italians call cannellini—and in this book so do we. It's vital to soak these beans overnight, rinse them and change the water several times to get rid of the chemicals that can upset your digestion.

ONION AND GARLIC

My friend Musa Dağdeviren, the scholar-chef who sparked the revival of regional Anatolian cooking (see Dinner chapter), was once asked to name the three ingredients he would take with him to a desert island. He said: 'Onions, garlic, and spring onions, because as long as I have them, I can make a delicious meal with anything else I find on the island.'

Onion was the key flavour-booster in Anatolian food long before the arrival of peppers from the Americas, and it remains dominant. Every home-style Turkish appetiser or main course has onion or garlic or both at its heart, often with leek as well.

My preference is to use red onions in salads and white or brown onions in cooking, and always to sauté onions for 5 minutes longer than garlic.

It's common in Turkey to use the green shoots of fresh garlic, which are most readily available in spring. They look like thin spring onions. In some recipes, we've suggested garlic shoots, but if you can't find them, toss whole spring onions in equal amounts of olive oil and finely crushed garlic to achieve a similar flavour.

We love leeks in winter, particularly braised in olive oil as part of a *meze* spread, or as wrappers instead of pastry around mince or rice parcels.

PARSLEY AND OTHER HERBS

Anytime I talk about parsley in this book, I mean the flat-leaf kind English-speakers call continental or Italian parsley. You never see the curly type in Turkey, but you see the flat-leaf kind everywhere. Don't feel compelled to follow the Turkish habit of sprinkling it on anything savoury. I know parsley is good for you, but I fear it is used too often as decoration and in my restaurant I have to spend a lot of time picking it off dishes my cooks send out of the kitchen.

Mint is our second favourite herb, used fresh in salads and dried as decoration on soups and dumplings. It is hardly ever associated with lamb—Turks regard that as an English eccentricity, preferring to use oregano or thyme (which is also used to make an invigorating tea in the southeast). We like to use bay leaves with fish, marjoram with chicken, and wild weeds (nettles) with eggs and pastries—but only on the west coast.

Herbal teas are central to Turkish life, seen as suitable treatments for colds, anxiety and stomach upsets. Wild thyme (*zahter*) tea is popular in the southeast for aiding digestion, and you'll also find teas made with linden, mountain sage and wild nettles.

THE EQUIPMENT YOU SHOULD HAVE

- Big sharp knife for mincing (ideally a *zırh* or a mezzaluna knife)
- Large, thick wooden board
- Long tongs for the barbecue
- Mortar and pestle
- Baking trays for pastries
- Plastic wrap
- Paper towel
- Baking paper
- Aluminium foil
- Skewers—bamboo and three sizes of metal (round, narrow-flat, wide-flat)
- Small and large clay pots for baking
- Wooden spoons
- Mixer/ blender/ food processor
- Whisk
- Regular rolling pin
- Thin (stick) rolling pin
- Wide heavy-based saucepans
- Pizza stone or unglazed terracotta tile
- Charcoal grill (broiler) or wood-fire barbecue
- Muslin (cheesecloth), for straining
- Ideally, a pomegranate seeder
- Turkish coffee pot (*cezve*)
- Spice grinder
- Sealable jars (for pickles and preserves)

Turkish home cooking is about doing what's comfortable with the equipment that's available, so if you don't have any of the above, adapt with what's in your cupboard.

THE WINES OF ANATOLIA

It is believed that the first place in the world where wine was made was Anatolia—by those reliable old Hittites, around 6000 years ago. The Hittites used the Sumerian term *viyana* for the alcohol derived from grapes—a word which some Turkish scholars think was the origin of a name to the capital of Austria (just as the Persian word *ungur* for grapes, gave a name to the capital of Turkey, Ankara).

Jewish and Muslim texts tell us that the first crop planted by Noah after he got off the ark was grapes, so his family could celebrate with a cup of wine. That supposedly happened on the southeastern side of Anatolia. Nowadays, excellent red wines are still made in that hot, dry climate.

The Greeks who conquered Troy thought the west-coast town of Nysa was the birthplace of white wine—and of the drunken demigod known to them as Dionysos (Dionysius) and to the Romans as Bacchus. Around 3000 years ago, white wines from western Anatolia were exported all around the Mediterranean in giant two-handled jugs called *amphoras*, some with a capacity of 75 litres (over 15 gallons). Thousands of *amphoras* have been found in ships that sank in the Aegean Sea, stamped with details of the wine's quality, including a recommendation that it be diluted in the proportion two cups wine to five cups water, or improved by the addition of honey.

Wine became a key component of celebrations for every ethnic, tribal or religious group that ever ruled Anatolia. Even some Ottoman sultans, supposedly devout Muslims, consumed vast quantities at palace banquets, while publicly disapproving of it for their subjects.

But in the nineteenth century the Turkish wine industry went into a decline, as drinkers decided they preferred to swallow *rakı* with their *meze*. By the time I was at university and ready to start my drinking life, wine (sold in bottles with plastic stoppers) was regarded as a poor man's tipple, suitable only for alcoholics who couldn't afford *rakı*.

The comeback started in the 1990s (despite a government determined to tax it out of existence), when some visionary Turkish companies sought the help of French winemakers to make better use of ideal climatic conditions in particular regions of Anatolia. Nowadays, if you visit a wine-tasting shop such as Sensus, near Istanbul's Galata Tower, you'll be surprised how many Turkish wines can match the best of America, Australia, Italy and France.

Many Turkish winemakers simply replicate the international clichés of chardonnay, sauvignon blanc, cabernet sauvignon and shiraz. They taste fine, but for the visitor they don't represent a uniquely Anatolian experience. You should look for wines made from the local white grapes called emir (from the cold middle of the country), narince (from Tokat in Central Anatolia), and misket (from the Aegean coast). My favourite whites are Suvla Kınalı Yapincak and Sevilen Isabey Narince.

I think Turkish reds are much more advanced and complex than Turkish whites. My favourites are Sevilen Plato Kalecik Karası and Kavaklıdere Prestige Boğazkere.

The red grapes to look for are *öküzgözü* (literally 'ox-eye', grown in Eastern Anatolia near Malatya) and *boğazkere* ('savoury throat', grown in the southeast, near Diyarbakır). I'm particularly pleased to see *kalecik karasi* making a comeback in the vineyards near Ankara. That was the grape used by the Hittites (and probably Noah), so it could well be the oldest wine in the world. Dionysos would approve.

Somer's mum Ülkü with her signature fava *meze*.

A BEGINNER'S GLOSSARY

Here are a few terms you'll encounter in Turkey that might not turn out to be quite as you expect:

Ayran (pronounced 'eye-run'): The other national drink (after *rakı*), made with *yoğurt*, salt and water.

Baklava: A sweet made with filo pastry layered with pistachios (sometimes walnuts) and soaked in sugar syrup (not honey).

Börek: Savoury pastry (called *yufka*) that has been rolled, stuffed or layered with (usually) feta, spinach and/or lamb mince.

Çay (pronounced 'ch-eye'): Tea, served with all shopping experiences and much more popular than Turkish coffee.

Çorba (pronounced 'chorba'): Soup, served for breakfast, lunch and dinner, sometimes approaching the thickness of stew.

Dolma: Anything stuffed, most often peppers, eggplant and zucchini, but occasionally lamb ribs, intestines and melons.

Dondurma: Ice cream, the best kind being the stretchy *maraş* (pronounced 'maraşh') made with mastic gum and *salep* (wild orchid stems).

Gözleme (pronounced 'goz-lem-eh'): A kind of savoury pancake, usually stuffed with feta, spinach and/or lamb mince.

Helva: A sweet, often made with semolina or flour (at home) or with tahini and soapwort root (in shops, where it's sold in sticky blocks).

Kahve (pronounced 'kah-weh'): Turkish coffee, and please wait for the grounds to settle (see Afternoon Tea chapter).

Kaymak ('keye-muk'): Clotted cream, made with buffalo, cow's or sheep's milk.

Kebap: Char-grilled meat, usually on a skewer. *Döner kebap* is the vertical version.

Köfte (pronounced 'kof-tuh'): Usually translated as 'meatball'—minced meat kneaded into various shapes, often with bulgur wheat.

Kokoreç (pronounced 'koko-rezh'): A kind of char-grilled sausage made with lamb offal wrapped in lamb intestines, often sold in street stalls.

Lokanta: A casual eatery, ideal for a cheap lunch, where most dishes are displayed on counters and served lukewarm.

Lokum: Turkish delight.

Mantı (pronounced 'mantuh'): Dumplings usually stuffed with beef mince and served with garlic *yoğurt* and pepper sauce.

Meyhane (pronounced 'may-huh-neh'): A bar that serves small tasting plates called *meze*, accompanied by aniseed-flavoured alcohol called *rakı*, or wine if you insist.

Muhallebici (pronounced 'moo-hah-lebee-zhee'): A pudding shop, selling milk- and rice-based desserts.

Pastane (pronounced 'pas-tah-neh'): a pastry shop, selling biscuits and syrupy sweets.

Pastırma: Dried spiced beef, usually served in thin slices as a cold cut.

Pide ('pee-deh'): A kind of bread roll, often stuffed with cheese or mince, sold in shops called *pideci* ('pee-day-zhee').

Restoran: Less casual than a *lokanta*, open for lunch and dinner, where you're likely to see a menu and a wine list.

Salça (pronounced 'salcha'): A flavouring paste, usually made with tomato or pepper.

Salep: A hot drink for winter, made with powdered orchid tubers, thought to be an aphrodisiac.

Sucuk ('soo-jook'): A spicy dried sausage, usually made of beef and usually fried.

Tarator: A paste of walnuts, garlic and day-old bread, usually served with fried seafood.

THE TEN TOP TECHNIQUES

DOLMA AND SARMA (STUFFING AND ROLLING)

Most English-speakers are familiar with a Greek dish called dolmades, which they take to be vine leaves filled with seasoned rice. In Turkey, that's not a *dolma*, that's a *sarma*. *Dolma* means 'stuffed' and *sarma* means 'rolled'. Turks will stuff anything that can be made to have a space in the middle, and anything they can't stuff (like leaves from grapevines, spinach, or cabbage) they will roll.

Records from the sultan's palace show that in the fifteenth century Turks were stuffing onions, apples and intestines; in the sixteenth century, zucchini (courgettes), eggplant (aubergine) and butternut pumpkin (squash); in the seventeenth century, mackerel, watermelon and *barbunya* (red mullet); in the eighteenth, leeks, spinach and quince; and in the nineteenth, melon, okra and lamb ribs.

You'll find most of those recipes here, though we've occasionally expanded upon the two standard fillings (rice, onion and lamb mince or rice, cinnamon, currants and pine nuts).

SALÇA (PASTE-MAKING)

The array of dishes that can be called 'Turkish cuisine' evolved in a time-rich, cash-poor society. Because of harsh climate variations in the eastern

half of the country, people had to find ways to make ingredients last across four seasons. So they perfected techniques for drying, pickling, brining, preserving and pulverising products that were plentiful in late summer.

The pulverising process is called *salça* in Turkish—a word that entered culinary dictionaries only in the nineteenth century, even though it's derived from the Latin *salsa*. Before that, the word *palude* was used for pastes, sauces and reductions that were thickened with starch. For me, *salça* means a concentration of one ingredient—a paste, perhaps with salt as a preservative.

The most popular *salça* is made with peppers. On the farm of my traditionalist friend Musa, they pick the peppers in the morning, remove the stalks and seeds, and toss them into a purpose-built pepper mincer. Then they simmer the mince in huge pots over a wood fire until most of the water has evaporated.

To make your own pepper salça (pepper paste) at home:

Remove the stalks and seeds from the capsicums (peppers) and boil the chopped pieces in a little water for 1 hour (with the lid on the pot). Strain the capsicum and purée the pieces in a blender, then simmer the purée for 1 hour with the lid off.

For every kilogram of capsicum, stir in 2 tablespoons of olive oil and 1 teaspoon of salt. Pour the paste into clean glass jars while still warm, top with olive oil and seal.

FIRIN (BAKING)

The local baker in an Anatolian village is the home cook's best friend. You can send him any dish and he will cook it for you in his wood-fire stone oven, taking a share of the food as payment if you're not flush with funds.

In the southeastern town of Gaziantep, I spent a morning in the bakery of Aydın Kilitoğlu, who's had twenty-nine years' experience with heat. His place is as big as the average bedroom, but he produces 3000 pides a day. His eleven-year-old son Samet (opposite) works as an apprentice during school holidays—just as Aydın did with his own father.

Locals kept coming in with trays of eggplants, peppers and even *kebaps* that would normally be done over charcoal but which he quickly finishes in his oven. He charges 1 lira per tray, regardless of what the customer has put on it. Some people were bringing him 'new' dishes, such as pizzas they'd constructed at home, and he was enjoying the challenge of deciding where in the oven the pizza tray should go, and how long it should stay there.

If you don't have a stone wood-fire oven, the best way to get close to Aydın's effect is to turn your oven up to full blast for at least 30 minutes before you put in your baking tray (or pizza stone, or unglazed terracotta tile).

If you're using a metal oven tray, the best way to avoid your pide dough sticking is to spread a bit of flour on the tray and bake it for about 5 minutes before putting the ball of dough on the flour.

Samet, eleven-year-old son of the owner of Asri Bakery in Gaziantep, learning how to make pide.

The 'Spice Girl', Bilge Kadıoğlu, in her shop in 'Area 51' of Istanbul's Spice Market.

TENCERE (STEWING)

Turks don't make stocks or reductions for storage. We simmer whatever meat we need on the day we're going to eat it, and boil the accompanying rice in that water when the meat is removed. We might make a second dish from the leftovers, but essentially it's all consumed within 24 hours.

But we do love slow cooking. The tradition of *güveç* (clay pot) cooking started in rural households, which would have a fire pit outside the house—a hole in the ground called a *tandır*. You would light a fire in the bottom and hang a clay pot over the fire, slowly simmering a mixture of any ingredients you could find. If you could afford it, you would line the sides of the pit with clay, and bake dough on the hot sides, making a loaf that was called *nan* in Ottoman.

In the nineteenth century, an iron device called a *kuzine* became the centrepiece of every Turkish home. It was a wood-fire stove, useful for warming the house, but also used for stewing, brewing tea, even roasting chestnuts. The cook would leave a clay pot full of ingredients on the top all day long and everybody tucked in when they got home at night.

The trick with *güveç* cookery is layering the pot so that the ingredient that will take the longest is at the bottom, while the one needing least heat is at the top.

KURUTMA (DRYING)

In delicatessens called *şarküteri* all over Turkey, you'll see red tubes that look like salami and red slabs that look like leather hanging from hooks. The sausage is called *sucuk*, spiced beef inside a lamb intestine, and the leather is a marinated beef fillet called *pastırma*.

The word *pastırma* (adapted to *basturma* in Greece and pastrami in New York) simply means 'pressed', but that reveals nothing of the long and complex process of drying and coating in paste that produces Turkey's ubiquitous answer to prosciutto.

Kayseri in central Anatolia is the capital of *pastırma*-making. It is thought to be the first place meat was wind-dried in the world, some time before the Romans arrived. These days the master-driers are said to be people of Armenian background. Afyon on the Aegean coast is the capital of *sucuk*-making.

In this book we've given a couple of recipes for non-traditional *pastırma* and a suggestion for *sucuk* without the intestine, but we're happy for you to use store-bought general versions.

In food markets across the land you will see small purple pouches hanging on strings from the roof beams. They are dried eggplants, waiting to be stuffed. Most likely they came from the Oğuzeli area in southeastern Anatolia, where summer is perfect for growing baby eggplants and drying them. In the season, they pick the eggplants (and zucchinis) early in the morning, scoop out the flesh and leave them to hang in the 35°C (95°F) heat for 24 hours. That's all it takes. But if it rains, the eggplants will become spotted and unsellable, and the grower will need to start again.

BAHARAT (SPICING)

For 1000 years Constantinople was the end point of the spice route. Some spices were literally worth their weight in gold because they were thought to be miracle cures for a variety of ailments. Now they are flavour boosters.

In a quiet corner of Istanbul's spice market, identified as number 51, you'll encounter a shop called Ucuzcular (Cheapies), run by Bilge Kadıoğlu (opposite). She'll tell you her first name is pronounced 'like Bill Gates—but without the money'. She'll tell you she doesn't mind being called the 'Spice Girl'. She'll tell you the term 'Area 51' is appropriate, echoing the section of a US air force base where UFOs are allegedly hidden, because in the marketplace she's an alien—the only woman to run a shop, and the only shopkeeper to charge the same prices to locals as to visitors. She's an honest broker in one of the world's oldest professions.

When I'm there, I always buy my *salep* powder (made from orchids) and *mahlep* powder (made from white cherry seeds) from Bilge. She also turns her spices into perfumes and oils for the skin.

Bilge's two most traditional spice mixes are spot on: *dolma baharı* (a blend of cinnamon, allspice, black pepper and pimento, to be stirred through rice) and *köfte baharı* (a mixture of cumin, black pepper, pimento, dried oregano and dried coriander, to be kneaded into minced meat). They are extraterrestrial. In this book we'll try to show you how to replicate their effect.

TURŞU (PICKLING)

A local movie called *Happy Days*, made in the 1970s, exposes one of the most divisive issues in Turkish society. It shows a married couple at odds over the best way to pickle vegetables. The husband says lemon, the wife says vinegar. They divorce and then get back together, but never reach agreement. Both as a chef and as a married man, I know you can never win an argument with a woman, so I mostly go with vinegar.

That also puts me on the side of the first published picklers. A fourteenth-century nutrition book contains recipes for preserving cucumber, eggplants, onions and beetroot in a vinegar marinade. In the seventeenth century, Greek *meyhanes* started pickling a fish called *lakerda*, its saltiness probably boosting alcohol sales.

The Turkish technique seems simple:

For every 1 litre (35 fl oz/4 cups) of water you need 100 ml (3½ fl oz) of vinegar and 3 tablespoons of natural rock salt (not iodised). But the devil is in the detail—you must make sure your glass jar is sterilised, the vegetables are of premium quality, not overripe, and evenly placed in the jar, and you must wait at least 5 weeks before eating them. You can throw in a few chickpeas to speed fermentation, but be sure to remove them after 1 week. The ideal temperature of the room where you store your pickles is 20°C (about 70°F). For every two degrees Celsius below that, wait another week.

REÇEL (PRESERVING)

There are more jams in Turkey than there are fruits, because we often make several types from the one ingredient—for example, orange rind marmalade and orange jam, or unripened fig jam, fresh fig jam and dried fig marmalade.

Some recipes are simple—as in, boil 1 kg (2 lb 4 oz) of berries with 800 g (1 lb 12 oz) of sugar for 30 minutes, adding the juice of half a lemon to prevent crystallisation. Some are more elaborate, like the rose petal jam we discuss in the Breakfast chapter.

The word *reçel* (jam) comes from the Persian *ricar*, which suggests an origin a little to the east of Anatolia. But we know the Romans were making marmalade with fruit and honey before they arrived in Byzantion, so we could also credit an influence from the West. The crusaders supposedly took jam-making recipes from Istanbul to northern Europe in the thirteenth century, and by the sixteenth century the futurologist Nostradamus was using them to impress the French royal family. Eat jam with pide and clotted cream.

KÖFTE (KNEADING)

This is what they do for entertainment in the southeastern town of Şanlıurfa: watch an expert make *çiğ* (chee) *köfte*. While a band plays and singers emote, the master sits on the floor and kneads a mixture of raw veal, bulgur and spices in a large tray for up to an hour. Moving his shoulders in time to the music, he produces hundreds of meatballs, which are served to the guests sitting around the musicians. The guests roll the pieces of *köfte* in lettuce leaves, and munch on them as they watch the floor show. The sweat from the master's hands has become part of the flavour. In a sense, sweat is the most important ingredient in any *köfte*, because it symbolises how much effort you've put into the kneading.

Köfte is often translated as 'meatball' but it comes from a Persian word that simply meant 'mashed'. The name implies no particular ingredient, which can be raw or cooked, meat, fish or veg. You work with shoulders and (thoroughly washed) hands for as long as it takes to produce a smooth patty. When you think it's ready, knead it for another 10 minutes.

In the centre of Sultanahmet Square, just near the Topkapı Palace, you will see rows of *köfte* sellers claiming to be 'the original', 'the historical' and 'the traditional'. The best, the first and the original does not display any of those adjectives. It's called Selim Usta (Selim the Master) and it dates from 1920. Selim's *köfte* is made from spiced beef and served with bean and onion salad.

KEBAP (GRILLING)

A common folk myth goes that *kebap* cooking was invented in the twelfth century by Turkish soldiers who skewered meat on their swords and cooked them over a fire. But an archaeological dig in Santorini, Greece, found *kebap* cookers called 'fire dogs' (with a hotbox carved into the shape of a dog) that were in use 3700 years ago. So it's one of humanity's most ancient forms of cooking, now evolved into a fine art.

First you must decide the form in which your lamb, beef or chicken will be cooked—whole, in lumps or minced into patties. Any mincing must be done with a giant sharp knife called a *zırh*. Then you must blend in your flavouring—a sophisticated mix of herbs, peppers, onions, spices and (with meat *kebaps*) lamb fat, which will drip out of the meat and turn into a fragrant smoke that will further complicate the ultimate flavour.

And it's not just a matter of sticking it on a fire. The wood or charcoal must be lit 1 hour in advance and allowed to die down to embers, so there will be no flames in contact with the meat.

Turks like to go to specialist *kebap* houses for their charcoal hits. Australians claim to be barbecue kings, so *kebap* cooking at home should be easy for them. If you don't own a charcoal grill, we offer some *kebap* recipes that can be cooked in the oven. But you'll be missing a lot of flavour.

HOW TO TALK TURKEY

After the republic was formed in 1923, Turks moved from the confusing Arabic alphabet to the much simpler Latin alphabet. In this book, we've used the Turkish spellings of dishes and locations.

The names might seem difficult at first, especially since the alphabet has twenty-nine letters, but the spelling is logical and phonetically consistent, once you get the hang of it.

All letters are read as they are written, and they always have the same sound. A/a B/b C/c Ç/ç D/d E/e F/f G/g Ğ/ğ H/h I/ı İ/i J/j K/k L/l M/m N/n O/o Ö/ö P/p R/r S/s Ş/ş T/t U/u Ü/ü V/v Y/y Z/z

A few letters are pronounced differently from the English alphabet:

A/a = as in far
C/c = as in joke
Ç/ç = as in chair
E/e = as in set
G/g = as in goat
Ğ/ğ = silent g, not pronounced but it extends the preceding vowel
I/ı = (without a dot) pronounced as the last syllable in button
İ/i = (with a dot) as in sit
J/j = as in measure
Ö/ö = as in bird
Ş/ş = as in shut
Ü/ü = as in cube
V/v = like w, as in water

So, for example, *köfte* (meatball) is pronounced 'kirf-teh'; *sütlaç* (rice pudding) is 'soot-latch'; *mantı* (dumpling) is 'mantuh'; *gözleme* (pancake) is 'gers-lemeh'; *yoğurt* is 'yoh-ourt'; *keşkül* (almond pudding) is 'kesh-kool'; kahvaltı (breakfast) is 'kah-waltuh'; and baklava is 'bah-klawa'.

At Karadeniz in Istanbul's Beşiktaş market, the *döner kebap* starts the morning as a 100 kilo ball of meat and slims down as the day proceeds.

BREAK FAST

LIGHT STARTS & BANQUETS

BREAKFAST

They love a big breakfast banquet in the far east of Anatolia. In the city of Van (pronounced 'wahn'), they'll take three hours to consume as many as forty-one courses, and then eat nothing else for the rest of the day. Most of the courses will be small—like a dish of olives, a few slices of watermelon, a pot of rose jam and bread rolls in various shapes—but they add up to a feast. There's a famous Turkish romantic poem, written by Yılmaz Erdoğan in 2002, in which an ardent suitor tells his sweetheart: 'I'd love the chance to have breakfast with you in a breakfast salon in Van.'

Now please don't imagine this is typical of all of Turkey—or even that it's an ancient tradition. Our word for breakfast is *kahvaltı*, which literally translates as 'coffee after'. It implies that breakfast is something that puts a layer on your stomach before your first coffee of the day, and in most Istanbul homes most mornings that means white cheese, fruit, *yoğurt* and bread from the local bakery. The egg dishes will come out at weekends.

Even the wealthy Ottomans of the sixteenth century didn't go in much for breakfast, preferring to have some soup and leftovers from last night's banquet around 11 am, in what these days we would call brunch.

Outside of Istanbul today, there is huge regional variation in morning behaviour. In the gourmet town of Gaziantep, in southeastern Turkey, they like to eat liver *kebap*s or a fiery soup of lamb, rice and chilli. Along the Black Sea they dip their bread into a kind of cheese fondue. In central Anatolia they love *böreks*—pastries usually stuffed with feta and spinach. In ancient Tarsus, they serve warm humus with bread for dipping. All of them drink tea with their first meal of the day, and have coffee after.

And in Van, they've only been doing the big breakfast since the 1940s, when it was introduced in a salon called Sütçü Kenan (which we could translate as 'Milkman Ken') to showcase the vast variety of cheeses from the region. Milkman Ken's breakfast banquet was quickly copied by other cafés in his town, and then by breakfast salons (*kahvaltı evi*) in Istanbul.

Four years ago, I started offering a 'Van breakfast' on Sunday mornings in my restaurant in Sydney. It's been a huge success. This chapter shows you how you can create your own Van breakfast, or any part thereof, at home.
For the record, these are the courses I serve in my version of the Van breakfast:

1. Pide bread
2. Pomegranate molasses
3. Bazlama bread
4. Poğaça pastry
5. Simit (a kind of pretzel)
6. Kaymak (clotted cream)
7. Honey
8. Rose jam
9. Sour cherry jam
10. Fig jam
11. Quince jam
12. Feta (goat's cheese)
13. Kashkaval (sheep's cheese)
14. Tulum (sheep's cheese aged in goat skin)
15. String cheese
16. Lor cheese (a kind of ricotta)
17. Labne balls (*yoğurt* cheese)
18. Unsalted butter
19. *Sucuk* (sausage)
20. Cigar *böreks*
21. Spinach *böreks*
22. *Paçanga* (*pastırma böreks*)
23. Cracked green olives
24. Black olives
25. Sliced tomatoes
26. Cucumbers
27. Olive paste
28. Tomato ezme (crushed with chilli)
29. *Muhammara* (pepper dip)
30. *Pastırma* (cold cuts of spiced beef)
31. Barbecued haloumi
32. Menemen (scrambled eggs)
33. Watermelon
34. Melon
35. Grapes
36. Mulberry leather (dehydrated grape molasses)
37. *Katmer* (sweet *börek*)
38. Red grapes
39. Turkish delight
40. Baklava
41. Tahini *helva*

Now you can make your own.

The Sunday Van breakfast at Efendy restaurant in Sydney.

SESAME RINGS

What pretzels are to New Yorkers, simit *are to Istanbulians, who buy them from street stalls all day long and munch them between appointments.*

They are at least 600 years old—Topkapı Palace documents from 1593 include bulk orders for simid-i halka *(round simits). They have entered the language of metaphor. A Turk who hates his job will say: 'I'd be better off selling* simit'. *Protesters trying to dissuade police from breaking up a demonstration will shout: 'Sell* simit *and leave with honour.'*

There are bakeries that cook nothing but simit—in wood-fire ovens, of course, at 300°C (570°F/ Gas 10+). And there are cafés, usually with titles such as 'Palace of Simit', that serve them with melted cheese, tomato and other unnecessary additions. Personally, I would never sit down to eat simit, and I would never cook them at home if I was in Istanbul. But outside my homeland, you need a recipe.

SERVES 8

2 teaspoons dry yeast
2 teaspoons sugar
300 g (10½ oz/2 cups) plain (all-purpose) flour,
    plus extra for dusting
1 tablespoon vegetable oil, plus extra for greasing
45 ml (1½ fl oz) thickened (whipping) cream
1 teaspoon salt
350 g (12 oz/1 cup) grape molasses
140 g (5 oz/1 cup) sesame seeds
butter and feta, to serve (optional)

Mix the yeast and the sugar in a bowl with 250 ml (9 fl oz /1 cup) of lukewarm water and then set aside for 5 minutes. It should start to form bubbles. Add another 125 ml (4 fl oz/½ cup) of water and combine.

Sift the flour into a mixing bowl, make a well in the middle and pour in the yeast mixture, vegetable oil and thickened cream. Knead the dough for 5 minutes to make a soft and stretchy dough, adding more flour if the dough is sticky. Cover the bowl with a damp cloth and rest for 1 hour. It should expand.

Preheat the oven to 230°C (450°F/Gas 8).

Add the salt to the dough and knead for 3 minutes. Sprinkle some flour on your work surface. Divide the dough into eight pieces and roll into balls. Rest for 3 minutes. With floured hands, pull each ball in half and roll each half into a strip about 50 cm (20 in) long. Twist the two strips around each other into braids. Pull the braided

dough around into a circle. Stick the ends together, wetting the dough if necessary to help it hold.

Dilute the grape molasses in 170 ml (5½ fl oz/ ⅔ cup) of water.

Place a frying pan over low heat. Add the sesame seeds and toast, tossing constantly, until the seeds turn golden brown. Turn onto a tray and set aside

Pour the grape molasses into a shallow bowl. Dip the braided dough into the molasses, one at a time. Turn to coat both sides. Shake off the excess liquid then toss each braid in the sesame seeds, making sure both sides are evenly coated.

Line a baking tray with baking paper and brush with oil. Arrange the *simit* on the tray and bake for 20 minutes until golden brown and crusty.

Serve warm with butter and feta, or at room temperature as part of a breakfast spread.

BAZLAMA
PAN-FRIED BREAD

Bazlama is the simplest form of bread in the world—it doesn't even require an oven. The technique is probably at least 3000 years old. In Turkish villages, lumps of dough are spread on a sac (pronounced 'sazh'), which is like an upturned wok resting over hot coals. You could try that, or use a frying pan instead.

Unlike most breads, bazlama involves little preparation time. You could leave it to rise overnight, or you could wake up on a Sunday morning, decide 'Lets do a bazlama brunch', invite your friends, leave the dough to rise while you're showering and tidying up, and fry your bread while your guests are sitting down.

Because it contains yoğurt it has a rich flavour and an interesting texture—soft inside and crunchy outside. You'd serve it with jams or cheeses (which you would need to make earlier).

SERVES 4

2 teaspoons dry yeast
1 teaspoon sugar
600 g (1 lb 5 oz /4 cups) plain (all-purpose) flour, plus extra for dusting
1 teaspoon salt
125 g (4½ oz/½ cup) plain *yoğurt*
vegetable oil, for frying
butter, jam or cheese, to serve

Put the yeast and sugar in a bowl with 250 ml (9 fl oz/1 cup) of lukewarm water, then set aside for 5 minutes. It should start to form bubbles.

Sift the flour into a mixing bowl, make a well in the middle, and pour in the yeast mixture. Knead the dough for 1 minute, then add the *yoğurt*. Knead for a further 10 minutes or until the dough has reached, as we say in Turkey, 'the softness of an earlobe'. Cover the bowl with a damp cloth and rest in a warm place for 2 hours. The ball of dough should double in size.

Add the salt to the dough and knead for 3 minutes. Sprinkle some flour on your work surface and divide the dough into four balls. Return the dough to the bowl, cover with a damp cloth and rest for 10 minutes.

Place one ball of dough on the work surface and, using floured hands or a rolling pin, flatten into a round about 10 cm (4 in) wide and 1 cm (½ in) thick. Repeat with the remaining dough balls.

Heat 1 tablespoon of vegetable oil in a frying pan for 1 minute over medium heat and swirl gently to coat. Add one round of dough and cook for 1 minute. Turn the round over and cook for 1 minute more or until golden brown, then transfer onto paper towel. Repeat with the remaining three rounds, adding more oil to the pan as required.

Serve the *bazlamas* with butter, jam or cheese.

TIRNAKLI PİDE
FINGER PIDE

Let me say it again—pide bread is different from pita, which is a Greek term for the unleavened bread that wraps around kebaps (better known as lavaş in Turkish). In Istanbul, pide is a treat you enjoy for one month of the year—when you break your fast after sunset during the month of Ramadan. In lucky southeastern Anatolia they get to have pide all year round, because it's their main form of bread. The cooks augment it with a coating of yoğurt, deposited on the top with dancing fingers, like concert pianists—hence the name 'finger pide'. The accompaniments for pide are infinite—jam is only the beginning.

SERVE 4

3 teaspoons dry yeast
500 g (1 lb 2 oz/3⅓ cups) plain (all-purpose)
    flour, plus extra for dusting
50 ml (1⅔ fl oz) sunflower oil
½ teaspoon *mahlep* powder
    (ground white cherry seeds) (optional)
2 teaspoons salt
25 g (1 oz) plain *yoğurt*
1 tablespoon nigella seeds
1 tablespoon sesame seeds
50 g (1¾ oz) wholemeal flour
    (if using a baking tray)

Dissolve the yeast in a bowl with 250 ml (9 fl oz/1 cup) of lukewarm water. Set aside for 5 minutes. It should start to form bubbles.

Sift the flour into a mixing bowl, make a well in the middle and pour in the yeast mixture. Add 375 ml (13 fl oz/1½ cups) of water, the sunflower oil and *mahlep* powder, and knead for 5 minutes to form a soft dough. Cover the bowl with a damp cloth and rest in a warm place for 1 hour. The ball of dough should double in size.

Add the salt to the dough and knead for 3 minutes. Sprinkle the extra flour on your work surface. Divide the dough into five pieces and roll into balls. Return the dough to the bowl, cover with a damp cloth and leave to rest for 30 minutes.

Preheat the oven to its maximum temperature (as close to 300°C/570°F as possible). If you have a pizza stone or unglazed terracotta tile, place it in the oven to heat.

Place one ball of dough on the work surface and, using floured hands or a rolling pin, flatten into a round about 10 cm (4 in) wide and 2 cm (¾ in) thick. Repeat with the remaining dough balls.

Mix the *yoğurt* and 25 ml (¾ fl oz) of water together in a bowl. Dunk both your hands in the mixture and then, using four fingers of each hand joined together, hop your fingertips across the dough vertically and then horizontally to make indentations across the top of each round. Dip your fingers into the *yoğurt* regularly to keep them wet.

Mix the nigella and sesame seeds together and sprinkle them evenly onto each round. Put the bread on the pizza stone or tile and place on the middle rack of the oven. If you don't have a stone or tile, sprinkle the wholemeal flour on a baking tray lined with baking paper and place the rounds on the flour. Cook for 5 minutes at 300°C (570°F/Gas 10+) (or 6 minutes at 250°C/500°F/Gas 9 or 7 minutes at 200°C/400°F/Gas 6) until brown on top and golden on the sides.

Serve warm as part of a breakfast spread.

The harbour at Bodrum, Aegean coast.

POĞAÇA

BALKAN-STYLE BRIOCHE STUFFED WITH POTATO AND CHILLI

The Turkish word poğaça *(pronounced 'poe-uchah') comes from the same root as the Italian word* focaccia*: the Latin* panis focacius*, which means bread cooked in the hearth. That suggests it must have been a favourite of the Romans during their time in Constantinople. In the mid-seventeenth century, the travel writer Evliya Çelebi reported in his memoir* Seyahatname *(Tales of the Journey) that a sweet version of* poğaça *had been popular in the sultan's palace 100 years earlier but was introduced as street food by Balkan immigrants, who would heap hot ashes over the dough, let it bake, then scrape the bread clean and serve it with cheese or lamb mince. (The description sounds rather like damper, a favourite of Australian bushies in the nineteenth century.)*

My version of this recipe could not have been eaten by the Emperor Constantine, since potatoes only reached Turkey from South America in the eighteenth century. I think poğaça *tastes even better when the mash melts into the dough.*

SERVES 4

---

1 teaspoon dry yeast
2 teaspoons sugar
70 g (2½ oz) butter
1 egg
125 g (4½ oz/½ cup) plain *yoğurt*
300 g (10½ oz/2 cups) plain (all-purpose) flour, plus extra for dusting
3 boiling potatoes (such as desiree)
2 teaspoons salt, plus extra for boiling the potatoes
1 teaspoon freshly ground black pepper
2 teaspoons chilli flakes
1 heaped tablespoon shredded *kaşar* (or mozzarella)
⬛ vegetable oil
1 egg ⬛
1 tablespoon nigella se⬛
1 tablespoon sesame seeds

Mix the yeast and the sugar in a bowl with 125 ml (4 fl oz/½ cup) of lukewarm water and set aside for 5 minutes. It should start to form bubbles.

Whisk the butter, egg and *yoğurt* together in a bowl. Sift the flour into a mixing bowl, make a well in the middle, pour in the yeast mixture and stir through. Add the *yoğurt* mixture and knead vigorously for 10 minutes to make a soft, stretchy dough. Cover the bowl with a damp cloth and rest in a warm place for 2 hours to expand.

Preheat the oven to 200°C (400°F/Gas 6).

Peel and quarter the potatoes, then place in a large saucepan, cover with salted water and bring to the boil. Cook for 15 minutes or until the ⬛ ⬛nder, then drain well. Add half the salt, t⬛ ⬛hilli flakes and cheese, and roughly mash.

Add the remaining salt to the rested dough and knead to combine. Sprinkle some flour on your work surface. Divide the dough into eight pieces and roll into balls. Place one ball of dough on the work surface and, with floured hands or a rolling pin, flatten into a round about 10 cm (4 in) wide and 1–2 cm (about ½ in) thick. Repeat with the remaining dough. Add 1 tablespoon of the mashed potato mixture in the middle of each round. Fold over one side to create a half moon shape. Press lightly around the edges to seal.

Line a baking tray with baking paper and brush with vegetable oil. Arrange the *poğaças* on the tray. Brush the pastry with oil and the tops with egg yolk, and sprinkle on the seeds. Bake for 30 minutes or until golden brown.

Serve warm, two per person.

BALIKLI EKMEK
BLACK SEA CORNBREAD WITH LEEKS AND WHITEBAIT

When I led my first gourmet tour of Turkey in 2013, we visited the tranquil Istanbul suburb of Anadolu Kavaği—the last stop for the Bosphorus ferries—lined with casual seaside restaurants looking out to the Black Sea and up to Yoros Castle. We sat down to a fish feast.

Walking back to the ferry, we passed an unassuming bakery, and one of my guests noted a snack I'd never seen before—cornbread that seemed to be stuffed with sardines and leeks. He bought some for everyone and they declared it the highlight of the day. So I researched it and recreated it for this book.

Hamsi is the most prized fish of the Black Sea—somewhere between an anchovy and a sardine. I decided to substitute baby whitebait, because hamsi don't swim far beyond the Bosphorus and sardines might be too strong for breakfast.

SERVES 8

½ bunch silverbeet (Swiss chard)
½ bunch dill
½ bunch flat-leaf (Italian) parsley
2 leeks
2 onions
2 tablespoons butter
2 tablespoons dried mint
500 g (1 lb 2 oz) whitebait
2 teaspoons baking powder
1 kg (2 lb 4 oz) maize flour
250 ml (9 fl oz/1 cup) olive oil, plus extra for brushing
1 egg
1 tablespoon salt

Wash the silverbeet and remove the stalks. Finely chop the leaves. Remove the stalks from the dill. Pick the leaves from the parsley. Remove the roots and green outer layer from the leeks, then rinse to remove any dirt. Finely chop the leeks, parsley and onions separately.

Melt the butter in a frying pan over high heat. Add the onions and cook for 3 minutes or until soft. Add the leeks and cook for 3 minutes, then add the silverbeet and cook for a further 5 minutes. Remove from the heat, turn into a bowl and leave to cool.

Preheat the oven to 180°C (350°F/Gas 4).

When the silverbeet mixture has cooled, stir in the parsley and dried mint. Add the whitebait and mash together with a fork.

Mix the baking powder with 300 ml (10¾ fl oz) of warm water. Sift the flour into a mixing bowl, make a well in the middle and pour in the baking powder mixture. Stir thoroughly and then add the whitebait mixture, olive oil, egg and salt. Knead for 5 minutes, or until it forms a rough dough.

Line a 30 x 20 x 4 cm (12 x 8 x 1½ in) baking tray with baking paper and brush with olive oil. Press the dough into the tray. Sprinkle the dill over the top and press it in. Brush the top with oil and bake for 45 minutes.

Take the tray out of the oven and make three knife cuts across the top of the bread to ensure even cooking. Brush the top and the slits with more oil and bake for a further 45 minutes or until golden brown.

Turn off the heat, leaving the bread in the oven, and rest for 30 minutes.

Slice or break the warm cornbread into chunks and serve.

KAYMAK AT PANDO'S

Everything moves slowly at Pando's—particularly Pando Şestakof, who is ninety. When a young businessman on his way to work sits at an outside table for a plate of *kaymak* and asks: 'Could you rush the order?' Pando replies: 'Here it runs at my speed.' Then he shuffles inside and painstakingly scoops the pure white treasure onto a steel plate and drizzles it with honey. He picks up a plastic basket containing half a loaf of bread, roughly chopped, and takes a full five minutes to shuffle back outside with the two plates.

That ritual has been going on in this place since 1895, when Pando's grandfather came from Bulgaria and set up a shop called Hayat (Life) to sell the products of his dairy farm. He became the favoured supplier to the Dolmabahçe Palace, where the sultan lived in summer. After the revolution that palace became the residence of President Atatürk, and Pando's father continued to provide the *kaymak*.

When Pando and his wife Yuanna inherited the shop, they sold the farm and started buying their milk from the best water buffalo farmers in the neighbourhood. Pando opens his café at 8 am, seven days a week, and closes when he runs out of *kaymak*. Then he goes home to make some more for tomorrow.

Pando's little shop is a geographical reference point in the neighbourhood. For the past thirty years, visitors asking the way somewhere won't be given a street name but instead be told 'Go 20 metres past Pando's and turn left'. He's at a kind of crossroads in Beşiktaş market, one of the last surviving local markets in Istanbul. As recently as twenty years ago, nearly every suburb had a jumble of shops and stalls like this. But more than a hundred local markets have shrunk to a handful, replaced by shopping centres with escalators instead of lane ways and supermarkets that sell flavourless commercially processed *kaymak*.

Here's how Pando makes his clotted cream (and you'll quickly see why we adapted the recipe):

Use unpasteurised and unhomogenised buffalo milk (which has a fat content of about 8 per cent, while cow's milk has 3 per cent).

Pour it into a baking tray over a wood fire and slowly cook it. Never let it boil. After about four hours it will start to develop a skin.

Every few hours, skim off the skin and put it into a separate tray. The skin is the kaymak. Over 48 hours you will get 100 g (3½ oz) of kaymak from 1 kg (2 lb 4 oz) of buffalo milk. You can drink the watery milk that is left behind.

To accompany our recipe on the following page, we've suggested rose jam—because that's how Pando used to serve it back in the 1960s. Nowadays, he prefers honey, but he always keeps a pot of rose jam for nostalgic customers.

Pando Şestakof delivers the tea that must accompany his precious *kaymak*.

YALANCI KAYMAK

YALANCI KAYMAK

CLOTTED CREAM WITH ROSE JAM

The Turkish name for this dish translates as 'Liar's kaymak', because our recipe will not end up tasting the same as the kaymak that has been served for 100 years in my favourite breakfast café in Istanbul—Pando in Beşiktaş markets. There the kaymak is made with water buffalo milk that has been slowly simmered until it's thick and luscious.

In this recipe, I've included cornflour as a thickener, on the assumption that you will be using pasteurised milk. If you have access to creamy unpasteurised milk, lucky you, because you can eliminate the cornflour and come closer to the Pando experience (see page 52).

SERVES 4

KAYMAK

60 g (2¼ oz/½ cup) cornflour (cornstarch)
250 ml (9 fl oz/1 cup) full-cream (whole) milk (preferably high-fat such as Jersey or buffalo)
500 ml (17 fl oz /2 cups) thickened (whipping) cream
50 g (1¾ oz) butter

ROSE JAM

50 pink rose petals
500 g (1 lb 2 oz) sugar
1 teaspoon citric acid powder

pide bread, to serve (to make your own, see page 45)

First make the *kaymak*. Whisk the cornflour, milk and cream together to dissolve the starch. Transfer to a baking tray, preferably a stainless steel ¼ gastronorm tray (26.5 x 16.3 x 2 cm/10⅓ x 6½ x ¾ in). Place the tray over very low heat and whisk for 5 minutes—being careful not to let the mixture stick. Add the butter and continue to whisk for 15 minutes or until it thickens to a pudding consistency. Remove from the heat and leave to rest for 30 minutes, then transfer to the fridge.

To make the jam, first peel the petals from the pink roses. If using organic (non-sprayed) roses, wash under cold running water. If using commercial roses, blanche in boiling water for 15 seconds, soak in cold water in the fridge for 12 hours, and then strain and wash under cold running water. Discard any brown or spotty petals. Cut the white patch off the bottom of each petal and slice any large petals in half. Pat the petals dry with paper towel. Place a layer of petals in a bowl, sprinkle with sugar, add another layer and repeat the process until all the petals are coated with the sugar. Cover with plastic wrap and refrigerate overnight.

Pour 500 ml (17 fl oz/2 cups) of water into a heavy-based saucepan and add 1 tablespoon of sugar. Slowly bring to the boil, stirring frequently.

Add the sugared rose petals and simmer for 20 minutes, stirring occasionally. Add the citric acid and simmer for a further 10 minutes, scooping off any scum that forms on the surface. To test the thickness of the jam, scoop a spoonful onto a cold plate. It should form a gel. If it's still runny, simmer for a further 5 minutes or until it thickens.

Remove the jam from the heat and leave to cool to room temperature, then transfer to a jar with a tight-fitting lid* and set aside. (Do not put in the fridge.)

Spread 2 tablespoons of jam on a plate and top with a large dollop of *kaymak*. Serve with pide.

NOTE

Stored properly, the rose jam will keep for up to 6 months. Cut a piece of baking paper slightly larger than the jar cap, brush liberally with olive oil and place it between the jar and the cap before sealing tightly. This will prevent mould forming on the jam.

Pando's wife, Yuanna Şestakof.

LABNE
MINTED YOĞURT BALLS

When I first heard of a Middle-Eastern cheese called labne I was intrigued, but I refrained from using it in my restaurant because I thought it was Lebanese. Then I discovered that the name comes from laban, *an Egyptian-Arabic word for 'milk', that it is just strained* yoğurt, *treated with a little lemon and salt; and that it can be found all over Turkey under the name* süzme. *The Lebanese like to dip their labne in zaatar, and the Egyptians dip them in dukka, but I thought I'd be Turkish and use mint and sumac.*

**MAKES ABOUT
15 BALLS**

1 garlic clove
1¼ tablespoons salt
1.4 kg (3 lb 2 oz) plain *yoğurt*
juice of ¼ lemon
1 mint stalk
500 ml (17 fl oz/2 cups) extra virgin olive oil
3 tablespoons dried mint
3 teaspoons sumac
2 teaspoons chilli flakes
1 tablespoon dill tips (or dried dill)

Crush the garlic with 1 teaspoon of salt, then mix with the *yoğurt* and lemon juice.

Place the *yoğurt* mixture on a sheet of muslin (cheesecloth), tie up the corners and hang over a pot for 12 hours to drain. The *yoğurt* should thicken to a cream cheese consistency.

Mould the thickened *yoğurt* into spheres about the size of a ping-pong ball. This quantity should make about fifteen balls.

Gently place the labne into a large jar with the fresh mint, cover with olive oil, and then set aside to rest for at least 24 hours.

When you're ready to serve, combine the herbs and salt on a plate and roll the balls in the mix, one at a time. Serve on a platter in the middle of the table for people to help themselves.

NOTE
Labne can be kept in the fridge for up to 1 month.

SİGARA BÖREĞİ

ROLLED PASTRY CIGARS WITH FETA AND PARSLEY

This is the first of three recipes for böreks, *the pastries that got their name from a Turkish verb meaning 'to twist'. You can tie yourself in knots trying to fold the pastry as neatly as a Turkish cook. We suggest you just relax and try to make shapes that vaguely resemble cigars (this recipe) or spirals (the next recipe) or square parcels (the third recipe).*

The word börek *is very old—there's a reference to a sugar* burek *in a twelfth-century book called* Danişmendname, *about the conquest of Anatolia by the Turks, which presumably means we can call* böreks *'the breakfast of conquerors'.*

The cigar börek *is the simplest form, and can be made with commercial* yufka *(or two layers of filo) instead of rolling out your own pastry. From one sheet of* yufka *you can make eight to twelve cigars, which you could freeze and then deep fry (without defrosting) when you need them.*

Normally sigara böreği *are stuffed with just feta and parsley, but I find mint a refreshing addition.*

MAKES 8

CHEESE FILLING
1 bunch flat-leaf (Italian) parsley
1 bunch mint
300 g (10½ oz) sheep's feta
1 egg
1 tablespoon sweet paprika

WRAPPING
1 sheet *yufka*, about 80 x 80 cm (31½ x 31½ in) (if you cannot buy *yufka*, or prefer to make your own, see page 27)
1 egg white

sunflower oil, for frying

First make the filling. Pick the mint and parsley leaves (discarding the stalks) and finely chop. Mash the feta with a fork. Break the egg into a small bowl and whisk. Add the feta, parsley, mint and paprika, and stir to a chunky paste.

Place the *yufka* on a board and cut across four times to create eight wedges (or cut eight times, into 16 wedges, to make cigarillos). Next, fill and fold your cigars. Place the egg white in a bowl. With the round edge of one *yufka* segment facing towards you, place a strip of filling across the pastry, about 5 cm (2 in) from each edge. Fold the round edge over the strip of filling and press down. Then, fold over about 5 cm (2 in) of pastry from the left side, leaving a straight edge. Finally, fold over a 5 cm (2 in) flap from the right side, leaving a straight edge. Using a pastry brush, brush the top triangle of pastry with egg white and roll the folded part tightly over to make a cigar shape. Repeat this process with the seven other segments.

Place a deep frying pan over high heat and add enough sunflower oil to cover the *böreks* (about 3 cm/1¼ in deep). Add a drop of water to the oil. If it sizzles, the oil is ready. Carefully add four *böreks* and fry for 2 minutes or until lightly golden. Remove the *böreks* from the pan with a slotted spoon and place on paper towel to absorb the excess oil. Repeat with the remaining *böreks*.

Serve immediately.

ISPANAKLI KOL BÖREĞI

ROLLED PASTRY WITH SPINACH AND FETA

The Turkish word kol means 'arm', and presumably gets into the Turkish name for this börek because each roll of pastry is bent to look like an arm coming round to hug you. It would make more sense to call this a spiral or a labyrinth, since that is how it looks when all the arms are linked together.

My maternal grandma, who came from Yugoslavia, was a master of the 'arm börek', and she made giant spirals to feed a large family. In later life, she used an electric börek cooker, called a drum oven, which was a cylinder with doors on the side and shelves onto which you could place multiple layers of börek.

Spinach is the traditional filling, but you can use kale, silverbeet or even minced lamb.

SERVES 8

250 g (9 oz) English spinach
1 onion
4 spring onions (scallions)
120 ml (4 fl oz) sunflower or vegetable oil
1 tablespoon chilli flakes
1 tablespoon salt
1 teaspoon freshly ground black pepper
1 tablespoon dried mint
150 g (5½ oz) feta
80 ml (2½ fl oz/⅓ cup) milk
1 egg
1 tablespoon plain *yoğurt*
2 sheets *yufka* (if you cannot buy *yufka*, or prefer to make your own, see page 27)

Wash the spinach thoroughly. Remove the stalks, then finely chop the leaves. Finely slice the onion. Wash the spring onions, then remove the roots and green outer layer. Finely chop.

Put 2 tablespoons of oil in a frying pan over medium heat. Add the onions and cook for 3 minutes. Add the spring onions and cook for 3 minutes more. Add the spinach and cook for a further 3 minutes, then remove from the heat. Mix in all the herbs and spices and leave in the frying pan to cool. Grate the feta into the cooled spinach mixture.

Preheat the oven to 180°C (350°F/Gas 4).

Whisk the milk, egg, *yoğurt* and 2 teaspoons of oil in a mixing bowl.

Unfold a sheet of *yufka* and slice it down the middle to create a half moon shape.

Brush a quarter of the egg mixture onto each half moon of *yufka*. Spread a quarter of the spinach mixture along the flat side of the half moon, making a strip about 5 cm (2 in) wide. Fold the strip over and tightly roll the *yufka* into a tube about 80 cm (31½ in) long.

Brush a 20 cm (8 in) wide baking tray with the remaining oil. Place the rolled *börek* onto the tray and pull it around into a circle, with the ends overlapping. Make another *börek* and join that to the inside end of the previous circle, so that it forms a smaller ring inside the first one. Add two more *börek* tubes so you have a spiral of smaller and smaller rings.

Bake for 20 minutes or until the *börek are* golden. Turn off the heat, leaving the tray in the oven, and rest for 10 minutes.

Cut across the spiral four times to make eight wedges, and serve.

KÜRT BÖREĞI

KURDISH-STYLE ROLLED PASTRY WITH HAZELNUTS

The Turkish name for this pastry—kürt böreği—suggests it is a Kurdish speciality, but you should not expect to find it in eastern Anatolia, where the Kurds live. The name seems to have arisen because it's the kind of dish Istanbul chefs imagine Kurds might eat. To confuse the issue further, I've boosted it with hazelnuts and crème pâtissière, which makes it more like the kind of rich pastry they love on the Black Sea.

SERVES 4

ROLLED PASTRY
120 g (4½ oz/1 cup) hazelnuts
1 kg (2 lb 4 oz) plain (all-purpose) flour (plus extra for dusting), or 3 sheets frozen puff pastry
2 eggs
1 tablespoon baking powder
125 ml (4 fl oz/½ cup) vegetable oil
125 g (4½ oz/½ cup) plain *yoğurt*
150 g (5½ oz) butter, plus extra for greasing
1 tablespoon cinnamon powder
3 tablespoons icing (confectioners') sugar

CRÈME PÂTISSIÈRE
310 ml (10¾ fl oz fl oz/1¼ cups) milk
3 egg yolks
3 tablespoons cornflour (cornstarch)
2 tablespoons plain (all-purpose) flour
30 g (1 oz/¼ cup) icing (confectioners') sugar
1 vanilla bean, or 1 teaspoon vanilla extract

Preheat the oven to 180°C (350°F/Gas 4).

Place the hazelnuts on a baking tray and bake for 5 minutes. Remove from the oven and leave to cool. When the nuts are cool enough to handle, remove the skin, transfer to a food processor and grind coarsely.

To make the crème pâtissière, warm the milk in a saucepan over low heat for about 10 minutes until it reaches a low simmer, preferably using a simmer mat. Try to keep the temperature around 70°C (160°F) if you have a food thermometer, being careful not to let the milk start to boil.

Meanwhile, combine the egg yolks, cornflour, flour and icing sugar in a mixing bowl and whisk until smooth. Ladle about 125 ml (4 fl oz/½ cup) of the warm milk into the yolk mixture, whisk together, and then pour into the saucepan with the remaining milk. Whisk slowly for another 2 minutes, then remove from the heat. Slit the vanilla bean lengthways, scrape the seeds into the mixture and stir through. Discard the skin. Put the bowl in the fridge to cool.

Sift the flour into a mixing bowl, make a well in the middle, break in the eggs and then add the baking powder, vegetable oil and *yoğurt*. Knead the dough for about 10 minutes, or until the dough is soft and stretchy. Cover the bowl with a damp cloth and rest for 1 hour to expand.

Sprinkle some flour on your work surface. Divide the dough into twenty pieces and roll into balls. With floured hands or a rolling pin, flatten one ball into a round 20 cm (8 in) wide and 2–3 cm (about 1 in) thick. Repeat with the remaining dough.

Melt the butter in a frying pan over medium heat (or microwave for 30 seconds). Brush each round with the butter and then place the rounds on top of each other to make a stack. Press the stack down and spread the dough out with a rolling pin, as thin as possible. Brush with butter and roll into a log. Slice into three equal pieces, wrap each piece in plastic wrap and refrigerate for 1 hour to rest.

Preheat the oven to 180°C (350°F/Gas 4).

Remove the chilled dough from the fridge (or freezer if using store-bought puff pastry) and leave to warm to room temperature. Grease a 30 x 20 x 4 cm (12 x 8 x 1½ in) baking tray with butter. Roll out the first piece of puff pastry to the size of the tray. Remove the crème pâtissière from the fridge and spread onto the pastry, then sprinkle one-third of the hazelnuts over the top.

Roll out the second and third pieces of puff pastry to the size of your tray, and brush the top with butter. Place the second puff pastry layer on top of the first, sprinkle with another third of hazelnuts, and then place the final pastry layer on top.

Cut the stacked dough into 8 cm (3¼ in) squares. Bake for 25 minutes or until golden on top. Remove from the oven and leave to cool slightly.

Sprinkle the remaining hazelnuts on top of the *börek*, dust with cinnamon and icing sugar, then serve warm.

KUYMAK
BLACK SEA FONDUE

This is a speciality of the Laz people who live along the Black Sea in northern Anatolia. People from other parts of Turkey say two things about the Laz people: the women are very beautiful and the men are very smart before midday. The Laz are famous for creating hundreds of recipes from a fish similar to a sardine called hamsi, *but this is one of the few sardine-free recipes. It's a kind of fondue into which you dip bread, but the maize flour gives it more of a hearty porridge consistency than a Swiss fondue. It prepares you to face the harsh climate along that windy coast.*

SERVES 4

2 tablespoons butter
½ teaspoon salt
½ teaspoon freshly ground black pepper
100 g (3½ oz) maize flour
115 g (4 oz/¾ cup) shredded mozzarella
1 tablespoon grated parmesan
½ teaspoon smoked paprika
pide bread, to serve (to make your own, see page 45)

Combine the butter, salt, pepper and 500 ml (17 fl oz/2 cups) of water in a saucepan over high heat and bring to the boil. Reduce the heat and add the maize flour. Cook for 10 minutes, stirring constantly. Add the cheeses and stir in to melt.

Top with paprika and serve hot in the pot, with pide for dipping.

KATMER
PISTACHIO PANCAKES WITH CLOTTED CREAM

When the suffix -ci (pronounced 'zhee') is added to a Turkish noun it means 'a maker of' that thing. Thus a katmerci is a maker of katmer, the crunchy pancake that is a speciality of Gaziantep, in southeastern Anatolia. The supreme katmerci in that foodie city is a man named Mehmet Özsimitci, whose surname translates as 'maker of genuine simits'. That tells you that one of his ancestors was a specialist in the pretzel/bagels that every Turk consumes as a street snack.

Somewhere along the line, Mehmet's family swapped from making simits to making katmers, adding greatly to the happiness of the world. Outside his shop, at the end of an arcade in the modern part of the city, Mehmet displays a slogan that translates as 'Katmer is not a product of a pastry shop but a culture of master Zekeriya'. Zekeriya is Mehmet's father, who these days sits at the cash register while Mehmet supervises his team of young pastry rollers and dances around the outside tables, taking orders and chatting to customers.

He'll tell you that katmer is best consumed with tea rather than coffee (and he'll order you a tea from the shop next door); that katmer is traditionally the first meal eaten by a bride and groom after their wedding night (to restore their energy); and that half his daily production goes to home delivery—transported by moped across Gaziantep and by mail to homesick Turks all over Europe.

I hope my recipe does him justice.

SERVES 4

---

2 sheets chilled filo pastry, about 40 x 27 cm (16 x 10¾ in) each
2 tablespoons ghee (to make your own, see page 21)
2 tablespoons thick (double) cream, or *kaymak* (see page 54)
2 heaped tablespoons ground pistachios
1 tablespoon sugar

Take the filo sheets out of the fridge and leave to warm to room temperature for 1 hour. Spread one sheet out on a large work surface and overlap with another sheet to create a 40 x 40 cm (16 x 16 in) square of filo. Paint a little ghee where the sheets overlap, and join them together.

Leaving a margin of about 10 cm (4 in) around the edges, dot nine dobs of cream onto the filo to make a square about 20 cm (8 in) wide. Sprinkle the pistachios and sugar over the cream, and then fold the four edges of pastry over to make a square parcel about 20 cm (8 in) wide.

Pour 1 tablespoons of ghee into a frying pan and swirl to coat. Place the pan over medium heat and let the ghee warm for about 10 seconds. Drop the filo parcel into the pan (wrap-side down) and cook for 2 minutes or until golden. Using two spatulas or large knives, turn the pancake over and cook for 1 minute more.

Cut the *katmer* into eight squares and serve two per person as part of a breakfast spread.

Mehmet Özsimitci, third-generation master of the art of *katmer* making.

At Zekeriya Usta, the art of *katmer* making begins with sprinkling and tossing sheets of buckwheat dough to make the thinnest possible fila.

PESTİL
GRAPE LEATHER STUFFED WITH WALNUTS

Pestil is fruit juice that has been dried into strips. Although the process originated as a way of preserving summer ingredients to last through winter, it has now become the candy bar of central Anatolia. Rolled around nuts, it goes in a kid's backpack to be consumed at school as a nutritious morning snack. We're suggesting you make pestil *from grape juice, but you can get tasty results with mulberries, plums or apricots. If you're planning to keep your* pestil *strip for any length of time, roll it up in baking paper so it does not stick.*

MAKES 16

GRAPE LEATHER
500 g (1 lb 2 oz) red grapes
1 star anise
1 cinnamon stick
3 cloves
1 heaped tablespoon cornflour (cornstarch)

WALNUT AND FIG FILLING
5 dried figs
150 g (5½ oz/1⅓ cups) walnuts

Wash the grapes and remove any stalks.

Place a large saucepan over low heat and then add the grapes, star anise, cinnamon stick and cloves. (Don't add any water.) Press down with a potato masher to push out some of the juices. Bring the grape mixture to the boil and then simmer for 15 minutes, pressing down regularly to release the juices.

Take the grape mixture off the heat and leave to cool. Put a muslin (cheesecloth) over another saucepan and pour all the grape pulp into the muslin. Tie the edges of the muslin together and squeeze the bag to extract all the juice—it should yield about 300 ml (10½ fl oz).

Preheat the oven to 100°C (200°F/Gas ½).

Place the grape juice in a saucepan over medium heat and bring to the boil. Put the cornflour in a bowl and mix in 250 ml (9 fl oz/1 cup) of the hot grape juice and then pour the mixture back into the pan. Continue to cook for 15 minutes, stirring regularly, until the mixture thickens to a custard-like syrup.

Line a baking tray, including the sides, with baking paper. Pour the syrup into the tray (it should be about 5 mm/¼ in deep).

Tap the tray to remove any air bubbles from the syrup. Bake for 5 hours, checking every hour to ensure the edges are not becoming too dry. If they appear crusty, use a pastry brush to apply a little water.

Remove the tray from the oven and leave to cool slightly. When the grape leather is cool enough to handle, carefully lift the baking paper edges to remove it from the tray and transfer to a board to cool completely.

Next, make the stuffing. Put the figs in a bowl, cover with hot water and leave to soak for 15 minutes. Transfer the figs to paper towel, drain for 10 minutes, and then remove the stalks. Put the figs in a food processor, add the walnuts and coarsely combine.

Cut across the grape leather to make four equal strips. Spoon a line of filling along the middle of each strip. Roll each strip, lengthways, to create a log about 20 cm (8 in) long, pressing down to keep it sealed. Slice the log into four equal pieces and serve as part of a breakfast spread.

LIVER KEBAPS

You've got to get up pretty early in the morning to catch Ali Haydar. Around 6 am should do it. If you wait till 8, you might find he has sold out of his speciality and gone home. This speciality is lamb liver kebaps—another breakfast tradition of southeastern Anatolia that baffles visitors from Istanbul.

Ali opens his little kebap shop, just down the hill from Gaziantep Castle, immediately after the dawn prayer, which means around 5 am in the summer and around 6 am in the winter. Gradually the customers arrive to sit on the tiny stools outside the shop. Some sit at an angle that suggests they are on the way home from a night of drinking. Others are straight-backed and alert, suggesting they are just out of the nearby mosque and on their way to work.

Inside the shop, Ali, in a light-blue butcher's jacket, risks setting fire to his moustache as he uses a sheet of cardboard to fan the coals of his charcoal grill. He closely watches his skewers and, at the moment the exterior turns crunchy while the inside stays pink, he lifts them away from the coals and wipes them into a mitten of flatbread. When all his livers (and his hearts, lungs and kidneys) have been cooked and consumed by customers, he heads home. In the afternoon he visits the offal market (distinguished by a large sign announcing 'Cleaned Heads') and collects the ingredients to be prepared overnight for the next morning's feast.

SERVES 4

KEBAPS
2 lamb livers, about 300 g (10½ oz)
250 ml (9 fl oz/1 cup) milk
4 mild green or red chillies
1 teaspoon cumin
1 teaspoon hot paprika
1 teaspoon chilli flakes
1 teaspoon salt
250 g (9 oz) butter, softened

PARSLEY SALAD
1 bunch flat-leaf (Italian) parsley
1 red onion
1 tablespoon sumac
1 teaspoon chilli flakes
2 teaspoons pomegranate molasses
   (to make your own, see page 24)
1 tablespoon olive oil

4 store-bought pita breads (or make a *lahmacun* base and fold it over, see page 106), to serve

Soak the lamb livers in milk overnight, covered, in the fridge.

Remove the bowl of livers from the fridge and set aside.

To make the parsley salad, pick the leaves off the parsley and roughly chop. Discard the stems. Finely slice the red onion and place in a salad bowl. Add the parsley, sumac, chilli flakes, molasses and olive oil, and mix well.

When you're ready to cook the livers, remove them from the bowl, pat dry with paper towel and clean off the membrane and sinews. Roughly cut each of the cleaned livers into 16 cubes about 2 cm (¾ in) across—the size of a bird's head, as we say in Turkey.

Preheat the barbecue grill to very high. If using bamboo skewers, soak in water for 15 minutes.

Slit down one side of each chilli and remove the seeds. Slice across each chilli to make six pieces about 1 cm (½ in) wide. Mix the cumin, paprika, chilli flakes and salt in a bowl, then stir in the softened butter. Using your hands, rub the pieces of lamb liver in the spiced butter to coat well.

Next, make the *kebaps* by alternately threading four pieces of liver and three chilli chunks onto each skewer—with the chilli keeping the liver pieces apart. Repeat to make eight *kebaps*.

Put the skewers on the grill and cook for 2 minutes on each side, turning the skewers once. The livers are ready when they start to form a crust.

Partly slit through the pita bread so that it can open like jaws. Spread any leftover spiced butter inside the bread. Next, holding a skewer in your left hand and a pita in your right hand, use the pita like a baseball mitten to wrap round the skewer and pull the row of liver and chilli pieces off. Repeat so each pita contains the liver from two skewers. Open the bread again and add a heaped tablespoon of salad between the two strips of liver. Close the bread and serve immediately.

Ali Haydar's liver stall at 6 am, just after morning prayers.

İNCİR UYUTMASI
THE SLEEPING FIGS

'While shepherds watched their flocks by night, all seated on the ground, they also soaked their figs in milk, and then some sleep they found.' That's essentially the back story of this dish. I love its name—the Sleeping Figs—because it suggests the gentle process of warming the milk and resting the pudding overnight.

A version of this dessert, called teleme, *has been a typical goat herder's snack popular for thousands of years in northwestern Anatolia. They'd milk their goats, add a few drops of sap from fresh figs to the milk, mix it for a few minutes and let it set into* yoğurt. *Then they would slice fresh figs through it. Of course, that restricted the pleasure to early autumn, when figs are at their best. Our version uses cow's milk, walnuts and dried figs to make a healthy breakfast for all seasons.*

SERVES 4

10 dried figs
500 ml (17 fl oz/2 cups) milk
2 fresh figs
2 tablespoons grape molasses
60 g (2¼ oz/½ cup) walnuts

Put the figs in a bowl, cover with hot water and leave to soak for 15 minutes. Transfer the figs to paper towel, leave to drain for 10 minutes, then remove the stalks. Roughly chop each fig into about six pieces and then set aside.

Warm the milk in a saucepan over low heat until it reaches a low simmer, preferably using a simmer mat. Try to keep the temperature around 70°C (160°F) if you have a food thermometer, being careful not to let the milk start to boil.

Add the chopped figs and, using a hand-held blender, mix to a purée. Simmer for a further 5 minutes. (If you don't have a stick blender, pour the mixture into a blender and pulse until smooth, then pour it back into the saucepan and warm for a further 7 minutes).

Half fill four small bowls with the fig purée. Put the bowls in a cool spot, cover with a tea towel (dish towel) and rest for 2 hours. Cover the bowls with plastic wrap and place in the fridge overnight.

When you're nearly ready to serve, preheat the oven to 180°C (350°F/Gas 4).

Cut each fresh fig into quarters. Place them on a baking tray with the skin side down. Brush each fig piece with grape molasses, then bake for 5 minutes until slightly soft but still semi-firm.

Roughly chop the walnuts using a food processor, or by hand. Remove the fig purée cups from the fridge. Place two fig quarters on each cup and sprinkle the crushed walnuts over the top, then serve.

MENEMEN

SMASHED EGGS WITH BULLHORN PEPPERS AND TOMATO

Menemen is a famous breakfast dish in Turkey—the nearest thing we do to scrambled eggs—but nobody can agree on the perfect version. It varies from village to village and from house to house—even in the Aegean town called Menemen, which is not necessarily its place of origin. There is constant debate among chefs and domestic cooks on whether to use butter or oil, whether to include onions or garlic, whether to include peppers or tomatoes, and whether to leave the eggs whole for the eater to smash, or scramble them as part of the cooking process.

I prefer to use oil, because I want to cook the onions and peppers without burning the butter. I add the tomatoes at the last minute so they taste fresh. And I prefer my eggs stirred not scrambled. You can join the debate and vary the dish to your taste.

SERVES 4

4 ripe tomatoes
2 green bullhorn peppers (or 1 large green capsicum/pepper)
1 red onion (optional)
2 tablespoons olive oil
4 eggs
1 teaspoon salt
1 teaspoon freshly ground black pepper
1 tablespoon chopped flat-leaf (Italian) parsley

Score a shallow cross in the base of each tomato. Put the tomatoes in a heatproof bowl and cover with boiling water. Leave for 30 seconds, then transfer to a bowl of cold water and peel the skin away from the cross. To seed, cut the tomato in half and scoop out the seeds with a teaspoon. Chop the tomatoes into 1 cm (½ in) dice.

Cut the peppers in half and discard the stems and seeds. Chop the peppers into 1 cm (½ in) pieces. If you are using an onion, finely slice it.

Heat the olive oil in a frying pan over medium heat. Add a drop of water to the oil. If it sizzles, the oil is ready. Add the onion and cook for 5 minutes. Add the chopped peppers and cook for a further 5 minutes, or until soft. Break the eggs into the pan and cook for 30 seconds. Add the tomatoes, salt and pepper. Stir two or three times to mix in the eggs, but don't blend. Cook over medium heat for a further 3 minutes until the egg whites are set.

Sprinkle with parsley and serve the *menemen* in the pan for people to help themselves.

SUCUKLU YUMURTA
SPICY SAUSAGE WITH EGGS

There is nothing sophisticated about this recipe, but I had to include it because it's one of the most common breakfasts all over my land. It's our answer to Britain's bacon and eggs. A wife might say of her husband: 'He's so hopeless, he can't even cook sucuk *and eggs'.*

You can buy sucuk *everywhere in Turkey, so nobody would bother to make it at home. But if you can't find it near you, you could use the recipe we offer here (or substitute chorizo). Bear in mind that this won't taste exactly like a professional* sucuk, *since that is stuffed into intestine casings, then hung and dried for a month. But it will be tasty.*

SERVES 4

SUCUK*

2 garlic cloves, crushed
250 g (9 oz) minced (ground) veal or beef
150 g (5½ oz) minced (ground) lamb
1 teaspoon cumin
1 teaspoon dried oregano
2 teaspoons chilli flakes
2 teaspoons smoked paprika
1 tablespoon capsicum (pepper) paste
   (see page 32)
1 teaspoon salt
1 teaspoon freshly ground black pepper

1 teaspoon butter
1 teaspoon salt
4 eggs
pide bread, to serve (to make your own,
   see page 45)

To make your own *sucuk,* crush the garlic into a fine paste. Put the garlic into a mixing bowl, add the ground meat and spices, and knead for 10 minutes.

Using a rolling pin, flatten the meat mixture into a strip about 1 cm (½ in) thick and then roll it into a log about 4 cm (1½ in) wide. Wrap tightly with plastic wrap, squeezing all the air out, then freeze for 1 hour.

Remove the *sucuk* from the freezer, remove the plastic wrap, and slice off twenty thin slices (about 5 mm/¼ in thick). Put the remaining *sucuk* in the fridge where it will keep, wrapped in plastic, for 2 weeks.

(If using store-bought *sucuk* or chorizo, soak in hot water for 15 seconds, then peel off the skin. Slice into twenty thin slices.)

Place a frying pan over medium heat. Add the *sucuk* and spread out into a single layer. Add the butter (and 1 tablespoon of water if the *sucuk* seems dry) and salt, then cook for 1 minute. Once the *sucuk* begins to sizzle, take out eight slices from the middle of the pan and break the eggs into the space created. Put the eight *sucuk* back on top of the eggs.

Cook for 3 minutes, or until the egg whites begin to set, the sides curl, and the yolk is soft but still formed in the centre. If you prefer your eggs more cooked, cover with a lid and simmer for 1 minute more.

Place the *sucuk* in the middle of the table—the Turkish way—for people to help themselves. Serve with pide.

NOTE

Instead of making your own *sucuk* you can use 100 g (3½ oz) of store-bought *sucuk* or chorizo if you prefer.

ÇILBIR
POACHED EGGS IN GARLIC YOĞURT AND PAPRIKA

In Ottoman times, çılbır *was the generic term for poached eggs, done all sorts of ways. Palace records from the fifteenth century show that a version of* çılbır *containing poached eggs and onion was cooked for the mighty sultan Mehmet II. The imperial cooks kept improving on it over the years. This recipe, with garlic* yoğurt, *was a favourite of the second-last sultan in the empire, Abdulhamid II, in the early twentieth century, and became the gold standard for* çılbır *in homes and restaurants across Anatolia.*

SERVES 4

1 garlic clove (or chopped garlic shoots)
500 g (1 lb 2 oz/2 cups) plain *yoğurt*
½ small red capsicum (pepper)
125 ml (4 fl oz/½ cup) white vinegar
8 eggs
2 tablespoons butter
½ tablespoon aleppo red pepper flakes (or chilli flakes)
4 teaspoons smoked paprika
pide bread, to serve (to make your own, see page 45)

Crush the garlic and mix it with the *yoğurt* (if the taste of raw garlic in the morning is too strong for you, you could leave out this step, and instead fry a little garlic or chopped garlic shoots later with the capsicum). Set aside at room temperature.

Remove the seeds from the capsicum and finely chop.

Divide the *yoğurt* mixture into four bowls.

Put 1 litre (35 fl oz/4 cups) of water and the vinegar in a deep frying pan over high heat. Bring to the boil, then reduce the heat to a gentle simmer. Carefully break in the eggs, one at a time, with a maximum of three eggs poaching at a time. Cook for 2–3 minutes, or until the whites are set and the yolks are still soft and runny.

While the eggs are poaching, melt the butter in a saucepan, add the red pepper flakes, paprika and capsicum (and garlic, if you've saved it for this step) and cook for 3 minutes.

When ready to serve, scoop the eggs out of the simmering water with a slotted spoon and place two in each bowl, on top of the *yoğurt*. Pour a light stream of the melted butter and peppers over the eggs. Serve with pide.

KAYGANA
CRETAN EGGS WITH WILD WEEDS

There's a joke about a salad farmer who is having a tea in the village café. A neighbour comes in and says: 'There's a goat in your field'. The farmer says: 'Don't worry, he won't eat much'. Shortly afterward, the neighbour returns and says: 'There's a cow in your field'. The farmer keeps sipping his tea and says: 'Don't worry about it'. Then the neighbour returns and says: 'There's a man from Crete in your field'. The farmer leaps up and rushes back to save his field before everything green has been stripped.

People of Cretan background are famous for eating the dark-green weeds that grow wild along the Aegean coast and that were ignored for centuries by Turkish cooks. This egg dish uses the kind of wild (and tame) greens the Cretans have taught the Turks to love.

SERVES 4

1 cup of any or all of these, mixed:
   nettles, curly endives, chicory, dandelion
   greens, round radicchio, beetroot (beet) leaves,
   wild rocket (but not witlof)
3 spring onions (scallions)
1 onion
80 ml (2½ fl oz/⅓ cup) olive oil
1 teaspoon salt
1 teaspoon freshly ground black pepper
1 teaspoon hot paprika
4 eggs
pide bread, to serve (to make your own,
   see page 45)

If you are using nettles, use gloves to handle them. To remove the sting, put in a heatproof bowl and cover with boiling water for 30 seconds. Transfer to cold water for 30 seconds. Pick the green leaves and discard the stems.

Clean and finely chop the endives and the chicory, discarding the woody stems. Wash the spring onions, then remove the roots and green outer layer. Finely chop the onion.

Heat the olive oil in a non-stick frying pan over medium heat, then add the onion and brown for 5 minutes. Add the spring onions and cook for another 3 minutes, then add the wild leaves in this order (from toughest to softest): endives, chicory, radicchio, nettle, dandelion, beetroot leaves, wild rocket. Lightly fry for about 5 minutes to let any excess water evaporate. Add the spices and stir. Make four wells in the mixture and break an egg into each well. Continue to cook until the whites are set but the yolks are still runny.

Serve the *kaygana* in the pan for people to help themselves. If the yolks spread into the mixture, so much the better. Serve with pide.

FIERY LAMB AND RICE SOUP

Take a whole sheep, skin it and gut it. Boil it for 12 hours. Shred all the meat. Boil the same weight of rice. Put some rice, a handful of meat and a hell of a lot of garlic and chilli into a bowl. Put it over an open flame so the fat on the surface catches fire. Serve.

That's not the recipe we're suggesting for beyran, but it's what Mustafa Hasırcı and his team do every day at Metanet, just behind the central spice market in Gaziantep, southeastern Turkey. The restaurant's name means 'endurance' or 'fortitude', which is presumably what you need to eat this spicy soup every day for breakfast as many citizens of Gaziantep do (only tourists think of having beyran for lunch).

Mustafa certainly has endurance. For the past forty years he's been getting up every day at 4 am to make his soup—following in the footsteps of his father, the founder of Metanet. Mustafa has earned the title usta, which means 'master of your craft'. He has no equal in Gaziantep.

Our soup is a modified version of Mustafa's masterwork, and we won't tell anybody if you decide to have it for lunch or dinner.

SERVES 4

1 lamb neck, about 1 kg (2 lb 4 oz)
220 g (7¾ oz/1 cup) medium-grain rice
2 teaspoons salt
4 garlic cloves, crushed
1 tablespoon chilli flakes

Put the lamb neck in a large saucepan with 1 litre (35 fl oz/4 cups) of water, then cover, and bring to the boil. Reduce the heat and simmer for about 1½ hours.

Lift out the neck and place on a rack or plate to cool. Do not discard the cooking water. When the lamb is cool enough to handle, strip off the meat and discard the bones. Shred the lamb into small strips and set aside.

Pour the rice into the pot of lamb-flavoured water and bring it back to the boil over medium heat. Cook the rice for 15 minutes, then add the salt, garlic, shredded lamb and chilli flakes. Increase the heat to very high and boil rapidly for 1 minute to spread the red-chilli colour through the liquid. Serve immediately, while very hot.

Mustafa Hasırcı preparing mutton for beyran soup at Metanet, Gaziantep.

Lunch heaven: one of Musa Dağdeviren's three Çiya restaurant in Kadıköy, Istanbul.

LUNCH

CASUAL & REGIONAL

LUNCH

Traditionally in Turkey, lunch was no big deal. People ate before they went out to work in the fields, and carried with them simple snacks such as bread, olives and cheese. In the late nineteenth century, cheap eateries started appearing in the cities, where tradesmen and shopkeepers could grab a soup, a stew, and maybe a *börek* or a *kebap*. These places came to be called *lokanta* (from the Italian word *locanda*).

In the 1980s, the lunchtime habit of going quick and casual made Turks in Istanbul an easy target for the American fast-food chains, and for a while it looked as if the midday formula of soup-stew-*kebap* was going to turn into Coke-fries-Big Mac.

Then Musa Dağdeviren appeared and went in exactly the opposite direction. He travelled round the countryside and spoke to farmers, bakers, butchers, picklers, pastrymakers and home cooks, and figured out how to recreate Turkey's vast regional diversity in a commercial kitchen.

Now his three *lokantas*—Çiya, Çiya Sofrası and Çiya Kebap—in the Istanbul port suburb of Kadıköy are packed every lunchtime with people desperate to test how many of the fifty dishes on display can be crammed into their bellies, and looking forward to returning three months later to find the new season has brought a different array of 'forgotten' recipes. Young chefs have been inspired by Musa's 'rediscoveries' to open bistro-style *lokantas* across Istanbul.

Musa grew up in a family of bakers in southeastern Anatolia, and moved to Istanbul in the late 1970s to operate the wood-fire oven in his uncle's *kebap* house. He became obsessed with preserving the great regional repertoire that seemed to be disappearing in the rush towards 'modernisation'. Here's a rough translation of his philosophy:

I travel all over the country to cook with people in their homes and also study old books to find new leads. I get very excited when I discover new poor-people's dishes, because I believe only poor people can create great food. If a man has money, he can buy anything, but a person who has nothing must create beauty from within.

Since he opened his first Çiya in 1987, Musa has regularly found himself in dispute with the Turkish food establishment, which is prone to engage in nationalist myth-making and wishful thinking about our cuisine. He fights fantasies with facts, publishing a quarterly magazine called *Yemek ve Kültür* (Food and Culture), which funds scholarship on the origins of Anatolian dishes. He's setting up a cooking school and research centre, with a seed bank that will preserve native ingredients.

Luckily for me, Musa opened his first restaurant close to my father's tailor shop in Kadıköy, back when I was a teenager who carried a McDonald's cup to school to show how cool I was. Çiya became my favourite eating place and Musa became my food hero.

Many of the dishes in this chapter, whether rustic, regional or urban, were inspired by Musa's food philosophy. You would be more likely to find them in Turkish homes far from Istanbul rather than in restaurants—unless you were lucky enough to live in Kadıköy.

Musa at one of his Çiya restaurants, with candied pumpkins, eggplants and olives.

PİRPİRİM AŞI
PURSLANE AND ANCIENT GRAINS STEW

Vegetarians are always surprised by how many interesting dishes the land of lamb lovers can offer. In season, this stew appears regularly on the famous 'Fifty Bowl' display table at Çiya restaurant in Istanbul's Kadıköy market, using the kind of grains humans have been boiling for millennia. While it is likely that lentils and chickpeas originated in Anatolia, black-eyed peas are recent arrivals—brought from Africa in the fifteenth century for palace chefs eager to surprise the sultan.

The sour-salty green purslane, which contains more omega-3 than any other leafy vegetable, is Turkey's favourite weed, usually consumed fresh in summer and dried in winter. In the first great work on botany, written in the fourth century BC, the Greek philosopher Theophrastus advises sowing purslane in mid-spring so you can enjoy it in summer. If you can't find purslane, the best substitute is baby rocket (arugula).

SERVES 4

95 g (3¼ oz/½ cup) dried chickpeas
95 g (3¼ oz/½ cup) black-eyed beans
110 g (3¾ oz/½ cup) green lentils
45 ml (1½ fl oz) olive oil
1 onion
2 garlic cloves
1 tomato
½ tablespoon capsicum (pepper) paste
　(see page 32)
90 g (3¼ oz/½ cup) coarse bulgur
2 teaspoons freshly ground black pepper
1 bunch purslane (or baby rocket/arugula)
juice of ½ lemon
1 teaspoon sumac
1 tablespoon butter
2 teaspoons dried mint
2 teaspoons chilli flakes
pide bread (to make your own,
　see page 45), to serve

Cover the chickpeas with water and soak overnight. Cover the black-eyed beans with water and also soak overnight.

Strain, then rinse the chickpeas and black-eyed beans. Rinse the lentils. Boil the chickpeas in plenty of water for 20 minutes, covered, and then add the black-eyed beans and lentils and boil, covered, for another 40 minutes.

Heat the olive oil in a saucepan over medium heat. Add the onion and cook for 3 minutes, then add the garlic and cook for 1 minute more. Cut the tomato in half and then grate it into the onion, discarding the skin.

Add the three pulses to the onion mixture. Dilute the capsicum paste in 250 ml (9 fl oz/1 cup) of warm water and add it to the mix. Add the bulgur and the pepper. Bring to the boil, then reduce the heat to a simmer.

Pick the leaves from the purslane and add them, whole, to the stew. Simmer, covered, for 10 minutes. Add the lemon juice and stir in the sumac, then turn off the heat.

Melt the butter in a frying pan over medium heat. Add the mint and stir for 1 minute. Add the chilli flakes and stir for 1 minute more.

Divide the stew into four bowls and drizzle with mint butter. Serve with pide.

ANALI KİZLI

'MOTHER AND DAUGHTER' (DUMPLING AND CHICKPEA STEW)

This complex combination of large and small dumplings in a lamb and chickpea stew comes from Malatya in eastern Anatolia, an area best known for apricots. The mothers are a mixture of beef and bulgur stuffed with minced lamb. The daughters are not big enough to have stuffing. You won't find this dish in many restaurants—only home cooks (and my friend Musa) have the time to do it properly.

For the mums' outer coating it's important to choose beef with a low fat content and to knead it thoroughly so it dissolves into the bulgur.

SERVES 4

BASE
50 g (1¾ oz/¼ cup) dried chickpeas
400 g (14 oz) lamb leg
2 onions
1 tablespoon butter
1 tablespoon olive oil
1 tablespoon capsicum (pepper) paste
   (see page 32)
10 flat-leaf (Italian) parsley leaves, finely chopped
juice of ½ lemon

STUFFING
1 onion
1 tablespoon butter
150 g (5½ oz) minced (ground) lamb
½ tablespoon tomato paste (to make your own,
   see page 24)
½ tablespoon capsicum (pepper) paste
   (see page 32)
½ teaspoon salt
½ teaspoon freshly ground black pepper
½ teaspoon cumin

SHELLS
250 g (9 oz) fine bulgur
200 g (7 oz) lean minced (ground) beef
1 egg
1 tablespoon tomato paste (to make your own,
   see page 24)
1 tablespoon butter
½ tablespoon cornflour (cornstarch)

TOPPING
2 tablespoons butter
½ tablespoon dried mint
½ tablespoon chilli flakes

Cover the chickpeas with water and soak overnight.

Strain and rinse the chickpeas, place in a saucepan with 500 ml (17 fl oz/2 cups) of water and simmer, covered, for 1 hour.

While the chickpeas are simmering, make the stuffing. Finely chop the onion. Melt the butter in a saucepan over medium heat. Add the onion and cook for 3 minutes until soft. Add the minced lamb and cook for 2 minutes more.

Put the remaining ingredients in a bowl and mix with 125 ml (4 fl oz/½ cup) of water. Stir the mixture into the onion and minced lamb, and bring to the boil, then simmer, with the lid on, for 5 minutes. Set the stuffing aside.

Next, make the shells. Put all the ingredients in a mixing bowl. Slowly add 45 ml (1½ fl oz) of warm water. Wet your hands and knead for 5 minutes to make a smooth paste.

Mould the shell mixture into spheres about the size of a ping-pong ball. Put a ball in your palm

and with the fingers of the other hand, make a well in the mixture. Place a teaspoon of stuffing in the middle and fold the shell back around it. Repeat to make sixteen balls. With the rest of the bulgur mixture, make about forty smaller chickpea-size balls.

Now, make the base. Chop the meat from the leg of lamb into small cubes, removing any sinews and most of the fat. Finely chop the onions. Melt the butter in a frying pan over medium heat. Add the olive oil and, when sizzling, cook the onion for 5 minutes until translucent. Add the capsicum paste and fry for 1 minute. Add the cubed lamb. Cook for 2 minutes, then add 250 ml (9 fl oz/1 cup) of water. Bring to the boil and simmer for 5 minutes.

Add the small balls (daughters) and the large balls (mothers), chickpeas and parsley to the lamb mixture. Bring back to the boil, then reduce the heat and simmer for 10 minutes. Add the lemon juice. Divide the mothers and daughters onto four plates, with the cubed lamb underneath.

For the topping, place a frying pan over medium heat and melt the butter. Add the dried mint and chilli flakes and sizzle for 4 minutes. Drizzle the mint and chilli butter over the *analı kizli* and serve.

TÜRLÜ
SUMMER VEGETABLE CASSEROLE

The Turkish word türlü *means 'with variety', and implies that you can use any kind of vegetable that's available in summer. This is sometimes called the Turkish ratatouille, but* türlü *has many more ingredients than the French dish, and you can even include lamb or beef and still call it* türlü.

You need to layer the ingredients in a deep pot (traditionally clay), with the slowest-cooking vegetables at the bottom, and simmer it for a long time. So yes, it's a casserole, which is normally thought of as a winter warmer. But this version, which includes green beans and okra, is perfect served cold on the hottest day, with a side of rice pilav and yoğurt. It tastes even better the next day.

SERVES 4

1 long eggplant (aubergine)
1 zucchini (courgette)
1 boiling potato
2 onions
3 garlic cloves
1 carrot
2 green bullhorn peppers (or 1 large green capsicum/pepper)
1 red capsicum (pepper)
150 g (5½ oz) green beans
100 g (3½ oz) okra
3 ripe tomatoes
45 ml (1½ fl oz) olive oil
1 thin slice of ginger
1 teaspoon salt
1 teaspoon freshly ground black pepper
rice pilav (see page 27), boiled rice or plain *yoğurt*, to serve (optional)

Preheat the oven to 180°C (350°F/Gas 4).

Peel the eggplant and zucchini and chop both into 3 cm (1¼ in) pieces. Wash and peel the potato, and chop into 3 cm (1¼ in) cubes. Finely slice the onions and chop the garlic. Peel the carrot and cut into 1 cm (½ in) pieces. Seed and chop the bullhorn pepper and capsicum into pieces about 3 cm (1¼ in) long. Cut the tips off the green beans and chop into 3 cm (1¼ in) pieces.

Cut the stalks off the okra. Score a shallow cross in the base of the tomatoes, then transfer to a heatproof bowl and cover with boiling water. Leave for 30 seconds, then plunge in cold water and peel the skin away from the cross. Roughly chop. Very finely chop the ginger.

Heat the olive oil in a large saucepan over medium heat. Add the onion and cook for 5 minutes, or until soft. Add the garlic and fry for another 2 minutes. Add the ginger, vegetables, salt, pepper and 500 ml (17 fl oz/2 cups) of water. Seal the pan with foil, then put the lid on. Simmer for 20 minutes. Turn off the heat and leave to rest for 20 minutes without opening the lid.

Serve warm with rice pilav or boiled rice, or cold with *yoğurt* on a hot summer day.

BEEF GOULASH

There's too much mythology and not enough research in discussions about food in Turkey. Turkish chefs like to claim the Hungarians got their word 'goulash' from the Turkish term kul aşi *(which means 'common man's dish'—a stew served to soldiers 300 years ago). But, if they'd bothered to check, they'd find that in Hungarian the word* gulyas *means a 'cattle herder', and since the ninth century, the Hungarian herders have been in the habit of carrying beef and vegetables and making a kind of stew out in the field.*

Throughout the seventeenth century, the soldiers of the Ottoman Empire regularly met the soldiers of the Austro-Hungarian Empire in battles for the control of Vienna. Presumably, the Turkish troops were eating kul aşi *on one side while the Hungarians were eating goulash on the other. Both would have been flavouring their stews with peppers, which arrived from the Americas in the early 1500s and were first cultivated by Turks living in Budapest.*

SERVES 4

500 g (1 lb 2 oz) topside or chuck steak
2 tablespoons plain (all-purpose) flour
2 onions
4 garlic cloves
2 tomatoes
2 green bullhorn peppers (or 1 large green capsicum/pepper)
1 carrot
2 boiling potatoes
1 parsnip
2 tablespoons vegetable oil
1 tablespoon capsicum (pepper) paste (see page 32)
½ tablespoon tomato paste (to make your own, see page 24)
1 bay leaf
8 celery leaves, chopped
1 tablespoon cumin
1 tablespoon chilli flakes
1 tablespoon salt
1 tablespoon freshly ground black pepper
rice pilav (see page 27), to serve

Chop the beef into cubes about 3 cm (1¼ in) wide. Toss in the flour, then shake off the excess.

Finely chop the onions and the garlic. Roughly chop the tomatoes. Remove the stalks and seeds from the peppers and chop. Chop the carrot, potatoes and parsnip.

Heat the vegetable oil in a heavy-based saucepan over medium heat. Add the onions and garlic and sauté for 3 minutes. Increase the heat to medium–high and brown the beef cubes evenly for 5 minutes. Add the tomatoes, peppers, capsicum paste and tomato paste. Stir for 2 minutes. Add the bay leaf, celery leaves and 750 ml (26 fl oz/3 cups) of water, then bring to boil.

Add the vegetables and the spices. Continue to boil over medium heat for about 15 minutes, or until the potato and parsnip are soft.

Serve with rice pilav.

PAPARA
GRANDMA'S BREAD AND BEEF STEW

I learned this dish from my mother's mother, who died in 2010 at the age of 103. Living through two world wars and three military coups, she raised three kids by herself. She knew how to survive, how to improvise and how not to waste a single grain.

I remember when she made papara the first time, from leftover bread, rice and a handful of minced meat. The origin of the dish is uncertain, but it is part of the peasant culture of Anatolia and the Balkans. In Istanbul during the seventeenth century, there were shops that sold 'papara cubed bread' as an ingredient for this dish—because, of course, the rich gourmands didn't have stale bread of their own.

SERVES 4

375 g (13 oz/1½ cups) plain *yoğurt*
1 onion
2 tablespoons vegetable oil
200 g (7 oz) minced (ground) lamb or veal
500 ml (17 fl oz/2 cups) beef stock
1 tablespoon tomato paste (to make your own, see page 24)
3 slices stale bread
2 tablespoons butter
185 g (6½ oz/1 cup) leftover rice (optional)
2 garlic cloves
1 teaspoon chilli flakes
1 teaspoon sweet paprika
1 tablespoon dried mint

Preheat the oven to 180°C (350°F/Gas 4).

Place the *yoğurt* on a sheet of muslin (cheesecloth) and tie up the corners. Hang the muslin over a pot for 3 hours to allow the *yoğurt* to thicken.

Finely chop the onion. Heat the vegetable oil in a frying pan over medium heat. Add the onion and sauté for 3 minutes. Add the meat and cook for 5 minutes. Add the beef stock and bring to the boil. Mix in the tomato paste and simmer for 15 minutes.

Chop the stale bread into 2 cm (about 1 in) cubes. Melt half the butter in a frying pan over medium heat. Brush the bread with the melted butter, then roast in the oven for 5 minutes, or until golden.

Add the bread to the minced meat and mix it through. If you want to thicken it with rice, stir that into the mixture now. Simmer for 5 minutes.

Pour the *papara* into a serving bowl.

Crush the garlic into a smooth paste using a mortar and pestle (or in a bowl with a wooden spoon) and fold it into the *yoğurt*. Pour the garlic *yoğurt* over the dish.

Melt the remaining butter in a small frying pan, add the chilli flakes and paprika, and sizzle for 2 minutes. Pour the butter mixture onto the *yoğurt*. Top with dried mint and serve.

Every village has a day of the week devoted to a fresh food market where local farmers' wives offer their produce. Opposite: the local market also sells many brands of olive oil.

KARNIYARIK

'SPLIT BELLY' (BAKED EGGPLANT STUFFED WITH BEEF)

As a chef, I often get asked: 'What would be your last meal?' I always reply: 'My grandmother's karnıyarık'. *She put something in there that I have never been able to replicate.*

The name 'split belly' is not a reference to what this dish will do to you, but to what you need to do to the eggplant. This dish first appeared in the nineteenth century on palace menus, but now it's a lokanta *favourite.*

There's a mistaken belief that the next recipe, İmam bayıldı *('The priest fainted'), is just a vegetarian version of this one. The recipes both include eggplant and they look alike, but the other ingredients and the cooking methods are different. And the priest fainted years before the belly got split.*

SERVES 4

---

4 long eggplants (aubergines)
135 ml (4½ fl oz) vegetable oil,
   plus extra for greasing
1 onion
1 garlic clove
250 g (9 oz) minced (ground) beef
1 tomato
2 tablespoons tomato paste (to make your own,
   see page 24)
½ tablespoon sugar
4 cherry tomatoes, halved
4 long sweet chillies (or 1 green bullhorn pepper)
½ tablespoon capsicum (pepper) paste
   (see page 32)
½ teaspoon freshly ground black pepper
½ teaspoon salt
10 flat-leaf (Italian) parsley leaves
rice pilav (see page 27) or boiled rice, and plain
   yoğurt, to serve

Slice three strips off the skin of each eggplant, starting about 2 cm (¾ in) below the top and finishing 2 cm (¾ in) above the base. The eggplants should now look like they're wearing striped pyjamas.

Heat 125 ml (4 fl oz/½ cup) of the vegetable oil in a frying pan over high heat. Add a drop of water to the oil. If it sizzles, the oil is ready. Carefully add the eggplants and cook for 2 minutes on each side, or until the exposed flesh is golden. Place the eggplant on paper towel to absorb the excess oil.

Preheat the oven to 180°C (350°F/Gas 4).

Finely dice the onion and slice the garlic. Heat the remaining ½ tablespoon of vegetable oil in a saucepan over medium heat. Add the onion and cook for 5 minutes or until translucent. Add the garlic and cook for 2 minutes more. Add the beef and cook for 3 minutes, stirring regularly.

Cut the tomato in half and grate it over the mixture, discarding the skin. Dilute 1 tablespoon of tomato paste in 1 tablespoon of water and stir it into the beef. Cook for 3 minutes more, stirring regularly.

Slit each eggplant lengthways, starting 2 cm (¾ in) from the tip and finishing 2 cm (¾ in) from the base. With the slit facing upwards, use the back of a tablespoon to push the slit open and give the eggplant a canoe shape. Brush a baking tray with oil. Put the eggplant boats into the greased tray. Add a pinch of sugar to each eggplant and fill each boat with the beef mixture. Cut the chillies in half (or cut the bullhorn pepper in quarters) and remove the stalks and seeds. Place 1 sweet chilli (or a slice of bullhorn pepper) and 1 halved cherry tomato on top of the beef stuffing in each eggplant.

Dilute the remaining 1 tablespoon of tomato paste and the capsicum paste in 250 ml (9 fl oz/1 cup) of boiling water. Spoon the liquid over the eggplants to prevent them drying out while baking. Put the *karnıyarık* in the oven and bake for 20 minutes, until the pepper starts to brown.

Serve one boat per person, hot, with rice pilav or boiled rice, and *yoğurt* on the side.

İMAM BAYILDI

'THE PRIEST FAINTED' (BRAISED EGGPLANT STUFFED WITH PEPPERS AND TOMATOES)

Why did this dish (first discussed in an 1844 cookbook) make the priest faint? Some say it was with pleasure, some say because of the extravagant amount of oil in it and some say because it used up every ingredient in his pantry. The story I like comes from Moveable Feasts: The History, Science and Lore of Food, where Gregory McNamee says the imam married the daughter of an olive oil seller. Every day after the wedding she made him an eggplant dish cooked in her father's olive oil. On the thirteenth day the oil ran out and her husband collapsed in shock.

Most Turkish cooks would start this dish by frying the eggplant, but the famous Istanbul chef Şemsa Denizsel of Kantin showed me what she says is the original method—steaming the eggplants in a pot with the stuffing mixture before filling them. This makes them a lot lighter, and more delicious. With this recipe, the imam might have lasted a few more days.

SERVES 4

4 tomatoes
25 flat-leaf (Italian) parsley leaves
4 onions
1 teaspoon salt
1 teaspoon sugar
4 long eggplants (aubergines)
150 ml (5 fl oz) olive oil,
    plus extra for greasing
16 garlic cloves, whole and peeled
1 red bullhorn pepper (or ½ large red
    capsicum/pepper)

Score a shallow cross in the base of the tomatoes, then transfer to a heatproof bowl and cover with boiling water. Leave for 30 seconds, then plunge in cold water and peel the skin away from the cross. Cut the tomatoes in half and scoop out the seeds with a teaspoon. Roughly chop.

Finely chop the parsley leaves. Put the onions, tomato, parsley, salt and sugar in a large saucepan and knead the mixture for 2 minutes.

Slice three strips off the skin of each eggplant, starting about 2 cm (about 1 in) below the top and finishing 2 cm (about 1 inch) above the base. The eggplants should now look like they're wearing striped pyjamas. Put them on top of the mixture. Pour in the olive oil and simmer over low heat for 30 minutes, with the lid on. Add the garlic cloves and simmer for another 20 minutes.

Remove the eggplants from the pan and slit lengthways, starting 2 cm (¾ in) from the tip and finishing 2 cm (¾ in) from the base. With the slit

facing upwards, use the back of a tablespoon to push the slit open and give the eggplant a canoe shape. Brush a baking tray with oil. Put the eggplant boats into the greased tray. Remove the garlic cloves from the tray and set aside. Spoon the onion mixture from the pan into each eggplant.

Remove the stalk and seeds from the pepper and cut into four slices, lengthways. Place one slice of pepper and four garlic cloves on top of each canoe. Spoon the remaining sauce over the top, then set aside until you're ready to serve.

Serve the *imam bayıldı* at room temperature, or do what I do in my restaurant and reheat them in a 180°C (350°F/Gas 4) oven for 10 minutes.

PASTIRMALI KURU FASULYE

BAKED WHITE BEANS WITH SPICE-CURED BEEF

The beans in this recipe are native to South America and didn't reach Anatolia until the eighteenth century. But they quickly became a staple food.

Stewed white beans in tomato sauce is the cheapest and most popular snack in lokantas throughout Turkey, and generally served with rice and pickles.

Back in 1960, a political columnist named Çetin Altan kept having his columns banned or heavily censored by the government. In exasperation, he finally began a column with the words 'Let's talk about the benefits of white beans'. That phrase has become a kind of code to signal when a journalist is being censored.

Don't try to rush this preparation. If you don't soak the beans overnight and change the water several times, be prepared for digestive difficulties.

SERVES 6

500 g (1 lb 2 oz) dried cannellini beans
1 tablespoon dried oregano
1 teaspoon cumin
2 onions
2 tablespoons vegetable oil
1 tablespoon tomato paste (to make your own, see page 24)
1 tablespoon capsicum (pepper) paste (see page 32)
2 teaspoon salt
1 teaspoon freshly ground black pepper
1 tomato
3 green chillies
2 tablespoons butter
150 g (5½ oz) thinly sliced *pastırma*

Wash the beans, transfer to a large saucepan and cover with water. Bring to the boil. Change the water and then leave to soak overnight.

Strain and rinse the beans thoroughly. Put the beans back in the pan and cover with water (to about 5 cm/2 in above the beans). Stir in the dried oregano and cumin. Bring to the boil, then reduce to a simmer and cook for 20 minutes, or until the water evaporates from the top and the beans are soft but not mushy.

Meanwhile, place a clay pot or casserole dish in the oven and preheat to 180°C (350°F/Gas 4).

Roughly chop the onions. Heat the vegetable oil in a deep frying pan over medium heat. Add the onion and cook for 5 minutes, or until translucent. Stir in the tomato paste, capsicum paste, salt and pepper. Strain the beans and add them to the pan. Cook for 15 minutes.

Slice the tomato into rounds. Remove the stalks from the chillies and slit down one side to remove the seeds. Chop the chillies into pieces about 1 cm (½ in) wide.

Carefully take the pot out of the oven. Add the butter and pour in the bean mixture. Spread the slices of *pastırma* over the top, then layer with the tomato and chilli. Put the pot back in the oven and cook, covered, for 10 minutes.

Serve the *pastırmalı kuru fasulye* in the pot for people to help themselves.

Hatice Kalan and friends tell stories and prepare tiny *yuvalama* at Yörem restaurant, Gaziantep.

YUVALAMA
'STORYTELLER SOUP' (LAMB AND BEEFBALL SOUP)

Because this dish takes a long time, it was traditional in the town of Gaziantep to hire a professional storyteller to keep the cooks entertained while they rolled hundreds of tiny balls of meat and rice. Yuvalama is consumed in vast quantities during the three-day eating festival called Bayram that follows Ramadan.

The word yuvalama means 'rolled', and it is said that it takes one person four hours to roll 1 kilo of meatballs. Few restaurants serve yuvalama these days, because their kitchen staff just don't have the time, but it remains a signature dish at the Gaziantep restaurant Yörem. Hatice Kalan, a rare female restaurateur in this male-dominated town, sits rolling and storytelling through the afternoon with a bunch of friends and employees. The meatballs they make go into her soup (decorated with a yin and yang of mint oil and paprika oil) and also get sold as takeaway to locals who add them to their own soups at home—grateful not to do all that rolling themselves (but missing out on the stories).

SERVES 4

95 g (3¼ oz/½ cup) dried chickpeas
440 g (15½ oz/2 cups) medium-grain rice
1 tablespoon salt
750 g (1 lb 10 oz) plain *yoğurt*
250 g lean minced (ground) beef
1 teaspoon white pepper
165 g (5¾ oz/1 cup) rice flour
2 onions
2 tablespoons vegetable oil
400 g (14 oz) lamb (preferably lamb leg), trimmed and cubed
1 egg
2 tablespoons butter
1 tablespoon dried mint
½ tablespoon chilli flakes

Cover the chickpeas with water and soak overnight. Cover the rice with water, add half the salt, and also soak overnight.

Place the *yoğurt* on a sheet of muslin (cheesecloth) and tie up the corners. Hang the muslin over a pot for 3 hours to allow the *yoğurt* to thicken.

Strain and rinse the chickpeas, place in a saucepan with 500 ml (17 fl oz/2 cups) of water and simmer, covered, for 1 hour.

Strain and rinse the rice, then blend in a food processor or blender. Transfer the rice to a mixing bowl and add the beef and white pepper. Knead the mixture with wet hands for at least 5 minutes, or until it becomes a thick paste—almost like a dough.

Spread the rice flour onto a baking tray. Shape the dough into chickpea-size balls, regularly dipping your hands into the rice flour on the tray to keep them dry. You can roll the balls between your palms three or four at a time. Even so, this will take a long time, so enlist other family members to help, or have a storyteller ready. When all the mixture has been made into balls, space them out on the rice flour so they don't stick together.

Roughly chop the onions. Heat the vegetable oil in a saucepan over medium heat. Add the onion and cook for 2 minutes. Add the cubed pieces of meat and brown for 5 minutes, stirring regularly. Add 1 litre (35 fl oz/4 cups) of water, bring to the boil and simmer, covered, for 20 minutes.

Toss the rice balls lightly in the flour and add them to the lamb. Simmer, covered, for another 15 minutes.

Whisk the *yoğurt* and egg in a bowl, then whisk in 250 ml (9 fl oz/1 cup) of the lamb cooking liquid. Slowly pour the *yoğurt* mixture into the pan, whisking constantly. Add the chickpeas. Bring the liquid back to the boil and simmer, covered, for 5 minutes.

Melt the butter in a frying pan over medium heat. And the mint and chilli flakes and stir for 2 minutes.

Ladle the soup into four bowls, drizzle the mint and chilli butter over the top and serve.

LAHMACUN

THIN-CRUST PIDE WITH SPICY LAMB TOPPING

When I say thin-crust pizza is Italy's answer to lahmacun (pronounced 'lah-mahjun'), I'm not trying to start a fight. The idea of putting spiced mince on a disc of dough would have occurred to human beings long before there were nations called Italy or Turkey—or for that matter Armenia, Greece or Syria—all of whom have claimed to be the originators of this addictive pastry. What we do know is that nowadays lahmacun is a speciality of the town of Şanlıurfa, in southeastern Turkey, where they pride themselves on the crispness of their bases.

Lahmacun should not be confused with the heavier kıymalı pide, well known in and out of Turkey for the thickness of its dough and the coarseness of its meat topping. For lahmacun you need a light touch.

In Şanlıurfa, they turn out hundreds of lahmacuns every lunchtime from big stone ovens. The best way to get the same effect at home is to use a pizza stone or an unglazed terracotta tile, and to ensure your oven is preheated to the max.

SERVES 4

BASE

200 g (7 oz/1⅓ cups) plain (all-purpose) flour, plus extra for dusting

1 teaspoon salt

70 g (2½ oz/½ cup) wholemeal flour (if using a baking tray)

TOPPING

2 tomatoes

1 red capsicum (pepper)

75 g (2⅔ oz) capsicum (pepper) paste (see page 32)

5 garlic cloves

½ bunch flat-leaf (Italian) parsley

2 teaspoons chilli flakes

1 teaspoon freshly ground black pepper

1 teaspoon salt

200 g (7 oz) minced (ground) lamb (about 25 per cent fat)

RED ONION AND SUMAC SALAD (OPTIONAL)

½ red onion, finely sliced

1 teaspoon salt

1 tablespoon sumac

1 tablespoon extra virgin olive oil

juice of ½ lemon, plus extra to serve

Preheat the oven to its maximum temperature (as close to 300°C/570°F as possible). If you have a pizza stone or tile, place it in the oven. Or leave your baking tray in the oven so it will preheat.

Sift the flour into a mixing bowl and add the salt. Make a well in the middle and slowly pour in 125 ml (4 fl oz/½ cup) of lukewarm water. Knead the dough for 5 minutes. Sprinkle some flour on your work surface and then divide the dough into four balls. Cover the bowl with a damp cloth and leave to rest.

Score a shallow cross in the base of the tomatoes, then transfer to a heatproof bowl and cover with boiling water. Leave for 30 seconds, then plunge in cold water and peel the skin away from the cross. Cut the tomato in half and scoop out the stalks and seeds with a teaspoon. Roughly chop. Remove the seeds from the capsicum and roughly chop. Coarsely blend the tomatoes and capsicum with the capsicum paste, garlic, parsley, chilli flakes, pepper and salt. Combine the mixture with the lamb mince and stir thoroughly.

Place a ball of dough on the floured work surface and, with floured hands or a rolling pin, flatten into a round about 25 cm (10 in) wide and less than 5 mm (¼ in) thick. Repeat with the remaining dough balls.

Using a tablespoon, thinly spread the lamb mixture onto the rounds. Then press in with your hands.

If you are using a baking tray, take it out of the oven and put a piece of baking paper over it. Dust the baking paper with a little wholemeal flour. Place the rounds of dough on the baking paper and bake for about 5 minutes, or until the edges are crisp.

Meanwhile, if you are making the salad, finely slice the onion and place in a bowl. Sprinkle with salt and sumac, add the lemon juice and olive oil, then mix together with your hands.

Sprinkle the salad over the lahmacuns, squeeze on some lemon juice, and serve.

A butcher shop in Gaziantep preparing lamb to mince with peppers for the topping of *lahmacun* (page 106).

SAMSUN PİDE
PIDE WITH FOUR CHEESES

Samsun is a city on the Black Sea famous for its pide (a thick form of flatbread that's not the same as pita or pizza). The defining qualities of a Samsun pide are: the dough contains the highest quality butter, flour and eggs; it is rolled out by hand, not with a rolling pin; it is pulled into a boat shape that can hold a stuffing; and it is baked in a wood-fire oven. In this case, the passengers on the boat are cheeses, tomatoes and a fried egg, but don't get hung up on finding four different cheeses—three or even two will do, as long as they contrast in texture and flavour. And by the way, we do not agree with the claim by some bold Turks that our pide gave birth to Italy's pizza.

SERVES 4

DOUGH

1 tablespoon dry yeast
1 teaspoon sugar
300 g (10½ oz/2 cups) plain (all-purpose) flour, plus extra for dusting
150 g (5½ oz/1 cup) strong flour
50 ml (1⅔ fl oz) milk
1 teaspoon salt

FOUR-CHEESE FILLING

4 tablespoons each four different cheeses—such as feta, *kaşar* (or provolone or mozzarella or any semi-hard yellow cheese), *tulum* (or aged ricotta or any sharp crumbly white cheese) and gorgonzola (or any piquant mouldy cheese)
1 egg
2 teaspoons chopped oregano

TOPPING

2 large tomatoes
2 green bullhorn peppers (or 1 large green capsicum/pepper)
4 eggs
2 tablespoons vegetable oil

spoon salad (see page 130), to serve

Dissolve the yeast in 50 ml (1⅔ fl oz) of lukewarm water. Stir in the sugar and set aside for 5 minutes. It should start to form bubbles.

Sift the flours into a mixing bowl, make a well in the middle and pour in the yeast mixture and the milk. Knead the dough for 10 minutes, or until it reaches earlobe softness. Cover the bowl with a damp cloth and rest for 30 minutes to let the dough rise.

Add the salt to the dough and knead for 3 minutes. Place the dough on a floured work surface and form it into a cylinder. Then cut it into four equal pieces. Rest for another 10 minutes.

Meanwhile, preheat the oven to 200°C (400°F/ Gas 6). If you have a pizza stone or tile, place it in the oven. Or leave your baking tray in the oven so it will preheat.

Crumble the four cheeses together in a mixing bowl. Break the egg into the bowl and fold it through the cheeses. Pick the oregano leaves off the stalk and finely chop, then stir the oregano through the cheese mixture.

Place the dough on the floured work surface and, with floured hands or a rolling pin, flatten it into an oval about 30 x 20 cm (12 x 8 in) wide and 5 mm (¼ in) thick. Repeat with the remaining dough.

Spoon a thick strip of cheese filling into the middle of each oval, leaving a 5 cm (2 in) gap around the edge. Fold over the two longer edges so they touch the filling but don't cover it. Join the folded edges at the top and bottom to make a boat shape. Press each end into a point and twist to close tightly.

Finely slice the tomatoes. Halve the pepper, remove the stalk and seeds, and finely slice. Put six slices of tomato and four slices of pepper on each pide, and break an egg into the middle.

If you are using a baking tray, take it out of the oven and put a piece of baking paper over it. Dust the baking paper with a little flour. If you are using a pizza stone or tile, sprinkle a little flour on it. Place the pides on the baking paper (or stone or tile) and brush the tops with oil. Bake for 15 minutes or until golden brown.

Serve warm with a spoon salad.

ÇİĞ BÖREK
HALF MOON PASTRY WITH BEEF AND CHILLI

My ancestors are Tartars who moved to central Anatolia from an area that is now close to Russia on the Black Sea. This is one of their dishes. Using raw beef (the meaning of the word çiğ in the Turkish name), you must knead it tenderly before stuffing inside yoğurt *pastry in a half moon shape. It is vital to seal the pastry tightly, so the meat steams inside without making contact with the frying oil.*

SERVES 4

2 tablespoons plain *yoğurt*
100 ml (3½ fl oz) vegetable oil
2 teaspoons salt
juice of ½ lemon
1 egg
750 g (1 lb 10 oz/5 cups) plain (all-purpose) flour, plus extra for dusting

STUFFING
1 brown onion
250 g (9 oz) minced (ground) beef
1 tablespoon chilli flakes
1 tablespoon freshly ground black pepper
½ tablespoon salt
5 ice cubes
500 ml (17 fl oz/2 cups) vegetable oil
ayran (see page 136) or basil lemonade (see page 189), to serve

Mix the *yoğurt*, vegetable oil, salt and lemon juice in a bowl. Break the egg into the mixture and whisk. Sift the flour into the mixture, add 250 ml (9 fl oz/1 cup) of water and knead for 10 minutes into a soft dough. Cover the bowl with a damp cloth and rest for 30 minutes.

Sprinkle a little flour on your work surface and divide the dough into ten pieces, then roll into balls. Return the dough to the bowl, cover again with a damp cloth and rest for 15 minutes.

Finely chop the onion. Combine it with the minced beef, chilli flakes, pepper and salt.

Wrap the ice in a tea towel (dish towel) and crush into small pieces. Add the crushed ice to the meat mixture and knead until it dissolves. The meat mix should be very moist, but not runny. If it seems watery, pour off the excess water.

Place a ball of dough on the floured work surface and, with floured hands or a rolling pin, flatten into a round 25 cm (10 in) wide and about 2 mm (about ⅟₁₆ in) thick. Imagine each round is two half moons joined together. Put 2 tablespoons of the meat mix in the middle of the right half moon, leaving a 5 cm (2 in) gap around it. Fold the other half of the dough over. Dip your fingers in water and press down all around the edges to tightly seal the package. Fold 1 cm (½ in) of the outer edge over to 'double lock' it. This ensures the filling will stay moist when cooked. Repeat with the remaining dough and stuffing.

Heat the vegetable oil in a deep frying pan over high heat. Add a drop of water to the oil. If it sizzles the oil is ready. Add the *böreks*, two at a time, and cook for 2 minutes until they start to puff up. Turn over and cook for 1 minute more, or until the *böreks* have golden-brown spots. Scoop the *böreks* out of the oil and rest on paper towel. Repeat with the remaining pastries.

Serve two *böreks* per person, with a glass of *ayran* or basil lemonade.

TALAŞ BÖREĞİ
FLAKY PASTRY WITH LAMB AND PEAS

The puff pastry in this dish is what the French would call a mille-feuille *(thousand leaves)—which suggests the dish appeared in Turkey with European influences during the past 300 years. In the absence of an origin story, I'll tell a personal one. When I was at high school I used to jump the fence to eat lunch in the neighbouring high school because its cook made fabulous flaky* börek. *When I graduated, I pretended to be an old boy of the other high school so I could attend their reunions and eat the flaky* börek, *which became famous throughout Istanbul and caused other high schools to start serving the dish at their own reunions. As with most French-influenced dishes, the use of too much butter is essential, along with infinite patience.*

SERVES 4

600 g (1 lb 5 oz/4 cups) strong flour
1 teaspoon salt
juice of ½ lemon
210 ml (7½ fl oz) soda water
155 g (5⅔ oz/1 cup) fresh shelled peas
1 small sweet potato
1 baby carrot
1 brown onion
500 g (1 lb 2 oz) lamb backstrap or trimmed
    lamb leg
2 tablespoons plain (all-purpose) flour,
    plus extra for dusting
2 tablespoons vegetable oil,
    plus extra for greasing
½ bunch flat-leaf (Italian) parsley
½ teaspoon salt
1 teaspoon freshly ground black pepper
250 g (9 oz) butter
2 eggs
wild thyme salad (see page 133) and *ayran*
    (see page 136), to serve (optional)

To make the dough, sift the strong flour into a mixing bowl. Make a well in the middle and add the salt and lemon juice. Slowly add the soda water and 80 ml (2½ fl oz/⅓ cup) of water. Knead for 5 minutes into a hard dough. Cover the bowl with a damp cloth and rest for 30 minutes.

Put the peas in a heatproof bowl and cover with boiling water. Leave for 1 minute, then plunge them into iced water for 30 seconds. Strain and set aside.

Peel and chop the sweet potato into 1 cm (½ in) cubes. Peel and chop the carrot into 1 cm (½ in) rounds. Finely slice the onion. Chop the meat into 2 cm (¾ in) cubes. Toss in the plain flour, then shake off the excess.

Heat the vegetable oil in a frying pan over medium heat. Add a drop of water to the oil. If it sizzles, the oil is ready. Add the chopped lamb and brown for 2 minutes. Add the onion, carrot and sweet potato and sauté for 3 minutes. Reduce the heat and simmer for 5 minutes. Finely chop the parsley. Add the peas, parsley, salt and pepper to the pan and simmer for 5 more minutes. Remove from the heat.

Preheat the oven to 180°C (350°F/Gas 4).

Melt the butter in a small frying pan (or microwave for 30 seconds). Sprinkle some flour on your work surface. Divide the dough into four pieces and, using a thin rolling pin, roll out each piece as thinly as possible. Brush the butter onto the dough and fold each piece twice (to make four layers). Rest for 5 minutes. Roll each dough piece out, butter and fold again. Repeat the fold and butter process twice more. Finally, roll each piece of dough into a square, roughly 20 cm (8 in) wide and 5 mm (¼ in) thick, using your fingers to create the shape.

Separate the eggs and keep the whites and the yolks handy in two bowls. Spoon 3 tablespoons of the meat mixture into the middle of each square, leaving a margin about 6 cm (2½ in) wide on each side. Fold each corner in like an envelope, slightly overlapping them and brush the edges with egg white to help them stick together.

Line a baking tray with baking paper and brush with oil. Arrange the *böreks* on the tray, folded side down, and brush the tops with egg yolk. Bake for 30 minutes, or until golden.

Serve the *talaş böreği* warm, with wild thyme salad and *ayran*.

SU BÖREĞI

WATER PASTRY WITH FETA AND KALE

Although the börek translated as 'water pastry' is usually credited to the central Anatolian cities of Ankara and Çorum, ancient cookbooks reveal the Romans were layering lasagne, under the name laganum, in the first century—which was when they moved into Byzantion in northwest Anatolia. So we should probably credit the Romans with starting the fad for layering dough with cheese and greens between. Getting it right is a laborious process, because you must boil and butter each of the eleven layers, then fry or bake the whole thing. But the result is worth the effort, as our Italian culinary cousins would agree.

Normally in my restaurant I cook water börek in the oven in a rectangular tray, and slice it into squares (as shown in the picture opposite). For this recipe though, I'm suggesting you use a round, deep frying pan, and slice the börek into wedges, which makes it look less like lasagne but is easier to work with.

SERVES 4

8 kale leaves
1 bunch flat-leaf (Italian) parsley
3 garlic shoots (or 1 garlic clove)
1 heaped tablespoon plain *yoğurt*
250 g (9 oz) hard feta
4 eggs
2 teaspoons salt
500 g (1 lb 2 oz) strong flour
2 tablespoons olive oil
300 g (10½ oz) butter
ayran (see page 136), to serve

Put the kale in a heatproof bowl and cover with boiling water. Leave for 30 seconds, then plunge in cold water. Remove the white stalks and finely chop the leaves.

Discard the parsley stalks and finely chop the leaves. Finely chop the garlic shoots (or crush the garlic) and mix in a bowl with the *yoğurt*. Crumble the feta into the mixture.

Whisk the eggs in a deep mixing bowl. Add 1 tablespoon of water and the salt. Sift the flour into the bowl and mix well. Knead for 10 minutes, or until the mixture becomes a hard dough. Dust your work surface with flour and divide the dough

into eleven balls. Dust the dough with flour and rest in a bowl, covered with a damp cloth, for 15 minutes.

Flour a board and, using a thin rolling pin, roll each ball into a 30 cm (12 in) wide round. (Turning the dough on the work surface 90 degrees at a time will ensure a circular pastry.) You can stack the eleven sheets while you do the next step, but be sure to scatter plenty of flour between the sheets so they don't stick together.

Pour the olive oil into a large non-stick frying pan and brush to coat. (The pan should be at least 25 cm/10 in across and 10 cm /4 in deep.) Warm the butter in a small saucepan.

Fill a deep saucepan with water and bring to the boil. Using a thin rolling pin or the handle of a long wooden spoon, lift one round of dough at a time and dunk it into the pan for 2 minutes. Lift out and pat dry on a clean cloth. Repeat with the remaining rounds of dough.

Place a round of dough in the large oiled non-stick frying pan and brush with butter. Slice around it to remove any overlap, and scatter the sliced-off bits on top of it. Place another dough round loosely on

top, and brush with butter. Continue to stack to make six layers. Spread the kale and cheese mixture on the sixth layer, then continue to stack another four buttered layers. Cut the final (eleventh) layer to fit as a round over the top (discarding any leftover pastry). Pour the remaining butter on top.

Place the pan over medium heat and cook for 10 minutes, constantly tilting the pan to prevent the bottom layer sticking. Place a large plate over the frying pan and, with one hand on the plate and the other hand on the handle, upend the pastry onto the plate.

Brush the inside of the pan again with olive oil and slide the upturned *börek* into the pan—with the cooked layer now on top. Cook for 8 minutes.

Cut across the *börek* to make four quarters (with one wedge per person). Serve in the pan with glasses of *ayran* to accompany the meal.

CEVİZLİ ERİŞTE
EGG PASTA WITH WALNUT AND BOTTARGA

Here's another dish where we acknowledge an Italian connection. Italians are known in Turkey as makarnacı, *which literally translates as 'macaroni maker' or 'pasta maker', because the suffix -ci means 'maker of' or 'doer of'. On the same principle, an Argentinian is a* tangocu *(a maker of the tango) and Brazilians are* sambacı.*

What the Turks call erişte *is the kind of flat ribbon pasta the macaroni makers call tagliatelle or fettuccine. But we can trace the Turkish version as far back as the fifteenth century, when a central Anatolian doctor called Şirvani wrote that* erişte *should be made from flour kneaded with egg whites, cut into thin strips and dried in the sun. In the sixteenth century the palace chefs were boiling it in soup.*

The Turks like to eat their pasta bland, usually just tossing it with butter. I decided to boost the flavour with dried mullet roe—what the Italians call bottarga and what the Turks call mumlu havyar *(a word which sounds like caviar for a very good reason). The best* havyar *comes from the beautiful Dalyan region, at the point where the Mediterranean coast meets the Aegean coast. There they eat their bottarga with bread, and take their* erişte *straight.*

SERVES 4

EGG PASTA
3 eggs
150 ml (5 fl oz) milk
500 g (1 lb 2 oz) plain (all-purpose) flour (preferably durum wheat), plus extra for dusting
1 teaspoon salt, plus extra for cooking the *erişte*

WALNUT SAUCE
1 tablespoon butter
100 g (3½ oz) walnuts
1 teaspoon turmeric
45 ml (1½ fl oz) thickened (whipping) cream
100 g (3½ oz) sharp white cheese (such as barrel-aged feta)
1 tablespoon chopped tarragon
1 tablespoon finely grated bottarga (or 2 tablespoons fresh mullet roe)

Whisk the eggs and milk together with a fork. Sift the flour into a mixing bowl, make a well in the middle and add the salt. Pour in the egg mixture and knead for 10 minutes until it's stretchy. Cover the bowl with a damp cloth and rest for 30 minutes.

Knead the dough for 5 minutes, making sure there are no bubbles. Dust your work surface with flour and divide the dough into three balls. With floured hands or a rolling pin, flatten into a round 30 cm (12 in) wide and less than 5 mm (¼ in) thick. Repeat with the remaining dough. Rest in a warm spot (preferably in direct sunlight) for 30 minutes. (You could drape them over your clothesline, or over a rolling pin between two chairs).

Place the rounds on the floured work surface and cut into strips about 5 mm (¼ in) wide and 5 cm (2 in) long. Don't worry if the shapes are irregular. If you have a pasta machine, you can follow the same process and make the strips as if they were fettuccine.

Bring a large saucepan of salted water to the boil. Add the *erişte* and boil for 2 minutes. Melt the butter in a large frying pan over low heat, then add the walnuts, turmeric and cream. Toss the pasta in the sauce for 1 minute over low heat. Transfer to a bowl and grate the cheese over the top. Sprinkle on the chopped tarragon. Finely grate the bottarga over the top and serve.

KAYSERİ MANTI
TWICE-COOKED MINI BEEF DUMPLINGS

If I had to nominate three dishes that I am confident originated with the ethnic group called the Turks (who arrived in Anatolia from Central Asia in the eleventh century), I would say yoğurt, pastırma and the wrapped dumplings we call mantı *(pronounced 'mant-uh'). Mantı are often labelled 'the Turkish ravioli', but given their Asian origin, it would be more appropriate to call them 'the Turkish wonton'.*

Versions are served all around Turkey and in several countries to the northeast, but the most famous are the ridiculously small ones from Kayseri in central Anatolia. Apparently they were designed as a torture test by mothers-in-law, because 'a good bride should be able to make mantı *so small you can fit 40 of them on one spoon'. So I'm not being cruel here by asking you to cut the dough into 3 cm (1¼ in) squares—the usual size in Kayseri is around 1 cm (½ in) square.*

SERVES 4

EGG PASTA
375 g (13 oz/2½ cups) plain (all-purpose) flour, plus extra for dusting
½ teaspoon salt
2 eggs

BEEF MINCE STUFFING
2 onions
250 g (9 oz) lean minced (ground) beef
½ teaspoon nutmeg
1 teaspoon salt
1 teaspoon freshly ground black pepper

COOKING WATER
1 tablespoon butter
2 tablespoons olive oil
1 tomato
1 tablespoon tomato paste
   (to make your own, see page 24)
1 tablespoon salt

YOĞURT SAUCE
2 garlic cloves
500 g (1 lb 2 oz/2 cups) plain *yoğurt*

PAPRIKA BUTTER
4 tablespoons butter
2 tablespoons smoked paprika
1 tablespoon chilli flakes

1 tablespoon dried mint
1 tablespoon sumac

Sift the flour into a mixing bowl, make a well in the middle and add the salt. Break in the eggs. Add 3 tablespoons of water and knead for 10 minutes until the dough is stretchy. Cover the bowl with a damp cloth and rest for 30 minutes.

Meanwhile, to make the stuffing, grate the onions in a bowl, add the remaining ingredients and knead for 3 minutes to combine.

Dust your work surface with flour and divide the dough in half. Using a thin rolling pin, roll out each piece as thinly as you can, using plenty of flour to prevent sticking. Using a sharp knife or a rolling wheel, cut each dough sheet into 3 cm (1¼ in) squares.

Have a bowl of water handy for dipping your fingers. Using the tip of a teaspoon, place a lump of the filling, about the size of a chickpea, into the middle of one square. Wetting your fingers, pull the four corners of each square together above the filling and press the points together. Repeat with the remaining dough sheets. You should end up with about 200 small dumplings (50 per person). Warning: this will take a long time ...

Preheat the oven to 180°C (350°F/Gas 4).

Sprinkle some flour on a wide baking tray. Place the *mantı* on the tray as you finish them, making sure they don't stick to each other. Put the tray in the oven for 10 minutes to dry the *mantı* but not completely cook them.

To cook the *mantı*, heat the butter and olive oil in a saucepan over medium heat. Halve the tomato and grate it into the oil, discarding the skin. Add the tomato paste and stir for 2 minutes. Add 1 litres (35 fl oz/4 cups) of water and the salt, and bring to the boil. Reduce the heat to medium, add the *mantı* and boil for 8 minutes.

While the *mantı* are cooking, crush the garlic and mix with the *yoğurt*.

To make the paprika butter, melt the butter in a small frying pan. Stir in the smoked paprika and the chilli flakes and sizzle for 2 minutes.

Use a serving spoon to scoop the *mantı* into four bowls. Discard the cooking water. Pour 3 tablespoons of garlic *yoğurt* into each bowl, drizzle with paprika butter, top with a pinch of dried mint and sumac, and serve.

MARRIED AND FEASTED IN ANATOLIA

The next three dishes are served at wedding feasts in rural Turkey. Here's what happens first …

Boy meets girl. Boy tells his mother this girl might be the one for him. Mother makes inquiries in the village to check out girl's suitability, then contacts her mother, saying: 'We would like to visit you for a good reason.' Girl's mother has a pretty good idea what this means, and replies: 'Would you like to come over for afternoon tea?'

Girl's mother asks the girl if she's interested in the boy, and if she gets the reply 'It's up to you', she tells the father there may be an offer to consider. (If the girl is not interested, the afternoon tea would still go ahead, but it would not end happily.)

On the appointed day, boy's family brings Turkish delight and baklava, beautifully packaged. Girl's family serves tea and other pastries, on the principle ' *Tatlı ye, tatlı konuş*' ('Eat sweet, talk sweet').

Girl is not present during the family chat, but if the conversation goes well, her mother will ask her to make coffee for everybody. She might then put salt instead of sugar into the cup intended for her suitor, in order to test his manners. If he compliments her on the coffee, he will be a patient husband.

Assuming everybody is getting on well, boy and girl will now be allowed to go out together, accompanied by a chaperone, of course. This will progress to a small ring, which means they are 'promised', followed by a bigger ring, which means they are engaged. Girl's family will pay for the engagement party.

On the day before the wedding, girl will have her hands coloured with henna, and on the morning of the wedding, boy will be shaved by the town barber. Everyone in the village—and anybody who happens to be passing through town—will be invited to the festivities.

After the imam has conducted the formalities, the bride will then ride into the town square on horseback, carrying the possessions she will bring to the marriage and accompanied by drummers, clarinet players and car horns. And so the feasting begins.

This was where we came in. Photographer Bree Hutchins and I were chatting to a farmer selling peppers and eggplants in the markets at Bodrum, on Turkey's west coast. The young farmer took a liking to us (to be honest, more to Bree) and asked if we'd like to come to his cousin's wedding feast. We said of course.

We arrived on the third day of a five-day festival. The food was cooking in huge pots all around the square. They'd slaughtered cattle and sheep specially for the occasion, which they were roasting over open fires. The three dishes you are about to read about were a tiny part of the banquet.

The bride and her brother at a Yörük wedding in the
Aegean village of Milas.

DÜĞÜN CORBASI

WEDDING SOUP WITH CHICKEN AND YOĞURT

This is a yoğurt soup with chicken or lamb meat, usually cooked over an open fire and served early in a wedding feast for up to 1000 invited guests from surrounding villages. A wedding feast can continue for five days, with cooking duties alternating between the bride's family and the groom's family. This dish takes 24 hours to prepare, so better hope the bride doesn't change her mind.

SERVES 8

50 g (1¾ oz/¼ cup) dried chickpeas
500 g (1 lb 2 oz/2 cups) plain *yoğurt*
1 small chicken
220 g (7¾ oz/1 cup) medium-grain rice
1 teaspoon salt
1 egg
2 tablespoons plain (all-purpose) flour
2 tablespoons butter
2 teaspoons dried mint
2 teaspoons paprika

Cover the chickpeas with water and soak overnight.

Strain and rinse the chickpeas. Place the *yoğurt* on a sheet of muslin (cheesecloth) and tie up the corners. Hang the muslin over a pot for 3 hours to allow the *yoğurt* to thicken.

Put the chicken and chickpeas in a large saucepan, cover with water and boil, with the lid on, for 30 minutes. Take out the chicken and remove the skin. Strip off the meat and shred, then set aside. Put the chicken bones and skin back in the pan and boil for a further 15 minutes, with the chickpeas, to make a stock.

Put 500 ml (17 fl oz/2 cups) of the stock in another saucepan. Rinse the rice. Add the rice and salt to the pan and bring it to the boil. Boil for 10 minutes, until not quite soft.

Whisk the egg and flour together in a bowl. Add the *yoğurt* and 2 tablespoons of the warm chicken stock and combine.

Take the carcass and skin out of the stock, and discard. Add the *yoğurt* mixture to the stock and slowly simmer for 5 minutes, stirring constantly. Slowly pour in the strained rice and continue to stir. Bring to the boil over medium heat and add the shredded chicken. Reduce the heat and simmer for another 10 minutes.

Divide the soup into four bowls. Heat 1 tablespoon of butter in a frying pan. Once it sizzles, add the mint and stir for about 30 seconds. Drizzle it over the soup in splashes. Heat the remaining butter and add the paprika. Sizzle for 30 seconds, then drizzle it over the soup in spaces not covered by the mint butter.

Serve with pide (pee-day) and pride.

EZO GELİN

'EZO THE BRIDE'
(RED LENTIL AND BULGUR SOUP)

Ezo the Bride is a famous figure in Turkish folklore. Her real name was Zöhre Bozgeyik and she was born in 1909 in southeastern Anatolia. She married a local musician and, following the regional Berdel tradition, her brother married her husband's sister. A few years later, her brother divorced his wife, which meant that although Ezo dearly loved her husband, she had to follow local custom and separate from him. Beautiful Ezo was forced to travel to Syria and marry a distant relative and, according to a popular song, she died there in 1956 of sorrow and homesickness. Her deathbed wish was for her remains to be buried in her home village, Dokuzyol. This soup comes from a happy time in her life.

SERVES 8

1.5 litres (52 fl oz/6 cups) beef stock
2 onions
2 tablespoons sunflower oil
2 tablespoons tomato paste (to make your own, see page 24)
1 tablespoon capsicum (pepper) paste (see page 32)
1 teaspoon hot paprika
110 g (3¾ oz/½ cup) medium-grain rice
205 g (7¼ oz/1 cup red lentils
90 g (3¼ oz/½ cup) fine bulgur
2 mint sprigs
2 teaspoons salt
2 teaspoons freshly ground black pepper

PAPRIKA BUTTER
1 tablespoon butter
1 tablespoon hot paprika
1 bird's eye chilli, finely chopped (optional)

Put the beef stock in a pot and bring to the boil. Reduce to a simmer.

Meanwhile, finely chop the onions. Heat the sunflower oil in a frying pan over medium heat. Add the onion and cook for 3 minutes until soft. Dissolve the tomato and capsicum pastes in 250 ml (9 fl oz/1 cup) of the beef stock, add the hot paprika, and then stir into the cooking onions. Pour the onion mixture into the simmering beef stock.

Rinse the rice, red lentils and bulgur, then add to the pot. Cover and cook for 20 minutes, or until the lentils are soft. Ladle the soup into four bowls.

Chop the mint. To make the paprika butter, melt the butter in a small frying pan, add the paprika (and finely chopped chillies if you want extra heat), and sizzle for 1 minute.

Top each bowl with chopped mint and drops of paprika butter, and serve.

KEŞKEK
LAMB AND BARLEY PORRIDGE

Keşkek is now served at village weddings all over Anatolia, but it originated with the Yörük people (nomadic Turks from Central Asia). For the authentic version, you'd need a brass pot as big as a bathtub, a bonfire, and 200 single men with thick pounding poles. Traditionally, a whole sheep or cow is boiled with pearl barley, then pulled out of the pot so the bones can be removed, then put back in and pounded for about an hour by the single men of the village until it becomes a paste. This recipe is a compromise.

SERVES 8

1 kg (2 lb 4 oz) pearl barley
1 lamb neck, about 1 kg (2 lb 4 oz)
1 teaspoon salt
2 onions
1 tablespoon sunflower oil
3 tablespoons butter, melted
1 teaspoon ground cinnamon

TOMATO SAUCE
1 tablespoon butter
1 tablespoon tomato paste (to make your own, see page 24)
½ teaspoon salt
½ teaspoon freshly ground black pepper
1 teaspoon dried oregano

Cover the barley with water and soak for 8 hours.

Cut the lamb neck into four pieces and place in a large saucepan with the barley. Cover with water, bring to the boil and then cook for 1½ hours, or until the barley and meat are tender.

Scoop out the pieces of neck and remove the bones. Shred the meat. Strain the barley and combine it with the meat in a large bowl. Add the salt.

Dice the onions. Heat the sunflower oil in a frying pan over medium heat. Add the onion and sauté for 5 minutes, until translucent. Add the onion to the meat and barley, and pound the mixture with a wooden spoon until it reaches a paste-like consistency.

To make the sauce, melt the butter in a frying pan over low heat. Stir in the tomato paste, salt, pepper and oregano. When it sizzles, remove the pan from the heat.

Serve the *keşkek* in a big bowl in the middle of the table for people to help themselves. Pour the melted butter over the top and sprinkle on the cinnamon.

The groom's village (above) is empty because everybody is at the feast in the bride's village (opposite).

GAVURDAĞ
'SPOON SALAD' (CHOPPED TOMATO, WALNUT AND SUMAC SALAD)

This salad is served with kebaps all over Turkey, and is designed to be eaten with a spoon. It's just a finely chopped salad, with the tomato pieces no bigger than the pomegranate seeds, but you'll see it on menus in Istanbul described as the famous 'Gavurdağ' salad (apparently named after a mountain in southeast Anatolia). My friend Musa points out in his scholarly journal Yemek ve Kültür *(Food and Culture) that there's a trend in Turkey for chefs to give obscure names to standard dishes in an attempt to suggest authentic regional origins. This could well be one of those.*

SERVES 4

6 ripe tomatoes
1 red onion
1 bunch mint
½ bunch flat-leaf (Italian) parsley
115 g (4 oz/1 cup) walnuts
3 green bullhorn peppers (or 1 green
    capsicum/pepper)
1 green chilli
1 tablespoon sumac
2 tablespoons pomegranate molasses
    (to make your own, see page 24)
60 ml (2 fl oz/¼ cup) olive oil
1 teaspoon apple vinegar
1 teaspoon sea salt
150 g (5½ oz/½ cup) pomegranate seeds

Quarter the tomatoes, remove the white centres and then finely chop. Finely chop the red onion. Discard the mint and parsley stalks and finely chop the leaves. Finely chop the walnuts. Cut the bullhorn peppers and the chilli in half, and remove the seeds and stalks. Finely chop. Mix all the chopped ingredients together in a salad bowl.

Mix the sumac, molasses, olive oil, vinegar and salt together, pour onto the salad and toss.

Sprinkle the pomegranate seeds on top and serve.

ZAHTER SALATASI
WILD THYME AND BLOOD ORANGE SALAD

Wild thyme (zahter) grows near the southeastern city of Antakya (once known as Antioch, where the followers of Jesus were first called Christians). The locals use the fresh leaves to make salads and an invigorating form of tea, and use the dried leaves as a substitute for oregano in meat dishes. The region was formerly part of Syria, only added to the Turkish republic in 1938, so its food is surprising to most Turks. In addition to this salad, we can credit the Antakyans with künefe *(page 334) and* muhammara *sauce (page 247).*

SERVES 4

10 thyme sprigs
5 oregano sprigs
3 spring onions (scallions)
1 green chilli (optional)
1 garlic shoot (if available)
2 blood oranges
3 teaspoons olive oil
½ teaspoon sea salt

Pick the leaves off the thyme and oregano. Discard the stalks. Wash the spring onions, then remove and discard the roots and tough outer leaves. Finely chop. Remove the seeds and stalk from the chilli (if you are using it) and finely chop. Finely chop the garlic shoot. Mix together in a salad bowl.

Peel the oranges and divide into segments, removing the white pith. Add to the salad bowl. Splash on the olive oil and salt, toss together and serve.

BALIK EKMEK
WHITING SANDWICH WITH TARATOR

This is my attempt to recreate a memory. When I was a teenager, I used to buy sandwiches from fishermen who would moor their boats next to one of the pillars of the Galata Bridge, just across the road from Istanbul's spice market. They would fillet their catch and cook fish pieces over a little charcoal grill, then shove them inside pide. Nowadays, this has turned into a tourist experience, where colourful boats, permanently moored, sell frozen fish cooked on flat griddles.

You can come close to the original experience by walking across to the other side of the Galata Bridge and turning left into the fish market. There they sell genuine fish sandwiches from carts in the street. They use locally caught fish and cook them over charcoal. They then add salad and lemon—not the walnut tarator (sauce) in this recipe, which is my improvement on the memory.

SERVES 4

TARATOR
15 g (½ oz/¼ cup) breadcrumbs
60 g (2¼ oz/½ cup) walnuts
2 garlic cloves
juice of ½ lemon
pinch of salt
60 ml (2 fl oz/¼ cup) extra virgin olive oil

ROCKET SALAD
12 large rocket (arugula) leaves
1 bunch flat-leaf (Italian) parsley
1 red onion
1 tablespoon chilli flakes
1 tablespoon red wine vinegar
60 ml (2 fl oz/¼ cup) extra virgin olive oil
2 teaspoons salt
juice of ½ lemon

PAN-FRIED WHITING
8 school whiting
185 g (6½ oz/1¼ cups) plain (all-purpose) flour
2 teaspoons salt
1 teaspoon freshly ground black pepper
250 ml (9 fl oz/1 cup) soda water
250 ml (9 fl oz/1 cup) vegetable oil

pide bread, to serve (to make your own, see page 45)
şalgam, to serve (see page 136)

First make the *tarator*. Soak the breadcrumbs in 60 ml (2 fl oz/¼ cup) of water for 5 minutes.

Put the breadcrumbs, walnuts, garlic, lemon juice and salt in a food processor, and pulse. While you're pulsing, slowly add the olive oil— you are aiming for a spreadable paste like mustard, so add a little more water if it does not seem smooth enough.

Now make the salad. Remove the stalks from the rocket and the parsley. Finely chop the leaves. Finely chop the onion. Mix the leaves, onion, chilli flakes, red wine vinegar and oil together in a bowl, then add the salt and lemon juice.

Next, prepare the fish. Slice each fish through the stomach, removing the gut. Butterfly each fish and remove the spine and any bones. Cut off and discard the heads and tails and wash thoroughly. Pat the fish dry and dust in about 35 g (1¼ oz/ ¼ cup) of the flour.

Put the remaining flour in a mixing bowl and add the salt and pepper. Make a well in the middle and whisk in the soda water to make a batter.

Heat the vegetable oil in a deep frying pan over high heat. Add a drop of water to the oil. If it sizzles, the oil is ready.

Dip the fish in the batter, allowing the excess to drip off. Carefully lower the whiting into the hot oil and fry for 2 minutes on each side, or until golden. Using a slotted spatula, remove the fish from the pan and place on paper towel to absorb the excess oil.

Cut each pide in half. Spread the *tarator* on the top and bottom. Put the fillets from two fish on each sandwich, then 2 tablespoons of salad, then close the lid. Serve with a glass of *şalgam*.

ŞALGAM
PICKLED CARROT AND BEETROOT JUICE

There are certain elements of the Turkish culinary repertoire with which an outsider will have a love–hate relationship—lamb testicles, sheep's head soup, fried pickles, boza beer, rakı, and şalgam—the earthy refreshment in this recipe. I love şalgam—especially washed down with rakı, which is a pairing perfected in the Mediterranean town of Adana.

SERVES 16

1 round red turnip
1 beetroot (beet)
1 purple carrot
1 red or green chilli (optional)
165 g (5¾ oz/½ cup) rock salt
1½ tablespoons citric acid
100 g (3½ oz) dried chickpeas

Peel the turnip, beetroot and carrot. Quarter the carrots lengthways. Quarter the turnip and beetroot. If you want your *şalgam* hot, slit down one side of a green or red chilli so the liquid will pull the heat out of the seeds.

Put the vegetables (and the optional chilli) in a 4 litre (140 fl oz/16 cup) preserving jar. Dissolve the rock salt and citric acid in 250 ml (9 fl oz/1 cup) of lukewarm water. Pour into the jar. Wrap the chickpeas in a parcel of muslin (cheesecloth) and knot tightly. Put the muslin parcel into the jar. Fill the jar, to the brim, with water. Seal the lid tightly. Leave in a cool spot for 15 days.

After 15 days take out the chickpea parcel and discard. If you keep the jar in the fridge, you can drink the juice, or eat the pickled vegetables for up to 3 months.

AYRAN
MINTED YOĞURT SHAKE

Ayran is the most popular cold drink in Turkey. Religious conservatives call it THE National Drink—as opposed to rakı, alcohol of choice on any meze table. I love the frothy crema rural villagers used to achieve with the traditional method of shaking the yoğurt in a sheepskin or wooden barrel. I've found a simpler way using a cocktail shaker and a bit of milk.

SERVES 4

1 bunch mint
135 g (4¾ oz /1 cup) ice
750 g (1 lb 10 oz/3 cups) plain *yoğurt*
125 ml (4 fl oz/½ cup) milk
125 ml (4 fl oz/½ cup) soda water
1 tablespoon salt

Finely chop the mint. Put the ice and all the other ingredients in a cocktail shaker. Shake vigorously for 30 seconds. Strain into four glasses and serve.

ISLAK
KIDS' SOGGY BURGER

This is my adaptation of a relatively new street snack, usually found in takeaway joints around Taksim Square in Istanbul, and designed for consumption when you are drunk. It's a kind of slider, except the sauce is not inside the bun but all around it.

When I first tried islak, I asked the shopkeeper what was in the sauce. He said it was a trade secret. I hung around for a while, and soon saw him pouring the fat that had collected under his döner kebap rotisserie into a mixture of tomato and peppers. I decided not to replicate this, and instead boosted the sauce with ground herbs and spices, and a plum.

My kids love soggy burgers because they are messy and full of flavour. This version won't give them heart conditions.

SERVES 4

SPICE MIX*
1 teaspoon dried oregano
2 teaspoons ground coriander
2 teaspoons cumin
¼ teaspoon pimento
1 teaspoon sweet paprika
1 teaspoon hot paprika
¼ teaspoon freshly ground black pepper
1 dried bay leaf

KÖFTE
100 g (3½ oz) breadcrumbs
1 tablespoon white vinegar
1 onion
2 tablespoons chopped flat-leaf (Italian) parsley
200 g (7 oz) minced (ground) lamb mince
    (preferably from breast)
400 g (14 oz) minced (ground) veal
1 egg
1 teaspoon salt
1 tablespoon vegetable oil

8 brioches or burger buns

BURGER SAUCE
1 tablespoon butter
2 tablespoons tomato paste (to make your own,
    see page 24)
1 plum

500 ml (18 fl oz/2 cups) beef stock
1 teaspoon salt
1 teaspoon freshly ground black pepper
1 teaspoon dried mint

Using a spice grinder or a food processor, grind the oregano into a powder. Mix all the spices together with the bay leaf. You can keep this powder in a sealed container for up to 3 months.

Put the breadcrumbs in a mixing bowl and moisten with 1 tablespoon of water and the vinegar. Finely grate the onion into the bowl. Stir in the parsley. Add the lamb and veal, break the egg in, then add the salt and ½ tablespoon of the spice mix. Knead with wet hands for 10 minutes until the mixture turns into a paste.

Cover the bowl with a damp cloth or plastic wrap and rest in the fridge for 1 hour.

Divide the meat mixture into eight balls about the size of billiard balls. With wet hands, flatten each ball into a patty about 2 cm (¾ in) thick.

To make the sauce, melt the butter in a saucepan over medium heat, add the tomato paste and stir for 1 minute. Finely chop the plum and add. Add the beef stock, salt, pepper and mint, bring to the boil, then reduce over low heat for 10 minutes.

Heat the vegetable oil over medium heat. Fry four patties at a time for 4 minutes on each side, until brown, then place on paper towel to absorb the excess oil. Repeat with the remaining *köfte*.

Slice the buns in half. Put a patty in each bun. Dunk each bun into the hot sauce and squash down with a wooden spoon. Remove from the pan and serve two buns per person, with plenty of paper towels for wiping hands.

NOTE
If you have a spice mill, buy coriander, cumin and pimento seeds, and grind them with the dried oregano. Alternatively, buy all ingredients except the bay leaf in powder form.

TEKİRDAĞ KÖFTE
VEAL MEATBALLS WITH WHITE BEAN AND TAHINI SALAD

The west coast city of Tekirdağ is known for two things: its exceptional rakı, due to the grapes and water of the region; and its delicious köfte, consumed in eateries devoted to this one experience and recognised as the most beloved veal dish all across the land of lamb. Each köfte maker in town has a personal secret ingredient, a common one being lungs. You may be relieved to hear my secret ingredient is not lungs, but semolina.

The accompanying salad comes from much further south—the sea resort of Antalya, where they add tahini to everything.

SERVES 4

KÖFTE

3 tablespoons breadcrumbs
½ teaspoon bicarbonate of soda (baking soda)
1 onion
1 garlic clove
500 g (1 lb 2 oz) minced (ground) veal
    (about 20 per cent fat)
1 teaspoon cumin
1 teaspoon salt
½ teaspoon pimento
½ teaspoon freshly ground black pepper
½ teaspoon chilli flakes
1 egg
½ tablespoon fine semolina
4 long yellow chillies

WHITE BEAN AND TAHINI SALAD

390 g (13¾ oz/2 cups) dried
    white cannellini beans
½ teaspoon sugar
1½ teaspoons salt
3 tablespoons tahini
3 tablespoons olive oil
juice of 1 lemon
2 tablespoons apple cider vinegar
½ bunch flat-leaf (Italian) parsley
½ bunch spring onions (scallions)
1 French shallot (eschalot), chopped
8 cherry tomatoes
8 quail eggs
2 teaspoons sumac

Put the breadcrumbs in a mixing bowl and moisten with 2 tablespoons of water. Stir in the bicarbonate of soda. Finely grate the onion and crush the garlic. Put the meat in the mixing bowl and then add the onion, garlic and the remaining *köfte* ingredients. Knead with wet hands for 15 minutes until the mixture becomes a smooth paste. Cover the bowl with a damp cloth or plastic wrap and rest in the fridge overnight.

Cover the cannellini beans with boiling water and leave overnight.

Strain and rinse the soaked beans, place in a saucepan with the sugar, cover with water and bring to the boil. Strain the beans and discard the water. Cover again with even more fresh water, add 1 teaspoon of the salt and boil, covered, for 1 hour.

Strain the beans and then transfer to a large salad bowl.

Dilute the tahini in 2 tablespoons of water. Add the olive oil, lemon juice, vinegar and the remaining salt. Mix the tahini dressing through the beans.

Pick the leaves from the parsley and finely chop. Wash the spring onions, then remove the roots and tough outer leaves, and finely chop. Stir the parsley and spring onions through the salad. Finely slice the shallot. Sprinkle the pieces over the beans. Quarter the cherry tomatoes and spread them over the shallot.

Preheat the barbecue hotplate or a grill pan. Add a drop of water. If it sizzles, the grill is ready.

Bring a small saucepan of water to the boil, add the quail eggs and boil for 3 minutes. Remove with a slotted spoon and run them under cold running water. Remove the shells, slice in half and place the halves on top of the salad. Sprinkle a little sumac over the eggs.

Divide the ball of *köfte* into patties about 1 cm (½ in) thick and about 6 cm (2½) wide. Make indentations with your hand across the top. Put the patties on the barbecue and cook for 2 minutes on each side, until brown. (If you are using a grill pan, cook fir 4 minutes each side.) Char the yellow chillies until the skin is slightly blackened

Serve four *köfte* per person, with the bean salad and chilli.

KADINBUDU
'LADIES' THIGHS' (VEAL MEATBALLS WITH RICE AND EGGS)

Probably because of the puritanism of their governments over the centuries, Turks have expressed their fascination with anatomy in their approach to naming foodstuffs. There are treats called woman's bellybutton, vizier's finger, lady's lips, sluts' dumplings and brothel donuts. The plump patties in this recipe made from young cows obviously reminded some nineteenth-century chef of a pleasant experience. The first published mention of this kind of köfte, using mince, watercress and eggs, appears in a Persian dictionary published around 1800— under a more polite name.

SERVES 4

1 onion
2 garlic cloves
2 tablespoons vegetable oil
500 g (1 lb 2 oz) minced (ground) veal mince
110 g (3¾ oz/½ cup) medium-grain rice
2 teaspoons salt
1 teaspoon freshly ground black pepper
1 teaspoon cumin
1 teaspoon ground pimento
2 tablespoons chopped marjoram leaves
3 eggs
150 g (5½ oz/1 cup) plain (all-purpose) flour
250 ml (9 fl oz/1 cup) vegetable oil, for frying
spoon salad (see page 130), to serve

Finely chop the onion and garlic. Heat the vegetable oil in a frying pan over medium heat. Add the onion and garlic and sauté for 3 minutes, until soft. Add half the mince and stir. Cook for 5 minutes, to evaporate any water it puts out. Transfer to a mixing bowl.

Wash the rice under cold running water. Put 250 ml (9 fl oz/1 cup) of water in a saucepan. Add the rice and salt, and bring to the boil. Boil for 10 minutes, until soft. Strain.

Add the rice to the cooked mince, then add the spices and marjoram. Break 1 egg into the mixture.

Add the remaining (raw) mince. Knead with wet hands for 5 minutes to combine. Cover the bowl with a damp cloth or plastic wrap and rest in the fridge for 30 minutes. Divide the mixture into eight rounds, each about the size of an egg, then flatten each into a patty about 1–2 cm (½–¾ in) thick. Put the flour in a bowl. Lightly beat the remaining eggs in a separate bowl. Coat both sides of each patty in the flour and dip in the egg. Heat the vegetable oil in a frying pan over medium heat. Toss a drop of water into the oil. If it sizzles, the oil is ready. Carefully add the four patties to the pan and cook for 3 minutes on each side, or until golden brown. Using a spatula, remove the patties from the pan and place on paper towel to absorb the excess oil. Repeat with the remaining patties.

Serve two *kadınbudu* per person, with the spoon salad.

SİMİT KEBABI
LAMB KEBAPS WITH BARBECUED SALAD

Kebap restaurants in Turkey never buy lamb mince. They always make their own using leg and belly meat, and a mighty machete called a zırh. A kebap master will choose an apprentice by putting a piece of paper between the chopping board and the lamb and asking the candidate to mince the meat using only a zırh. If there are no cuts in the paper, the candidate gets the job.

With this kebap it's important to use the finest bulgur, which is known in Gaziantep as simit. This is not to be confused with the sesame rings we discussed in the breakfast chapter (see page 43). In Antep dialect, simit means the smallest grains of wheat that fit through a sieve. Their other name is elek altı, which means 'under the sieve'.

This is a perfect dish for a barbecue, because the salad is char-grilled along with the meat.

SERVES 4

LAMB KEBAPS
90 g (3¼ oz/½ cup) extra fine bulgur
1 teaspoon salt
1 teaspoon freshly ground black pepper
1 tablespoon cumin
1 teaspoon chilli flakes
10 mint leaves
600 g (1 lb 5 oz) minced (ground) lamb (about 30 per cent fat)
3 garlic cloves
½ onion

SALAD KEBAPS
4 tomatoes
4 shallots
4 green bullhorn peppers (or 2 large green capsicums/peppers)
8 garlic cloves
2 tablespoons pomegranate molasses (to make your own, see page 24)
1 tablespoon sweet paprika
1 tablespoon hot paprika
2 tablespoons tomato paste (to make your own, see page 24)
1 teaspoon salt
1 teaspoon pepper

1 piece pita bread, for holding the skewer

Put the bulgur, salt, pepper, cumin and chilli flakes in a mixing bowl. Add 60 ml (2 fl oz/¼ cup) of hot water. Knead the mixture with wet hands for 1 minute. Finely chop the mint leaves and stir through the mixture.

If you're using a charcoal grill, you should light it 1 hour before you want to cook. Burn the charcoal for at least 45 minutes and when the flames have died down, and the coals are glowing with a covering of white ash, the barbecue is ready. (If you're using a gas barbecue, turn it on to medium heat about 5 minutes before you're ready to cook.)

Put the lamb in a separate bowl. Finely grate the garlic and the onion, and add it to the mince. Add the bulgur mixture and knead with wet hands for 8 minutes, to make a smooth paste. Cover the bowl with a damp cloth and rest for 30 minutes.

Using eight thick metal skewers (ideally 2 cm/¾ in thick), divide the lamb and bulgur into four balls and squash each ball around a skewer, pressing the mixture so it spreads 5 cm (2 in) from the top to 10 cm (4 cm) from the bottom.

To make the salad, cut the tomatoes in half. Skin the shallots. Cut the bullhorn peppers in half. Push the salad pieces onto the four remaining skewers.

Place the eight *kebaps* on the charcoal grill or barbecue. Cook for 2 minutes, then when the meat on that side is seared, turn and cook the other side for 2 minutes. Turn again, and grill for another 2 minutes on each side. (The fat from the meat will drip on the charcoal and burn, but that smoke adds to the flavour.) Constantly check to see if the meat is at risk of falling off the skewer, and if so, turn it over. Take all the skewers off the heat.

Pull the salad ingredients off their skewers and pulse in a food processor to make a chunky purée. Add the pomegranate molasses, sweet paprika, hot paprika, tomato paste, salt and pepper, and stir.

Divide the salad mix onto four plates. Using the pita bread as a mitten, pull the *kebaps* off the skewers and place on top of the warm salad. Serve immediatley.

TAVUK ŞİŞ

CHICKEN KEBAPS WITH PRUNE ORZO PILAV

Chicken kebaps are mostly served with a rice pilav in Turkey. I find that a bit boring, and since I share the Ottoman taste for combining meat with dried fruits, I've added prunes. Sour plums are popular as summer fruits in Turkey, while the dried version (prunes) are handy in winter. We prefer damsin plums, which are named for their supposed point of origin—Damascus. They were brought to Byzantion by the Romans.

Instead of rice I've used a kind of pasta called orzo (the Italian word for barley) or risoni (which translates as 'big rice'). It's called kritharáki (little barley) by the Greeks and arpa şehriye (barley grains) by the Turks, but I most like the Arab name lisân al-uşfür, which translates as 'songbird tongues'.

SERVES 4

KEBAPS

8 chicken thigh fillets
4 thyme sprigs
250 g (9 oz/1 cup) plain *yoğurt*
100 g (3½ oz/½ cup) capsicum (pepper) paste
  (see page 32)
125 ml (4 fl oz/½ cup) olive oil
1 teaspoon cumin
1 teaspoon chilli flakes
1 teaspoon salt
1 teaspoon freshly ground black pepper

ORZO PILAV

80 g (2¾ oz/½ cup) blanched almonds
750 ml (26 fl oz/3 cups) chicken stock
2 tablespoons butter
2 tablespoons olive oil
270 g (9½ oz/2 cups) orzo pasta
½ teaspoon salt
½ teaspoon freshly ground black pepper
10 prunes, seeded and chopped
200 g (7 oz) crumbly feta

Cut the chicken thighs in half, crossways. Pick the leaves from the thyme sprigs and discard the stalks. Mix the *yoğurt*, capsicum paste, olive oil, cumin, chilli flakes, salt, pepper and thyme leaves in a large non-metallic bowl. Add the chicken and thoroughly coat in the *yoğurt* mixture. Cover the bowl with plastic wrap, transfer to the fridge and leave to marinate for at least 6 hours.

About 1 hour before serving, start making the orzo pilav. If you're using an oven rather than a grill, preheat it to 220°C (425°F/Gas 7).

Halve the almonds. Put the chicken stock in a saucepan over a low heat and bring to a simmer.

Meanwhile, melt the butter in a saucepan over low heat. Add the olive oil. When it begins to sizzle add the almonds and half the orzo. Brown for 3 minutes. Add the remaining orzo and stir for another 3 minutes. Add the heated chicken stock. Stir and add the salt and pepper. Bring the orzo to the boil, and simmer, covered, for 8 minutes.

Preheat the barbecue hotplate or a grill pan. Add a drop of water. If it sizzles the grill is ready.

Chop the prunes and stir them through the orzo mixture. Simmer, covered, for another 5 minutes. Turn off the heat and stir in the feta. Let the mixture rest, covered, for 10 minutes.

Meanwhile, prepare the *kebaps*. Using eight metal skewers (ideally 1 cm/½ in wide), push each skewer through two pieces of chicken and place them on the hot grill. Grill for 7 minutes on one side, then 5 minutes on the other side. (If you are using the oven, put the chicken pieces on an oven rack and bake for 10 minutes.)

Divide the orzo pilav onto four plates. Place two skewers on each portion of pilav and serve.

YAPRAK KEBAP
HOME-STYLE VEAL DÖNER KEBAP

Sadly, the world sees döner kebap (also known by the Greek word gyro or the Arabic word shawarma) as the pinnacle of Turkey's cooking culture. Tourists in Turkey are often told that this vertical way of grilling sliced meat was invented by the Iskender family in the 1860s in the town of Bursa as a way to avoid fat dripping onto the coals and creating a lot of smoke. In one tale we hear that Mr Iskender skewered slices of meat on his sword and stuck it in the ground next to a stack of burning wood. My scholarly friend Musa has discovered that this way of cooking was used throughout Anatolia and the Middle East long before Mr Iskender opened his restaurant.

The Iskender family from Bursa now has a chain of restaurants around Turkey, serving döner kebap with yoğurt, pide and their own barbecued tomato sauce. They call it Iskender kebap—a name that has been copied and a dish that has been bastardised all over the world. This recipe is my suggestion of how to get a similar effect when you don't have a vertical rotisserie. Most offerings outside Turkey use pressed mince. The real döner kebap should be made with slices of veal, with minced meat only used to stick the veal slices together.

SERVES 4

VEAL KEBAP
800 g (1 lb 12 oz) veal backstrap
8 onions
2 garlic cloves
1 tablespoon capsicum (pepper) paste (see page 32)
1 tablespoon plain *yoğurt*
1 tablespoon dried oregano
1 dried bay leaf
6 slices day-old bread (or 3-day-old pide bread)
2 tablespoons butter, plus extra for greasing

DÖNER KEBAP SAUCE
2 tablespoons butter, melted
2 tablespoons tomato paste (to make your own, see page 24)
500 ml (17 fl oz/2 cups) beef stock
½ tablespoon salt
1 teaspoon freshly ground black pepper
1 teaspoon sugar
1 teaspoon dried mint

250 g (9 oz/1 cup) plain *yoğurt*, to serve

The day before you are planning to serve this, clean the outer fat and sinews off the backstrap. Slice as thinly as you can, then pound each slice with the back of a wooden spoon (or a meat tenderiser if you have one) to make a slice about 8 cm (3¼ in) across and less than 5 mm (¼ in) thick. Cut the slices in half.

Finely grate the onions. Squeeze all the onion juice through a fine sieve or muslin (cheesecloth) into a non-metallic bowl.

Crush the garlic and add it to the onion juice, along with the capsicum paste, *yoğurt*, oregano and bay leaf. Mix well. Add the veal and coat in the onion mixture. Cover the bowl with plastic wrap, transfer to the fridge and leave to marinate overnight.

If you're using a charcoal grill, you should light it 1 hour before you want to cook. Burn the charcoal for at least 45 minutes and when the flames have died down, and the coals are glowing with a covering of white ash, the barbecue is ready.

(If you're using a gas barbecue, turn it on to medium–high about 5 minutes before you're ready to cook.)

Preheat the oven to 180°C (350°F/Gas 4).

Cut the bread into 2 cm (¾ in) cubes. Brush with butter. Grease a baking tray, place the bread in the tray and bake for 5 minutes until golden.

To make the sauce, melt the butter in a saucepan over medium heat, add the tomato paste, cook for 1 minute, add the beef stock, salt, pepper, sugar and mint, and then bring to the boil.

Cook the veal slices on the charcoal grill or barbecue for 2 minutes each side.

Divide the bread pieces onto four plates. Put five or six pieces of veal on each plate, pour over the sauce, dollop with *yoğurt*, and serve.

Turks prefer to eat lunch all day long outside casual 'salons' that serve *döner kebabs* sliced from a giant ball of meat and a vertical grill.

YENİ DÜNYA KEBABI
LOQUAT KEBAPS

This is one of the many seasonal kebaps of Gaziantep in southeastern Anatolia, appearing at the beginning of spring and served for only three weeks. It uses loquats picked just before they are ripe (if you can't find loquats, try to use almost-ripe apricots). Usually a family will layer the fruit and meat in their own baking tray and get the kids to carry the tray to the nearest bakery to be cooked in a wood-fire oven. At other times of the year they might layer garlic, shallots and eggplant (aubergine) with the meat.

There are two ways of cooking this dish: one over charcoal, the other in the oven. I mix both methods here, first giving the kebaps a smoky flavour on the barbecue, then finishing them off in the oven. If you don't have a barbecue, do the whole thing in the oven.

SERVES 4

500 g (1 lb 2 oz) lamb mince
   (with about 25 per cent fat)
1 teaspoon salt
1 teaspoon freshly ground black pepper
20 loquats (or apricots)
2 spring onions (scallions)
3 garlic shoots (or 1 garlic clove)
8 cherry tomatoes
2 tablespoons pomegranate molasses
   (to make your own, see page 24)
1 tablespoon sumac
1 tablespoon olive oil
1 tablespoon chilli flakes

pita bread, to serve

If you're using a charcoal grill, you should light it 1 hour before you want to cook. Burn the charcoal for at least 45 minutes and when the flames have died down, and the coals are glowing with a covering of white ash, the barbecue is ready. (If you're using a gas barbecue, turn it on to medium heat about 5 minutes before you're ready to cook.)

Put the lamb in a mixing bowl. Add the salt and pepper, and knead with wet hands for 2 minutes. Divide the meat into twenty balls about the size of walnuts.

Slit each loquat (or apricot) down one side, pull the halves partly apart and remove the seeds and the surrounding membrane. Stuff a ball of meat into each loquat.

Preheat the oven to 180°C (350°F/Gas 4).

Using four flat metal skewers (ideally 1 cm/½ in thick), push five loquats onto each skewer. Each loquat should have the open side facing upwards, so the skewer passes through both sides of the fruit and also the meat.

Put the *kebap* skewers on the charcoal grill or barbecue, with the open sides of the loquats facing upwards. Cook for 3 minutes on each side then remove from the heat. Remove the loquats from the skewers and put them in a round baking dish (preferably terracotta) leaving a space in the middle.

Wash the spring onions, then remove the roots and tough outer leaves. Roughly chop the spring onions and the garlic shoots (or garlic clove). Halve the cherry tomatoes and mix them with the spring onions and garlic shoots in a salad bowl. Add the pomegranate molasses, sumac, olive oil and chilli flakes. Toss the salad.

Make a mound of the tomato salad in the middle of the loquats (pushing the loquats to make it fit). Put the tray in the oven and cook for 15 minutes.

Serve with pita bread.

ALİ NAZİK
'THE GENTLE KEBAP' (LAMB AND SMOKED EGGPLANT)

The literal translation of the Turkish name for this dish is 'gentle Ali', leading to the theory that the creator was a chef named Ali. More likely, though, the name is a corruption of ala nazik *(good and gentle) or* eli nazik *(gentle hand). In the land of dubious etymologies, the name is often said to have come from an event in the early 1500s, when Sultan Selim I ate a dish of eggplant and lamb and asked: 'What gentle hand made this?' Hopefully the answer was a good chef named Ali.*

While I have adapted many of the regional recipes in this book to modern forms, this one is exactly as I first consumed it in Gaziantep. It won us the 'Best in Taste' award at the Taste of Sydney festival in 2012. Thanks, Ali.

SERVES 4

1 red capsicum (pepper)
700 g (1 lb 9 oz) lamb (at least 25 per cent fat), coarsely minced (ground)
1 teaspoon salt
1 tablespoon paprika
1 tablespoon chilli flakes
500 g (1 lb 2 oz/2 cups) plain *yoğurt*
4 large eggplants (aubergines)
juice of 1 lemon
4 garlic cloves
2 teaspoons salt
75 g (2²⁄₃ oz) butter

CHILLI AND CAPSICUM BUTTER
75 g (2²⁄₃ oz) butter
1 red capsicum (pepper), chopped
50 g (1¾ oz) chilli flakes

1 piece pita bread, for holding the skewer

Cut the capsicum in half and remove the stalk and seeds. Chop into quarters and pulse in a blender until finely minced. Transfer the capsicum to a mixing bowl and add the lamb, salt, paprika and chilli flakes. Knead the mixture for 5 minutes with wet hands to make a smooth paste. Cover the bowl with plastic wrap, transfer to the fridge and leave to marinate overnight.

Place the *yoğurt* on a sheet of muslin (cheesecloth) and tie up the corners. Hang the muslin over a pot overnight to allow the *yoğurt* to thicken.

In the morning, take the meat mixture out of the fridge and divide it into four balls, each about 180 g (6½ oz). Wrap the meat around four flat metal skewers (ideally 2 cm/¾ in thick). Squash each ball around the skewer, pressing the mixture so it spreads 5 cm (2 in) from the top to 10 cm (4 in) from the bottom. Once all four skewers are firmly covered, put them back in the fridge for at least 1 hour.

If you're using a charcoal grill, you should light it 1 hour before you want to cook. Burn the charcoal for at least 45 minutes and when the flames have died down, and the coals are glowing with a covering of white ash, the barbecue is ready. (If you're using a gas barbecue, turn it onto medium heat about 5 minutes before you're ready to cook.)

Char the eggplants on an open flame until the skin is blackened (see page 21). When they are cool, scoop out the flesh and put the pieces in a colander for 10 minutes to lose some of their water. Drizzle on the lemon juice to help them retain their colour.

Roughly chop the eggplant into a chunky purée. Crush the garlic with 1 teaspoon of the salt. Mix the strained *yoğurt* with the crushed garlic. Set aside.

To make the chilli and capsicum butter, melt the butter in a frying pan over low heat. Add the capsicum and chilli flakes. Cook for 2 minutes. Set aside.

Melt the butter in a frying pan. Add the chopped eggplants and the remaining salt. Heat the mixture for 1 minute then divide onto four plates. Spread the garlic *yoğurt* over the eggplant.

Put the *kebaps* on the charcoal grill or barbecue. Cook for 2 minutes, until the meat on one side has seared, then turn over and cook the other side for 2 minutes. Turn again, and cook for 2 minutes on each side. The fat will drip on the charcoal and burn, but that smoke adds to the flavour. Constantly check to see if the meat is at risk of falling off the skewer, and if so, turn it over.

Use the piece of pita bread as a mitten to grip the meat and pull it off the skewer. Cut the meat from each skewer into three and place the three pieces on the *yoğurt*. Pour the chilli and capsicum butter into a jug (pitcher) for people to help themselves and serve immediately.

AFTER NOON TEA

PUDDINGS, BAKLAVAS & SWEETS

AFTERNOON TEA

If you've a sweet tooth like the average Turk, these are the signs you'll be looking for as you wander through the streets of any Turkish town. A *tatlıcı* will sell you *helva*, Turkish delight and ice creams; a *şekerci* will sell confectionery; a *muhallebici* will sell milky puddings; and a *pastane* will sell pastries (often including baklava, but if you're a connoisseur of the prince of pastries, you should look for a *baklavacı*, which serves nothing else). And at street stalls in Tarsus, on the Mediterranean coast, you'll find the iced rosewater pudding called *bici bici* (pronounced 'beegee beegee').

A Turk would drink tea with any of those desserts, but if you insist on coffee, you should look for a sign saying 'Café', which will offer a European mix of snacks. If you see the older word *Kahve*, you'll encounter a hole in the wall where men play cards and backgammon.

As you'll gather, Turks have a sugary treat for every occasion. For example, on the tenth day of the month of Muharram in the Islamic calendar, they share a desert called *aşure*, which has up to forty-one ingredients, supposedly based on the dried fruits, nuts and pulses that Noah had in the cupboard when his ark finally settled on dry land. In Ottoman times, the fifteenth day of the month of Ramadan was associated with the gift of baklava to the janissaries—the soldiers of the sultan in the Topkapı Place. They were kept from staging military coups for two centuries by their annual sweet crunchy bonus.

There's even a pastry called *kerhane tatlısı*, which translates as 'brothel sweet' because it is sold outside houses of ill repute. If you buy one of these syrupy pretzels, the street seller won't wish you the usual *Afiyet olsun* (bon appétit) but rather *Beline kuvvet* (power to your back).

Sweet treats are more usually associated with the other end of the morality spectrum. In my parents' day, it was customary for a young man, seeking to get to know a young woman, to ask nervously: 'Would you like to meet me in the pudding shop?' The couple might bond over a *sütlaç* (rice pudding) and a house-made lemonade before he asked his mother to ask her mother if a marriage might be possible. Then the families would meet over pastries and Turkish delight. With tea, of course.

For 500 years, the Ottoman sultans were mad for rice puddings but their chefs showed off by inventing micro-thin filo pastry and forty-layer baklava some time in the late fifteenth century. In the nineteenth century, the fad for cakes spread from the palace to the people as French *pâtissiers* arrived in Istanbul to serve the tourist trade from Europe.

Lokum (Turkish delight) is a vital element in Turkish hospitality, surrounded by rituals. You never eat it before midday, and it's better with coffee than with tea. And you should never arrive at somebody's house without a package of it to conclude an afternoon.

A sacred site for pastry lovers is the Markiz Pastanesi in the Istanbul suburb of Beyoglu—not for the pizzas and *kebaps* it serves nowadays, but because it started life in the 1880s as Café Lebon, a magnificent art-nouveau salon where the former chef of the French Embassy served crunchy creamy confections to passengers from the Orient Express. His slogan was '*Chez Lebon, tout est bon*'.

In the early twentieth century, Albanian *patissiers* took over from the French, opening Inci (specialising in profiteroles); Sariyer Muhallebicisi (specialising in *sütlaç*, *aşure*, and *keşkül*); and Baylan in my suburb of Kadıköy (the first pudding shop I visited as a child—specialising in ice cream with caramel and bitter almonds).

Outside of Istanbul, certain regions are identified with certain desserts. The western town of Afyon is the place to go for *kaymak* (clotted cream, see page 54). For the crunchy cheesy pastry *künefe*, you'd go south to Antakya (formerly Antioch). For *dondurma* (stretchy ice cream), you'd move east to Kahraman Maraş.

Or you could stay in your own kitchen and make this chapter your journey through the sweet history of Anatolia.

Contrary to popular belief, Turks drink more tea than cofee—7.5 kilos per person a year—especially if they're retired gents meeting in the local *kahve*.

ASTARLI SÜTLAÇ
SAFFRON-LAYERED RICE PUDDING

This layered dessert is a speciality of the southeastern city of Gaziantep (best known for baklava). In the Turkish name, the word sütlaç *(pronounced 'sutlatch') means 'milky rice pudding' and the word* astarlı *means 'the lining of a jacket'.*

Saffron—either home-grown or imported from Persia—was an important ingredient in Ottoman cuisine, because it allowed the sultans to show off their wealth. Pretentious people got into the habit of leaving the saffron threads in the pudding so their guests could say: 'Wow, that must have cost a bit!' There's actually no reason to leave the threads in, since all the flavour and colour you need is extracted by the warm water within 20 minutes.

I like to decorate my astarlı sütlaç *with candied chickpeas, which you should be able to find in Middle Eastern food shops. But the dessert works perfectly well without them.*

SERVES 4

RICE PUDDING
100 g (3½ oz/½ cup) rice
1 piece mastic crystal (less than 1 g/¹⁄₂₅ oz)
1 tablespoon sugar
750 ml (26 fl oz/3 cups) milk
2 tablespoons rice flour
pinch of salt

SAFFRON TOPPING
5 saffron threads
1 drop geranium oil (or rose water)
1 tablespoon currants
1 tablespoon pine nuts
50 g (1¾ oz/¼ cup) rice
110 g (3¾ oz/½ cup) sugar
1 tablespoon rice flour

DECORATION (OPTIONAL)
20 candied or roasted chickpeas
4 tablespoons pomegranate seeds

Wash the rice in cold running water to remove the excess starch. Transfer to a saucepan, add 100 ml (3½ fl oz) of water, bring to the boil and simmer for 10 minutes. The rice will absorb most of the water.

Crush the mastic crystal into a powder, using a mortar and pestle or the handle of a knife, and then combine with the sugar. Heat the milk, mastic mixture and strained rice in a saucepan over medium heat, and bring to the boil. Combine the rice flour with 125 ml (4 fl oz/½ cup) of the boiling milk mixture and then add to the pan. Add the salt and simmer for 10 minutes, stirring constantly, to thicken. Remove the pan from the heat and leave to cool for 5 minutes, then divide the rice pudding equally between four 250 ml (9 fl oz/1 cup) glasses. Leave to cool completely at room temperature and then transfer to the fridge and chill for 30 minutes.

Next, make the topping. Put the saffron threads in a bowl and cover with 60 ml (2 fl oz/¼ cup) of warm water. Stir in the geranium oil and then leave to rest for 20 minutes. Discard the saffron threads and set aside.

Cover the currants in warm water, leave for 10 minutes and then strain. Toast the pine nuts in a frying pan over medium heat for 2 minutes, shaking the pan constantly to evenly brown.

Rinse the rice in cold running water to remove the excess starch. Transfer to a saucepan and add 125 ml (4 fl oz/½ cup) of water. Bring to the boil and simmer for 10 minutes. Add another 375 ml (13 fl oz/1½ cups) of water and half the sugar, and continue to simmer for 3 minutes, stirring constantly. Combine 125 ml (4 fl oz/½ cup) of the cooking liquid with the rice flour in a bowl. Discard the remaining rice mixture, and then pour the rice flour mixture into the pan. Add the remaining sugar and cook for a further 5 minutes, stirring occasionally. Add the saffron-infused liquid and simmer for a further 5 minutes until it starts to thicken. Add the currants and pine nuts, remove from the heat and leave to cool.

Remove the rice puddings from the fridge, cover with saffron topping and then refrigerate again for 1 hour.

Decorate the chilled *astarlı sütlaç* with the chickpeas and pomegranate seeds, and serve.

YALANCI KAZANDİBİ

'TRICKSTER'S POTSTICKER' (BURNT MILK AND MASTIC PUDDING)

In the Turkish title, the word kazandibi *means 'bottom of the pan', which I've loosely translated as 'potsticker'.* Yalancı *(pronounced 'yalanjuh') means a liar or trickster—the kind of person who'd promise a pudding that is usually made with chicken breast, but who'd then leave out the chicken breast. In other words, me and most of the pudding shops in modern Istanbul.*

The very last recipe in this book is a variant of that classic chicken breast pudding (called Tavuk göğsü). *In Turkey, it was customary to scrape up the bits left at the bottom of the pan after the chicken breast pudding had been served, fold them over neatly, caramelise the outside, and present them as a new dessert called 'bottom of the pan'. Nowadays, cooks usually leave out the chicken breast. I've followed the modern style because I wanted a dish suitable for vegetarians—or maybe just because I'm a trickster.*

SERVES 8

1 piece mastic crystal (less than 1 g/¹⁄₂₅ oz)
150 g (5½ oz) sugar
1 litre (35 fl oz/4 cups) milk
2 tablespoons rice flour
70 g (2½ oz) arrowroot powder
2 tablespoons butter, melted
100 g (3½ oz) icing (confectioners') sugar
1 tablespoon ground cinnamon

Crush the mastic crystal into a powder, using a mortar and pestle or the handle of a knife, and then mix with the sugar. Heat the milk and mastic mixture in a saucepan over medium heat. Meanwhile, add the rice flour and arrowroot to 250 ml (9 fl oz/1 cup) of water and stir to combine. Pour the arrowroot mixture into the milk and bring to the boil, then reduce to a simmer and cook, whisking constantly, for 5 minutes.

Brush a 30 x 40 x 4 cm (12 x 16 x 1½ in) baking tray with the melted butter. Sprinkle the icing sugar evenly over the tray. Place the tray over medium heat on the cook top and gently shake so that the sugar caramelises evenly but does not burn. Pour the milk mixture over the caramelised sugar. Remove the tray from the heat and tap it on a solid surface to make the pudding settle evenly. Put the pudding back over the heat and

gently shake so that the mixture cooks evenly. Once all corners of the pudding have started to brown and the pudding starts to bubble, take the tray off the heat and sit it in a larger tray of iced water. Leave to cool to room temperature and then place the pudding tray in the fridge for 1 hour to chill.

Remove the pudding from the fridge and cut it into six slices (once lengthways and twice across). Fold each strip of pudding over to expose the burnt underside. Push a plastic spatula under one end and roll about a third of the strip over the top. Repeat with the remaining strips.

Dust each snail with cinnamon and serve at room temperature.

ELMA ÇAYI
APPLE AND CINNAMON TEA

A cheap version of apple tea—over-sweetened and made with crystals instead of real fruit—is served to tourists in Istanbul's grand bazaar by carpet sellers who think it will help seduce visitors into paying twice as much as a carpet is worth. If you're not a good negotiator, it could be the most expensive tea you ever drink.

The first time I had apple tea was from a Turkish family in Australia—because the carpet sellers never saw any reason to serve it to me in Istanbul. I've been trying to perfect it ever since. You can use all the parts of the apple you would normally throw away, and the peppercorns, cloves and star anise add intriguing complexity. Genuine apple tea, with no hidden agenda, is the ideal accompaniment for the three little treats coming up next.

SERVES 4

2 apples
2 slices lemon
2 cinnamon sticks
2 black peppercorns
1 star anise
4 cloves
3 tablespoons honey, to taste

Preheat the oven to 100°C (200°F/Gas ½).

Thinly slice the apples across the core, place on a baking tray and bake for 1 hour until they are dried and browned.

Put the baked apple, lemon, cinnamon, black peppercorns, star anise and cloves in a saucepan with 1 litre (35 fl oz/4 cups) of water over low heat. Bring to the boil and simmer for 15 minutes, and then strain the tea into a teapot, gently pressing the apples. Sweeten with honey, then pour into tea glasses and serve.

ÇİKOLATALI HURMA
CHOCOLATE DATES

Purists would say this is not a very Turkish dish, since dates tend to come from Arab countries further to the south and east, and chocolate is a rare ingredient in our desserts (disappointing for a chocoholic like me). But we certainly use almonds and pistachios, so I've included them to appease the nationalists. Çikolatalı hurma has the great advantage of being easy to make with just a few minutes' notice—assuming your pantry is equipped with the right balance of Turkish and Arabic pleasures.

MAKES 16

16 dates (preferably medjool)
150 g (5½ oz/1 cup) slivered almonds
150 g (5½ oz) bitter chocolate (70 per cent cocoa)
70 g (2½ oz/½ cup) ground pistachios

Slit each date and remove the pit. Stuff the cavity with slivered almonds.

Bring 750 ml (26 fl oz/3 cups) of water to the boil in a large saucepan. Reduce the heat to a simmer and place a small metal mixing bowl over the pan, making sure it covers the sides like a lid but does not touch the water below. Line a baking tray with baking paper and set aside. Break the chocolate into small pieces and gradually add to the bowl, stirring constantly so that the chocolate melts but doesn't separate. Using tongs or a slotted spoon, place the dates, one at a time, in the hot melted chocolate and coat completely. Remove the chocolate-coated dates, place them on the prepared tray, and leave to cool slightly.

Put the pistachios in a small bowl. Dip the still-warm dates in the nuts to half cover, and then transfer to a clean tray. Put the tray in the fridge for 30 minutes for the chocolate to set, and then serve.

BADEM EZMESİ
BEBEK ALMOND TRUFFLES

Bebek, on the European side of the Bosphorus, is Istanbul's most expensive suburb, lined with elegant restaurants and bars that will charge you $25 for a cocktail.

That was where I came across almond truffles, served in wooden boxes emblazoned with the golden logo of a shop called Meşhur Bebek Badem Ezmesi (Famous Bebek Almond Paste). It opened in 1904 and it sells only almond confectionery. If you make my version, you'll save a fortune—even when you include the orange blossom water and hazelnut liqueur.

MAKES ABOUT 10

50 g (1¾ oz) sugar
4 drops lemon juice
½ teaspoon orange blossom water
150 g (5½ oz/1 cup) blanched almonds
1 tablespoon Frangelico (or hazelnut liqueur)
50 g (1¾ oz) dark cocoa powder

Bring 50 ml (1⅔ fl oz) of water to the boil over high heat. Add the sugar and stir to dissolve. Reduce the heat to a simmer, then add the lemon juice and the orange blossom water. Put the almonds in a mixing bowl and gradually add the syrup, in four batches, pounding the mixture with a wooden spoon each time. Add the Frangelico and then knead the mixture for 5 minutes until a smooth paste forms. Roll the almond truffles into about ten walnut-sized balls, coat with cocoa powder and serve.

CEZERYE
MERSİN CARROT AND COCONUT BALLS

Every city in Turkey makes a sweet they claim is 'a natural Viagra'. Cezerye (pronounced 'jez-air-yeh') is the natural Viagra of Mersin on the southeast coast. It was once the ancient Greek city of Zephyrion, and now it's Turkey's largest port.

I have no evidence to support the alleged aphrodisiac value of carrots, but you could say that this is one of the healthier deserts you can consume from the region of excessive sugar and butter. I confess I have added turmeric mainly for visual impact, because carrots outside of Turkey have a less vivid colour—and presumably less potency.

MAKES ABOUT 20

75 g (2⅔ oz/½ cup) hazelnuts
4 carrots
1 teaspoon honey
1 tablespoon cornflour (cornstarch)
110 g (3¾ oz/½ cup) sugar
4 cloves
1 teaspoon ground cinnamon
½ teaspoon allspice
½ teaspoon ground ginger
½ teaspoon turmeric
30 g (1 oz/½ cup) flaked coconut

Preheat the oven to 180°C (350°F/Gas 4).

Place the hazelnuts on a baking tray and bake for 5 minutes. Remove the tray and set aside to cool, then rub off the skins using your fingertips. Put the nuts in a food processor and coarsely grind.

Put the carrots and 250 ml (9 fl oz/1 cup) of water in a saucepan over high heat and boil for 10 minutes. Put 2 tablespoons of the boiling water in a bowl with the honey and cornflour and stir to combine.

Strain the carrots and then transfer to a blender. Add the sugar and blend into a purée. Put the carrot purée back in the pan over low heat and stir in the spices. Add the honey and cornflour mixture and then simmer for 10 minutes, stirring constantly. Remove the pan from the heat and discard the cloves. Add the hazelnuts and then leave to cool to room temperature.

Using a teaspoon, shape the mixture into small walnut-sized balls. It should make about twenty balls. Spread the coconut flakes on a tray and then roll the balls in the coconut to evenly coat. Put the tray in the fridge and leave until you are ready to serve.

Put the *cezerye* on a plate (with toothpicks, if you like, so that people don't have to use their fingers) and serve.

In Mersin market (southeastern Anatolia), this stall specialises in every kind of confectionery—fruit candies, nougat, dried fruits, dried molasses stuffed with nuts, and *lokum* (Turkish delight).

AŞURE
NOAH'S ARK PUDDING

This could well be the oldest pudding in the world. The Turkish name aşure means 'ten' because you're supposed to eat it on the tenth day of the first month of the Islamic calendar (which, being lunar, changes every year). It's staggering how many important events need to be remembered on that date—Moses crossed the Red Sea; Abraham's son Ishmael was born; Adam's plea for forgiveness was accepted by God; the prophet Jesus was born; and Noah's ark landed on Mount Ararat as the waters receded after the Great Flood.

It's the last event that explains why the full version of this pudding has forty-one ingredients. To celebrate his return to dry land after forty days on the water, Noah cooked up all the remaining supplies in the ark—nuts, pulses and dried fruits, but definitely no animals—and shared the resulting stew with everybody who had survived the flood. We've simplified Noah's recipe, but the spirit of generosity remains—you're supposed to offer this dish to anybody who could smell it cooking.

SERVES 16

---

100 g (3½ oz/½ cup) white haricot beans
100 g (3½ oz/½ cup) dried chickpeas
3 cloves
150 g (5½ oz) dried figs
200 g (7 oz) dried apricots
100 g (3½ oz) currants
100 g (3½ oz) sultanas
100 g (3½ oz) hazelnuts
50 g (1¾ oz/⅓ cup) blanched almonds
100 g (3½ oz) walnuts
350 g (12 oz/2 cups) pearl barley
880 g (1 lb 15 oz/4 cups) sugar
1 tablespoon cornflour (cornstarch)
250 ml (9 fl oz/1 cup) milk
1 tablespoon honey
zest of 1 orange

DECORATION
2 tablespoons cinnamon
4 tablespoons toasted sesame seeds
80 g (2¾ oz) walnuts, coarsely ground
80 g (2¾ oz) hazelnuts, coarsely ground
140 g (5 oz/1 cup) pistachios, coarsely ground
75 g (75 g (2⅔ oz/½ cup) dried apricots, finely chopped
200 g (7 oz) pomegranate seeds
zest of 2 oranges

Soak the white haricot beans and chickpeas in water overnight, in separate bowls. Strain and rinse under cold running water and then place the beans and chickpeas, together, in a saucepan. Cover with water, bring to the boil over medium heat, then boil for 40 minutes until they are soft.

Preheat the oven to 180°C (350°F/Gas 4).

Crack the cloves with a wooden spoon and soak in warm water for 1 hour. Finely chop the dried figs and apricots, and then place in a bowl with the currants and sultanas. Cover with lukewarm water and leave to soak for 30 minutes.

Place the hazelnuts on a baking tray and bake for 5 minutes. Remove the tray and set aside to cool, then rub off the skins using your fingertips. Halve the hazelnuts. Halve the almonds. Put the walnuts in a food processor and coarsely grind.

Wash the barley in cold running water to remove the excess starch. Half fill a saucepan with water and bring to the boil over high heat. Add the barley and cook for 10 minutes. Strain the barley, half fill the pan with fresh water and boil the barley again for 10 minutes. Strain the barley a third time, add

to the pan with 1.5 litres (52 fl oz/6 cups) of water and boil for a further 40 minutes. Add the strained chickpeas and beans and continue to boil for 10 minutes, stirring occasionally. Add the almonds and hazelnuts. Reduce the heat to a simmer and cook for 5 minutes, stirring slowly.

Next, add the strained dried apricots, sultanas, currants, figs and sugar. Dilute the cornflour in the milk, then add to the cooking mixture. Simmer for 3 minutes, stirring constantly. Add the strained cloves, honey and orange zest. Simmer for another 7 minutes until the mixture starts to thicken.

Divide the pudding into each serving bowl and then refrigerate for at least 2 hours.

Decorate the top of the pudding with cinnamon, sesame seeds, walnuts, hazelnuts, pistachios, chopped dried apricots, pomegranate seeds and orange zest, and serve.

NOTE
Aşure will serve four people over four meals, and can be stored in the fridge for a week.

The cradle of civilisation, just north of the Garden of Eden, the Euphrates River in southeastern Anatolia, and the sunken city of Halfeti.

STRAWBERRY AND ROSE SNOW CONE

It's traditional to sprinkle rosewater on the hands of mourners at the wakes that take place forty days after burials in Turkey. For that reason, many Turks associate the smell of rosewater with mourning. In the Mediterranean town of Tarsus, near the Toros mountains, they associate rosewater with an iced treat that is sold from carts in the streets. There, for five months of the year, the bici bici *hawkers would head up the hill and fill their carts with snow. Then they'd race back down, and for a lira coin you'd get a generous scoop of pudding and snow spread on a plate and soaked with a sweet syrup made from the petals of roses or pink tulips. Nowadays,* bici bici *is sold from refrigerated trucks all year round.*

SERVES 4

ROSE SYRUP
1 organic pink rose, about 20 petals (or non-organic rose petals thoroughly washed)
2 teaspoons citric acid
100 ml (3½ fl oz) grenadine (or raspberry cordial)

CANDIED ROSE PETALS
1 organic pink rose, about 20 petals (or non-organic rose petals thoroughly washed)
2 egg whites
60 g (2¼ oz/½ cup) icing (confectioners') sugar

PUDDING
60 g (2¼ oz/½ cup) cornflour (cornstarch)

TOPPING
150 g (5½ oz/1 cup) strawberries
100 g (3½ oz) icing (confectioners') sugar

DECORATION
2 tablespoons icing (confectioners') sugar

You could use a commercial rose syrup with this dish, but if you want to make your own, remove the petals from the pink rose and wash thoroughly. Sprinkle on the citric acid and place in a jar. Cover the petals with 200 ml (7 fl oz) of water, seal the jar tightly, and then rest in a sunny spot for 3 days.

Mix the grenadine with 125 ml (4 fl oz/½ cup) of the homemade rosewater. Now you have the rose syrup—you need 50 ml (1⅔ fl oz) for the granita, 50 ml (1⅔ fl oz) for the pudding, and 100 ml (3½ fl oz) for the topping. Discard the petals. The remaining rosewater will keep in the fridge for 3 months, and you can sprinkle it on other puddings—or use it at wakes.

Now make the granita. Mix 250 ml (9 fl oz/1 cup) of water with 50 ml (1⅔ fl oz) of the rose syrup in a small bowl, and then place in the freezer for 15 minutes. Remove the bowl and use a fork to break up any ice that has formed. Put the bowl back in the freezer and repeat the process three more times over the course of about 1 hour, to stop the granita from setting into a solid block. Once the granita has crystallised into pink ice fragments, freeze again for 2 hours.

Next, candy the rose petals. Cut the white parts off the petals. Lightly whisk the egg whites for 1 minute to make a smooth liquid. Brush each petal on both sides with egg white. Sprinkle both sides with the icing sugar.

Preheat the oven to 100°C (200°F/Gas ½).

Line a tray with baking paper. Place the petals on the tray and heat for 2 hours, with the oven door ajar. Remove the dried petals from the oven and leave to cool for 15 minutes.

Bring 625 ml (21½ fl oz/2½ cups) of water to the boil over medium heat. As it is heating, add the cornflour and whisk vigorously to combine. Continue to stir slowly for about 5 minutes, until the mixture thickens to a pudding-like consistency.

Put the remaining 150 ml (5 fl oz) of rose syrup into a squeeze bottle and squeeze about 50 ml (1⅔ fl oz) into swirls over the pudding. Line a dinner plate with baking paper and pour the pudding onto it, then refrigerate for 1 hour to set. Remove the pudding from the fridge, lift the pudding off the paper and cut into 2 cm (¾ in) cubes.

Wash the strawberries, cut off the stems and slice into quarters. Pat dry with paper towel and then sprinkle with the icing sugar.

Using four serving dishes, half-fill each dish with spoonfuls of the pudding. Add the sugared strawberries to the top of each pudding and then cover with granita. Shape the granita into a cone and decorate the base with five or six candied rose petals.

Sprinkle the icing sugar on top of each mound, to resemble a snowy peak, and then splash a little more rose syrup from the squeeze bottle around the granita for added colour, if you like. Serve immediately.

ÇATAL
FORK BISCUITS

The word çatal (pronounced 'chatal') means 'fork', and I can only imagine these savoury biscuits got their name because somebody thought they looked like a two-pronged fork joined together at the top (though if you ask me, they look more like spoons). You are supposed to eat them with your fingers, not with a fork.

The secret ingredient here is a spice powder called mahlep, *made from the seeds of the St Lucie cherry. Its flavour is between bitter almond and cherry. I'm suggesting you roll these biscuits in sesame and nigella seeds. That's mostly for visual impact, but also because they add complexity to the flavour and texture.*

MAKES 4

1 egg
100 g (3½ oz) butter
50 ml (1⅔ fl oz) olive oil, plus extra for greasing
50 g (1¾ oz) plain *yoğurt*
300 g (10½ oz/2 cups) plain (all-purpose) flour, plus extra for dusting
1 teaspoon *mahlep* powder (ground white cherry pits)
1 teaspoon baking powder
1 teaspoon salt
2 teaspoons nigella seeds
2 teaspoons white sesame seeds

Separate the egg white and yolk. Set aside the yolk. Gently melt the butter in a frying pan (or microwave for 30 seconds). Put the egg white in a bowl, add the olive oil, *yoğurt* and melted butter and whisk to combine.

Sift the flour into a mixing bowl, make a well in the middle and add the *mahlep*, baking powder, egg white mixture and salt. Knead the dough for 10 minutes, until smooth. Cover the bowl with a damp cloth and rest for 15 minutes.

Preheat the oven to 170°C (325°F/Gas 3).

Divide the dough into eight balls. Place a ball of dough on a floured work surface and, with floured hands, roll into 20 x 1 cm (8 x ½ in) lengths. Repeat with the remaining dough.

Set two pieces of the dough side by side and curve them towards each other like brackets. Join them together at each end to form an oval shape, and twist the tips to make sure they stay together. Repeat with the remaining dough to make four *çatals*. Brush the top of the dough with egg yolk and sprinkle with nigella and sesame seeds.

Line a baking tray with baking paper and brush with oil. Put the ovals on the baking paper and cook for 25 minutes or until golden brown. Remove *çatals* from the oven and rest for 10 minutes. Serve warm.

KAVALA KURABİYESİ
KAVALA COOKIES

Kavala is a town in Greece, not far from the border of Turkey. I wanted to include what Turks call Kavala cookies in honour of one of my food idols—the Sydney chef Janni Kyritsis, whose grandparents were expelled from Turkey in the 1920s as part of a government policy of monoculturalism. They ended up living in Kavala (just as my grandparents were expelled from Greece and ended up living in the Turkish town of Mürefte, where Janni's parents had started). But when I asked Janni if he was familiar with Kavala cookies, he looked blank. The people of Kavala, it seems, just call them almond cookies, and are unaware of their city's fame throughout my country.

MAKES ABOUT 16

300 g (10½ oz/2 cups) plain (all-purpose) flour, plus extra for dusting
150 g (5½ oz/1½ cups) almond meal
150 g (5½ oz) butter
150 g (5½ oz) icing (confectioners') sugar
1 vanilla bean
1 tablespoon baking powder
2 eggs
50 g (1¾ oz/½ cup) coarsely ground almonds
1 tablespoon vegetable oil, for greasing

Mix the flour and almond meal together in a non-stick frying pan over low heat for 3 minutes until it begins to bake, then remove from the heat and set aside.

Gently melt the butter in a frying pan (or microwave for 30 seconds). Pour the melted butter in a bowl and add 50 g (1¾ oz) of the icing sugar. Slice the vanilla bean and scrape the seeds into the butter mixture. Add the baking powder and eggs, and whisk to combine. Put the flour and almond mixture in a separate bowl. Make a well in the middle and pour in the butter and egg mixture. Knead for 5 minutes to make a soft dough. (If it seems too moist, add a little more flour.) Add the ground almonds and knead for 5 minutes more until it forms a coarse paste. Cover the bowl with a damp cloth and rest for 15 minutes.

Preheat the oven to 170°C (325°F/Gas 3).

Place the dough on a floured work surface and roll out the dough, using a rolling pin, into a sheet about 30 cm (12 in) wide and 1 cm (½ in) thick. Use the rim of a glass to cut the sheet into rounds, then slice each round in half to make sixteen half moons. (For a traditional shape, push the straight edge of the half moon inwards to create a crescent.)

Line a baking tray with baking paper and brush with vegetable oil. Add the half moons and bake for 25 minutes or until golden. Remove the tray from the oven and leave to cool for 10 minutes, then sprinkle generously with the remaining icing sugar and serve.

WHERE THE BEST BAKLAVA BEGINS

Undoubtedly, Anatolian cooks were playing around with dough, butter and beet-sugar long before the Ottoman Empire. The Romans in Constantinople and the Greeks in Byzantion loved their sweet pastries. But the ingredient that was added by the chefs in the Topkapı Palace in the fifteenth century was showmanship. They wanted their audience (the sultan, his family, his advisers and occasionally his bodyguards) to exclaim, 'My god, how can he roll out his filo so thin?' and 'My god, how does he have the patience to create forty layers, and still get it so light?' Nowadays, those questions are asked every day by the customers at İmam Çağdaş, the best baklava maker in Gaziantep, which is the best baklava town in Turkey.

Until I was twenty, I thought I was eating great baklava in Istanbul. Then the grandfather of one of my student friends arrived at our shared house with a beautifully wrapped box he'd bought in southeastern Turkey. As I tasted the contents, Şakir Dede, the grandfather, explained that the baklava at İmam Çağdaş was designed to satisfy the five senses:

1. The Look: High-domed with a golden top and glimpses of the fluorescent green of pistachio nuts;
2. The Smell: The richness of the butter and a hint of caramel and wood smoke from the baking;
3. The Touch: The syrup and butter should be so well absorbed that instead of being soggy the filo is crisp enough to crumble under your finger;
4. The Sound: You should hear 'the tune of the crunch' when you bite; and of course
5. The Taste.

I had to make the pilgrimage to Gaziantep where I met Telat Çağdaş and his son Burhan. Telat is the grandson of Hacı Hüseyin, who opened a bakery in Gaziantep in 1887 and began the legend. Telat spends all day in a fog of flour, supervising the thirty men who knead, roll out, sprinkle, layer, soak, bake and slice the precious product from 6 am to 3 pm every day.

While Telat runs the baklava factory upstairs, Burhan runs the 200-seat restaurant downstairs (which also serves excellent *kebaps*). Burhan's son, Telat Jr, looks after the cash desk.

The youngest workers are the twelve-year-old apprentices who come in before and after school to clean and carry, and bring cups of tea to the more senior workers. They can expect to rise, every two years or so, through these ranks: caretaker of ingredients; dough maker; dough roller (with the thinnest rolling pins in the world); baklava builder (layering with nuts and butter and sometimes clotted cream); wood-fire oven baker; slicer and folder; and syrup master.

The current syrup master has been working with the Çağdaş family for thirty years, and started at the age of twelve. Telat trusts him absolutely, but he still checks the syrup every day.

That perfectionism explains why the European Union has given the baklava of Gaziantep a 'Protected Geographical Indication' as a unique artisanal creation.

In Gaziantep, Telat Çağdaş and his grandson Telat Çağdaş Jr package their baklava to send all over the world.

The filo production room in Imam Çağdaş Baklava House, where the pastry is rolled so thin you can read a newspaper through it.

BAKLAVA

TRADITIONAL PISTACHIO BAKLAVA

The next three recipes are forms of baklava, which Turks rarely make at home. We hate to seem defeatist, but honestly, you're not going to be able to make your own filo pastry to anywhere near the standard of a place like İmam Çağdaş (see page 174)—even if you possess a huge marble table, a long thin rolling pin and the world's strongest shoulders.

At İmam Çağdaş, they aim to roll out the pastry so thin you could read a newspaper through it, but we don't expect you to manage that (although if you insist on trying, see page 27). For this recipe, just buy a couple of chilled packs of filo. You'll need at least forty-two sheets to make true baklava.

The recipe assumes your baking tray is what is known as a 'quarter pan', which is 33 cm long, 22 cm wide and 2 cm deep (13 × 8½ × ¾ in), so try to find filo of roughly those dimensions. If your tray is a different size, however, just cut the filo to fit. The most important ingredient of baklava is patience. Even with bought pastry, the recipe takes a long time—there are forty-two layers to butter, place and sprinkle. But the process is satisfying, and it's fun to get the kids to help.

SERVES 8

400 g (14 oz) ground pistachio kernels (preferably Turkish or Iranian, and definitely not salted)
500 g (1 lb 2 oz) ghee (to make your own, see page 21) or clarified butter
375 g (13 oz) chilled filo pastry (at least 42 sheets)
500 g (1 lb 2 oz) caster (superfine) sugar
juice of ¼ lemon

Put the pistachios in a blender and blend into a coarse powder. Gently melt the ghee in a frying pan (or microwave for 30 seconds).

Remove the top 12 layers of filo and place between two damp cloths, then set aside for the top of the baklava. Divide the remaining filo into two equal stacks and place each stack between damp cloths. Using a pastry brush, lightly brush the bottom and sides of a baking tray (traditionally 33 x 22 x 2 cm/13 x 8½ x ¾ in) with the warm ghee.

Place one filo sheet in the tray and lightly brush with ghee. Add two more layers,

brushing with ghee each time, and then lightly sprinkle 1 tablespoon of pistachios over the third filo layer. Reserve 2 tablespoons of pistachios to decorate the top. Repeat the process six more times, to make a 21-sheet stack.

Top this layer with a thick, 5 mm (¼ in) layer of pistachios. Continue the layering process—three sheets, then a light sprinkling of pistachios—four more times to make a 33-sheet stack. (Any broken or offcut pieces of filo can be used to make the middle layer of any trio.) Take the remaining nine filo layers and continue to stack, brushing between each sheet with ghee, but not adding pistachios.

Using a sharp knife, cut the baklava seven times lengthways and six times across to make forty-two portions. (The Turkish style is square, but you can also make rectangular blocks.) Reheat the remaining ghee and pour it between the cracks, and then set aside the pastry tray for 20 minutes to rest and absorb the ghee.

Preheat the oven to 180°C (350°F/Gas 4). Put the pastry in the oven and bake for about 30 minutes,

rotating the tray after 15 minutes to ensure even baking.

Meanwhile, make the sugar syrup. Heat 600 ml (21 fl oz) of cold water and the sugar in a saucepan over medium heat. Add the lemon juice and bring to the boil, then reduce to a low simmer and cook for about 20 minutes until the mixture becomes thick and syrupy, being careful not to let it caramelise. Check the pastry regularly and remove it once the top is golden brown.

Carefully place the baklava tray over medium heat for 1 minute, moving the tray around to ensure the base is evenly heated. Remove from the heat and pour the hot sugar syrup over the hot baklava. Leave to rest for 1 hour to absorb the sugar. Decorate the top with the remaining pistachios and serve.

NOTE
Leftover baklava can be kept for 4 days. Don't put it in the fridge, though, as this will ruin the texture.

SARIĞI BURMA
BLACK SEA ROLLED BAKLAVA

The name of this Ottoman recipe literally means 'rolled turban'. In the sultan's kitchen the cooks would twist the pastry into a shape that resembled what they saw on the heads of the aristocrats around them. We're giving you a simpler version, but keeping the name.

We've already said Gaziantep has the greatest makers of baklava in Turkey and therefore the world, but other parts of Turkey approach baklava in different ways. On the Black Sea they use hazelnuts and their own butter, and they make the baklava into a roll shape. I've decided to use walnuts instead of hazelnuts, because I'm not from the Black Sea.

MAKES 50 PIECES

500 g (1 lb 2 oz) plain (all-purpose) flour
3 eggs
100 ml (3½ fl oz) milk
100 ml (3½ fl oz) vegetable oil
3 tablespoons plain *yoğurt*
pinch of salt
1 tablespoon baking powder
1 tablespoon white vinegar
150 g (5½ oz) butter
100 g (3½ oz) potato flour
600 g (1 lb 5 oz) walnut kernels, roughly ground
500 g (1 lb 2 oz) sugar
juice of ¼ lemon

Sift the flour into a mixing bowl and make a well in the middle. In a separate bowl, whisk the eggs, milk, vegetable oil, *yoğurt*, salt, baking powder, vinegar and 50 ml (1⅔ fl oz) of water to combine. Pour the egg mixture into the flour. Knead for 10 minutes to make a smooth dough, then cover the bowl with a damp cloth and leave to rest for 15 minutes.

Melt the butter in a frying pan over high heat (or microwave for 30 seconds). Brush a baking tray with a little of the melted butter.

Divide the dough into ten billiard-sized balls. Dust your work surface with the potato flour to prevent sticking. Place a ball of dough on the work surface and flatten the dough using a thick rolling pin, being careful not to let the dough stick. Roll the dough out as thin as possible, stretching it into a square about 40 cm (16 in) wide, using your hands and the rolling pin. Brush the stretched dough with butter and sprinkle with 50 g (1¾ oz) of walnuts.

Place a straightened wire coat hanger (or a very thin rolling pin at least 50 cm/20 in long) across the dough sheet, on the edge nearest you, and roll the sheet into a tight cylinder around the wire. Push the cylinder ends towards each other and squeeze into a crinkly concertina shape about 30 cm (12 in) long. Lift it onto the prepared baking tray. Gently pull the wire out. Repeat with the nine

remaining balls of dough, tightly packing the concertinas into the tray. Preheat the oven to 180°C (350°F/Gas 4).

Cut across the row of concertinas four times to divide each cylinder into five rolls, each about 6 cm (2½ in) long. Reheat the remaining butter and then pour it over the pastry and between the cracks. Set aside the pastry tray for 10 minutes to rest and absorb the butter.

Bake for about 30 minutes, rotating the tray after 15 minutes to ensure even baking. Meanwhile, make the sugar syrup. Heat 600 ml (21 fl oz) of cold water and the sugar in a saucepan over medium heat. Add the lemon juice and bring to the boil, then reduce to a low simmer and cook for about 20 minutes until the mixture becomes thick and syrupy, being careful not to let it caramelise. Check the pastry regularly and remove it once the top is golden brown.

Carefully place the baking tray over medium heat for 1 minute, moving the tray around to ensure the base is evenly heated. Remove from the heat and immediately pour the hot sugar syrup over the hot pastry. Leave the *sarığı burma* to rest for 1 hour to absorb the sugar. Decorate the top with the remaining walnuts and serve.

SÜTLÜ NURİYE
'THE GENERAL'S COMMAND' (HAZELNUT AND MILK BAKLAVA)

When the last military coup happened in Turkey (in 1980) I was nine years old. One of the generals who took control of the government decided to involve himself in the details of daily life. He thought some baklava houses were overcharging, so he ordered all baklava houses to standardise their price.

One of the artisan baklava houses in Istanbul, Güllüoğlu, was not prepared to sacrifice quality for the sake of meeting cost regulations, so they decided to create a new type of baklava, with cheaper ingredients. They used hazelnuts instead of pistachios (which are three times the price). To make it a little creamier and lighter, they used milk syrup instead of sugar syrup.

The price controls were lifted many years ago but the revolutionary pastry can still be found as an option in the Güllüoğlu branch at Karaköy, the port across the water from Istanbul's spice market.

SERVES 8

250 g (9 oz) ghee (to make your own, see page 21) or clarified butter
300 g (10½ oz) sliced hazelnuts (or coarsely ground hazelnuts)*
375 g (13 oz) chilled filo pastry (at least 42 layers)
750 ml (26 fl oz/3 cups) milk
440 g (15½ oz/2 cups) sugar

Gently melt the ghee in a frying pan (or microwave for 30 seconds). Divide the sheets of filo into two equal stacks and place each stack between two damp cloths.

Using a pastry brush, lightly brush the bottom and sides of a 40 x 30 x 4 cm (16 x 12 x 1½ in) baking tray with a little of the warm ghee. Place the first filo sheet in the tray and lightly brush with ghee. Add another layer of filo, brush with ghee and continue to layer with the rest of one stack. Repeat the process until you have layered and buttered the first stack. (Any broken or offcut pieces of filo can be used towards the bottom of the stack),

and then cover with the hazelnuts, reserving 2 tablespoons of nuts to decorate the top. Continue to layer and brush the pastry in the baking tray using the second stack of filo.

Once all the pastry has been layered, cut the baklava using a sharp knife, five times lengthways and seven times across to make thirty-five blocks. Reheat the remaining ghee and pour it between the cracks, and then set aside the pastry tray for 20 minutes to rest and absorb the ghee.

Preheat the oven to 180°C (350°F/Gas 4). Bake the pastry for about 30 minutes, rotating the tray after 15 minutes to ensure even baking.

Meanwhile, make the milk syrup. Heat the milk and sugar in a saucepan over very low heat for 8 minutes, stirring constantly, being careful not to boil the milk (keep the temperature around 75°C/165°F if you have a thermometer). Check the pastry regularly and remove it once the top is golden brown.

Carefully place the baklava tray over medium heat for 1 minute, moving the tray around to ensure the base is evenly heated. Turn off the heat and pour over the warm milk syrup. Leave to rest for 1 hour to absorb the sugar. Decorate the top with the remaining hazelnuts and serve.

NOTE
Sliced hazelnuts are preferred for presentation, but if these are not available, use coarsely ground hazelnuts instead. To make these, preheat the oven to 180°C (350°F/Gas 4) and then roast 300 g (10½ oz) whole hazelnuts for 5 minutes, remove from the oven, leave to cool and then rub the skins off with your fingers. Finally, coarsely chop the nuts using a blender or food processor.

TULUMBA
OTTOMAN DONUTS

This snack, from the late Ottoman period, is soft inside and crunchy outside. Fried batter soaked in syrup is a favourite in Greece and the Balkan countries. Or you might consider it similar to Spanish churros or Egyptian balah el sham (Damascus dates). Tulumbas are particularly popular during the fasting month of Ramadan, where they give a sugar and carbohydrate hit for people who haven't eaten all day.

MAKES ABOUT 20 DONUTS

LEMON SYRUP
440 g (15½ oz/2 cups) sugar
juice of ¼ lemon

DONUTS
50 g (1¾ oz) butter
pinch of salt
1 tablespoon sugar
300 g (10½ oz/2 cups) plain (all-purpose) flour
3 eggs
1 tablespoon semolina
1 tablespoon cornflour (cornstarch)
1 litre (35 fl oz/4 cups) vegetable oil

Make the lemon syrup first. Put 500 ml (17 fl oz/ 2 cups) of water and the sugar in a saucepan over medium heat and bring to the boil. Add the lemon juice, lower the heat and continue to simmer for 10 minutes. Remove from the heat and pour the syrup into a deep bowl. Set aside.

In a separate saucepan, mix 500 ml (17 fl oz/2 cups) of water with the butter, salt and sugar, and bring to the boil over medium heat. Add the flour and continue to boil for 3 minutes, stirring constantly, to make a dough. Remove from the heat and stir to help it cool. Set aside.

Put the dough in a mixing bowl and stir in the eggs, one at a time, until combined. Knead for

3 minutes. Add the semolina and cornflour, and knead for a further 5 minutes to make a soft moist dough, adding 1 tablespoon of water if it seems dry. Cover the bowl with a damp cloth and set aside to rest for 15 minutes.

Push the dough into a piping bag with a star nozzle. Squeeze out a long line of dough and cut into 6 cm (2½ in) chunks. Pour the vegetable oil into a deep heavy-based saucepan. Add the *tulumbas* and place the pan over low heat. Once the oil starts bubbling, simmer for 5 minutes or until the donuts turn golden brown. Remove the *tulumbas* with a slotted spoon and transfer into the bowl with the lemon syrup. Leave to soak for 5 minutes, then remove from the syrup and serve.

KADAYIF DOLMA
APRICOT AND WALNUT DOLMAS

This traditional dish is from Erzurum, in eastern Anatolia, where they stuff it with walnuts. I've reduced the amount of syrup and boosted the stuffing with apricots. It uses the crunchy 'string' pastry called Kadayıf, which means there are interesting texture contrasts between the inside and the outside.

MAKES 20

SUGAR SYRUP
500 g (17 fl oz) sugar
¼ lemon

FILLING
250 g (9 oz) chopped walnuts
50 g (1¾ oz) dried apricot, finely chopped

PASTRY
50 g (1¾ oz) butter
300 ml (10½ fl oz) milk
2 egg yolks
500 g (17 fl oz) chilled fresh *kadayıf* pastry
1 litre (35 fl oz/4 cups) vegetable oil

DECORATION
2 tablespoons chopped walnuts

To make the syrup, put the sugar and 750 ml (26 fl oz/3 cups) of water in a saucepan over medium heat and bring to the boil. Reduce the heat, squeeze the quarter lemon into the water, and throw in the lemon skin. Simmer for 15 minutes and then remove the lemon skin and discard. Remove from the heat and set aside to cool. (Do not refrigerate.)

Put the chopped walnuts and apricots in a bowl and mix together.

Gently melt the butter in a frying pan over low heat (or microwave for 30 seconds). Transfer to a deep mixing bowl, add the milk and egg yolks and whisk to combine.

Loosen the pastry using your fingers and then roughly chop the strands. Using clean hands, take a handful of pastry and press together between your palms to make a round. Still holding the round in your palm, place 2 teaspoons of the walnut and apricot mixture in the middle and use your other hand to fold over the sides of the pastry and roll up the ends, and then squeeze into a tight tube. Dip your fist into the milk mixture, letting the pastry absorb some of the liquid through your fingers, pushing the pastry back inside your fist as it slightly expands. Shake off the excess liquid and then set aside on paper towel. Repeat with the remaining pastry to make about twenty rounds.

Heat the vegetable oil in a deep frying pan over high heat. Add a drop of water to the oil. If it sizzles the oil is ready. Carefully add the *dolmas*, ten at a time, and then fry for 3 minutes until golden and crunchy. Remove with a slotted spoon and transfer into the bowl with the syrup. Leave to soak for 2 minutes, then remove and serve, decorated with the chopped walnuts.

Murat Muhallebicisi (pudding shop) in Kadıköy,
Istanbul, famous for pastries and milk puddings.

BOZA

BOZA 'BEER' WITH TOASTED CHICKPEAS

Boza is a sweet slightly fermented drink that originated in the Balkans in the ninth century and is now associated with the suburbs of Istanbul. When I was a kid, I would look forward to hearing the cries of the food sellers who would pass by our house in the afternoon. The one I enjoyed the most came past at the end of a winter's day as the sky was darkening. He would stretch out the cry as long as he could: 'Bohhhhh-zaaaaa'. You would bring him a bottle, and the boza man would fill it by turning a tap in a big tank he carried on his back.

The street sellers are gone now. If you want to drink boza in Istanbul, you must go to the shop known as Vefa, which opened in 1876 in a suburb called Vefa. Between October and April they sell boza (and pickles). The rest of the year they sell grape sherbet, lemonade and ice cream. If it's a quiet day, they'll show you the glass from which Kemal Atatürk drank Vefa boza the year before he died (1937). Presumably he couldn't hear the cry of the street seller from inside his palace.

SERVES 8

120 g (4¼ oz) fine dark bulgur
25 g (1 oz) rice
175 g (6 oz) sugar
20 g (¾ oz) dry yeast
95 g (3¼ oz/½ cup) dried chickpeas
1 tablespoon olive oil, for greasing
1 tablespoon ground cinnamon

Wash the bulgur and rice in cold running water to remove the excess starch. Put the grains in a saucepan with 1 litre (35 fl oz/4 cups) of water over medium heat. Bring to the boil, reduce the heat, and simmer for 30 minutes, stirring regularly. Strain the liquid into another pan, pressing on the grains to extract as much juice as possible. Discard the boiled bulgur and rice. Put the pan over medium heat, add the sugar and bring to the boil, then remove from the heat.

Dilute the yeast in 125 ml (4 fl oz/½ cup) of warm water. Set aside for 5 minutes. It should start to form bubbles.

Slowly pour the yeast into the grain mixture, stirring constantly, then leave to cool to room temperature, stirring occasionally. Cover with a lid between stirs. Once completely cool, transfer the pan to a cool spot and leave to ferment for at least 24 hours. Every 6 hours or so, stir with a wooden spoon. Meanwhile, prepare the chickpeas.

Strain and rinse the soaked chickpeas, place in a saucepan, cover with water and bring to the boil over medium heat. Lower the heat and simmer for 30 minutes. Wash the cooked chickpeas and then strain and pat dry with paper towel.

Preheat the oven to 200°C (400°F/Gas 6). Grease a baking tray with the olive oil, then add the chickpeas and bake for 15 minutes. Remove the tray from the oven and gently shake it to roll the chickpeas around. Return the tray to the oven and bake for a further 15 minutes. Remove the tray and set aside to cool. Store the chickpeas in a covered container at room temperature until you are ready to add them to the *boza*.

After 24 hours, check the *boza*. Depending on the season, the temperature and the humidity, it may take up to 3 days for the drink to ferment. Once bubbles form on the top, it is ready.

Stir the *boza* with a metal spoon just before serving. Pour into four glasses, spoon the chickpeas over the top (or on the side for people to add themselves), sprinkle each glass with cinnamon and serve.

NOTE
Stored in the fridge, *boza* will keep for about 3 days.

LİMONATA
BASIL LEMONADE

Lemonade has been a staple for decades in pudding shops all over Turkey, and when my mother was young, the usual way to ask someone out on a date was to say: 'Would you like to have a lemonade together?' Limonata is currently making a comeback in Istanbul's coolest cafés. But do not confuse limonata with some commercial fizzy drink. It must be made in-house with fresh lemon juice.

The secret to a good lemonade is to rub the lemon skin with sugar before grating it—this sharpens the flavour. Normally we add fresh mint leaves, but I thought I'd twist the formula with a herb that is more unusual in Turkey—basil.

SERVES 4

8 lemons
220 g (7¾ oz/1 cup) sugar
about 30 basil leaves

Grate the zest from the lemons into a bowl. Sprinkle in the sugar and knead for 5 minutes to make a paste. Add 250 ml (9 fl oz/1 cup) of warm water and stir to dilute the paste.

Cut the lemons in half and squeeze out as much juice as you can. Transfer to a jug (pitcher) and set aside. Put the squeezed halves in a bowl, cover with warm water and leave to soften for 1 hour.

Discard the soaking water. Wrap the lemon pulp in muslin (cheesecloth) and squeeze out any remaining juice, then add to the jug. Add the sugared zest paste. Add 250 ml (9 fl oz/1 cup) of water and 270 g (9½ oz/2 cups) of crushed ice. Finely chop half the basil leaves and stir through the lemonade. Pour into glasses, top with a few whole basil leaves, and serve.

ŞEKERPARE
SEMOLINA DOMES

This is one I learned from my grandma, who would make vast quantities of
şekerpare (which means 'piece of sugar' in old Turkish) and invite twelve or more
people at a time to share it for afternoon tea or dinner. I like it because semolina
makes a lighter texture than you find in flour-based desserts.
It is vital to pour the syrup over the domes while they are hot, so there is
maximum absorption, and to leave plenty of space around each dome so they can
expand—along with your waistline.

MAKES 20

½ lemon
550 g (1 lb 4 oz/2½ cups) sugar
125 g (4½ oz) butter
300 g (10½ oz/2 cups) plain (all-purpose) flour
95 g (3¼ oz/½ cup) fine semolina
1 egg
1 tablespoon baking powder
2 tablespoons vegetable oil
20 blanched almonds

First, make the syrup. Using a fine grater or a microplane, grate the lemon zest into a bowl and set aside. Squeeze the lemon into a cup. Mix 440 g (15½ oz/2 cups) of the sugar and 625 ml (21½ fl oz/2½ cups) of water in a saucepan over medium heat and bring to the boil. Add the lemon juice, reduce the heat and simmer for a further 15 minutes. Remove from the heat and set aside to cool.

Gently melt the butter in a frying pan over low heat (or microwave for 30 seconds). Sift the flour into a mixing bowl and add the semolina. Make a well in the middle and pour in the butter. Break in the egg. Add the remaining sugar, then add the lemon zest and the baking powder. Knead for

5 minutes. Cover the bowl with a damp cloth and set aside to rest for 15 minutes.

Preheat the oven to 180°C (350°F/Gas 4).

Knead the dough again for 5 minutes, then divide into about twenty ping pong-sized balls. Brush the oil onto a baking tray. Place the balls on the tray and push into a dome shape. Push an almond into the top of each dome and then bake for 25 minutes.

Remove the *şekerpare* from the oven and pour the syrup over the top. Leave to cool for 15 minutes before serving.

LOKUM
TURKISH DELIGHT

With most classic dishes, the precise origin story is lost in the mists of history. With Turkish delight we can actually put a date on it. In the year 1777, a bunch of British businessmen visiting Istanbul gave the name to a sticky sweet they discovered in the shop of a cook named Bekir. He was calling it lokum, which was his abbreviation of an Arab phrase meaning 'throat relaxant'.

He told them he had created it when the sultan put out the word to confectioners that he was looking for a sweet that wouldn't break his teeth. Bekir won the contest with lokum flavoured with rosewater, and was appointed chef pâtissier in the kitchen of the Topkapı Palace. He then went on to open his own shop in the Bahçekapı district, near the railway station where the Orient Express ended its journey.

The British businessmen started selling Bekir's product in their homeland, and his shop became a place of pilgrimage for tourists from Europe. Confectioners all over Turkey (and Greece) started copying his lokum, flavouring it with seasonal ingredients from their neighbourhood. A painting of a turbaned Bekir feeding lokum to children (The Confectioner by Preziosi) now hangs in the Louvre, and the original shop, beautifully restored, is classified as a protected site. The people behind the counter will tell you lokum was the favourite sweet of Picasso, who said it helped his concentration.

I've attempted to reproduce the original recipe here, but to be honest, I'm not partial to rosewater (like most Turks). You can add any flavouring you like. I sometimes replace the rosewater with mint and cinnamon. A popular version replaces the almonds with twice-roasted pistachios. A friend of mine in Bodrum does a great version with the juice from local satsuma mandarins. Guess what they use in the Black Sea town of Safranbolu (the name means 'plenty of saffron').

MAKES ABOUT 75 PIECES

60 g (2¼ oz/½ cup) cornflour (cornstarch)
2 tablespoons rose water
600 g (1 lb 5 oz) caster (superfine) sugar
35 g (1¼ oz/¼ cup) slivered almonds
30 g (1 oz/¼ cup) icing (confectioners') sugar

Put 30 g (1 oz/¼ cup) of the cornflour in a bowl with the rose water and 2 tablespoons of water, and stir to combine. Put the caster sugar in a saucepan, add 500 ml (17 fl oz/2 cups) of water and bring to the boil over medium heat, then reduce the heat and simmer for 5 minutes until it starts to thicken. Add 2 tablespoons of the hot sugar syrup to the cornflour mixture and mix thoroughly. Add the thickened cornflour mixture to the pan. Add the slivered almonds and continue to cook, stirring constantly until the mixture is runny enough to pour but thick enough to set. To check the consistency, spoon a drop of the mixture into a glass of cold water. If it retracts into a ball, it is ready. (Or check using a thermometer. It is ready when the temperature reaches 115°C/240°F.)

Line a quarter gastronorm tray (22 x 33 cm/8½ x 13 in) with muslin (cheesecloth). Sprinkle the remaining cornflour evenly in the tray. Pour the mixture into the tray and then refrigerate for 1 hour to set.

Remove the tray from the fridge and remove the gel block by lifting the edge of the muslin. Place the block on a board, peel off the cloth and then slice into 3 cm (1¼ in) cubes using a sharp knife (or a steel ruler). Separate the blocks slightly and then sprinkle half the icing sugar over the top. Put the Turkish delight in an airtight container, and coat with the remaining icing sugar. Serve with Turkish coffee.

The *lokum* factory in Bodrum
(on the Aegean coast) specialises in
Turkish delight made with the juice of the
local satsuma mandarins.

TÜKENMEZ
THE NEVERENDING SHERBET

Tükenmez is a sustainable home version of the kind of sherbet you used to buy in the street from hawkers with tanks on their backs—still seen occasionally in some parts of eastern Turkey. The street sherbets were often made with tamarind or liquorice root, while the home version uses medlars. As you'll see in the ingredients list, I've suggested a variety of fruits that will contribute interesting notes to the taste, but you can keep adding cores and skins of any hard fruits that take your fancy. To get fermentation started, you need to keep the chickpeas in the water for at least five days. The liquid will continue to ferment gently once the chickpeas are removed, and you can keep refreshing the drink with water for three months. If it starts to taste like vinegar, use it as vinegar and make another batch.

SERVES MANY

1 red apple
1 granny smith (or sour green) apple
1 quince (or nashi pear)
1 pear
100 g (3½ oz) green grapes
200 g (7 oz) medlars (or loquats
    or firm red plums)
50 g (1¾ oz) dried or frozen sour cherries
    (or red grapes)
220 g (7¾ oz/1 cup) sugar
5 chickpeas

Quarter the apples, quince and pear without removing the seeds. Remove the stalks from the grapes. Mix all the fruits, including the medlars and sour cherries together in a bowl.

Put the mixed fruit into a 2 litre (70 fl oz/ 8 cup) jug (pitcher) with a sealing lid and then add the sugar. Wrap the chickpeas in muslin (cheesecloth) and add to the jug. Fill the jug with 1 litre (35 fl oz/4 cups) of water, up to the brim. Seal tightly and then store in a cool spot for 10 days before serving.

NOTE
Each time you want a drink of sherbet, pour it out and replace it with 250 ml (9 fl oz/1 cup) of water and 2 tablespoons of sugar. Stored in the pantry, the sherbet can be kept and replenished for up to 6 months.

KAHVE—TURKISH COFFEE WITH ADDED PATIENCE

When I was growing up, Istanbul was changing, adapting to a faster way of life, but my grandma was determined to keep making perfect coffee. She used a *cezve* (the traditional copper pot), which she placed over burnt charcoal for 15 minutes but regularly removed from the heat to ensure it did not overcook.

In my grandmother's day, a prospective wife was judged by her coffee-making skills—not just her technique, but more importantly her patience. If she's patient with her coffee, she will be patient with her husband—or so the men thought at the time. Now it's possible to judge a Turkish café on the same principle. A second-rate place will boil the coffee too quickly, degrading the taste and producing little of the froth that needs to form gradually and cover the top of the liquid.

These days, you don't need charcoal to make a perfect Turkish coffee. An electric or gas stove top works perfectly well—as long as you have the technique and the patience.

To make your own Turkish coffee, you will need a *cezve* (pronounced 'jezweh')—a heavy-based pot with a long handle, and you will need to buy finely ground medium-roast Arabica coffee (or, if you're a purist, you'd grind medium-roast beans in a cylindrical brass coffee mill called a *kahve değirmeni*). Here's the process:

1. Pour cold water into the pot—one cup for each person you are serving and an extra half cup 'for the pot'.
2. Add a heaped teaspoonful of the ground Turkish coffee for each cup and stir. The amount of coffee may be varied to taste, but don't forget, there should be a thick layer of grounds left at the bottom of each cup. Don't fill the pot too much.
3. If you need to add sugar, this is the time to do it. Check with your guests and if they say 'medium sweet', stir a teaspoon of sugar per cup into the cold water.
4. Heat the pot as slowly as you can—the lower the heat the better it will be. Make sure you watch to prevent the *cezve* overflowing when the coffee boils.
5. When it boils, pour some (not all) of the coffee equally between the cups, filling each cup about a quarter to a third of the way. This will ensure everybody gets a fair share of the foam forming on top of the brew, without which coffee loses much of its taste.
6. Put the pot back on low heat until the coffee boils again (which will be very soon). Distribute the rest of the coffee between the cups.

Since there is no filtering at any time during this process, you should wait for a few minutes before drinking your coffee while the grounds settle at the bottom of the cup.

HERE'S HOW TO ORDER *TÜRK KAHVESI* WHEN YOU'RE IN TURKEY:

Sade ('sah-DEH'): plain, no sugar (fairly bitter)

Az şekerli ('AHZ sheh-kehr-lee'): a little sugar (takes off the bitter edge; half a teaspoon per cup)

Orta şekerli ('ohr-TAH sheh-kehr-lee'): medium (about a teaspoon of sugar per cup)

Şekerli ('sheh-kehr-lee'): sweet (two teaspoons of sugar per cup)

You never order coffee with milk. If you enjoy a milky coffee and you're lucky enough to be in the east of Turkey, you could ask for *menengiç* ('men-en-GITCH'), which is made with crushed wild pistachio nuts, milk and sugar. There's no caffeine, so you can drink it all day.

In traditional cafés, coffee is cooked over charcoals that have been burning for more than an hour.

A *kahve* is a meeting place where men go to play cards, drink tea or coffee, and watch soccer games on TV. *Kahves* rarely serve food.

MEZE

SMALL PLATES
TO DRINK WITH

MEZE

Every great food culture has a tradition of small tasting plates served with a national drink. The Italians have antipasto, the French have hors d'oeuvres, the Spanish have tapas—all washed down with local wines. The Chinese have yum cha, served with tea. The Russians have *zakuski*, served with vodka.

And the Turks have *meze*, served with *rakı* (or occasionally wine or beer). *Mezes* are most likely to be served in a *meyhane*, which is a kind of bar/bistro/pub where people meet for a chat and a drink and a bite from sunset until well after midnight. During the Ottoman period, the *meyhanes* were often run by families of Greek or Armenian background, because those cultures do not have the Muslim aversion to alcohol.

There's an origin story for *meze* that sounds too good to be true. Supposedly the Ottoman sultans in the fifteenth century were a paranoid lot, fearful of being poisoned by foreign spies who sneaked into their kitchens, or by members of their own family. So they hired official food tasters, who would be given small helpings of every dish offered by the chef. They would have to be seen to swallow all of them and keep smiling before the sultan could begin his meal.

Other rich Turks thought they would look important if they followed the same ritual even when they weren't in fear of death threats and couldn't afford official tasters. So they started serving small quantities on small plates and called them *meze*, from the Persian word for 'a taste'.

The reason I'm dubious about this tale is that there were *meyhanes* in the Middle East long before the Ottoman emperors built their kitchens. The eleventh-century Persian poet Omar

Khayyam wrote this line: 'You say rivers of wine flow in heaven—is heaven a *meyhane* to you?' The rivers of wine would have flowed through Istanbul, a thriving trade hub, before the Muslims started cracking down on alcohol sales. Smart *meyhane*-owners would have served salty high protein snacks to make their customers thirsty and to line their stomachs so they wouldn't fall unconscious before ordering another drink.

The need for stomach lining became more pressing in the seventeenth century, when the favoured drink in *meyhanes* changed to *rakı*. *Rakı*, like wine, is made from grapes but, as it is distilled, it is much more alcoholic. Most people dilute *rakı* with water, which turns it white and explains its nickname—'lion's milk'. *Meyhanes* started boasting about the variety of *meze* they had available to keep the customer (relatively) sober.

The twentieth-century poet Nazım Hikmet wrote that a good *meze* table should feast the eye, the conversation should feast the brain, and the *rakı* should whet the palate: 'You can drink *rakı* with spicy or sweet, with cucumber, melon or cheese, with water or without water, in winter or in summer, in joy or in sorrow—the only thing you cannot drink *rakı* with is idiots.'

So here's a typical night out for me during my student years. You decide to meet your friends at a *meyhane* (a decision that might take a while,

because the second most divisive question in Istanbul, after 'What's your soccer team?' is 'Which is the best *meyhane* in town?').

You find a table and order your *rakı* (aniseed-flavoured), which arrives with a jug of water and a bucket of ice. A waiter comes around with a tray displaying cold *meze*—maybe melon and white cheese, *yoğurt* and mint, spicy tomato salsa, eggplant salad, marinated fish, braised vegetables, stuffed mussels—and you point at the ones you fancy. Musicians pass by and you might have to pay them to go away. Street sellers wander in and try to interest you in their wares.

After an hour or so, the waiter comes back and asks if you'd like any hot *meze*. He describes them, emphasising what's unique to the establishment, and maybe points to a tank from which a fish can be scooped out and grilled. You pick a few tastes and you order another bottle of *rakı*. Suddenly it's midnight. You stagger out and buy some *kokoreç* (stuffed intestines that look like sausage) from a street stall to help you sober up.

This chapter gives you the tools to create your own *meyhane*, complete with cocktails. Turks think of *meze* as sharing food, to be placed in the middle of the table as part of a spread, but any of the dishes in this chapter could be served on its own as a starter or first course for lunch or dinner. We have suggested ingredient quantities that will make enough for four, when you want to serve the dish as a course by itself. If the dish is part of a *meze* platter or party table, then each guest is likely to take a smaller quantity. So if one of our 'serves 4' dishes is served as part of a platter of three *mezes*, for example, then you could say it will serve twelve (or six greedy people).

This is party food and party drink, served with conversation. The only thing you cannot serve it with is idiots.

A typical laneway *meyhene* in Istanbul, where friends gather to chat, sing, get tipsy on *rakı* and eat an array of *mezes*.

SUCUKLU HUMUS
POMEGRANATE HUMUS WITH SPICY SAUSAGE

A well-made humus is a wonderful form of comfort food. But it's not Turkish. If you're offered it in Turkey you're probably in a place run by someone with an Arabic background. (This is not to say that I'm taking a side in the humus war. You won't catch me making a declaration on whether its origin is Syrian or Israeli or Palestinian or Lebanese. All I know is it's not Turkish.)

At my restaurant in Sydney, we try to change our menu every three months. The discussion with my cooks and waiters begins with me saying: 'Lets lose the humus—it's not Turkish.' My manager, Fatih, always replies: 'Leave it alone. It's been seven years, and the customers love it.' So I've compromised. I've turned an Arabic speciality into a Turkish dish by adding ingredients familiar to me— pomegranates to sweeten it, capsicum to colour it and sucuk (spicy beef sausage) to give it heat. My customers are right.

SERVES 6

HUMUS
200 g (7 oz/1 cup) dried chickpeas
1 teaspoon bicarbonate of soda (baking soda)
2 garlic cloves
60 ml (2 fl oz/¼ cup) lemon juice
1 tablespoon pomegranate molasses
   (to make your own see page 24)
1 tablespoon capsicum (pepper) paste
   (see page 32)
4 tablespoons tahini
½ teaspoon salt
125 ml (4 fl oz/½ cup) olive oil
½ teaspoon paprika

TOPPING
1 small cucumber
½ small red onion
½ red capsicum (pepper)
100 g (3½ oz) *sucuk* (or chorizo)
2 slices day-old sandwich bread

pide bread (to make your own, see page 45),
   grilled, or pita crisps, to serve

Put the chickpeas in a saucepan, cover with water and bring to the boil over high heat. Boil for 1 minute, and then strain. Put the chickpeas in a bowl with the bicarbonate of soda, cover with water and soak overnight.

Strain the chickpeas and rinse under cold running water for 5 minutes. Transfer to a saucepan, cover with plenty of water, and bring to the boil over medium heat. Cook for 1½ hours until the chickpeas are soft enough to mash with your fingers. Put the cooked chickpeas in a food processor and blend into a smooth paste. Finely crush the garlic and stir into the chickpea paste. Add the lemon juice, pomegranate molasses, capsicum paste, tahini, salt, olive oil and paprika and blend into a smooth purée. Spoon the humus into a bowl.

Peel the cucumber and finely chop. Finely chop the onion. Slice the red capsicum, remove the seeds and stalk, and finely chop. Chop the *sucuk* very finely. Chop the day-old bread into small cubes.

Put the *sucuk* in a small frying pan over low heat and bring to a simmer, then cook until the fat begins to sizzle and emerge. Add the bread cubes and capsicum, and cook for 2 minutes until crisp. Remove the *sucuk*, bread and capsicum from the pan and mix with the cucumber and red onion.

Using a spoon, swirl the humus so it looks like a whirlpool, and then scatter the *sucuk* mixture into the swirls. Serve the bowl of humus with grilled pide or pita crisps.

MUM'S BROAD BEAN PÂTÉ

My mother, who was a great home cook, became a professional restaurateur when I was sixteen. It was great experience for me to work in her meyhane as a kitchenhand while I was studying. I became the fallback cook every time she sacked her chef, which, on average, was about once a month. I got a crash course in meze preparation, barely having time to learn one new recipe from each chef before they disappeared.

One dish mum would never let anyone else touch was the fava, which she made with her own hands in spring, using a mixture of dried and fresh broad beans and adding black olive paste because she liked the colour contrast. She said fava should be like a cake—able to endure a long sitting at a meze table. If the cake collapses, it's a dip, not a fava.

In this recipe I have used dried beans, so you can make fava all year round, but if you're making it in spring, you could include fresh broad beans (double peeled).

SERVES 4

FAVA PURÉE
190 g (6¾ oz/1 cup) split broad beans
1 small onion
1 teaspoon salt
1 teaspoon sugar
70 ml (2¼ oz) olive oil, plus extra for greasing
2 tablespoons black olive paste
3 dill stalks

TOPPING
1 red bullhorn pepper (or ½ red capsicum/pepper)
¼ red onion
8 black olives, pitted
2 tablespoons olive oil

Wash the broad beans and then transfer to a bowl, add 750 ml (26 fl oz/3 cups) of water and soak overnight.

Rinse the soaked beans under cold running water. Heat the beans, onion, salt, sugar, 50 ml (1⅔ fl oz) of the olive oil and 750 ml (26 fl oz/ 3 cups) of water in a saucepan over medium heat for 15 minutes. Reduce the heat and simmer for 15 minutes, stirring regularly. Remove the pan from the heat and purée the mixture using a hand-held blender (or leave to cool slightly and blend in a food processor). Spoon half the purée into a bowl, add the olive paste and mix together thoroughly, then set aside.

Pick the leaves off the dill and discard the stalks. Fold the leaves into the remaining broad bean purée and leave to cool to room temperature.

Brush four teacups (or rice bowls) with the remaining olive oil. Half fill each cup with the broad bean–dill purée and refrigerate for 30 minutes.

Remove the cups from the fridge and fill the rest of each cup with the olive paste mixture. Refrigerate for a further 30 minutes.

Now make the topping. Slice the bullhorn pepper and discard the stalk and seeds. Finely chop the red onion. Finely chop the black olives. Mix the chopped ingredients in a bowl with the olive oil and then set aside.

Remove the cups from the fridge and upend each one onto its own plate. Use the back of a teaspoon to dent the top of each dome, spoon on the topping, then serve.

POOR MAN'S SAFFRON AND CARROT DIP

A meal in a meyhane usually starts with an assortment of cold plates, designed to sit on the table for hours. Most customers are there primarily to drink alcohol, and they may just pick at their food, expecting it to taste as good at midnight as it did when they sat down at 7 pm. Borani is a model of this kind of meze. The centrepiece is braised carrot, which lines the stomach nicely. I've called this a dip, but it's denser than the usual dips made with yoğurt and coloured with beetroot, chillies or parsley. This one is coloured with turmeric—known in Turkey as the poor man's saffron because it provides visual impact without the exotic fragrance.

SERVES 6

1 tablespoon caraway seeds
4 carrots
50 ml (1²⁄₃ fl oz) olive oil
1 teaspoon turmeric
2 garlic cloves
200 g (7 oz) plain *yoğurt*
2 dill stalks, finely chopped
pide bread, to serve (to make your own, see page 45)

Toast the caraway seeds in a frying pan over medium heat, shaking frequently, for about 2 minutes until fragrant.

Peel and grate the carrots. Heat the olive oil in a frying pan over medium heat. Add the grated carrots and sauté for 5 minutes. Add the caraway seeds and turmeric, sauté for 5 minutes more and then remove from heat.

Crush the garlic and mix it in a bowl with the *yoğurt*. Add the chopped dill and spiced carrots and mix together. Serve the bowl of *borani*, warm or chilled, with pide bread.

CHILLI AND CAPSICUM SALSA

I've translated the word ezme, which literally means 'crushed', as 'salsa' because it's chunkier than a sauce but runnier than a dip, and because it contains the New World ingredients chillies and tomatoes. The secret to making a great ezme is never to use a food processor. Instead, you should chop it finely just before you take it to the table.

Ezmes are served in kebap houses to lubricate the palate before the meat arrives. The waiter just plonks a few small plates on the table when you sit down, and you spoon them up while you discuss what kind of kebap you might order. The spiciest ezmes are made in Gaziantep.

SERVES 6

6 ripe tomatoes
4 green bullhorn peppers
    (or 2 green capsicums/peppers)
1 bunch flat-leaf (Italian) parsley
3 red onions
3 garlic cloves
1 tablespoon *isot* (or chilli flakes)
1 tablespoon capsicum (pepper) paste
    (see page 32)
50 ml (1²⁄₃ fl oz) pomegranate molasses
    (to make your own, see page 24)
100 ml (3½ fl oz) extra virgin olive oil
juice of ½ lemon
1 tablespoon sea salt
pomegranate seeds, to decorate (optional)
pide bread (to make your own, see page 45),
    grilled, to serve

Score a shallow cross in the base of the tomato. Put in a heatproof bowl and cover with boiling water. Leave for 30 seconds, then plunge in cold water and peel the skin away from the cross.

Cut the peeled tomatoes into quarters and scoop out the seeds. Slice the peppers and discard the stalks and seeds. Pick the parsley leaves and discard the stalks. Preferably using a mezzaluna, finely chop the tomatoes, parsley, peppers, red onions, garlic and parsley together into a chunky purée.

Drain off any excess water from the chopping board and then transfer the purée into a bowl. Add the *isot*, capsicum paste, pomegranate molasses, olive oil, lemon juice and sea salt, and stir well to combine.

Decorate with pomegranate seeds, if using, then serve the bowl of *antep ezme* with grilled pide.

PATLICAN SALATA
CHARRED EGGPLANT SALAD

If you've been in Turkey for more than a day, you've had a version of this salad, which would have arrived automatically when you sat down for lunch or meze. It's a candidate for the title of National Dish.

The flesh of the eggplant has a lovely texture but does not have much flavour of its own. It's a great carrier of flavours, though—particularly the smokiness that comes when the skin is burnt on a barbecue or char-grill or open gas flame. The other key flavour here is apple cider vinegar.

One of my closest friends is vegetarian by choice and allergic to eggplant. Life in Turkey is difficult for her.

SERVES 6

EGGPLANT SALAD
2 large eggplants (aubergines)
1 large red capsicum (pepper)
½ bunch flat-leaf (Italian) parsley
2 spring onions (scallions), finely chopped
1 teaspoon salt
½ teaspoon freshly ground black pepper
60 ml (2 fl oz/¼ cup) extra virgin olive oil
2 tablespoons lemon juice
1 tablespoon apple cider vinegar

POMEGRANATE TOPPING
2 tablespoons pomegranate molasses
   (to make your own, see page 24)
1 tablespoon extra virgin olive oil
20 pomegranate seeds

Pierce the eggplants with a fork and char the skins by placing the eggplants directly onto the flame of your stove. Using tongs, move the eggplant around to evenly blacken and then remove from the flame. Peel off the skins and put the eggplant pieces in a colander to drain for about 10 minutes.

Blacken the skin of the capsicum over an open flame in the same way. Put the capsicum in a bowl and cover with plastic wrap to sweat. Leave to cool. Once the capsicum is cool enough to handle, peel off the skin under cold running water. Discard the stalk and seeds.

Pick the parsley leaves, discard the stalks, and finely chop the leaves. Wash the spring onions, remove the roots and tough outer leaves, and finely chop. Roughly chop the eggplant into a chunky purée. Finely dice the capsicum. Mix the vegetables and parsley together in a salad bowl. Add the salt, pepper, olive oil, lemon juice and apple cider vinegar and mix thoroughly.

Mix the pomegranate molasses and olive oil together in a small jug (pitcher). Serve the *patlican salata* at the table for people to help themselves. Swirl the pomegranate dressing over the eggplant. Decorate with the pomegranate seeds.

ZEYTİN PİYAZI
GREEN OLIVE AND WALNUT SALAD

This dish appears on every meze table near the Aegean Sea. It's best made with what we call 'scratched green olives' (early harvested and lightly crushed before being soaked in salty water). They come from the Edremit area in the northwest.

The world's first known edible olives were cultivated in Anatolia 6000 years ago, long before anybody talked about nations called Greece or Turkey. These days Turkey is one of the largest olive oil producers in the world and arguably the most enthusiastic eater of olives in the Mediterranean.

The word piyaz *in the Turkish name comes from Ottoman times, and suggests a salad that contains onions. In fact, the onions are the least interesting part of this dish.*

SERVES 6

125 g (4½ oz) green olives
2 garlic cloves
125 ml (4 fl oz/½ cup) extra virgin olive oil
½ bunch flat-leaf (Italian) parsley
4 spring onions (scallions), chopped
50 g (1¾ oz) walnuts
½ green apple
1 red bullhorn pepper (or ½ red capsicum/pepper)
juice of 1 lemon
2 tablespoons pomegranate molasses
   (to make your own, see page 24)
1 teaspoon chilli flakes
½ tablespoon dried thyme

Slice the olives into quarters, and remove the seeds. Squash the garlic cloves and remove the skin. Put the olive slices and garlic in a small container with half the olive oil, and leave to marinate overnight

Finely chop the parsley leaves. Wash the spring onions, remove the roots and tough outer leaves, and finely chop. Roughly chop the walnuts. Slice the apple. Slice the bullhorn pepper, remove the seeds and the stalk, and finely chop. Transfer the olives from the garlic marinade into a large bowl. Add all the other ingredients and mix thoroughly. Serve the bowl of *zeytin piyazi* at the table for people to help themselves.

ÇIĞ KÖFTE
NIMROD'S VENISON TARTARE

Çiğ köfte (raw meatball) is usually made with veal because of its low fat content. But I'm suggesting you try venison because it is hallowed by history (and has an even lower fat content).

Let me take you back 4000 years to the city of Şanlıurfa in southeastern Anatolia. As the story goes, the ruler at the time was a man named Nemrut (translated as Nimrod in English) who was a great grandson of Noah. Nimrod became paranoid after a dream in which he was told he was about to be replaced by a leader named Abraham, who would try to persuade Nimrod to worship one god. So he ordered his solders to collect all the wood they could find so they could burn Abraham at the stake. When a hunter returned home to his village after killing a deer, his wife was unable to cook it because she, of course, had no wood. Instead, she chopped the raw meat and kneaded it with spices and bulgur— thereby presenting a new dish to the world. (And God saved Abraham by turning the fire to water—the site of which is recognised today by the famous pond in the middle of Şanlıurfa, full of sacred carp.)

SERVES 4

250 g (9 oz) venison loin fillet (or veal loin), trimmed
2 onions
5 garlic cloves
2 tablespoons capsicum (pepper) paste (see page 32)
½ tablespoon tomato paste (to make your own, see page 24)
4 heaped tablespoons *isot* (or chilli flakes)
1 tablespoon pimento
1 tablespoon cumin
½ tablespoon cinnamon
½ tablespoon salt
½ tablespoon freshly ground black pepper
450 g (1 lb/2½ cups) very fine bulgur
15 ice cubes
5 flat-leaf (Italian) parsley stalks
5 mint stalks
3 spring onions (scallions)
lettuce leaves (or pita bread), to serve

Finely cut the venison. Put the meat in a food processor and blend into a coarse paste, then transfer to a round baking tray with indentations on the bottom (or a mixing bowl). Finely grate the onions. Crush the garlic cloves. Add the capsicum and tomato pastes, onion and garlic to the meat and combine. Stir in the six dry spices. Knead the meat mixture for 10 minutes to make a smooth paste. Add 90 g (3¼ oz/½ cup) of the bulgur and three of the ice cubes, and continue to knead until the ice has melted. Repeat with the remaining bulgur and ice cubes until all the bulgur is well combined with the meat.

Pick the parsley and mint leaves and discard the stalks. Finely chop the leaves. Wash the spring onions, then remove the roots and tough outer leaves. Finely chop. Add the mint, parsley and spring onions to the veal mixture and knead for 10 minutes until it holds together as a large ball.

To make the *çig köftes*, take a handful of the mixture and squeeze tightly in your fist to make a log about 3 cm (1¼ in) across and 6 cm (1¼ x 2½ in) long. Repeat to make about thirty patties.

Place about three *köfte* in each lettuce leaf and serve on a platter for guests to help themselves.

MERCİMEK KÖFTESİ
RED LENTIL MEATBALLS

Here's another dish with history. The Bible tells how Esau, a hunter who normally ate venison, saw his brother Jacob eating a bowl of red lentils and was so hungry he offered to give up his inheritance for it.

This is a rare vegetarian version of köfte, *which is normally associated with raw veal or lamb, and is a staple winter dish in the eastern half of Turkey. Even if you love it as much as Esau, be careful not to overload, as bulgur will continue to expand in your stomach.*

SERVES 6

410 g (14½ oz/2 cups) split red lentils
175 g (6 oz/1 cup) fine bulgur
2 onions
2 tablespoons vegetable oil, for frying
1 tablespoon capsicum (pepper) paste
   (see page 32)
1 tablespoon tomato paste (to make your own,
   see page 24)
1 bunch flat-leaf (Italian) parsley
6 spring onions (scallions)
1 tablespoon cumin
1 tablespoon chilli flakes
1 tablespoon olive oil
2 teaspoons salt
1 cos lettuce
1 lemon

Wash the red lentils in cold running water, then place in a saucepan with 1 litre (35 fl oz/4 cups) of water and bring to the boil over high heat. Reduce the heat and simmer for 15 minutes, with the lid partly closed. Put the bulgur in a large mixing bowl and pour over the hot lentils and the cooking water. Rest for 15 minutes, covered, to soften the bulgur.

Finely chop the onions. Heat the vegetable oil in a frying pan over medium heat and then add the onion. Cook for 5 minutes until the onion is translucent. Meanwhile, mix the capsicum and tomato pastes in a small bowl with 1 tablespoon of water. Stir the mixture into the pan and cook for 3 more minutes until the whole mixture is mushy. Remove the pan from the heat and set aside.

Pick the leaves from the parsley, discard the stalks, and finely chop the leaves. Wash the spring onions, then remove the roots and green outer layer. Finely chop.

Once the bulgur has softened, stir in the parsley, spring onion, cumin, chilli flakes, olive oil, salt and onion mixture. Knead for 3 minutes and then divide the mixture into about twenty-four balls, using your hands. Slightly flatten each ball.

Wash the cos lettuce, and break it up into leaves. Place three *köftes* in each lettuce leaf.

Cut the lemon into 6 slices. Place on a platter with the *köftes* for guests to help themselves.

KISIR
BULGUR, MINT AND CUCUMBER SALAD

This salad is associated with southeastern Anatolia, but it has spread all round the country, with regional variations. In my mother's restaurant in Bodrum I learned to include pickles and pickle juice to add saltiness and contrast to the sweetness of the molasses. The trick here is to use just the right amount of boiling water—too little and the grain will be crunchy, too much and it will be mush. The Turkish name is strange—the word kısır *literally means 'infertile', which is hardly the case here.*

SERVES 8

200 g (7 oz) fine bulgur
60 ml (2 fl oz/¼ cup) extra-virgin olive oil
1 tablespoon tomato paste (to make your own, see page 24)
1 teaspoon capsicum (pepper) paste (see page 32)
3 large tomatoes
1 long green chilli
1 teaspoon chilli flakes
2 pickled cucumbers or gherkins
10 flat-leaf (Italian) parsley stalks, picked
10 mint leaves, chopped
5 spring onions (scallions)
2 tablespoons gherkin juice
1 teaspoon white pepper
juice of 1 lemon
1 teaspoon pomegranate molasses (to make your own, see page 24)

Bring 125 ml (4 fl oz/½ cup) of water to the boil water over high heat. Place the bulgur in a large bowl and pour over the boiling water. Leave to rest for 15 minutes. Stir the olive oil, tomato paste and capsicum paste into the bulgur.

Score a shallow cross in the base of each tomato, then transfer to a heatproof bowl and cover with boiling water. Leave for 30 seconds, then plunge into cold water and peel the skin away from the cross. Cut the tomatoes in half and scoop out the seeds with a teaspoon. Finely chop.

Slice the chilli and remove the stalk and the seeds. Finely chop. Finely chop the cucumbers, parsley leaves, mint leaves and spring onions. Add all the chopped ingredients to the bulgur and mix well. Finally, add the gherkin juice, pepper, lemon juice and pomegranate molasses. Stir and serve the *kısır* in the bowl for people to help themselves.

TOPİK
ARMENIAN CHICKPEA DOMES

Topik is a vegetarian dish originally consumed during Lent by the Armenian community, who are Orthodox Christians. Now it's one of the most treasured delicacies to go with a bottle of rakı *in Armenian* meyhanes. *As a child I fell in love with* topik *when our Armenian neighbours invited me to stay for supper while I was playing with their kids. I rediscovered it as a teenager in a* meyhane *called Madam Despina, which was opened in 1946 in the multicultural suburb of Kurtuluş by a Greek lady whose signature dish happened to be Armenian. She's been immortalised in a nostalgic folk song, which goes: 'Set the table, Madam Despina. Are we tipsy again? Did you just run out of* topik*? We love you anyway.' Madam Despina died in 2006, but she's still a hot* topik *in Istanbul.*

SERVES 6

SHELL
400 g (14 oz/2 cups) dried chickpeas
3 potatoes
½ tablespoon cinnamon
1 teaspoon salt
½ teaspoon freshly ground black pepper
1 teaspoon sugar
100 g (3½ oz) tahini

FILLING
10 onions
100 ml (3½ fl oz) olive oil
30 g (1 oz) currants
30 g (1 oz) pine nuts
1 teaspoon cinnamon
½ teaspoon salt
½ teaspoon freshly ground black pepper
½ teaspoon allspice
½ teaspoon sugar
250 g (9 oz) tahini

½ tablespoon cinnamon, to serve
juice of 1 lemon, to serve

Bring a large saucepan of water to a rapid boil. Add the chickpeas and blanch for 1 minute. Transfer the chickpeas into a bowl, cover with fresh water and leave to soak overnight.

The next day, start making the filling. Finely slice the onions. Heat the olive oil in a frying pan over medium heat. Add the onion and cook for 10 minutes until translucent and slightly caramelised. Reduce the heat and simmer for 2 hours with the lid partly closed, stirring occasionally.

Strain and rinse the chickpeas, and then rub in a rough cloth to remove as much skin as possible. Place the skinned chickpeas in a large saucepan, cover with plenty of water (at least three times the volume of chickpeas) and boil for 1 hour, without the lid. Remove the pan from the heat and leave to cool. Once the chickpeas are cool enough to handle, remove any more skin, using your fingers, and then set aside.

Cut the potatoes in half, place in a large saucepan, cover with salted water and bring to the boil. Cook for 15 minutes or until the potatoes are tender, then drain well. Leave to cool and then remove the skin.

Place the potatoes, chickpeas, cinnamon, salt, pepper and sugar in a food processor and blend to make a thick paste. Transfer to a mixing bowl, add the tahini and combine. Knead the mixture together for 2 minutes to make a smooth paste. Cover the bowl with plastic wrap and leave to rest for 10 minutes.

Meanwhile, place the currants in a bowl, cover with warm water, and leave to soak for 15 minutes. Toast the pine nuts in a frying pan over medium heat for 3 minutes, shaking often. Remove the onions from the heat. Strain the currants and then add to the onions. Add the pine nuts, cinnamon, salt, pepper, allspice and sugar. Stir in the tahini.

Cut twelve 30 cm (12 in) squares of plastic wrap.

To make the *topik*, put 4 tablespoons of the chickpea mash in the middle of a square of plastic wrap. Flatten the mash into a round about 15 cm (6 in) across, pushing outwards so the centre is thicker than the edge. Put 2 tablespoons of the onion mixture in the middle of the mash. Lift one corner of the plastic wrap and fold the mash over the filling. Bring the other three corners up to meet the first corner and fold the other edges over. Pull the four corners of plastic wrap together and form the mixture into a ball. Twist the corners of plastic into a strand. Tie a knot in the strand just above the ball. Repeat to make twelve balls. Place the parcels on a tray and refrigerate overnight to set.

When you are ready to serve, snip off the top of the plastic wrapping (below the knot) and take the balls out of the plastic wrap. Sprinkle a little cinnamon on top, and a few drops of lemon juice, then serve.

The Aegean village of Türkbükü, where geese, normally confined to fresh water, have been breeding in the salt water since they were left at the beach by Somer's stepfather in 1995.

MİDYE DOLMA
STREET HAWKER'S STUFFED MUSSELS

If you wander through the Istanbul suburb called Beyoğlu, you'll soon encounter men carrying circular aluminium trays full of mussels stuffed with spiced rice. Give the first man you see a lira and you'll get three or four mussels and a slice of lemon on a paper plate. You'll then become addicted, and feel compelled to go to the street called Nevizade where, with any luck, you'll find a meyhane that will serve you mussel dolmas sitting down.

When I came to Sydney, I met an Armenian lady named Bercük Anne, who made mussel dolma far superior to any I'd found in the streets of Istanbul. Her recipe had a lot of onions, spices and herbs, and very little rice. So here's how you can make the true Armenian mussel dolma better than any you'll find in the streets of Istanbul.

**SERVES ABOUT 4
(5 MUSSELS PER PERSON)**

5 onions
100 ml (3½ fl oz) vegetable oil, for frying
30 g (1 oz) currants
30 g (1 oz) pine nuts
110 g (3¾ oz/½ cup) short-grain rice
2 tomatoes
2 teaspoons freshly ground black pepper
2 teaspoons pimento
1 teaspoon cinnamon
5 flat-leaf (Italian) parsley stalks
3 dill stalks
20 black mussels
2 tablespoons tomato paste (to make your own, see page 24)
2 teaspoons capsicum (pepper) paste (see page 32)
2 tablespoons olive oil
4 lemons, cut into wedges, to serve

First make the stuffing. Finely chop the onions. Heat the vegetable oil in a frying pan over medium heat. Add the onions and cook for 5 minutes. Reduce the heat and simmer, covered, for 20 minutes, stirring occasionally.

Place the currants in a bowl, cover with warm water, and leave to soak for 15 minutes. Toast the pine nuts in a frying pan over medium heat for 3 minutes, shaking often.

Wash the rice under cold running water and then add to the simmering onions. Increase the heat to medium. Grate the tomatoes over the rice. Strain the currants and add to the pan. Add the pine nuts, pepper, pimento and cinnamon, and stir. Simmer the mixture for 5 minutes, then remove from the heat and leave to cool.

Pick the parsley leaves, discard the stalks and finely chop the leaves. Finely chop the dill. Mix the parsley and dill into the stuffing, then set aside.

Now, open the mussels. If you've bought the mussels in a vacuum bag, open the bag over a bowl to catch any liquid inside. Scrub the shells clean. Using a blunt knife, carefully force the point of the knife into the gap at the pointy end of each mussel, and slice through the meat so the shell opens with half the meat attached to each half shell—once you cut through the thick, round connecting muscle at the bottom of the mussel, it will be easy to open. Pour the juice into a bowl. Snip off the beards and, using your finger, remove any grit at the base. Spread the half shells to tear the muscle of the mussel, but leave the two halves connected. Put 2 teaspoons of the stuffing into the middle of each mussel and push the half shells together again.

Place a bread and butter plate, face down, in the bottom of a saucepan about 25 cm (10 in) wide.

Place the mussels in the pan, with the tips pointing outwards towards the edge of the pan with the shells slightly overlapping (to prevent them opening). Build a tight spiral of shells in the centre of the pan. There should be one layer of mussels. Strain the mussel juice through a sieve lined with a double layer of muslin (cheesecloth) three times, to remove any grit.

Mix 250 ml (9 fl oz/1 cup) of mussel juice in a small bowl with the tomato paste and capsicum paste. Pour the mixture over the mussels. Splash on the olive oil. Place another bread and butter plate over the mussels, then put the lid on the pan. Place the pan over medium heat and bring to the boil, then reduce the heat and simmer for 15 minutes.

Remove the mussels from the heat and leave to cool to room temperature. (You can also keep them in the fridge overnight.) Serve the *midye dolma* on a big platter with lemon wedges for guests to help themselves. The best way to eat them is with your hands, using the top shell to scoop the mixture out of the bottom shell.

SOMON PASTIRMA
SALMON PASTIRMA AND BABY ZUCCHINI

This is an example of the new Turkish cooking. When you say pastırma *to traditional Turks, they think beef. But the word simply means 'pressed', so there's nothing to prevent you from wrapping the wonderful paste around any form of protein.*

Since the process involves leaving the protein to dry for at least a week, you need to be careful if you're using seafood. For me, the fish that works best is salmon—it can absorb the flavours of the paste while retaining its own.

Unlike beef pastırma, *somon pastırma is kept in the fridge during the drying process, which means the coating will stay moist and crumble away when you're slicing the salmon. This is a good thing—it's the salmon you want to eat, not the wrapper.*

Because somon pastırma *has a strong taste, I decided to accompany it with the simple freshness of raw zucchini.*

SERVES 6

CURED SALMON
500 g (1 lb 2 oz) sashimi-grade salmon fillet
1 kg (2 lb 4 oz) rock salt
440 g (15½ oz/2 cups) caster (superfine) sugar
15 cloves garlic
3 tablespoons ground fenugreek
3 teaspoons cumin
2 tablespoons sweet paprika
1 tablespoon hot paprika
1 teaspoon ground coriander
1 teaspoon salt

ZUCCHINI AND DILL TOPPING
500 g (1 lb 2 oz) small zucchini (courgettes)
60 ml (2 fl oz/¼ cup) extra virgin olive oil
juice of 1 lemon
4 tablespoons dried *yoğurt* cheese
   (or crumbly feta)
2 dill stalks, picked and chopped

Place the salmon (which should already be skinned and filleted) on a board and remove any small bones, blood lines and white pieces of fat.

Spread a tea towel (dish towel) over a cake rack (or steamer tray or large colander). Sit the rack on top of a baking tray or large pan. You will use this for the drying process.

Mix the rock salt and caster sugar together in a bowl. Spread half the rock-salt mixture onto the towel-covered rack, about 1 cm (½ in) thick. Put the salmon fillet in the middle of the rack and cover it thoroughly with the rest of the rock salt mixture. Fold the muslin cloth over the top of the salt. Place a flat-bottomed tray over the salmon with a 3 kg (6 lb 12 oz) weight on top (using anything from a bag of potatoes to the *Oxford Dictionary*), to flatten out the salmon as it dries. Place the baking tray in the fridge and rest for 2 days.

Take the salmon out of the fridge, wash the salt off and plunge in iced water. Rest the salmon (in the water) in the fridge for 1 day.

Remove the salmon and pat dry. Put the salmon on a rack with a drip tray underneath and refrigerate for 24 hours. Turn the salmon over and return to the fridge for one more day.

Meanwhile, make the paste. Mix the garlic and spices and salt together in a blender to make a thick paste. If the mixture seems dry, drizzle about ½ teaspoon of water into the mix.

Remove the salmon from the fridge and coat it with the paste, making sure every part is completely covered. Put the salmon on the cake rack with the tray underneath, but without the muslin cloth, and return to the fridge for at least another 48 hours.

When you are ready to serve, finely slice the zucchini lengthways. Place in a bowl and toss with the olive oil, lemon juice and *yoğurt* cheese. Finely chop the dill and then add to the zucchini mixture. Thinly slice the *somon pastırma*, diagonally, to make at least 24 slices, and serve with the topping.

VODKA AND MUSTARD-CURED BREAM

This is another of my mum's specialities, perfected in her restaurant in Bodrum, where the visitors love their vodka cocktails and the favourite fish is levrek *(normally translated as 'sea bass'). At my restaurant, we use sea bream. I like using vodka as a curing alcohol because it has a neutral taste, which does not interfere with the hints of ginger, bay leaves and dill in the* votkalı levrek.

SERVES 4

20 whole black peppercorns
1 tablespoon sea salt
3 fresh or dried bay leaves
2 thin slices ginger
50 ml (1²/₃ fl oz) vodka
100 ml (3½ fl oz) lemon juice
1 tablespoon mild French mustard
4 fillets deep sea bream (or another firm
   white-fleshed fish, such as snapper or cod)
50 ml (1²/₃ fl oz) olive oil
3 dill stalks, finely chopped, for decoration

Mix all the ingredients, except the fish and olive oil, together in a bowl.

Place the bream on a board and remove any small bones and blood lines. Thinly slice each bream fillet into five 'leaves'. Place the fillet pieces in the bowl and cover with the marinade. Cover the bowl with plastic wrap, put in the fridge and leave for at least 6 hours (ideally, overnight).

Remove the fish from the bowl and place one fillet on each plate. Drizzle with olive oil, sprinkle on a little dill and serve.

AYVALI KEREVİZ

BRAISED CELERIAC WITH QUINCE AND ORANGE

It is thought that the Greek island of Samos, very close to the Turkish mainland, is where the ugly celeriac first grew. On that island, fossil remains of celeriac were found in a grove sacred to the goddess Hera created in seventh century BC. We're entitled to speculate that the warriors on both sides of the Trojan War were eating it. Homer writes in The Iliad *that the horses of Achilles' soldiers were eating what we assume were wild celeriac leaves.*

In Turkey, celeriac is better known than celery (which tends to appear mostly as sticks in bloody marys). It's often cooked with sour apples, but I agree with the Ottoman cooks in preferring to use quince if it's in season.

SERVES 4

½ lemon
1 celeriac (up to 500 g/1 lb 2 oz)
1 quince
1 onion
1 carrot
125 ml (4 fl oz/½ cup) olive oil
2 oranges
1 teaspoon sugar
2 teaspoons salt

Put 500 ml (9 fl oz/2 cups) of water in a bowl. Squeeze in the juice from the lemon and then add the lemon. Peel the celeriac and chop into pieces, roughly 2 cm (¾ in) square. Add the celeriac to the bowl. Cut the quince in half, remove the pit and thinly slice. Add the slices to the bowl and set aside.

Finely chop the onion. Finely chop the carrot. Heat the olive oil in a frying pan over medium heat. Add the onion and cook for 4 minutes, until soft. Add the carrot and cook for 2 minutes. Drain the quince slices and celeriac cubes, pat dry with paper towel and then add to the pan. Fry for 4 minutes until the mixture starts to change colour and softens a little.

Cut the oranges in halves. Finely grate the zest of one half into the mixture. Squeeze the juice from both oranges into a cup and add enough warm water to fill the cup. Pour the orange mixture into the pan and add the sugar and salt. Bring to the boil, then simmer, covered, for 15 minutes. Check the softness of the celeriac, and if it's still hard, simmer for another 10 minutes. Turn off the heat, and rest, covered, for 15 minutes.

Divide the *ayvalı kereviz* between four serving plates. Serve at room temperature.

ÇERKEZ TAVUĞU
CIRCASSIAN CHICKEN

Circassia is a mountainous region in southern Russia where walnut trees grow in abundance. In the nineteenth century, many Circassians were driven out of Russia and took refuge in parts of the Ottoman Empire where they proceeded to introduce new cooking techniques. Turks, who thought chicken came on skewers, now learned they could eat it cold, smothered in a walnutty paste.

Coriander is one of my pet hates, and I don't use it in my restaurant, but I've included it here to honour the Circassians, who brought it to Turkey.

SERVES 6

2 flat-leaf (Italian) parsley stalks
2 coriander (cilantro) stalks
1 onion, quartered
1 carrot, quartered
1 tablespoon salt
1 tablespoon black peppercorns
1 whole chicken (about 1.2 kg/2 lb 10 oz)
3 slices day-old sandwich bread
200 g (7 oz) walnuts
1 garlic clove
2 tablespoons sweet paprika
60 ml (2 fl oz/¼ cup) walnut oil
pide bread, to serve (to make your own, see page 45)

Pick the leaves off the parsley and coriander, and set aside. Put the parsley and coriander stalks in a saucepan. Add the onion, carrot, salt, peppercorns, chicken and about 3 litres (105 fl oz/12 cups) of water. Place the pan over high heat and bring to the boil, then reduce the heat and simmer, partly covered, for 1½ hours. Remove any scum that forms on the surface.

Take the chicken out of the pan, place on a rack and leave to cool to room temperature. Leave the cooking liquid in the pan and set aside.

Remove the skin from the chicken and pick the meat off the bones. Place the skin and bones back in the cooking liquid and bring to the boil over high heat. Continue to boil vigorously for 1½ hours, uncovered, so the liquid reduces to half its original volume.

Strain the bones, skin and vegetables out of the chicken stock, and discard. Shred the chicken meat and spread the pieces on a deep serving platter. Pour on 2 tablespoons of stock, cover with plastic wrap and place the platter in the fridge. Discard the crusts from the bread. Dunk the bread into the stock for a few seconds then squeeze out any excess liquid. Blend the bread, walnuts, garlic and 1 tablespoon of the paprika in a food processor. Gradually add some stock, tablespoons at a time, to make a smooth paste.

Remove the serving platter from the fridge. Put the chicken in a bowl, stir one-third of the paste through the chicken pieces, then spread them across the platter again. Chop the parsley and coriander leaves and mix them with the remaining paste, then pour this paste over the chicken. Mix the walnut oil and the remaining paprika together, and drizzle over the chicken.

Serve the *çerkez tavuğu* platter cold, with pide bread, for people to help themselves.

YAPRAK SARMA
SOUR CHERRY-STUFFED VINE LEAVES

The traditional cold vegetarian dolma *stuffing involves spiced rice with currants and pine nuts. In recent years, Turkish chefs have started replacing the currants with sour cherries, which contribute great colour as well as flavour. They may think they are doing something new, but actually a sour cherry-stuffing recipe appears in the first published Turkish cookbook,* Melceu't-Tabbahin *(The Cook's Shelter) from 1844—of course, those adventurous Ottomans thought of it first. This recipe was inspired by my friend Batur, whose* yaprak sarma *is a signature dish at his scholarly Ottoman restaurant Asitane (see page 306).*

SERVES 4

100 g (3½ oz/½ cup) sour cherries
   (dried, frozen or tinned), pitted
½ lemon
30 vine leaves
150 ml (5 fl oz) olive oil
2 tablespoons pine nuts
4 onions
185 g (6½ oz/1 cup) short-grain rice
1 tomato
½ teaspoon cinnamon
½ teaspoon allspice
½ teaspoon freshly ground black pepper
1 teaspoon salt
½ teaspoon sugar
5 mint stalks
2 dill stalks

If you are using dried sour cherries, soak them in warm water for 1 hour. If frozen, thaw for 30 minutes. If tinned, rinse to remove the syrup. Halve the sour cherries. Set aside. Zest the lemon half, and squeeze the juice. Set both aside.

If you are using fresh vine leaves, place them in a bowl, cover with boiling water, add 1 tablespoon of salt, and leave to soak for 10 minutes. If they are in brine, wash to remove the salt. Set aside.

Heat the olive oil in a frying pan over medium heat. Add the pine nuts and fry for 2 minutes. Finely slice the onions, add to the pan and cook for 5 minutes until soft. Wash the rice under cold running water and then add to the onion mixture. Grate the tomato into the rice, sauté for 2 minutes and then reduce the heat to a simmer. Stir in the cherries, cinnamon, allspice, pepper, salt, lemon zest and sugar. Add 50 ml (1⅔ fl oz) of water and simmer for 5 minutes. Remove from the heat—the rice should be softened but still slightly crunchy. Finely chop the mint and dill, add the lemon juice and combine with the rice mixture.

Pat the vine leaves dry with paper towel. Snip off any stems and, if the spine in the centre of the leaf is woody, soften it by crushing with the back of a knife. Put aside the five least attractive-looking leaves.

Next, stuff the vine leaves. Put a leaf on a board, shiny side down. Put a strip of rice mixture in the middle of the vine leaf, fold over the base of the leaf, then fold over each long side and roll into a çigar shape, about 6 cm (2½ in) long. Repeat to make about 25 stuffed vine leaves.

Place a bread and butter plate face side down in the bottom of a saucepan. Spread the five reserved vine leaves over the back of the plate. Arrange the stuffed leaves in a tightly packed spiral shape on top of the plate. Thinly slice the half lemon and scatter over the vine leaves. Put another bread and butter plate on top. Add 250 ml (9 fl oz/1 cup) of warm water and bring to the boil over medium heat. Reduce the heat and simmer, partly covered, for 30 minutes.

Remove from the heat, leave to cool and then serve, or keep in the fridge for up to 3 days.

BAKLALI ENGİNAR
BRAISED ARTICHOKES WITH BROAD BEANS

Artichokes are common in the Greek-influenced western part of Turkey—the easterners have barely heard of them. But the artichoke fields that once fed the Ottoman palace have in recent years been turned into shopping centres. Now artichokes are grown way out of town.

If you're in Istanbul in early spring, make sure you try a type of artichoke called bayrampaşa, *which is the name of the suburb where they used to grow. They are sold already cleaned by street sellers, soaking in lemon water to retain their colour. They have a wider heart than most artichokes, and lend themselves to stuffing with broad beans. Once summer comes around, their texture becomes too woody for eating.*

Artichokes became a staple on meze *tables because Turkish drinkers believe these vegetables have liver-cleansing properties.*

SERVES 6

6 globe artichokes
½ lemon
1 teaspoon salt
10 spring onions (scallions)
175 g (6 oz/1 cup) fresh broad beans
125 ml (4 fl oz/½ cup) olive oil
1 teaspoon salt
2 teaspoons sugar
2 dill stalks, leaves only

Clean the artichokes, discard the stalk and remove the leaves until you reach the heart. Put the hearts in a large bowl and cover with water. Cut the lemon and squeeze the juice into the water. Add the two squeezed lemon quarters and the salt, and set aside.

Wash the spring onions, remove the roots and tough outer leaves, and then slice into 3 cm (1¼ in) pieces. Make a slit in each broad bean skin, place them in a saucepan, cover with water, and bring to the boil. Boil for 5 minutes. Strain the beans and leave to cool, then double peel.

Place the spring onions in a saucepan. Add the broad beans and the drained artichoke hearts. Add the olive oil, salt, sugar and 375 ml (13 fl oz/1½ cups) of water, and then bring to the boil over high heat. Reduce the heat and simmer for 15 minutes, covered, until the broad beans are soft.

Lift the lid and scoop 2 tablespoons of the spring onion and broad bean mixture over the top of each artichoke heart. Simmer, covered, for another 15 minutes. Remove the lid and place 2 dill leaves on each artichoke. Cover again, turn off the heat, and leave to rest for 15 minutes.

Carefully lift each artichoke with its bean and onion topping out of the pan and place on a serving platter for people to help themselves.

MÜCVER
NETTLE AND FETA FRITTER

Usually the classic dish called mücver *is made with zucchini, dill and feta. In some parts of the country they add carrots or spinach. I decided to sharpen the flavour with the wild weeds that grow near Bodrum, the west-coast resort town where my mother had her restaurant.*

Turks who use wild weeds in their cooking were probably originally taught by the descendants of the Cretans, who used to live along the Aegean coast (until they were expelled in the 1920s). If you can't find nettles, you could substitute spinach.

This is the first of three zucchini dishes, which can complement each other when served together. You can use the zucchini skins you peel off in this recipe for the next one.

SERVES 4

ZUCCHINI PATTIES
15 flat-leaf (Italian) parsley stalks
10 dill stalks
3 spring onions (scallions)
50 g (1¾ oz) hard feta
20 g (¾ oz) parmesan
1 egg
35 g (1¼ oz/¼ cup) plain (all-purpose) flour
1 teaspoon freshly ground black pepper
2 zucchini (courgettes)
½ teaspoon salt
30 nettle leaves (or 3 spinach stalks)
60 ml (2 fl oz/¼ cup) olive oil

MINT YOĞURT
1 garlic clove
130 g (4⅔ oz) plain *yoğurt*
1 teaspoon dried mint

Pick the parsley leaves, discard the stalks, and finely chop the leaves with the dill. Wash the spring onions, remove the roots and tough outer leaves, and finely chop. Grate the feta and parmesan.

Whisk the egg in a mixing bowl. Add the flour, feta, parmesan, dill, parsley and pepper, and mix together to make a runny paste.

Peel the zucchini (and reserve the skins for the next dish, *kaskarikas*, if you like). Finely grate the zucchini. Place the zucchini shreds in a colander and sprinkle on the salt. Leave for 5 minutes—the salt will help extract the moisture from the shreds. Wrap the zucchini in muslin (cheesecloth) and tightly squeeze out the excess water.

If you are using nettles, use gloves to handle them. To remove the sting, put in a heatproof bowl and cover with boiling water for 30 seconds. Transfer to cold water for 5 minutes. Pick the green leaves and discard the stems. Pat the leaves dry with paper towel and then roughly chop. (If using spinach instead, wash thoroughly and remove the stalks, then chop.)

Mix the zucchini and nettle (or spinach) with the flour and egg mixture. Divide this dough into eight small patties, flattening them in your palm.

Heat the olive oil in a frying pan over high heat. Add a drop of water to the oil. If it sizzles the oil is ready. Add the patties, four at a time, and fry for 2 minutes on each side until golden. Transfer to paper towel to drain the excess oil.

Crush the garlic and mix in a small bowl with the *yoğurt* and dried mint. Place the patties on four plates and serve with the mint *yoğurt*.

KAŞKARİKAS
ZUCCHINI AND GOAT'S CHEESE SALAD

This dish was brought to the Ottoman Empire by the Sephardic Jews who migrated to Anatolia when they were expelled from Spain in the sixteenth century. Some of their descendants lived in my apartment block in Istanbul when I was growing up, and sometimes I was lucky enough to be invited to dinner when they made kaşkarikas. They tossed zucchini skins with almonds and pine nuts, and served yoğurt on the side. I decided to make it a more complete salad in this version, adding goat's cheese.

SERVES 6

2 zucchini (courgettes), skin only
   (see previous recipe)
1 sour plum, halved (or 3 crushed unripened
   grapes or 1 teaspoon lemon juice)
2 tablespoons olive oil
½ teaspoon salt
pinch of sugar
2 tablespoons slivered almonds
1 tablespoon soft goat's cheese

Cut the zucchini skins into 5 cm (2 in) long strips. Put the strips in a small saucepan and just cover with water. Add the sour plum (or grapes or lemon juice). Add the olive oil, salt and sugar, then bring to boil over high heat. Reduce the heat and simmer for 5 minutes until the skins are soft. Remove from the heat and leave to cool to room temperature.

Serve in a salad bowl with slivered almonds, and a dollop of soft goat's cheese.

ÇİÇEK SARMA
AEGEAN STUFFED ZUCCHINI FLOWERS

You don't say no to my friend Musa Dağdeviren, the custodian of Turkish traditional values in cooking. So when he told me to meet him outside his Istanbul restaurant at 5 am, I stayed up all night to be on time. We jumped in his pickup truck and drove for an hour to his farm in the country. The sun was just coming up. He wanted to show me the perfect moment to pick zucchini flowers for stuffing—the moment when they open to the sun. He'd brought a pot of his own rice stuffing and we filled the flowers, steamed them and ate them that morning. Two years later I saw a documentary about Middle Eastern cooking hosted by the London chef Yotam Ottolenghi, in which he enjoyed the same experience.

You might not be able to pick your flowers at sunrise, but you can come close to the experience if you choose male zucchini flowers (the ones with no zucchini attached), which taste better because they have not had to expend any energy producing fruit. This recipe is not Musa's stuffing—it's a simpler version they use on the Aegean coast.

SERVES 4

5 spring onions (scallions)
5 flat-leaf (Italian) parsley stalks
5 dill stalks
5 mint stalks
220 g (7 oz/1 cup) short-grain rice
100 ml (3½ fl oz) olive oil
1 teaspoon salt
½ teaspoon white pepper
½ teaspoon sugar
1 tomato
½ onion
16 zucchini flowers (preferably male)
½ lemon

Wash the spring onions, then remove the roots and tough outer leaves. Finely chop. Pick the leaves from the parsley, dill and mint and finely chop. Set aside the stalks. Wash the rice under cold running water, drain and place in a bowl. Add half the olive oil, spring onion, salt, pepper, sugar and herb leaves, and mix together with the rice. Grate the tomato into the mixture.

Remove any stalk from each zucchini flower, gently fold back the petals and stuff with a tablespoon of the stuffing. Fold the largest petal over to cover the mixture, then fold over the remaining petals.

Put a 20 cm (8 in) plate face down in the bottom of a large saucepan (about 25 cm/10 in wide). Scatter the parsley, dill and mint stalks over the plate. Place the half onion in the middle of the plate. Surround it with the zucchini flowers, stem side facing up, flowers down. Add the remaining olive oil and 50 ml (1⅔ fl oz) of warm water. Bring to the boil, then cover and simmer for 20 minutes. Check after 15 minutes and add another 50 ml (1⅔ fl oz) of water if the pan seems to be drying out. Turn off the heat and squeeze the lemon half over the flowers. Rest, covered, for 15 minutes.

Serve warm.

TURŞU KAVURMA
FRIED GREEN BEAN PICKLES

If you find this dish in a meyhane, you'll know the chef is from the Black Sea. Pickling is an ancient tradition all over Anatolia, a way of preparing vegetables at the end of summer to feed the family over the harsh winter months, but the Black Sea is the only area where they pickle vegetables and then pan-fry them. In addition to green beans (usually the flat kind) they fry pickled cabbage and silverbeet roots. But green beans are the best.

SERVES 4

1 kg (2 lb 4 oz) green beans
2 red chillies
4 garlic cloves
160 g (5⅔ oz/½ cup) rock salt
50 ml (1⅔ fl oz) white vinegar
4 chickpeas
1 onion
60 ml (2 fl oz/¼ cup) vegetable oil
1 tablespoon capsicum (pepper) paste
   (see page 32)

Wash the beans and cut off the ends. Bring 500 ml (17 fl oz/2 cups) of water to the boil in a saucepan, add the beans and simmer for 4 minutes. Strain the beans and then plunge into iced water for 2 minutes. Strain the refreshed beans and then arrange them, upright, in a 2 litre (70 fl oz/8 cup) preserving jar.

Cut a slice along each chilli (but leave the seeds and the stalks) and push between the beans. Peel two of the garlic cloves and place them, whole, in the jar. Dissolve the rock salt in 500 ml (17 fl oz/2 cups) of water. Add the vinegar to the brine, then pour the mixture into the jar. Put the chickpeas on top of the beans. Seal tightly and store for 1 week at room temperature

Remove the chickpeas from the jar, scoop off any froth on top of the water and then store for 1 more week (or a few days longer if the weather is cold).

A day before you want to serve the fried pickles, take out about 250 g (9 oz/2 cups) of the beans, and rest them in water overnight.

Pat the soaked beans dry and cut into 5 cm (2 in) lengths. Finely slice the onion and crush the remaining garlic. Heat the vegetable oil in a frying pan over medium heat. Add the onion and fry for 3 minutes until soft. Add the garlic and capsicum paste, and fry for 2 more minutes, stirring regularly. Add the beans, stir through the onions, and simmer, covered, for 5 minutes. Serve the *turşu kavurma* warm on a platter for people to help themselves.

NOTE
You can keep the remaining *turşu kavurma* in a jar for up to 3 months at room temperature, and enjoy them as a side dish whenever you feel like pickles.

THE BROTHERS OF ORFOZ

An evening walk along the waterfront in the west-coast town of Bodrum is likely to be at first a charming experience and then a depressing one. Beneath the fifteenth-century Castle of Saint Peter, you stroll along a pebbly beach lined with candle-lit tables put out by the local eateries. The gentle waves are lapping just short of the table legs.

It's idyllic until the waiters start beckoning and shouting: 'Check out our menu. We got schnitzel, we got pizza, we got Greek salad, we got waffles, we got kebabs.'

Well, an optimist would say at least 20 per cent of their repertoire is Turkish. Bodrum, once the site of one of the seven wonders of the ancient world (the Mausoleum of Halicarnassus), is now a tourist haven that could be anywhere in the Mediterranean. But to get back to Anatolia, you need only round the corner just past the beach, behind the museum of Turkey's favourite singer, Pasha of Bodrum, Zeki Muren, and look for a sign

that says 'Orfoz'. There you'll find what might be the best seafood *meze* bar in the country.

Orfoz is run by the Bozçağa brothers—Çağri is the cook and Çağlar is the host (and also a cook). Their parents were bakers, but they'd both gone off and studied chemical engineering at university before they realised their real passion was experimenting with food. So they opened Orfoz in 2003.

When I remark that the bistros along the waterfront do not seem very Turkish, Çağlar says: 'Well, you could say that in Orfoz we are not doing Turkish cuisine either—we are just doing *our* cuisine. We cook local seafood in the best way we can think of.'

There's no written menu. In the great tradition of *meyhanes*, Çağlar just keeps bringing dishes and asking what we'd like. But afterwards he's happy to write down, in a mixture of Turkish and English, what he gave us. Here's what he wrote down after our meal:

Kecirpeynir—Goat cheese with own local cold pressed olive oil

Sardalya sasimi—fish, sashimi, sardine

Smoked eel

Sea snails with wine sauce patlangoz

Fish soup from grouper fish fresh leaves of celery

Mixed salad

Fresh clams and local oysters

Oysters with parmesan cheese

Mussels in casserole wine parsley garlic olive oil

Rice with seafoods cinnamon

Eggplant in oven (garlic, pepper, olive oil)

Grilled octopus

Baby calamary with onion and garlic

Shrimps in olive oil

Mother's cookie and cream caramel

Seasonal fruits

Çağlar insists that Orfoz is just a *meze* bar with a large wine list. Anywhere else in the world, it would be called a great restaurant.

Çağlar (left) and Çağrı Bozçağa preparing *kidonya*, one of their unique shellfish *mezes*.

Local scampi served in Orfoz in Bodrum on the
Aegean coast.

KADAYIF KARİDES
CRUNCHY PRAWNS

Many Turks would have trouble recognising this dish as part of their cuisine. Kadayıf pastry is mostly used for desserts (in a sugar and cheese confection called künefe) and jumbo prawns are not a common ingredient across the country—being pretty much confined to the area around Mersin on the Mediterranean coast. But I still claim this for my culture because the recipe was a gift from my Aunty Meral, who suggested the idea of wrapping prawns in pastry when I first opened my restaurant in Sydney in 2007. It went down a treat with Australians, who love to throw a 'shrimp' on the barbie.

Kadayıf pastry is not easy to make at home, so we suggest you buy it ready-made. In Turkey it's manufactured in an elaborate process whereby thin streams of batter are drizzled onto a spinning hot plate, so they dry instantly and form bunches. Its full name is tel kadayıf, which translates as 'string dough'. It is similar to Italian vermicelli, so if you can't find kadayıf, you could buy vermicelli or fresh angel hair pasta instead. You'd soften the pasta in boiling water for a minute, drain it, add the ghee and orange, and bunch it together in ribbons about 1 cm (½ in) wide, ready to wrap around the prawns.

SERVES 4

MUHAMMARA SAUCE
2 tablespoons olive oil
2 red bullhorn peppers (or 1 red capsicum/
   pepper)
2 garlic cloves, lightly roasted
50 g (1¾ oz) walnut kernels
1 teaspoon *isot* pepper (or chilli flakes)
1 teaspoon ground cumin
pinch of salt
1 tablespoon capsicum (pepper) paste
   (see page 32)
1 tablespoon lemon juice
1 tablespoon pomegranate molasses
   (to make your own, see page 24)
20 pomegranate seeds

8 fresh king prawns
1 tablespoon ghee (to make your own,
   see page 21)
juice of ½ orange
1 teaspoon orange zest
100 g (3½ oz) *kadayıf* pastry (or vermicelli
   or fresh angel hair pasta)
2 teaspoons sumac, for decoration

First make the *muhammara* sauce. Rub half the olive oil on the bullhorn peppers and roast over an open flame on your cook top, using tongs to rotate the skin and evenly char. (If you prefer a milder garlic taste to raw garlic, you can repeat with the garlic cloves.) Transfer the peppers to a bowl, cover the bowl with plastic wrap, and leave to sweat for 15 minutes. Peel the skin from the peppers and remove the stalk and seeds. Roughly chop.

Put the chopped peppers, garlic, walnuts, *isot*, cumin, salt, capsicum paste, lemon juice, pomegranate molasses and the remaining oil in a blender and pulse for 15 seconds to make a coarse paste. Stir in half the pomegranate seeds.

Preheat the oven to 180°C (350°F/Gas 4).

Remove the heads from the prawns. The best way to do this is to straighten the body with one hand and twist the head 90 degrees with the other hand, gently pulling the head off so that the black thread along the spine comes away. Peel off the skin but leave the tail on.

Put the ghee in a frying pan over low heat and warm it slightly (so you can still put a finger in it). Add the orange juice and zest. Place the *kadayıf* in a mixing bowl and gently loosen the pastry, slowly adding the ghee mixture and smearing it through with your fingers so it's evenly spread. When the dough is softened, pull it apart into ribbons about 1 cm (½ in) wide.

Wrap a *kadayıf* ribbon tightly around each prawn, starting at the tail and pressing the strands of dough into the prawn flesh. Keep the wrapping in a neat single layer to ensure even cooking. Place the prawns in a baking tray and cook for about 5 minutes, or until the pastry is golden brown. If your oven cooks unevenly, turn the tray round once during cooking.

Spread a heaped tablespoon of the sauce on four plates. Sit two prawns on top of the sauce, tails up. Sprinkle over a little sumac and a few more pomegranate seeds and serve.

MİDYE TAVA
BOSPHORUS-STYLE MUSSELS WITH TARAMA

If you wanted a glass of beer and a plate of fried food to soak up the alcohol, you'd go to a birane *rather than a* meyhane. *The dish you're most likely to find there is deep-fried mussels, where beer appears in the batter as well as in a glass.*

The tradition is to serve the mussels with a tarator *(dipping sauce) made with stale bread, walnuts and garlic. Our refined version includes the roe of grey mullet, which makes it a* tarama *(what the Greeks call a* tarama salata*).*

In Turkey, tarama *is always light beige, because that's the colour of the roe. I was surprised to find in Australia that* tarama salata *is pink—and then I learned that it is often artificially coloured. I do not recommend that you buy commercial* tarama salata *to serve with this dish. If you can't find the grey mullet roe, make a simple* tarator *by replacing the roe with 100 g (3½ oz) of walnuts.*

SERVES 4

TARAMA SAUCE
2 thick slices white bread
100 g (3½ oz) mullet roe
1 garlic clove, roughly chopped
juice of 2 lemons
250 ml (9 fl oz/1 cup) olive oil
250 ml (9 fl oz/1 cup) vegetable oil

MUSSELS
16 blue mussels, scrubbed
60 g (2¼ oz/½ cup) chickpea flour (besan)
100 ml (3½ fl oz) lager beer
1 egg, separated
75 g (2⅔ oz/½ cup) plain (all-purpose) flour
1 teaspoon salt flakes
1 teaspoon freshly ground black pepper
vegetable oil, for shallow-frying

First make the *tarama* sauce. Remove the crusts from the bread and discard. Roughly chop the bread. Put the bread pieces in a mixing bowl and add about 125 ml (4 fl oz/½ cup) of water to just cover. Leave to soak for 1 minute, then remove the bread and squeeze out the water. Transfer to a food processor, add the roe, garlic and half the lemon juice, and pulse to make a paste. Mix the two oils together and gradually drizzle them into the mixture as it's processing. After you've added about 100 ml (3½ fl oz) of the oils, loosen the mixture with 2 tablespoons of ice-cold water. Keep adding oil and iced water in similar amounts to completely emulsify, and finish by adding the remaining lemon juice. Set aside.

Sniff each mussel and if it has a strong smell, discard it. Place the mussels in a bowl and cover with boiling water. When they start to open (after about 5 minutes), scoop them out of the water. Using a knife with a point but a blunt edge, force open any shells that are not open enough and then pull all the mussels out of their shells. Snip off the beards and place the mussels on paper towel to drain.

Using eight 20 cm (8 in) long bamboo skewers, put two mussels, lengthways, on each skewer. Sift the chickpea flour into a wide bowl, pour in the beer and egg yolk and mix well. Whisk the egg white until soft peaks form and fold it into the flour mixture.

Sift the plain flour in a separate bowl and mix in the salt and pepper.

Pour the vegetable into a frying pan, about 2 cm (¾ in) deep and heat over medium heat. Add a drop of water to the oil. If it sizzles the oil is ready. Toss the mussel skewers through the flour, shake off any excess flour, then dip in the batter. Fry four skewers at a time in the hot oil, using tongs to turn after 1 minute, then cook for 1 minute more until golden brown. Place the cooked skewers on paper towel to absorb the excess oil.

Spread 2 tablespoons of *tarama* sauce onto one side of four plates. Place two skewers (four mussels) next to the sauce and serve.

SÜBYE KOKOREÇ
SAUTÉED SQUID WITH GREEN CHILLIES

Kokoreç is my favourite street food, made with lamb intestines, but you may be relieved to hear there are no lambs or intestines in this dish. I've used the word in the Turkish name because the squid has a similar texture to the intestines, and the spicing is the same. We use green chillies as a colour contrast to the red bullhorn peppers. I prefer squid to calamari in a dish like this because of its softer texture. Calamari is better stuffed, as you'll see on page 287.

SERVES 4

3 garlic cloves
2 green chillies
2 red bullhorn peppers (or 1 red capsicum/pepper)
3 spring onions (scallions)
4 oregano stalks
1 tomato
500 g (1 lb 2 oz) squid, cleaned
2 tablespoons olive oil
1 tablespoon capsicum (pepper) paste (see page 32)
1 teaspoon sea salt
1 teaspoon freshly ground black pepper
1 teaspoon ground cumin
1 tablespoon dried thyme
pita bread (to make your own, see page 45) or baby cos lettuce, to serve

Finely slice the garlic. Slice the chillies and the peppers, and remove the seeds and stalks. Wash the spring onions, then remove the roots and tough outer leaves. Finely chop. Pick the leaves from the oregano and finely chop. Finely chop the tomato.

Finely chop the squid, including the head and tentacles.

Heat the olive oil in a wok over high heat. Add the garlic, spring onion, chilli and pepper. Fry for 3 minutes. Add the squid, capsicum paste, salt, pepper, cumin and thyme. Fry for 5 minutes, stirring constantly. Add the oregano and tomato, stir and then remove from the heat.

Serve hot in open pita bread or in baby cos lettuce, on a large platter for people to help themselves.

KÖMÜRDE AHTAPOT
MEDITERRANEAN GRILLED OCTOPUS

Octopus is one of the most common ingredients on any Aegean seaside meze table. At 3 pm in the coastal towns you'll see kitchen workers emerge from the restaurants and throw handfuls of octopus against the rocks beside the sea, to tenderise them ahead of the 6 pm rush.

My mum used to automate the process by putting them in an old top-loading washing machine with some rocks and churning them for an hour (without washing powder!). Luckily, in fish markets now you can buy them already tenderised.

I love cooking octopus whole with its tentacles on. My good friend İvgen, from Evgenia meyhane in Bodrum, gave me a version of this recipe which has the octopus boiling with mulberry-tree branches before it's char-grilled. She says it makes the octopus melt in your mouth. For convenience, ecology and flavour, I've substituted oregano. No mulberry trees were harmed in the making of this dish. I can't say the same for the octopus.

SERVES 4

1 kg (2 lb 4 oz) octopus, cleaned
250 ml (9 fl oz/1 cup) red wine
1 teaspoon dried oregano
1 garlic clove
185 ml (6 fl oz/¾ cup) olive oil
1 tablespoon dark soy sauce
4 spring onions (scallions)
juice of 1 lemon
3 flat-leaf (Italian) parsley stalks, leaves only, finely chopped
1 small bunch of fresh cranberries (optional)

Put the octopus in a bowl with the red wine and oregano, and leave to marinate for 2 hours.

If you're using a charcoal grill, light it 1 hour before you're ready to cook. Burn the charcoal for at least 45 minutes and when the flames have died down, and the coals are glowing with a covering of white ash, the barbecue is ready. (If you're using a gas barbecue, turn it on to medium–high about 5 minutes before you're ready to cook.) If you are using the oven, preheat to 200°C (400°F/Gas 6).

Remove the octopus from the marinade, place it on a board and stretch it out into a tube shape. Tightly wrap the octopus tube in three layers of foil. Discard the marinade.

Place the foil-wrapped octopus on the grill and cook for 2 hours, turning every 30 minutes (or cook in the oven for 1½ hours).

Crush the garlic and mix together in a bowl with 125 ml (4 fl oz/½ cup) of the olive oil and the soy.

Remove the octopus from the heat, unwrap from the foil and brush with the oil and soy mixture. Brush the spring onions with the same mixture. If you're using a charcoal barbecue, put the octopus and spring onions over the coals for 2 minutes on each side. Or sear the octopus and spring onions in a frying pan over high heat for 2 minutes each side until the octopus skin darkens.

Cut the octopus and divide it among four plates. Or place the octopus, whole, on a serving plate for people to help themselves as part of a *meze* platter. Decorate with the spring onions and drizzle with the lemon juice and the remaining oil. Top with parsley and serve. If it's the season for fresh cranberries, you can decorate the plate with a few of them.

Opposite: The signs in the Istanbul fish market say 'Calamari fish' (top left) and 'Real grey mackerel kilo 10.Lira'. Mullet is often used for pickling, drying, or stuffing as *dolma*.

PIRASA SARMA
LEEKS STUFFED WITH CHICKEN AND CHESTNUTS

Chestnuts are a favourite Turkish street food in winter, sold from wood-fired braziers by hawkers who probably sell ice cream in the summer.

Bursa, a town near Istanbul, is famous for its chestnuts (and its Iskender kebap—see page 45). It is in the foothills of Mount Uludağ, which has forests full of chestnut trees.

In this meze, I've paired the chestnuts with leeks, another winter ingredient. It involves a fair bit of folding, as you're required to turn a tube into a triangle. Don't get hung up on a perfect fold. Anything vaguely resembling a three-sided parcel will do, as long as you eat it quickly.

SERVES 4

9 chestnuts
3 large leeks
220 g (7¾ oz/1 cup) short-grain rice
1 French shallot (eschallot)
50 ml (1⅔ fl oz) olive oil
3 garlic cloves, crushed
300 g (10½ oz) minced (ground) chicken
1 tomato
1 tablespoon tomato paste (to make your own, see page 24)
1 tablespoon capsicum (pepper) paste (see page 32)
2 teaspoons freshly ground black pepper
1 teaspoon allspice
1 teaspoon cumin
2 teaspoons salt
50 g (1¾ oz) craisins (dried cranberries)
5 flat-leaf (Italian) parsley stalks
5 dill stalks

CAPSICUM SAUCE
1 tablespoon butter
1 tablespoon capsicum (pepper) paste (see page 32)
1 tablespoon pomegranate molasses (to make your own, see page 24)
1 teaspoon salt

You can use frozen or tinned chestnuts, as long as they are skinned. If using fresh chestnuts, cut a cross in the flat base, place in a saucepan of boiling water and boil for 10 minutes. Remove from the pan and leave to cool, then peel the skin off. Roughly chop the chestnuts.

Remove the roots and green tops from the leeks, then rinse to remove any dirt. Slice down one side of each leek and peel off the outer two layers. Wash these thoroughly, flatten them out and place them across the bottom of a saucepan.

Peel off another four layers of each leek and place in a separate saucepan. Reserve the remaining white centres. Add 750 ml (26 fl oz/3 cups) of salted water to the second pan, bring to boil and then simmer for 5 minutes until the leek sheets are translucent and soft. Transfer to a bowl of iced water for 2 minutes to refresh. These twelve pieces are the leek skins you are going to stuff.

Wash the rice under cold running water. Finely chop the cores of the leeks and finely chop the French shallot. Finely crush the garlic. Heat the oil in a frying pan over medium heat. Add the chestnut pieces and the shallots. Fry for 1 minute, then add the chopped leeks, garlic and the minced chicken and fry for 2 minutes more. Add the rice,

then grate in the tomato. Fry for 2 minutes, then add the tomato paste, capsicum paste, spices and cranberries, and stir to combine. Add 125 ml (4 fl oz/½ cup) of boiling water and simmer for 5 minutes, covered. Turn off the heat. Stir in the chopped parsley and dill, close the lid, and leave to rest for 15 minutes.

Pick up one sheet of leek skin and put a heaped tablespoon of mixture onto one side. Fold the edges over to make a tight triangular parcel. Repeat to stuff the remaining leek skins.

Put the parcels into the first leek-skin covered pan, folded sides down, on top of the spread skins. Pack them in tightly. Add 250 ml (9 fl oz/1 cup) of warm water and put a small bread and butter plate on top to hold the parcels down. Put the lid on and simmer for 30 minutes over low heat.

Meanwhile, make the sauce. Melt the butter in a frying pan over low heat. Add the capsicum paste, pomegranate molasses and salt, and stir to combine. Simmer for 5 minutes.

Remove the parcels from the pan. Place three parcels on each plate. Drizzle the capsicum sauce over the top and serve.

ÖRDEK GÖZLEME
DUCK AND SOUR CHERRY GÖZLEME

The stuffed pancakes known as gözleme are hard to find in Istanbul—even though they are well known outside Turkey. They are associated with the Yörük people who live in mountainous regions. Yörük means 'walker' or 'nomad', but the Yörüks are not gypsies. They walked into Anatolia around 800 years ago and set up agricultural communities. Nowadays, Yörük women with scarves round their heads arrive in small towns with their tents made of horsehair and fry gözleme stuffed with spinach and cheese, potatoes or minced lamb.

I decided to make the concept upmarket by including duck, which nobody would do in Turkey. Strictly speaking, this dish is not a meze (they don't serve gözleme in meyhanes), but in my restaurant I serve it as part of my meze selection.

SERVES 6

4 onions
2 carrots
9 garlic cloves
1 kg (2 lb 4 oz) duck legs
4 dried bay leaves
1 tablespoon salt
1 tablespoon black peppercorns
½ bunch flat-leaf (Italian) parsley
½ bunch mint
200 g (7 oz) haloumi
125 ml (4 fl oz/½ cup) olive oil
80 g (2¾ oz) blanched almonds
2 tablespoons capsicum (pepper) paste
    (see page 32)
200 g (7 oz/1 cup) sour cherries, pitted
juice of ½ lemon
1 sheet *yufka*, 60 cm (24 in) wide (or 12 sheets
    of filo about 30 x 40 cm/12 x 16 in)
1 egg
4 tablespoons butter

Cut two of the onions into quarters, quarter the carrots, squash five of the garlic cloves, and place in a large saucepan. Add the duck legs, bay leaves, salt and peppercorns, cover with water and bring to the boil over medium heat. Reduce the heat and simmer for 1½ hours until the legs are fully cooked.

Meanwhile, chop the remaining onions and crush the remaining garlic. Pick the leaves from the parsley and mint, and finely chop. Coarsely grate the haloumi.

Remove the duck legs from the cooking liquid. Leave to cool slightly and then pull the meat off the bones. Shred the duck meat, and discard the bones and cooking liquid.

Heat the olive oil in a frying pan over medium heat. Add the almonds and toast for 2 minutes, shaking the pan constantly to evenly brown. Add the chopped onions and cook for 5 minutes until translucent. Add the garlic, capsicum paste and the duck meat. Cook for a further 3 minutes. Remove the pan from the heat and leave to cool.

Halve the sour cherries. Stir them into the duck mixture and then add the parsley, lemon juice, mint and haloumi. Stir to combine.

Cut the *yufka* into six wedges. (Or if you're using filo, overlap two sheets to make a square, painting a little melted butter where they overlap to help them stick together.)

Divide the duck mixture into six portions and put one portion in the middle of each wedge of *yufka* (or each square of filo). Whisk the egg.

Fold the three points of the *yufka* wedges over the filling to make a triangular parcel, or fold the four corners of the filo over the filling to make a square parcel. Paint some egg onto the last layer to stick the parcels together.

Heat 1 tablespoon of the butter in a frying pan over high heat. Add one *gözleme* and fry for 3 minutes on the multi-layered side of the parcel, then flip over and cook the other side for 1 minute. Place on paper towel and repeat with the remaining *gözleme* and butter. Serve hot on a platter for people to help themselves.

İÇLİ KÖFTE
TARSUS LAMB AND BEEF DUMPLINGS

İçli köfte literally means 'a meatball with something inside'. The word içli is also poetic language for 'deeply felt', and I've seen this translated on Turkish tourist menus as 'sentimental meatballs'.

Tarsus is a historic city in south-central Turkey, in the middle of the wheat and cotton belt. It was where Cleopatra met Mark Antony. Biblical scholars know it as the home of Saul who became Saint Paul. No doubt he ate these dumplings, which are known as kibbeh on the Arab peninsula.

Tarsus has many citizens of Arab descent, who moved to the area in the nineteenth century and introduced this dish, using the wheat of the area. Their version is different from the standard form because it is boiled instead of fried, so it's healthier.

SERVES 6

LAMB FILLING
4 onions
80 ml (2½ fl oz/⅓ cup) vegetable oil
4 cloves garlic
500 g (1 lb 2 oz) lamb mince
2 tablespoons capsicum (pepper) paste
  (see page 32)
2 teaspoons salt
2 teaspoons freshly ground black pepper
1 tablespoon chilli flakes
1 teaspoon ground cinnamon
1 teaspoon allspice
150 g (5½ oz) walnuts

BULGUR SHELLS
500 g (1 lb 2 oz) fine bulgur
200 g (7 oz) lean ground (minced) beef
1 tablespoon cornflour (cornstarch)
1 teaspoon salt
2 teaspoons capsicum (pepper) paste
  (see page 32)
50 g (1¾ oz) butter
1 egg
80 ml (2½ fl oz/⅓ cup) vegetable oil

YOĞURT AND TAHINI TOPPING
200 g (7 oz) plain *yoğurt*
1 tablespoon tahini
pinch of sumac

First make the filling. Finely chop the onions. Crush the garlic. Heat the vegetable oil in a frying pan over medium heat. Add the onion and cook for 5 minutes until translucent, then add the garlic and fry for 2 minutes more. Add the mince and fry for 5 minutes, stirring frequently. Add the capsicum paste, salt, pepper, chilli flakes, cinnamon and allspice, and fry for a further 3 minutes. Remove the pan from the heat and leave to cool. Put the walnuts in a blender and coarsely chop. Transfer the filling mixture into a bowl, add the walnuts and mix together, then refrigerate for 2 hours.

Now make the wrapping. Put the bulgur in a heatproof bowl and cover with 750 ml (26 fl oz/3 cups) of boiling water. Leave to soak for 30 minutes, then drain.

Mix the mince, cornflour, salt, capsicum paste and butter into the bulgur. Break the egg into the mixture and knead for 10 minutes, to make a smooth paste.

Mix 125 ml (4 fl oz/½ cup) of water with the vegetable oil. Wet your palm with the oily water, and place a ping-pong-ball-sized lump of the beef mixture in your palm. Press it into a pattie the size of your palm. Partly close your fist to turn the pattie into a cup, and put a heaped tablespoon of the lamb mixture in the middle. Fold the wrapping around the mixture to make a ball. Transfer the ball onto a tray. Repeat to make twelve balls and then refrigerate for 2 hours.

Bring about 3 litres (105 fl oz/12 cups) of water to the boil in a saucepan over high heat. Carefully add the dumplings, six at a time, and cook for 5 minutes until the skin is firm and crusty. Remove each batch of dumplings from the pan with a slotted spoon and place on paper towel.

Mix the *yoğurt* and tahini together in a small bowl.

Place the *icli köfte* on a serving plate. Spoon a tablespoon of the *yoğurt* and tahini topping over each dumpling, decorate with a pinch of sumac, and serve.

KURU DOLMA
STUFFED DRIED EGGPLANT

You see the dried shells of baby eggplants hanging in markets all over eastern Turkey, and you can safely assume they came from a village called Oğuzeli, near Gaziantep, which specialises in emptying and drying eggplants, zucchini and capsicums at the end of summer, ready to be stuffed during winter.

Of course the stuffing in this recipe can be used with fresh baby eggplants. Just slice off the top, hollow out the core (leaving thickish walls) and fill it with the stuffing. You can use the scooped out flesh to make the eggplant salad on page 213.

SERVES 4

DOLMA
1 green capsicum (pepper)
4 red capsicums (peppers)
10 mint leaves, finely chopped
10 flat-leaf (Italian) parsley leaves
1 garlic clove
175 g (6 oz/1 cup) fine bulgur
150 g (5½ oz) ground (minced) lamb
100 g (3½ oz/½ cup) chickpeas, boiled
1 tablespoon pomegranate molasses
    (to make your own, see page 24)
1 teaspoon cumin
1 tablespoon capsicum (pepper) paste
    (see page 32)
1 teaspoon salt
1 teaspoon white pepper
50 ml (1⅔ fl oz) olive oil
1 tomato
1 pack dried eggplants (aubergines), about
    20 pieces (or 10 fresh eggplant/aubergines)
3 red capsicums, extra
1 onion

TOMATO AND CAPSICUM
   COOKING LIQUID
1 tablespoon tomato paste (to make your own,
    see page 24)
1 tablespoon capsicum (pepper) paste
    (see page 32)
2 tablespoons olive oil
juice of ½ lemon

YOĞURT SAUCE
125 g (4½ oz/½ cup) plain *yoğurt*
2 tablespoons tahini
2 teaspoons sumac

Remove the stalks and seeds from the green capsicum and 1 red capsicum and finely chop. Finely chop the mint and parsley leaves. Crush the garlic to a paste.

Put the bulgur in a bowl, cover with 125 ml (4 fl oz/½ cups) of water and leave to soak for 20 minutes. Stir in the mince, chickpeas, pomegranate molasses, cumin, capsicum paste, parsley, chopped capsicum, salt, pepper, oil and garlic. Halve the tomato and grate it into the mixture. Discard the skin. Mix the mince mixture together well and then set aside.

Put the dried eggplants in a bowl, cover with warm water and leave to hydrate for 6 minutes. Remove from the bowl and pat dry with paper towel. Stuff each of them with 1 to 2 tablespoons of the stuffing, until it is three-quarters full.

Cut the remaining 3 red capsicum in half and remove the stalks and seeds. Cut the halves into pieces to fit inside the top of the eggplants. Push the capsicum lids on top of the stuffing, shiny side up. These will stop the stuffing from falling out when the eggplant swells during cooking. Peel the onion but leave whole.

Using a deep 25 cm (10 in) wide pot, place a 20 cm (8 in) wide dinner plate upside down at the bottom of the pan. Sit the eggplants, capsicum-lids upwards, around the inside of the pot, with the onion in the centre to create a tight fit.

To make the cooking liquid, mix the tomato and capsicum pastes, and olive oil in 500 ml (17 fl oz/2 cups) of water. Pour the liquid over the eggplants and add the lemon juice. Bring to the boil over high heat, then reduce to a simmer and cook, covered, for 45 minutes.

Meanwhile, mix the *yoğurt*, tahini and sumac together in a small bowl.

Spoon 2 tablespoons of the cooking liquid onto four plates. Add five *kuru dolma* to each plate, distribute the sauce on top and serve.

PAÇANGA
PASTIRMA BÖREKS

I used to joke that the word paçanga *(pronounced 'pachanga') sounds like a Spanish dance, and when we were researching this book, I got two shocks. First, it is the name of a type of music popular in Cuba since the late 1950s; and second, there are scholars who claim the dish was brought to Anatolia by Jews escaping the Spanish Inquisition in the sixteenth century. I hope that's true, because then this dish would represent a blend of three communities that contributed greatly to Turkish cuisine—the Armenians, with their* pastırma*-making skills; the Bulgarians, with their dairy farming; and the Spanish Jews, with their sophisticated technique (and the name).*

MAKES 8

1 sheet *yufka* (see page 27) (or 4 sheets of filo)
65 g (2⅓ oz/½ cup) shredded aged *kaşar* (or aged mozzarella)
1 tomato
2 green chillies, about 10 cm (4 in) long
8 pieces beef pastırma (or another cold cut of meat, including corned beef)
3 eggs
1 teaspoon salt
250 ml (9 fl oz/1 cup) vegetable oil
60 g (2¼ oz/1 cup) breadcrumbs

Cut the *yufka* into eight wedges. Grate the cheese. Halve the tomato and thinly slice. Remove the stalks from the chillies but leave the seeds. Finely slice.

Divide the *pastırma* or cold meat into strips about 3 cm (1¼ in) wide and 10 cm (4 in) long. Place a strip across each segment of *yufka*, about 5 cm (2 in) from the bottom. On top of the strip, put 4 slices of tomato, 2 tablespoons of cheese, and 1 teaspoon of chilli pieces. Whisk the eggs and the salt together in a bowl. Fold the *yufka* base over the strip of filling, then fold in the sides (about 3 cm/1¼ in flap). Tightly fold up the parcel, but before you finish the rolling, brush the top triangle of pastry with a little of the egg mixture to make the roll stick. Set aside the eight parcels.

Heat the vegetable oil in a deep frying pan over medium heat. Add a drop of water to the oil. If it sizzles the oil is ready. Dunk the *böreks* into the egg mixture, two at a time, then roll in the breadcrumbs. Pan-fry the rolls for 2 minutes on each side until golden. Place on paper towel to absorb the excess oil and then repeat with the remaining *börek*. Serve on a platter for people to help themselves.

THRACE-COOKED VEAL LIVER

Thrace is a region that overlaps Greece, Bulgaria and Turkey. In the Turkish part, the town of Edirne (named after the Roman emperor Hadrian) is known for two things: olive oil wrestling and the livers of the cattle that grow in the neighbourhood. The liver is sliced very long and thin so that it looks like leaves (yaprak) and is always pan-fried. One thing I learned from an Edirne liver master was to rest the liver in milk to drain the excess blood and soften the taste. I've had customers who have never enjoyed liver turn into converts when they try this.

SERVES 4

LIVER
1 veal liver (about 200 g/7 oz)
250 ml (9 fl oz/1 cup) milk
75 g (2⅔ oz/½ cup) plain (all-purpose) flour
50 g (1¾ oz) unsalted butter
1 teaspoon salt
3 dried whole red chillies
1 teaspoon hot paprika
1 teaspoon freshly ground black pepper
1 teaspoon *isot* (or chilli flakes)
1 teaspoon thyme
1 teaspoon ground cumin

SUMAC SALAD
½ red onion
1 tablespoon sumac
3 flat-leaf (Italian) parsley stalks, chopped

Peel the thin skin off the liver. With a very sharp knife, slice the liver into about eight leaves, about 5 mm (¼ in) thick. Place the livers in a bowl, cover with the milk and leave to rest for 1 hour. Pat the liver strips dry with paper towel.

Sift the flour into a bowl. Roll the liver in the flour to coat well. Shake off any excess flour.

Heat the butter in a frying pan over medium heat until it begins to sizzle. Add the liver and cook for 2 minutes on each side until the corners are crisp. Sprinkle on the salt and chillies and sauté quickly, then remove the pan from the heat.

Mix the paprika, black pepper, *isot*, thyme and cumin together in a large bowl. Toss the cooked slices of liver into the mixed spices.

Thinly slice the red onion, place in a bowl and add the sumac and chopped parsley. Knead the onion mixture for 1 minute to mix the juice of the onion with the parsley. Place the liver slices on a large plate, add a dollop of onion salad on top, and serve.

KOÇ YUMURTASI
RAM'S EGGS

When I put testicles on the menu many people thought I was trying to create a sensation, but I was actually making a point about sustainability. When I was growing up, Turkey was going through economically tough times, and it was important not to waste anything. The butchers would reserve offal for the families that had young children, as a source of protein. I grew up eating liver, kidneys, brains and testicles, and anyone looking at my height today would say that they must have been a great source of nutrition. Nowadays, when the food elite talks about sustainable eating, I like to ask: 'How did we go from fillet steak to fried crickets without using the rest of the animal first?'

SERVES 4

4 ram testicles
1 slice day-old white sandwich bread
50 ml (1⅔ fl oz) milk
80 g (2¾ oz/½ cup) blanched almonds
1 garlic clove, peeled
juice of ½ lemon
1 tablespoon white vinegar
2 teaspoons sea salt
1 tablespoon extra virgin olive oil
2 tablespoons butter
1 teaspoon ground cumin
1 teaspoon *isot* (or chilli flakes)
2 teaspoons sumac, to decorate

It's likely you will have bought the testicles frozen. Let them thaw for 15 minutes. Chop off the top and bottom. Remove the translucent skin and the white membrane, then cut the soft meat in half lengthways. Set aside.

Put the bread in bowl, cover with the milk and leave to soak for 5 minutes. Discard the crusts and squeeze the bread to remove excess liquid.

Put the almonds, garlic, lemon juice, vinegar, salt and the bread in a food processor and purée, slowly adding the oil. If it's too thick, add 2 teaspoons of water.

Melt the butter in a frying pan over low heat. Add the half testicles, cut side down, and sauté for 2 minutes. Turn, sprinkle on the cumin, *isot* and remaining salt, and fry for 1 minute more. Remove from the pan and rest on paper towel.

Spread 1 tablespoon of the almond and garlic sauce on one side of each plate, with pieces of testicle on the other side. Sprinkle with the sumac and serve.

KOKTEYLLER
KOKTEYLLER
THREE COCKTAILS

Let me tell you a secret: I've mixed more drinks in Turkey than I've cooked hot dinners. I was trained as a bartender before I became a chef and, like most of my generation of Turkish hospitality students, I was inspired by the movie Cocktail *(starring Tom Cruise and Bryan Brown). I found mixing drinks with 'flair' was a great way to get tips and to pick up chicks. Then I got serious and added cooking to my repertoire. When I opened my restaurant in the Sydney suburb of Balmain, one of my first customers was Bryan Brown, who lives round the corner.*

These three flashy mixtures give a nod to traditional Turkish ingredients—rakı, pomegranate and figs—and two of them have Turkish puns in their names (the Nar *in* Narito *means pomegranate, and the* Inci *in* Incini *means fig). But they were all created within a mile of Bryan Brown.*

**MAKES 3
INDIVIDUAL COCKTAILS**

MIDNIGHT EXPRESS

1 heaped teaspoon Turkish coffee
15 ml (½ fl oz) Kahlua
30 ml (1 fl oz) brandy
10 ml (¼ fl oz) barrel-aged *rakı*
1 piece of *pashmak* (Persian fairy floss)

Boil the Turkish coffee with 70 ml (2¼ fl oz) of water in a pot over medium heat. Strain three times through a tea strainer lined with muslin cloth to yield 15 ml (½ fl oz) of triple-strained Turkish coffee.

Half fill a cocktail shaker with ice. Add the kahlua, brandy, *rakı* and coffee. Shake vigorously for 1 minute. Strain into a long glass. Decorate with *pashmak* and serve.

NARITO

1 lime or small green satsuma mandarin
5 ml (⅛ fl oz) pomegranate molasses
  (to make your own, see page 24)
6 mint leaves
2 tablespoons pomegranate seeds
30 ml (1 fl oz) light rum
15 ml (½ fl oz) pomegranate liqueur
60 ml (2 fl oz/¼ cup) pomegranate juice
soda water, to top up

Quarter the lime or satsuma. Place in a cocktail shaker with the pomegranate molasses, mint and pomegranate seeds. Mash the mixture with what bartenders call a muddler. Add the rum, pomegranate liqueur and pomegranate juice. Shake vigorously for 1 minute. Serve in a tall cocktail glass, topped up with soda water.

INCINI

½ fresh fig in season or 1 teaspoon fig jam
30 ml (1 fl oz) Hendricks gin
15 ml (½ fl oz) Cointreau
10 ml (¼ fl oz) fresh lemon juice

GARNISH
1 candied fig (from fig jam)
5 pieces lemon zest

Muddle the fresh half fig in a shaker or put in the fig jam. Add the gin, Cointreau and lemon juice. Half fill the shaker with ice. Shake vigorously for a minute. Double-strain into a martini glass with the candied fig and lemon zest, and serve.

A busker on Istiklal Street in Beyoğlu, centre of Istanbul's bohemian culture and nightlife.

DINNER

TRADITIONS & INNOVATIONS

DINNER

For most Turks, dinner is the most important meal of the day, particularly during the thirty nights of Ramadan (spelt 'Ramazan' in Turkish). That's the month when adult muslims are expected to refrain from eating, drinking, smoking or having sex from dawn to sunset.

When the drums and cannons signal that the sun has set, the faithful sit down to a feast called *iftar*, which begins with easily digested foods such as dates and olives, then moves on to lavish lamb and eggplant stews, and concludes with cinnamon-flavoured rice puddings and baklava.

Paradoxically, although Ramadan is the month for fasting, Turks tend to put on weight then, because they have a gourmet party every night—either at home or in *lokantas* and *restorans* that set up trestle tables in the street to provide instant gratification to the desperate fasters.

The other 335 nights of the year, Turks have the leisure to contemplate the way their dining scene is changing, and the rise of what is being labelled 'the new Anatolian cuisine'.

The classic European image of a 'restaurant', serving starter, main course and dessert from a written menu, with matching wines, is not part of the Turkish tradition. Until the twenty-first century, our approach to meals outside the home mostly involved going to eateries that specialised in one type of cooking (just *kebaps*, say, or just *köfte*, or just grilled fish, or just *pide*), and sharing dishes delivered to the middle of the table in no particular order, apart from the broad principle of 'cold first, then hot'.

There was no tradition of hero-worshipping chefs. Eateries were chosen for the friendliness of

the host or the celebrities that might be seen there. Chefs saw their job as perfecting the standard recipes of their predecessors, not creating their own works of art.

If people wanted to show off, they would look for restaurants purporting to offer Italian, French, Japanese or whatever was that year's international fad. They saw no reason to spend big money on anything described as Turkish.

Then a bunch of radicals came along and applied to Anatolian food a concept known in English-speaking societies as 'fine dining' or in French-speaking societies as *nouvelle cuisine*.

Mehmet Gürs was the first of the fine dining pioneers, and became internationally known. With a Turkish father and a Finnish mother, and eight years' kitchen training in the United States, he was bound to come up with something unusual when he opened his first restaurant, Downtown, in 1995 (which had evolved by 2006 into the very posh Mikla on top of the Marmara Pera Hotel). Here's how Mehmet summarises his philosophy:

The Anatolian kitchen is not restricted to the Turkish or the Ottoman kitchen. All products of different ethnic origins and religions of Anatolia, the birthplace of cultures during a very long span of time before and after the Ottoman Empire, constitute the kitchen of this region. Wine born in this region is an indispensable part of the New Anatolian kitchen. Diversity of ingredients and revitalisation of endangered and almost extinct rich resources is as important as the methods used ... Respect the elders and listen to them, yet do not be crushed by them and do not be afraid to turn age-old ideas upside down.

Other pioneers include Şemsa Denizsel, who moved from advertising to cooking and opened her Kantin in 2000; US-trained Didem Şenol, whose restaurant Lokanta Maya sets the bar a lot higher than all preceding *lokantas*; Maksut Aşkar, who started his career as a bartender in one of Mehmet's restaurants and now runs a bistro called neolokal where he reinvents traditional recipes with his unique touch; and Civan Er, who studied international relations in London before opening Yeni, which means 'new'. I've detailed how to find these places at the end of this book.

Thanks to chefs like them, it's possible for visitors to Istanbul to enjoy sophisticated Turkish dinners that use contemporary methods but respect the produce and have regional authenticity. That's an approach I share. But in addition, I've had to develop my style in a land thousands of miles from Turkey. I've found those adaptations exciting, and I hope the fun I've had comes across in this chapter.

Mehmet Gürs prepares for dinner at Mikla, one of Istanbul's most innovative restaurants.

BADEM ÇORBASI
COLD ALMOND AND GRAPE SOUP

The almond, now grown along the Aegean and Mediterranean coasts, is another delicacy that was cultivated first in Anatolia (and one of only two nuts to be mentioned in the holiest Christian, Jewish, and Muslim texts—the other being the pistachio).

I first had the cold version of this sixteenth-century Ottoman dish in Şemsa Denizsel's famous Kantin restaurant in the posh Istanbul suburb of Nişantaşi. She was inspired by Spanish cuisine in deciding to include grapes. I like the addition of unripened green almonds (picked in late spring before the outer skin becomes tough and inedible) because they give a sour balance to this mellow soup.

SERVES 4

50 ml (1²⁄₃ fl oz) almond milk
1 slice thick sandwich bread
2 garlic cloves
160 g (5²⁄₃ oz) blanched almonds
1 teaspoon sea salt
125 m (4 fl oz/½ cup) olive oil
60 ml (2 fl oz/¼ cup) white wine or sherry vinegar

TOPPING
3 garlic cloves
2 teaspoons lemon juice
pinch of sugar
80 ml (2½ fl oz/⅓ cup) olive oil
2 green almonds (optional)
180 g (6⅓ oz/1 cup) green seedless grapes

Put the almond milk in a saucepan with 50 ml (1²⁄₃ fl oz) of water. Bring to the boil and then turn off the heat. Cut the crusts from the bread and discard. Soak the bread in the boiled almond milk for 2 minutes. Squeeze the excess milk out of the bread and set the milk aside to cool.

Dry-fry the garlic (unpeeled) in a frying pan over medium heat for 4 minutes, shaking the pan constantly to evenly brown. Remove from the heat and leave to cool slightly. Peel away the skin and any burnt spots.

Place the blanched almonds, soaked bread, toasted garlic and salt in a food processor, and blend to make a fine paste. Slowly mix in the oil, then the almond-milk water, and then 200 ml (7 fl oz) of cold water. Pour the soup into a large bowl and stir in the vinegar. Chill in the fridge for 30 minutes.

Next, make the garlic chips. Finely slice the garlic lengthways into about eighteen thin pieces. Drizzle with lemon juice and sprinkle with sugar.

Heat the olive oil in a frying pan over high heat. Add a drop of water to the oil. If it sizzles, the oil is ready. Add the garlic to the pan and fry for 3 minutes until it's golden brown. Scoop the chips out with a slotted spoon and place on a paper towel to drain the excess oil.

Quarter the green almonds. Cut the grapes in half. Divide the *badem çorbasi* soup into four bowls. Decorate with the halved grapes, almond pieces and garlic chips. Serve chilled.

KIRLANGIÇ ÇORBASI

SCORPIONFISH SOUP

When I was growing up, this delicacy made with the ugliest fish I'd ever seen was a speciality of my father. He is a devoted sailor and amateur fisherman, and we spent our summers in the seaside village of Bayramoğlu, an hour from Istanbul. He'd go out on the water all day in his small boat, and come back with a catch that always included scorpionfish. They are bony and hard to clean, so there's no point trying to turn them into fillets. Best to cook them before you remove the flesh.

Like many Turkish soups, this is enriched at the end with a terbiye—a word that translates as 'teaching good manners'. The basic ingredients of a terbiye are egg and lemon, sometimes with yoğurt or flour added. Old-school chefs would call this 'binding' the soup, but we prefer to say we're polishing it to perfection.

SERVES 4

1 scorpionfish, about 1.5 kg (3 lb 5 oz)
   (or any rockfish)
1 garlic clove
1 onion, quartered
1 potato
1 carrot
¼ celeriac
1 celery stalk
½ bunch dill
½ bunch flat-leaf (Italian) parsley
125 ml (4 fl oz/½ cup) dry white wine
1 egg yolk
100 ml (3½ fl oz) olive oil
juice of 1 lemon
1 teaspoon salt
1 teaspoon freshly ground black pepper

Clean the fish, removing the guts and gills. Place on a board and chop into three pieces.

Put 1.5 litres (52 fl oz/6 cups) of salted water in a saucepan. Add the fish, whole peeled garlic clove and onion, and bring to the boil over high heat. Continue to boil for 20 minutes, uncovered. Turn off the heat, remove the fish from the pan and rest for 20 minutes. Remove the flesh from the bones and set the flesh aside. Return the bones and head to the pan, bring back to the boil and then boil over high heat for 15 minutes.

Peel the potato, carrot and celeriac and roughly chop. Remove the leaves from the celery and set aside. Chop the celery stalk.

Strain the hot fish liquid into another pot and discard the bones, garlic and onion. Add the vegetables and bring back to the boil, then reduce the heat and simmer for 20 minutes.

Pick and chop the celery, dill and parsley, add to the original pan with the fish and mix together. Add the wine and boil vigorously for 2 minutes to let the alcohol evaporate. Add 250 ml (9 fl oz/ 1 cup) of the soup and bring to the boil over high heat. Boil for 5 minutes.

Put 250 ml (9 fl oz/1 cup) of the soup in a bowl with the egg yolk and whisk to combine. Return the soup to the pan and simmer for 5 minutes, stirring frequently.

Mix the olive oil, lemon juice, salt and pepper in a bowl. Divide the fish into four bowls. Pour a ladle of the soup over each lump of fish. Drizzle a little lemony oil over each bowl and serve.

KELLE PAÇA
SHEEP'S HEAD SOUP

This is a dish to help you sober up at 4 am and in Istanbul is likely to be found in an offal specialist that is closed during daylight hours. These places, in the more colourful suburbs, catch the customers who stagger out of a meyhane in a confused condition after midnight and look after them until the breakfast cafés start opening around 6 am.

I first encountered kelle paça when I was seventeen at an eatery called Apik in the abattoir district Dolapdere. It's filled with Romany musicians, prostitutes, and characters you would not want to meet in a dark alley. In my merry condition at the time, I found the scene intriguing, and was happy to go along with the Turkish conviction that the gelatine and protein in this dish helps you sober up.

Clearly, this recipe depends on you being able to source a whole sheep's head. If you can't, leave out the head and make the soup with lamb knuckles and brains.

SERVES 4

---

1 sheep's head, skin off, top of skull removed

BRAIN
1 teaspoon white vinegar
2 teaspoons salt
1 egg
1 tablespoon plain (all-purpose) flour
pinch of freshly ground black pepper
125 ml (4 fl oz/½ cup) vegetable oil, for frying

SOUP
1 onion
2 lamb knuckles
1 tablespoon salt
3 tablespoons plain (all-purpose) flour
2 tablespoons lemon juice
1 egg

GARLIC SAUCE
2 cloves garlic
juice of 1 lemon
70 ml (2¼ fl oz) red wine vinegar

Remove the brain from the head and wash under running water. Remove the outer membrane. Put the brain in a saucepan and cover with water. Add the vinegar and half the salt, and bring to the boil over high heat. Reduce the heat to medium and boil for 5 minutes. Strain off the water and put the brain in a bowl. Cover with cold water and then transfer to the fridge to cool.

To make the soup, peel and halve the onion. Put the head, minus brain, and knuckles in a saucepan, add the onion halves and add enough water to cover. Add the salt. Boil for 1½ hours over medium heat, partly covered with the lid. Skim any scum off the surface.

Remove the sheep's head from the pan and remove the tongue. Return the head to the pan and set aside the tongue. Continue to cook for another 20 minutes. Remove the head and knuckles from the pan and leave to cool on paper towel. Strip all the meat off the head. Take the meat from the knuckles and remove the fat. Set aside in a bowl.

Peel the outer layer from the tongue and remove any connective tissue from the base. Thinly slice the tongue.

Strain the stock into another saucepan to remove the onion and any floating scum. Put the stock and all the meat back in the original pan and place over low heat. When the soup is warm (not boiling), scoop out 250 ml (9 fl oz/1 cup) of the liquid and mix in a bowl with the flour, lemon juice and egg. Whisk together and then add to the soup. Increase the heat to medium and bring to the boil. Reduce the heat to a simmer.

Remove the brain from the fridge, strain off the water, and slice into four pieces. Mix the egg, flour, remaining salt and pepper, and 1 tablespoon of water in a bowl, and then coat the pieces of brain in the mixture.

Heat the vegetable olive oil in a frying pan over medium heat. Add a drop of water to the oil. If it sizzles the oil is ready. Place the brain pieces in the pan and fry for 2 minutes on each side until golden. Using a slotted spoon, scoop four heaped spoons of meat out of the soup and place each in a bowl. Put one piece of brain on each mound of meat. Ladle the soup around each mound.

To make the sauce, crush the garlic and mix together with lemon juice and red wine vinegar. Drizzle a little of the sauce over each bowl and serve.

KARPUZ SALATASI
WATERMELON AND FETA SALAD

European writers in the seventeenth century associated stuffed watermelons (under the name 'Turkish pumpkins') with the luxurious life of the Ottoman emperors, although the watermelon had originated in southern Africa and seems to have arrived in Turkey with Arab traders. Nowadays, the biggest watermelons in the world are grown on the banks of the Tigris River, in a region called Diyarbakır. The 'First International Traditional Watermelon Festival' was held there in 2012. In 2013, they changed the name of the event to the 'Diyarbakır Culture and Watermelon Festival'. I met a grower named Adil Aydın, who proudly displayed a watermelon weighing 49.5 kilos (110 lb). Asked who would need a watermelon that size, he replied: 'In my area, we have big families.'

SERVES 4

¼ watermelon, about 1 kg (2 lb 4 oz)
400 g (14 oz) feta (mild and creamy)
1 piece mastic crystal (less than 1 g/¹⁄₂₅ oz)
   (or 1 teaspoon mastic liqueur or Sambuca)
2 tablespoons balsamic vinegar
1 tablespoon extra virgin olive oil
juice of ½ lemon
20 purslane (or baby rocket/arugula) leaves
20 mint leaves

Skin and seed the half watermelon and cut it into 2 cm (¾ in) cubes. Keep the seeping juices in a bowl to add to the dressing. Cut the feta into 2 cm (¾ in) cubes. Put the mastic in a bowl and crush with the watermelon juice. Add the vinegar, olive oil and lemon juice and mix well.

Toss the watermelon, feta, purslane and mint together in a salad bowl and drizzle over the dressing. Serve with grilled fish or sardine 'birds' (see page 294).

EFENDY SALATA
FIG AND HAZELNUT SALAD

This has been the house salad ever since I opened my Sydney restaurant in 2007. It was one of my team's first creations, and I must confess it has one non-Turkish ingredient—mustard, with the seeds left in. If it's winter and figs are out of season but you're desperate to serve this, you could soak dried figs in warm water for 15 minutes. It won't be quite as luscious as the fresh version, but it will still be delicious.

SERVES 4

135 g (4¾ oz/1 cup) hazelnuts
6 fresh figs
150 g (5½ oz) wild (or baby) rocket (arugula)
65 g (2⅓ oz/½ cup) crumbly goat's feta

MUSTARD DRESSING
2 tablespoons olive oil
1 tablespoon seed mustard
1 tablespoon grape molasses
1 tablespoon red wine vinegar
2 teaspoons lemon juice

Preheat the oven to 180°C (350°F/Gas 4).

Put the hazelnuts in a baking tray and roast for 5 minutes. Remove from the oven and leave to cool. Rub the skins off. Crush the hazelnuts or roughly grind in a food processor

Mix all the dressing ingredients in a bowl.

Remove the stalks from the figs and slice each fig into six pieces, lengthways. Toss the rocket and nuts in a salad bowl with the dressing. Crumble the feta and sprinkle over the salad. Top the salad with the fig slices and serve.

KANGURMALI TARAK

LIME-MARINATED SCALLOPS WITH KANGAROO PASTIRMA

This dish commemorates the pivotal historical event shared by Australia and Turkey, and combines ingredients from these two great cultures. Gallipoli, in northwest Turkey, is a popular scuba-diving area, and a major source of scallops. It is best known to Australians as the site of an attempt in 1915 to secure territory in Turkey, which had joined the First World War on Germany's side.

Australia's major public holiday each year is 25 April, which was when the Australian and New Zealand troops (called ANZACs) took part in the ill-fated Allied assault on the Turkish peninsula. They were repelled by the Turks under General Mustafa Kemal Atatürk, who went on to create the Turkish republic out of the ruins of the Ottoman Empire.

When I came to live in Sydney, I was curious to see how kangaroo meat would respond to the drying and preserving process we call pastırma. *It turns out that kangaroo works even better than beef, because it's almost fat-free.*

SERVES 4

500 g (1 lb 2 oz) kangaroo fillets
1 kg (2 lb 4 oz) rock salt
500 g (1 lb 2 oz) caster (superfine) sugar
15 garlic cloves
1½ teaspoons salt
3 tablespoons ground fenugreek
3 tablespoons ground cumin
1 teaspoon ground fennel
2 tablespoons sweet paprika
1 tablespoon hot paprika
8 tarragon leaves
4 mint leaves
juice of 1 lime
1 teaspoon white pepper
1 teaspoon grape molasses
1 tablespoon olive oil
1 teaspoon *rakı*
12 sea scallops (or 6 large scallops)

Place the kangaroo fillets on a board and, using a sharp knife, remove any sinews. Using a cake rack (or steamer tray or a large colander), cover the rack with muslin (cheesecloth) or a tea towel (dish towel). Place the rack in a baking tray or large pan. You will use this for the drying process.

Mix the rock salt and caster sugar in a bowl. Spread half the rock salt mixture onto the muslin-covered tray, about 1 cm (½ in) thick. Put the kangaroo fillets in the middle of the rack and thoroughly cover with the rest of the rock salt mixture. Fold the muslin cloth over the top of the salt. Place a flat-bottomed tray over the fillets with a 3 kg (6 lb 12 oz) weight on top (using anything from a case of beer to wine bottles) to flatten out the kangaroo as it dries. Place the baking tray in a cool spot for 2 days, checking occasionally that the accumulated water does not reach the meat.

Unwrap the meat and wash off the salt. Place the meat in a bowl, cover with water and leave to rest for 24 hours.

Remove the meat from the water and pat dry with paper towel. Put the kangaroo on a rack with a drip tray underneath and refrigerate for 24 hours. Turn the fillets over and return to the fridge for one more day.

Next, make the paste. Mix the garlic, 1 teaspoon of the salt, fenugreek, cumin, fennel and paprika in a blender. If the mixture seems dry, drizzle about ½ teaspoon of water into the mix.

Remove the kangaroo from the fridge and coat with the paste, making sure every part is completely covered. Put the kangaroo on the cake rack with the tray underneath, but without the muslin cloth, and return to the fridge for at least another 5 days.

When you are ready to serve, slice through the fillet, diagonally, as thinly as possible (about 1–2 mm/¹⁄₃₂–¹⁄₁₆)—use a slicer if you have one. Finely chop the tarragon and mint leaves. Put the lime juice in a small bowl and mix in the mint, tarragon, white pepper, grape molasses, olive oil, *rakı* and the remaining sea salt. Slice the scallops into rounds about 1 cm (½ in) thick, and rest them in the marinade for 2 hours.

Divide the scallop slices among four plates, top each with a slice of kangaroo and serve.

KALAMAR DOLMA
STUFFED BABY CALAMARI

As you've gathered by now, we Turks will stuff anything. We love baby calamari because, when cleaned, they form little pouches—just waiting to be filled. To make life more challenging, I decided to fill the pouches with an elaborate stuffing, using other seafood that would either eat or be eaten by calamari.

You may be surprised to see soy sauce among the ingredients here, and yes, it's not typically Turkish. I first encountered this mixture of cream and soy in the meyhane *of my friend Ivgen, in Bodrum, and mistook it for a form of tahini. It turned out Ivgen had successfully brought together the two ends of the spice route.*

SERVES 4

1 kg (2 lb 4 oz) small calamari
  (about 6–8 cm/2½–3¼ in each), cleaned
1 tablespoon white vinegar
100 g (3½ oz) prawns, peeled
100 g (3½ oz) firm white flesh fish (such as ling,
  blue eye trevalla, mahi mahi)
1 garlic clove
60 ml (2 fl oz/¼ cup) olive oil
100 g (3½ oz) rice
½ teaspoon salt
1 teaspoon sugar
1 tablespoon turmeric
50 g (1¾ oz) butter
50 g (1¾ oz) grated *kaşar* (or mozzarella)
10 tarragon leaves, chopped
10 mint leaves, chopped

CREAM SAUCE
50 g (1¾ oz) butter
3 garlic cloves
1 tablespoon soy sauce
150 ml (5 fl oz) pouring (whipping) cream

We recommend you buy the calamari cleaned, but if you prefer to use whole calamari, remove the tentacles, the cartilage in the middle and the skin, and thoroughly wash the bodies (you can use the tentacles, chopped, as part of the stuffing).

Put 1 litre (35 fl oz/4 cups) of water and the vinegar in a saucepan over high heat and bring to the boil. Add the calamari tubes, reduce the heat to medium and cook for 25 minutes. Scoop the tubes out of the water and place on a board to cool. Reserve the cooking liquid.

Peel and clean the prawns, then finely chop. Check there are no bones in the fish fillets, then finely chop.

Finely slice the garlic. Heat the olive oil in a frying pan over medium heat. Add the garlic and cook for 1 minute. Wash the rice under cold running water, then add to the pan. Stir for 1 minute to coat the rice with the oil. Add the chopped fish, prawns and the salt and sugar. Stir for 1 minute to combine.

Put 250 ml (9 fl oz/1 cup) of the reserved cooking liquid in a small bowl and stir in the turmeric. Add the turmeric liquid to the rice mixture and cook, covered, for 5 minutes. Remove from the heat and leave to rest, with the lid on, until it cools to room temperature.

Finely chop one of the calamari tubes (and the legs, if you've kept them) and add to the rice. Stir in the butter, cheese, and the chopped tarragon and mint leaves.

Use a teaspoon to stuff the rice into the remaining calamari tubes (about 2–3 teaspoons per tube). Tightly pack the calamari tubes into a saucepan, with the wide open ends facing upwards. If the calamari seem too loosely packed and are at risk of falling over, put a large (washed) potato in the middle and pack the calamari around it. Pour 250 ml (9 fl oz/1 cup) of the cooking liquid into the pan, so that the liquid comes about two-thirds of the way up the tubes. The tops should be at least 2 cm (¾ in) clear of the liquid. Cover with the lid and simmer for 20 minutes over low heat.

Meanwhile, make the sauce. Melt the butter in a saucepan over low heat. Halve 2 garlic cloves. Add to the pan, increase the heat to medium and cook for 3 minutes. Add the soy sauce and reduce the heat to a simmer. Add the cream and simmer, uncovered, for 5 minutes, stirring regularly until the mixture starts to bubble. Remove from the heat.

Put 2 tablespoons of the sauce onto each plate. Lift the calamari tubes out of the pan, divide between the plates, sitting them on top of the sauce, and serve.

KARİDES GÜVEÇ
PRAWN AND HALOUMI CASSEROLE

The word güveç (pronounced 'goo-wetch') means a clay pot in which traditional casseroles are made. The usual version of karides güveç, *served in restaurants and* meyhanes *in Turkish coastal cities, uses small prawns or shrimps, but because I live in Australia, I have the luxury of easy access to prawns of significant size. Using bigger prawns also saves shelling time.*

The mushrooms keep the casserole moist when it's cooking, and help prevent the prawns from drying out. You need only bake the güveç in the oven for long enough to let the haloumi melt, without overcooking the prawns.

SERVES 4

12 cherry tomatoes (multi-coloured, if possible)
1 long green chilli
2 green bullhorn peppers
   (or 1 green capsicum/pepper)
3 onions
3 garlic cloves
12 prawns
80 ml (2½ fl oz/⅓ cup) vegetable oil, for frying
400 g (14 oz) small mushrooms
   (such as Swiss brown or button)
200 g (7 oz) haloumi
50 g (1¾ oz) butter
1 teaspoon salt
1 teaspoon freshly ground black pepper

Hlave the cherry tomatoes. Slit along the chilli and the bullhorn peppers and remove the stalks and seeds. Finely chop. Finely slice the onions. Finely chop the garlic.

Remove the heads from the prawns. The best way to do this is to straighten the body with one hand and with the other hand twist the head 90 degrees, gently pulling the head off so that the black thread along the spine comes away. Peel off the skin but leave the tail on.

Preheat the oven to 180°C (350°F/Gas 4).

Heat half of the vegetable oil in a frying pan over medium heat. Add a drop of water to the oil. If it sizzles the oil is ready. Add the prawns and sear for 30 seconds on each side. Remove from the pan and set aside on paper towel. Add the remaining oil to the pan, immediately add the onion and cook for 3 minutes. Add the garlic and sauté for 1 minute. Add the chilli and pepper and fry for 3 minutes. Halve the mushrooms. Toss them into the pan, add the salt and pepper and simmer for 3 minutes. Remove from the heat and stir in the halved cherry tomatoes.

Put three prawns in each of four ovenproof bowls. Divide the mushroom mixture between each bowl. Cut the haloumi into four slices. Place one slice in each bowl. Put a dollop of butter on each slice of haloumi. Bake for 7 minutes until the haloumi is melted and slightly burnt around the corners. Serve hot.

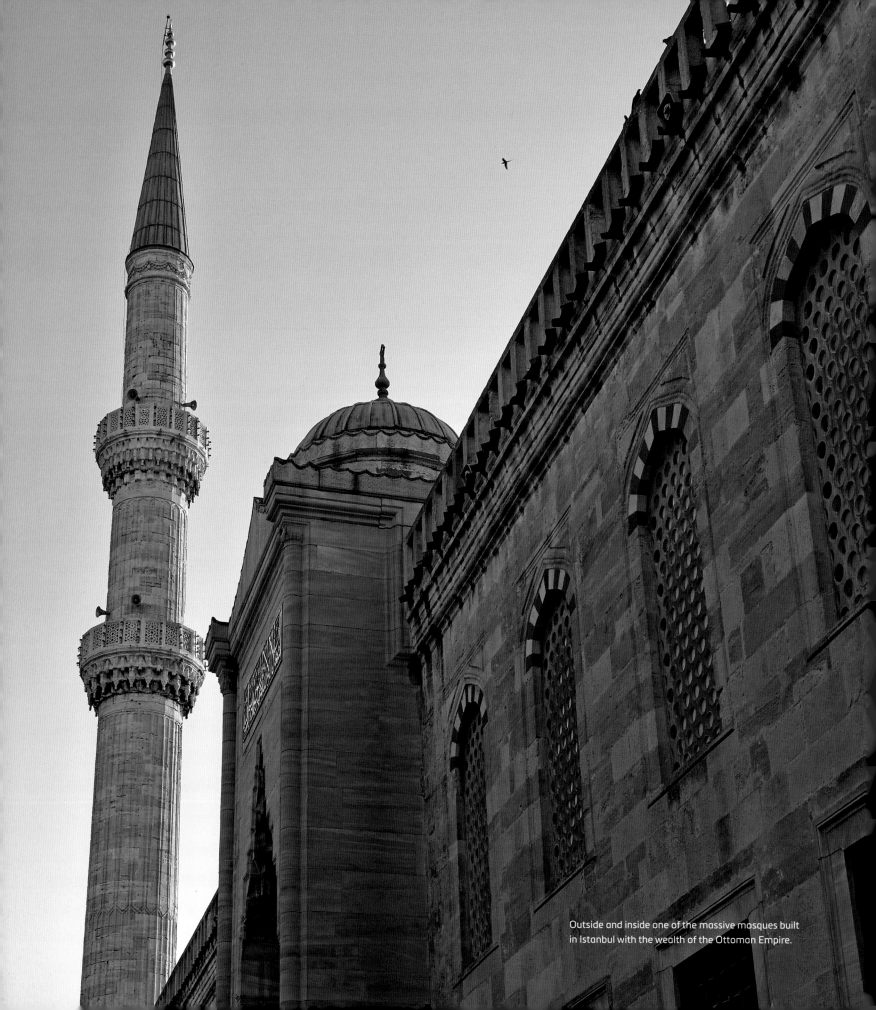

Outside and inside one of the massive mosques built in Istanbul with the wealth of the Ottoman Empire.

ASMADA ZARGANA
CHAR-GRILLED GARFISH
IN VINE LEAVES

The traditional recipe involves stuffing and wrapping hamsi *(similar to a
European anchovy), the most prized fish of the Black Sea region, but they are
impossible to find outside of the Black Sea. You could make this dish with
sardines, or small red mullet, but I prefer garfish because it's milder in taste and
can absorb some of the saltiness of the vine leaves. Because they're cooked on the
barbecue or grill, the vine leaves will char a little. That just adds flavour.*

SERVES 4

15 fresh or preserved vine leaves
10 flat-leaf (Italian) parsley leaves
10 mint leaves
2 garlic cloves
2 tablespoons pine nuts
juice of ½ lemon
12 garfish (about 1 kg/2 lb 4 oz),
   butterflied, heads and tails on
2 tablespoons olive oil
2 lemons, cut into 8 wedges each, to serve

If you're using a charcoal grill, light it 1 hour before
you're ready to cook. Burn the charcoal for at least
45 minutes, and when the flames have died down
and the coals are glowing with a covering of white
ash, the barbecue is ready. If you're using a gas
barbecue, turn it on to medium heat about
5 minutes before you're ready to cook. Or use
a frying pan.

If the vine leaves are fresh, place in a bowl, cover
with boiling salted water and soak for 10 minutes.
If they are in brine, wash thoroughly to remove
most of the salt.

Crush the parsley leaves, mint leaves, garlic,
pine nuts and lemon juice with a mortar and
pestle. Open out each fish and place a tablespoon
of the stuffing inside, then close the two halves of
the fish.

Spread the vine leaves out flat on a board, shiny
side down. Roll each garfish in a vine leaf. If the
vine leavs are small, add half of another vine leaf.
Drizzle the vine leaves with the olive oil and cook
on the grill, close to the heat, for 2 minutes on
each side until the vine leaves are charred. If you
don't have a barbecue, heat the olive oil in a
heavy-based frypan over high heat. Add a drop of
water to the oil. If it sizzles the oil is ready. Place
the wrapped fish in the pan and cook for
4 minutes on each side.

Serve the *asmada zargana* with the lemon
wedges. You should eat the vine leaves.

HAMSİ KUŞU
SARDINE BIRDS

This is very much a hands-on recipe, requiring you to squeeze three egg-coated fish fillets into the shape of a bird (or what must have looked like a bird to the Black Sea chef who named this dish centuries ago). There's a song about this dish, by local folk singer Volkan Konak, which goes: 'I wish I was a hamsi bird, so I could fly up into the branches, and the mothers-in-law wouldn't eat me.'

The strong-flavoured fish called hamsi *(similar to a European anchovy) is the staple protein of the Black Sea region. In the season (autumn and winter) you find them everywhere in Istanbul, and you can buy them in the fish markets for as little as 2 lira a kilo.*

Because they're so plentiful, hamsi *appear in hundreds of Turkish recipes—in simple dishes like pan-fried* hamsi *with cornflour, some more complicated ones (like this recipe), and some totally weird, like the cornbread in our breakfast chapter (see page 51) or 'hamsi jam' (which everyone mentions but nobody admits to having eaten). The best substitute for* hamsi *outside Turkey is sardines.*

SERVES 4

1 tablespoon roasted hazelnuts
30 wild rocket (arugula) leaves
2 onions
290 ml (10 fl oz) olive oil
2 tablespoons rice
2 teaspoons salt
½ teaspoon sugar
1 teaspoon freshly ground black pepper
zest of 1 lemon
18 sardines, butterflied, tails on
4 tablespoons maize flour
2 eggs

watermelon salad (see page 280)
   to serve (optional)

Finely chop the roasted hazelnuts. Finely chop the wild rocket. Finely slice the onions.

Heat 2 tablespoons of the olive oil in a saucepan over medium heat. Add the onions and cook for 5 minutes until soft and translucent. Wash the rice under cold running water, then add to the onion. Stir for 1 minute. Add 250 ml (9 fl oz/1 cup) of hot water and the salt. Bring to the boil and then simmer, covered, for 15 minutes. Stir in the hazelnuts, sugar, pepper and lemon zest. Remove from the heat and leave to rest, covered, for 15 minutes.

Slice six of the sardines into two fillets each, so you have twelve lids to go on the 'birds'. Toss all the sardines (halves and whole), in the maize flour.

Now stuff the birds. Holding a butterflied sardine in your hand, place a little less than 1 tablespoon of filling between the halves, and push them gently together. Repeat with the other eleven butterflied sardines. Put a half-sardine lid on each stuffed sardine, to make a triangle shape. Squeeze the pieces together.

Whisk the eggs in a bowl. Heat the remaining olive oil in a frying pan over high heat. Add a drop of water to the oil. If it sizzles the oil is ready. Dip the birds into the egg and carefully place in the hot oil. Fry for 2 minutes on each side until golden. Place on paper towel to absorb the excess oil.

Serve three *hamsi kuşu* per person, with watermelon salad if you like.

DİL ŞİŞ
SKEWERED SOLE WITH BRAISED FENNEL

Partly out of laziness, partly out of convenience, Turkish restaurants outside Turkey have made swordfish on skewers a clichéd dish, but they're not doing their country any favours. Charcoal works best with an oily fish that doesn't dry out as easily as swordfish, so inevitably most swordfish skewers turn out dry and overcooked.

Putting something on a skewer doesn't make it Turkish. What does is the right application of techniques and flavourings to a fresh ingredient. Sole, like most fish fillets, is much more suitable for pan-frying, and rolling the fillets before skewering means you can achieve a crispy outside and a juicy inside.

SERVES 4

16 sole fillets (or other flat fish)
125 ml (4 fl oz/½ cup) olive oil
8 bay leaves
4 spring onions
1 red onion
1 lemon
12 bay leaves
1 small fennel bulb
zest of 1 orange
2 teaspoons salt
1 teaspoon sugar
1 teaspoon plain (all-purpose) flour
juice of 2 oranges
2 tablespoons butter
1 teaspoon white pepper

Ask your fishmonger to slice four fillets each from four soles. Lay the fillets on a board. Slice the spring onions into 4 cm (1½ in) tubes. Heat 1 tablespoon of the olive oil in a frying pan over medium heat. Add the spring onions and cook for 2 minutes, shaking the pan constantly. Remove from the heat.

Put a spring onion across the bottom of each fillet and roll the fillet around it. Now make the skewers. Cut the red onion in half, crossways. Reserve one half to use with the fennel. Cut the remaining half into eight pieces. Cut the lemon in half, then slice that half into three rounds about 1 cm (½ in) wide, then slice each round into quarters. Reserve the remaining half of the lemon for the sauce.

Each skewer will contain four rolls of fish, three small pieces of lemon, three bay leaves, and two pieces of onion that will form brackets at either end of the skewer. Take one piece of onion and push onto the skewer. Add one roll of fish, then one bay leaf, one piece of lemon, then fish again, bay leaf again, lemon, fish, bay leaf, lemon, fish, and finally the other onion bracket. Make three more skewers the same way.

Remove the outer layer from the fennel and slice the remaining bulb into four rounds, lengthways. If the fennel came with the green fronds attached, keep them for decoration. Finely slice the remaining half onion and any remaining pieces not used for the skewers.

Heat 2 tablespoons of the olive oil in a frying pan over medium heat. Add the onion and fry for 1 minute. Add the fennel pieces and fry for 1 minute, then stir in the zest, salt and sugar. Mix the flour into the orange juice. Reduce the heat to a simmer. Add the orange juice mixture and enough water to cover the fennel. Close the lid and simmer for 15 minutes. Check the fennel; if it is not soft, simmer for another 10 minutes.

In a separate, large 30 cm (12 in) frying pan, heat all but 2 tablespoons of the remaining olive oil with the butter over medium heat. Add a drop of water to the oil. If it sizzles the oil is ready. Add the skewers and cook for 4 minutes on each side until golden brown.

Place a quarter of the fennel mixture on each plate. Place a skewer on top. Juice the remaining half lemon, and combine the juice with the remaining olive oil and the white pepper. Drizzle a little over each skewer. Decorate with fennel tips (if you have them) and serve.

USKUMRU DOLMASI
'FORGET-ME-NOT' MACKEREL WITH BARBERRIES

In this dish you are required to reach down the throat of a fish and pull out its insides, including the bones, in order to make it empty enough to satisfy the Turkish compulsion to stuff everything they see.

Uskumru dolmasi is one of the oldest surviving Ottoman seafood recipes, mentioned in seventeenth century palace documents, and nicknamed unutma beni (don't forget me) because meyhanes in past centuries would send plates of stuffed mackerel to the homes of their regular customers on the last night of the fasting month of Ramadan, to remind them of what they'd been missing. It was the earliest form of advertising by letter box drop, but we doubt if anybody rejected it as junk mail.

SERVES 4

4 blue mackerel, whole

BARBERRY STUFFING
50 g (1¾ oz) dried barberries (or currants)
1 large onion (about 250 g/9 oz), chopped
200 ml (7 fl oz) olive oil
100 g (3½ oz) pine nuts
1 teaspoon ground cinnamon
1 teaspoon allspice
3 teaspoons salt
20 flat-leaf (Italian) parsley leaves, finely
    chopped, plus extra to garnish

MACKEREL COATING
150 g (5½ oz/1 cup) plain (all-purpose) flour
3 eggs
190 g (6¾ oz/1 cup) fine polenta
300 ml (10½ fl oz) olive oil

POMEGRANATE DRESSING (OPTIONAL)
1 tablespoon pomegranate molasses
    (to make your own, see page 24)
1 tablespoon olive oil
20 pomegranate seeds
10 parsley leaves, finely chopped

Clean the blue mackerel by removing the gills and the organs without a knife. You need to push your fingers into the throat of the fish and hook them under the gills. Pull gently so the gills and the attached organs come out. Use scissors to cut off the fins, being careful not to tear the skin. Wash thoroughly.

Gently massage the fish on each side for 5 minutes to soften the flesh until you can feel the spine. Gently break the tail, turning it 90 degrees, up then down, without puncturing the skin. Push the points of a pair of scissors through the gill hole and use them to sever the head from the spine. You can now remove the spine from inside the fish. Cover the fish with a dry cloth so you can hold it with one hand. With the other hand, reach through the gill hole and, with your thumb and forefinger, gently pull out the spinal bones. Scrape off any meat that's attached to the spine and put in a bowl. Using a cocktail spoon, remove all the flesh from inside the fish and add to the bowl.

Put the barberries in a bowl, cover with water and leave to soak for 15 minutes. Finely chop the onion. Meanwhile, heat the oil in a large frying pan over medium heat. Add a drop of water to the oil. If it sizzles the oil is ready. Sauté the pine nuts

for 2 minutes, then add the onions and fry for 3 minutes. Add the fish meat, spices, salt, parsley and barberries and fry for another 2 minutes, stirring constantly. Remove from the heat and leave to cool for 5 minutes.

Stuff a quarter of the mixture into each fish, using a long-handled cocktail spoon. Pack the stuffing in tightly, and use your fingers to mould it into a fish shape.

Now make the coating. Sift the flour into a bowl. Lightly whisk the eggs in a separate bowl. Put the polenta in a third bowl. Heat the oil in a frying pan over medium heat. Add a drop of water to the oil. If it sizzles the oil is ready. Coat each fish with flour. Dip in the egg. Thoroughly coat with polenta. Carefully place the stuffed fish in the pan, two at a time, and cook for 8 minutes each, giving them a quarter turn every 2 minutes until the skin is golden brown and crisp. Drain on paper towel.

If using, mix the pomegranate molasses, olive oil, pomegranate seeds and parsley together in a small jug (pitcher).

Serve the *uskumru dolmasi* hot, splashed with a little olive oil and parsley and, if you like, the pomegranate dressing.

BAMYALI BARBUNYA
PAN-FRIED RED MULLET WITH OKRA

This late-summer dish is a combination of two much-loved ingredients in Turkey. There's the pretty pink sweet-tasting fish, which is called barbunya *by the Turks and Greeks,* triglia *by the Italians, and red mullet or goatfish by the unpoetic English. And there's the green bullet called* bamya *by the Turks and Arabs, ladies fingers' by Malaysians, okra by the English and gumbo by the people of Louisiana.*

Okra are edible seed pods that originated in Africa. They had become a fad food by the fifteenth century in the Ottoman Empire, when the sultan in Istanbul organised palace war games between teams named 'the cabbages' and 'the okras'. Okra is very good for you, but it's not popular because when cooked it puts out a slime that some people don't like. Here's the solution to the slime: use very small pods. If you can't find small okra, choose medium-sized ones (no longer than 10 cm/4 in or they'll have a woody texture) and soak them for 30 minutes in 1 litre (35 fl oz/4 cups) of water with 100 ml (3½ fl oz) of vinegar and 2 tablespoons of salt. Rinse them well, peel off the skin, and remove the woody stalk.

SERVES 4

2 French shallots (eschalots)
2 garlic cloves
1 red capsicum (pepper)
1 carrot
1 green tomato or 2 tablespoons
  unripened grapes
300 g (10½ oz) okra
80 ml (2½ fl oz/⅓ cup) olive oil
125 ml (4 fl oz/½ cup) verjus
juice of ½ lemon
½ teaspoon sugar
1 teaspoon white pepper
2 teaspoons salt
16 small red mullets
75 g (2⅔ oz/½ cup) plain (all-purpose) flour
1 teaspoon freshly ground black pepper
250 ml (9 fl oz/1 cup) vegetable oil
1 lemon

Finely slice the French shallots and garlic. Remove the stalk and seeds from the red capsicum and roughly chop. Roughly chop the carrot. Quater the green tomato. Cut the stalks off the okra.

Heat the olive oil in a saucepan over medium heat. Add the shallots and carrot and fry for 3 minutes. Add the garlic and fry for 2 more minutes. Add the okra, tomato and capsicum, and fry for 1 minute. Add the verjus, lemon juice, sugar, white pepper and half the salt, and bring to the boil. Add 250 ml (9 fl oz/1 cup) of warm water, reduce the heat and simmer, covered, for 10 minutes.

Clean and scale the red mullet. Sift the flour into a bowl and mix in the remaining salt and the black pepper. Coat the red mullets in the flour. Shake the fish to remove the excess flour.

Heat the vegetable oil in a frying pan over medium heat. Add a drop of water to the oil. If it sizzles the oil is ready. Carefully add the mullet, four at a time, and fry for 2 minutes on each side until the skin is golden brown and crisp. Transfer to paper towel to remove the excess oil.

Cut the top and bottom off the lemon and slice into 8 rounds. Place the lemon in the frying pan and cook for 1 minute on each side each side until it starts to caramelise.

Spread the okra mixture on one half of each plate, and place four red mullet on the other half. Decorate with the lemon rounds and serve.

The moped rider must have gone swimming at Bodrum beach. Opposite: Fishing from Istanbul's Galata Bridge, with beer houses serving local seafood on the lower deck.

MERCAN BUĞULAMA
WHOLE SNAPPER IN CELERIAC MILK

One day when I was a kid, my father came home very late saying my stepmother was in hospital with food poisoning, because 'she ate yoğurt and fish together'. That started my fascination with combining seafood and dairy.

It's a common myth in Turkey that milk and fish don't mix, but if it were true, there'd be nobody left alive in the west coast town of İzmir (formerly known as Smyrna and very close to Troy). All along the promenade there, restaurants compete to offer the best version of sütlü balık (literally 'fish in milk'). Normally it's done with fillets, but I always prefer to use whole fish if I can. I've included celeriac here, because it adds a great flavour to the milk.

SERVES 4

1 celeriac
500 ml (17 fl oz/2 cups) milk
1 white onion
4 celery stalks
2 tarragon stalks
4 caperberries
1 snapper (about 1 kg/2 lb 4 oz), cleaned
2 tablespoons thickened (whipping) cream
250 ml (9 fl oz/1 cup) dry white wine
juice of 1 lemon
½ bunch chives
3 silverbeet (Swiss chard) leaves

Peel the celeriac and cut it into rounds about 1 cm (½ in) thick. Place the rounds in a bowl, add the milk and leave to rest overnight in the fridge. Remove the celeriac from the bowl and pat fry with paper towel. Reserve the milk.

Preheat the oven to 180°C (350°F/Gas 4).

Slice the onion. Pick the celery leaves and tarragon leaves. Chop the stalks off the caperberries and slice in half.

Clean and scale the fish, if necessary. Place the fish on a board and slice through the belly to open a pocket for the stuffing. Stuff with celery and tarragon leaves, onion and caperberries.

Place the celeriac rounds on the bottom of a baking tray. Place the snapper on top. Mix the soaking milk with the cream and white wine, and pour over the fish. Add the lemon juice and chives on top of the fish. Cover with silverbeet leaves, then cover the baking tray tightly with foil. Bake for 40 minutes.

Serve the *mercan buğulama* on a serving platter, pouring any remaining juice over the fish, for people to help themselves.

THE OTTOMAN EXPERIMENT

Batur Durmay happily admits that his restaurant, Asitane, is an indulgence. 'We didn't open this place to make a lot of money', he says. 'I just have to be sure I get it right.' Getting it right means ensuring the dishes on his menu are what you could have eaten had you been invited to a banquet with the sultan at the Topkapı Palace around 1700.

Asitane was set up by Batur's family in 1991 so they'd have an interesting place to take clients in their primary business, which was making steel moulds for heavy industry. Batur, the most obsessive foodie in a family of gourmets, was tasked with unearthing recipes that displayed the opulence and diversity of one of the greatest empires in history.

He soon encountered a problem. Before the year 1844 (when the first cookbook in the Turkish language was published), the Ottoman kitchen workers did not write down recipes. But they were meticulous record keepers, giving names to every dish served at banquets and noting the ingredients purchased for the pantry. Batur found a particularly helpful document from 1539 listing the 100 dishes served at a circumcision ceremony for the sons of Süleyman the Magnificent.

He hired scholars to dig further into the palace records and chefs to theorise on how the ingredients must have been combined and served, and ultimately came up with more than 300 dishes that he is confident would be recognisable to a time traveller from the seventeenth century.

Modern Turks have an ambiguous relationship with the Ottoman Empire. They are proud that for 500 years, their ancestors were the fairly humane rulers of a collection of countries now called Albania, Bulgaria, Egypt, Greece, Hungary, Iran, Iraq, Israel, Jordan, Lebanon, Macedonia, Romania, Saudi Arabia, Syria and Tunisia. They are annoyed that after 200 years of decline, the Ottoman caliphs had become so decadent by the early twentieth century that they dragged Turkey into The First World War on the wrong side, and ended up losing what was left of this great empire.

Whether they admire or disapprove, they are fascinated by the lavish lifestyle the Ottomans created for themselves, especially since the success in 2011 of a TV melodrama called Muhteşem Yüzyil (Magnificent Century), about the life of Sultan Süleyman the Magnificent. Batur was a food consultant for the series.

The Istanbul eating scene is now enjoying an Ottoman revival. Batur estimates there are 200 restaurants that claim to serve the food of the emperors. Many of them think that all they have to do is cook meats with dried fruits, or serve spiced rice in several colours, or give fancy names to standard *kebaps*.

Some places have sent spies to Asitane, to steal Batur's recipes. But Batur is fighting back. Occasionally he includes a dish on his menu that contains typically Ottoman ingredients but has no background in any scholarship. He invents a name that sounds as if it might have been used in the sixteenth century, and then waits to see how long it takes for that name to appear on the menus of his competitors. Then he has a little word to them about laziness and plagiarism.

Fortunately, he now has plenty of customers who recognise the work his researchers and cooks have put into ensuring authenticity. Asitane has become so popular that he finds himself seriously at risk of financial success.

Batur Durmay recreates dishes served to the
seventeenth-century sultans at Asitane restaurant,
in Istanbul's historic Fatih district.

FİRİKLİ BILDIRCIN
SUPER FREEKEH QUAILS

My family used to keep quails in cages on the balcony of our apartment in Istanbul because my father believed eating their eggs would help my stepsister's asthma.

Quails are thought to have originated in China, but they were cultivated for food by the Egyptian pharaohs and became popular in Anatolia during the Seljuk period (in the eleventh and twelfth centuries). We don't know how the Seljuks cooked them, because they weren't big on written records, but a few hundred years later, this recipe was created by the Ottomans, which explains the carob glaze. Before the arrival of chocolate from the Americas in the seventeenth century, carob was the sultans' favourite sweetener. Nowadays, grape and pomegranate molasses have become more fashionable than carob molasses, but I think the thick caramel flavour contrasts beautifully with the smoky freekeh (which I've used as stuffing instead of the Ottomans' rice).

SERVES 4

FREEKEH STUFFING
50 g (1¾ oz) green lentils
1 onion
2 tablespoons olive oil
250 g (9 oz) freekeh
1 teaspoon chilli flakes
1 tablespoon capsicum (pepper) paste
   (see page 32)
500 ml (17 fl oz/2 cups) chicken stock
1 tablespoon butter
pinch of salt
pinch of pepper

COATING
80 ml (2½ fl oz/⅓ cup) vegetable oil
4 tablespoons carob molasses
1 teaspoon hot paprika
5 sage leaves

8 quails
4 tablespoons butter

Soak the lentils overnight or simmer for 30 minutes, and then drain.

Finely chop the onion. Heat the olive oil in a frying pan over medium heat. Add the onion and fry for 5 minutes until soft. Add the freekeh and the lentils and fry for a further 3 minutes, stirring regularly. Add the chilli flakes, capsicum paste, stock and butter. Stir thoroughly and bring to the boil, then add the salt and pepper. Cover and simmer for 15 minutes. Remove from the heat and leave to rest, covered, for 15 minutes.

Wash the quails. Sizzle 1 tablespoon of the butter in a frying pan over medium heat. Add the quails, two at a time, and cook for 2 minutes on each side until the skin crisps up. Add a new tablespoon of butter for each two quails. Leave to rest on paper towel.

Preheat the oven to 180°C (350°F/Gas 4).

Using a tablespoon, stuff each quail with the freekeh and lentil mixture.

Now make the coating. Mix the vegetable oil, carob molasses and paprika together in a bowl. Finely chop the sage leaves, add to the carob mixture and combine. Brush the quails thoroughly in the coating, retaining a little of the molasses mixture to serve.

Pour 250 ml (9 fl oz/1 cup) of water into a baking tray. Sit the quails in the water. Bake for 25 minutes until golden brown. After 10 minutes of baking, spoon some of the liquid from the tray over the quails to keep them moist.

Serve two quails per person, with a tablespoon of the molasses mixture drizzled over each plate.

KAVUN DOLMASI
STUFFED MELON WITH CHICKEN AND CASHEWS

Melon has been one of the staples of Anatolian cuisine since Roman times, and was probably first cultivated near what is now eastern Turkey. The Ottoman palace chefs apparently liked the theatre of being able to lift the lid and expose the filling. They adopted the Persian fascination for mixing meat and fruit, and mostly used lamb mince in the stuffing, but I think that's too heavy for the delicate fruit, so I changed it to chicken.

I like to use Galia melon (developed in Israel in the 1970s) because it's almost perfectly round, but if you can't find it, go for rockmelon, and choose the smallest one you can find.

SERVES 4

50 g (1¾ oz) craisins (dried cranberries)
2 onions
10 parsley stalks
10 mint stalks
50 ml (1⅔ fl oz) vegetable oil
75 g (2⅔ oz) almonds
75 g (2⅔ oz) cashews
300 g (10½ oz) chicken mince
1½ teaspoons salt
1 teaspoon freshly ground black pepper
½ teaspoon allspice
½ teaspoon cinnamon
1 Galia melon, rockmelon or honeydew
    (about 1 kg/2 lb 4 oz)
2 tablespoons butter
50 ml (1⅔ fl oz) olive oil

Put the cranberries in a bowl, cover with warm water and leave to soak for 15 minutes. Finely chop the onions. Pick and chop the mint and parsley leaves.

Heat the vegetable oil in a frying pan over medium heat, add the onions and cook for 4 minutes. Add the almonds and cashews, and fry for 1 minute. Add the chicken mince and fry for 5 minutes, stirring regularly until the chicken is evenly golden brown. Add 1 teaspoon of the salt and the spices. Drain the cranberries, add to the pan and stir. Remove the pan from the heat.

Preheat the oven to 180°C (350°F/Gas 4).

Slice the cap off the melon, about 2 cm (¾ in) below the top. Scoop out and discard all the seeds. Mix the butter with a pinch of salt and rub inside the cavity. Push in the stuffing mixture. Place the cap back on, secured with two toothpicks. Rub the olive oil all over the outside of the melon and bake for 35 minutes.

Remove the cap and serve the whole melon at the table. Scoop out four servings, or slice into quarters.

PERDELİ PİLAV
VEILED RICE

This is a kind of chicken and rice pie, which originated in Siirt, a city in southeastern Turkey. In the classical version they simply mixed the chicken into the spiced rice and wrapped pastry around it, but I find that quite dry.

It makes a spectacular presentation if you upend the pie and unveil layers of different ingredients inside—caramelised onions on top, which keep the other layers moist, then a layer of shredded chicken, and under that the spiced rice.

SERVES 4

FILLING
125 ml (4 fl oz/½ cup) olive oil
10 brown onions
5 saffron threads
440 g (15½ oz/2 cups) medium-grain rice
1½ tablespoons butter
100 g (3½ oz) flaked almonds
1 tablespoon cinnamon
2 teaspoons allspice
2 teaspoons freshly ground black pepper

CHICKEN STOCK
2 onions
2 carrots
1 small chicken (less than 1.8 kg/4 lb)
1 tablespoon salt

PASTRY
450 g (1 lb/3 cups) plain (all-purpose) flour, plus extra for dusting
250 g (9 oz) butter
3 eggs
½ teaspoon baking powder
1 teaspoon salt
2 tablespoons vegetable oil, for greasing
5 blanched almonds, halved

First, get the onion confit started for the filling. Heat the olive oil in a saucepan over low heat. Finely slice the onions, add to the pan and fry, covered, for 10 minutes. Move the lid so it's partly open and simmer 1½ hours, stirring occasionally. The confit onions should reduce to half the size of the uncooked onions

Next, make the chicken stock. Halve the onions and carrots, and place in a large saucepan with the chicken. Cover with salted water and boil, partly covered, for 30 minutes over medium–low heat. Turn off the heat and transfer the chicken to a board. Leave to cool slightly. When the chicken is cool enough to handle, strip off the skin and all the meat. Shred the meat into thin strands and set aside. Put 375 ml (13 fl oz/1½ cups) of the warm chicken stock in a bowl, add the saffron and set aside to soak. Put the chicken skin and bones back in the pan and return to the heat. Simmer, without the lid, so the stock reduces.

Now, make the 'veil'. Sift the flour into a mixing bowl. Make a well in the middle. Melt the butter in a frying pan over medium heat (or microwave for 30 seconds). Whisk the eggs in a bowl. Whisk the butter into the egg, then whisk in the baking powder and salt. Fold the egg mixture into the flour and knead for 5 minutes. Sprinkle some flour on your work surface and roll the dough into a ball. Return the dough to the bowl, cover with a damp cloth and rest in a warm place for at least 30 minutes.

Now cook the rice. Rinse the rice under cold running water. Melt the butter in a medium saucepan over medium heat. Stir in the flaked almonds, and fry for 2 minutes. Add the rice and toss it in the butter for 1 minute, to coat. Remove the saffron threads from the bowl of stock and discard. Mix the cinnamon, allspice and pepper into the saffron liquid. Add the liquid to the rice and stir. Add 500 ml (17 fl oz/2 cups) of the simmering chicken stock. Bring the rice to a boil.

Reduce the heat and simmer, covered, for 15 minutes. Remove from the heat and leave to rest, covered, for 15 minutes.

Preheat the oven to 180°C (350°F/Gas 4).

Place the dough on a floured work surface. Roll into a round sheet about 60 cm (24 in) wide. Paint half the vegetable oil inside a 25 cm (10 in) cake tin to grease well. Place the half almonds around the bottom of the cake tin in any pattern you like. Line the tin with the pastry sheet so the sides of the sheet come up and overlap the rim of the tin. There should be about 12 cm (4½ in) of pastry hanging over the edge (this will be folded over the rice).

Remove the onion confit from the heat. Scoop out the onions with a slotted spoon and spread them over the pastry in the tin. Add a layer of chicken meat over the onion, then spoon in the rice so it fills to about 1 cm (½ in) below the rim. Fold the pastry over the rice. If it doesn't completely cover the rice, squeeze the pastry out with your fingers so it stretches across. Brush on the remaining vegetable oil. Cook the 'pie' in the oven for 20 minutes until golden. Lift the cake tin out of the oven and turn the pie out onto a baking tray. Put the baking tray in the oven and cook for another 10 minutes.

Serve the whole pie at the table, slicing it into eight wedges (two per diner).

ÖRDEK SARMA
DUCK AND SILVERBEET PARCELS

When I came to Sydney I found duck was a popular meat with Australians, and I started serving this dish in winter. It is a modern variation of a Black Sea dish, where silverbeet is usually wrapped around lamb mince and rice. There they'd never use duck, which is a meat cooked at home by the wives of hunters, or freekeh, which is from the southeast. My justification for the change is that spit-roasted duck was served in Istanbul at the circumcision ceremony for the son of Sultan Mehmet II, in 1457. That's the rule: when challenged, quote the Ottomans.

SERVES 4

4 duck legs
1.5 litres (52 fl oz/6 cups) chicken stock
190 g (6¾ oz/1 cup) freekeh
2 tablespoons dried barberries (or cranberries)
1 red capsicum (pepper)
1 onion
1 garlic clove
2 tablespoons butter
2 tablespoons olive oil
4 tablespoons flaked almonds
125 ml (4 fl oz/½ cup) dry sherry
½ teaspoon cinnamon
1 teaspoon pimento
1 teaspoon salt
1 teaspoon freshly ground black pepper
2 teaspoons capsicum (pepper) paste
   (see page 32)
2 teaspoons tomato paste (to make your own,
   see page 24)
10 silverbeet (Swiss chard) leaves

SAUCE
2 garlic cloves
1 tablespoon olive oil
1 tablespoon smoked paprika
250 g (9 oz/1 cup) plain *yoğurt*

Put the duck legs and chicken stock in a large saucepan. Bring to the boil over medium heat, then reduce the heat and simmer, covered, for 1 hour.

Remove the legs from the pan and place on a board to cool slightly. When the legs are cool enough to handle, remove the meat. Put the skin, sinews and bones back in the pan and simmer, with the lid off, for another 5 minutes. Remove from the heat.

Put the freekeh in a bowl and cover with 375 ml (13 fl oz/1½ cups) of warm strained stock. Leave to rest for 30 minutes. Put the barberries in a bowl. Cover with warm water and leave to soak for 15 minutes. Halve the capsicum, remove the stalk and seeds, and finely chop. Finely chop the onion and the garlic.

Melt the butter in a frying pan over medium heat. Add the olive oil. Add the flaked almonds and onion and cook for 2 minutes. Add the garlic and fry for 1 minute. Add the duck pieces and fry for 2 minutes. Add the sherry, cinnamon, pimento, salt and pepper. Increase the heat to high for 3 minutes to cook out the alcohol.

Put the capsicum and tomato pastes in a bowl, add 125 ml (4 fl oz/½ cup) of the warm chicken stock and stir to combine. Add the mixture to the duck and stir. Add the strained freekeh and capsicum to the duck mixture, and stir. Bring to the boil, then turn off the heat. Strain the

barberries and stir into the duck and freekeh stuffing. Leave to cool, covered, for 10 minutes.

Wash the silverbeet leaves under cold running water. Put the silverbeet in a bowl and cover with boiling water. Leave for 2 minutes, then plunge in iced water for 1 minute to refresh. Remove the stalks. If the leaves are large, cut them in half (so you can make two parcels). You should have at least ten leaf pieces. Put the two largest leaves aside (to line the bottom of the cooking pot). Place 3 tablespoons of the freekeh and duck mixture across each leaf, about 4 cm (1½ in) from the bottom. Fold in the edges around the stuffing and tightly roll the leaf up. Repeat to make eight parcels.

Cover the bottom of a saucepan with the two reserved leaves. Place the eight parcels on the leaves. Pour in the chicken stock to almost cover the parcels. Weigh the parcels down with a plate. Bring to the boil, then reduce the heat and simmer, covered for 20 minutes.

Meanwhile, make the sauce. Crush the garlic. Heat the olive oil in a frying pan over medium heat. Add the crushed garlic and paprika. Fry for 3 minutes, stirring constantly. Remove from the heat and leave to cool. Transfer to a bowl and mix in the *yoğurt*.

Place a quarter of the *yoğurt* sauce on each plate. Scoop out the parcels with a slotted spoon then add two to each plate and serve.

KABURGA DOLMASI
ROASTED LAMB RIBCAGE

This is a hearty dish, designed to entertain an extended family or lots of friends. It's a speciality of the beautiful southeastern city of Mardin, which was carved out of a sandstone mountain 6000 years ago.

I first tried this dolma at Cerciş Murat Konaği, Mardin's most famous restaurant (now with a branch in Istanbul), which also serves wine made from white cherry pits in clay jugs. Mardin's cooking has influences from the Kurds, the Assyrians and the Armenians.

Try to use spring lamb, which has sweeter flesh than a grown up sheep. And you'll need good stitching skills, because tightly stitching the skin is important to keep the flavours inside the ribcage.

SERVES 8

2 kg (4 lb 8 oz) uncleaned lamb ribcage (skin on)

STUFFING

1 lamb liver (about 120 g/4¼ oz)
4 onions
80 ml (2½ fl oz/⅓ cup) olive oil
70 g (2½ oz/½ cup) pistachio kernels
440 g (15½ oz/2½ cups) coarse bulgur
1 teaspoon salt
1 tablespoon freshly ground black pepper
2 tablespoons capsicum (pepper) paste
   (see page 32)
3 tablespoons craisins (dried cranberries)
2 teaspoons allspice
2 teaspoons cinnamon
15 basil leaves

COATING

20 oregano leaves
1 tablespoon plain *yoğurt*
1 teaspoon dried chilli flakes
1 tablespoon butter
½ teaspoon salt
½ teaspoon freshly ground black pepper
1 tablespoon capsicum (pepper) paste
   (see page 32)

First make the stuffing. Remove and discard the skin from the lamb liver, and roughly chop into small pieces. Finely slice the onions. Heat the olive oil in a frying pan over medium heat Add the onions and cook for 3 minutes. Add the lamb liver and cook for 1 minute, stirring constantly, then add the pistachios and bulgur and fry for 1 minute, stirring to coat. Add the salt and pepper and 250 ml (9 fl oz/1 cup) of warm water, and stir.

Dilute the capsicum paste in 250 ml (9 fl oz/1 cup) of water, and add to the pan. Add the cranberries, allspice and cinnamon. Cover and simmer over low heat for 10 minutes. Remove from the heat. Finely chop the basil and stir into the mixture. Leave the mixture to rest for 10 minutes, covered.

On the wider side of the ribcage, lift the skin away from the ribs to create a pocket for the stuffing. Push the stuffing into the cavity so the skin forms a dome. Stitch up the skin at the top. Ideally, you should use what chefs call a 'trussing needle', but any large needle and strong thread will do. This will stop the stuffing falling out during the boiling process.

Sit the stuffed ribcage in a large saucepan, ribs facing upwards, and pour in enough water to almost cover. Bring to the boil and then simmer, covered, for 2 hours. Add more water after 1 hour, if necessary.

Preheat the oven to 200°C (400°F/Gas 6). Transfer the ribcage to a board and leave to cool.

Finely chop the oregano leaves. Place in a bowl and mix with the *yoğurt*, chilli flakes, butter, salt, pepper and capsicum paste. Spread the *yoğurt* paste over the ribcage. Place the ribcage in a baking tray, skin side up, and roast for 20 minutes until it's brown and crisp.

Serve the *kaburga dolması* on the tray at the table. Remove the stitches and discard the cotton. Carve down the middle and open to reveal the stuffing. Spoon out the stuffing and add a chunk of meat for each person.

GOAT AND DATES IN BAKED YOĞURT

Along with cubed and deep-fried spiced liver, this goat stew is one of two famous Albanian dishes that influenced the cuisine of Anatolia. It is named after the city of Elbasan, which means 'crushing fist', presumably because Mehmet II built a huge fortress there to keep the Albanians under control in the fifteenth century.

Strangely, you'd have a hard time finding either this dish or the fried liver in modern Albania, where waiters are inclined to say 'They do that in Turkey—we don't do it any more'. It's their loss. If you can't find goat, use lamb.

SERVES 4

835 g (1 lb 13 oz) plain *yoğurt*
3 French shallots (eschalots)
3 garlic cloves
500 g (1 lb 2 oz) goat (shoulder meat)
1 tablespoon butter
1 tablespoon black peppercorns
1 teaspoon salt
10 basil leaves
1 bay leaf
12 dates, pitted
500 ml (17 fl oz/2 cups) beef stock
3 egg yolks
450 g (1 lb/3 cups) plain (all-purpose) flour
1 tablespoon sweet paprika
mixed cress salad, to serve (optional)

Place the *yoğurt* on a sheet of muslin (cheesecloth) and tie up the corners. Hang the muslin over a pot overnight to allow the *yoğurt* to thicken.

Quarter the French shallots. Finely chop the garlic. Remove any fat from the goat shoulder and cut the meat into 3 cm (1¼ in) cubes. Melt the butter in a frying pan over high heat. Add the meat and fry for 2 minutes, turning to evenly brown. Add the shallots and fry for 2 minutes. Add the garlic, peppercorns, salt, basil and bay leaf and fry for 2 minutes. Add 250 ml (9 fl oz/1 cup) of water. Bring to the boil, then reduce the heat and simmer, covered, for 45 minutes. It should reduce and thicken. Pour the goat stew into a casserole dish. Sprinkle the dates over the stew.

Preheat the oven to 180°C (350°F/Gas 4).

Gently warm the stock in a saucepan to about 35°C (95°F). Put the egg yolks in a bowl. Sift in the flour and whisk. Add the flour mixture to the *yoğurt*. Stir in the beef stock. Warm the *yoğurt* mixture over low heat, constantly whisking, but remove it from heat as soon as you see bubbles forming (you do not want it to boil). Pour the mixture over the meat and add the paprika. Place the casserole dish in the oven and bake for 40 minutes.

Serve in the casserole dish at the table with a mixed cress salad, for people to help themselves.

Bodrum's marina and the Castle of Saint Peter,
a former Crusader fortress, at night.

DANA PİRZOLA
ROAST VEAL CUTLETS AND CAULIFLOWER PURÉE

Cauliflower, which was known as 'rose cabbage' in Ottoman times, is much loved in Turkey—pickled, sautéed or boiled for salads. But in the past, it was never puréed, and certainly never served with parmesan. And you'd hardly ever encounter veal cutlets in Turkey—cattle are mostly used for dairy farming, and the meat minced when the milk runs out.
So we'd have to call this an example of 'the new Istanbul cooking'.

SERVES 4

250 ml (9 fl oz/1 cup) olive oil
4 thick veal cutlets
1 celeriac (or 3 potatoes)
2 carrots
1 onion
1 garlic bulb
4 French shallots (eschalots)
250 ml (9 fl oz/1 cup) dry red wine
2 tablespoons fennel seeds
4 thyme stalks
1 tablespoon salt
1 tablespoon freshly ground black pepper

CAULIFLOWER PURÉE

1 cauliflower
2 tablespoons butter
2 tablespoons plain (all-purpose) flour
125 ml (4 fl oz/½ cup) pouring (whipping) cream
1 teaspoon white pepper
1 teaspoon nutmeg
50 g (1¾ oz/½ cup) grated parmesan

DATE MOLASSES GLAZE

4 tablespoons butter
4 tablespoons date molasses (or grape molasses)
1 teaspoon ground cumin
1 teaspoon freshly ground black pepper
½ teaspoon salt

Preheat the oven to 200°C (400°F/Gas 6).

Heat a splash of the olive oil in a frying pan over high heat. Add the cutlets and sear for 1 minute on each side. Remove from the heat and set aside.

Skin the celeriac and roughly chop. Roughly chop the carrots. Quarter the onion. Quarter the garlic bulb, leaving the skins on. Roughly chop the French shallots.

Pour the wine and remaining olive oil into a deep baking pan, then add the cutlets, in a single layer. Spread the chopped vegetables, fennel seeds and thyme stalks over the cutlets. Sprinkle on the salt and pepper and pour in enough water to cover the vegetables. Tightly cover the pan with foil and bake for 3½ hours.

Meanwhile, chop the cauliflower into florets, discarding the stalk. Put the cauliflower in a saucepan, cover with water and boil for 30 minutes over medium heat. Scoop out the cauliflower pieces with a slotted spoon and transfer to a food processor. Pulse to a thick liquid.

Melt the butter in a saucepan over medium heat and stir in the flour. Continue to stir for 3 minutes to remove any lumps. Pour in the cream. Stir for 2 more minutes to make a smooth sauce. Add the cauliflower, white pepper and nutmeg. Whisk for 5 minutes over low heat. Add the grated parmesan and whisk for another 5 minutes to make a smooth purée. Divide the purée among four plates.

Remove the baking tray from the oven. To make the glaze, melt the butter in a frying pan over low heat. Scoop out 125 ml (4 fl oz/½ cup) of the liquid from the baking tray and add it to the butter. Stir in the molasses, add the cumin, pepper and salt. Lift out the veal cutlets, one at a time, and glaze them in the molasses mixture, about 1 minute on each side.

Place one cutlet on top of the cauliflower purée and serve with the vegetables.

EFENDY BEĞENDY
BRAISED BEEF CHEEKS AND EGGPLANT PURÉE

There are as many folk stories about the origin of Turkish dishes as there are combinations of lamb and eggplant. The story I like about this dish is that it was served to the French empress Eugenie when she passed through Istanbul on her way to the opening ceremony of the Suez Canal in 1869. Eugenie's personal chef got together with the sultan's chef and added béchamel sauce to the original palace recipe. It then was named Hünkar Beğendi ('the sultan liked it')—probably because all possible combinations of the words for lamb and eggplant had been used up.

I solved the lamb-repetition problem by using beef cheeks (rare in Turkish cuisine) and I've lightened the mash by not using flour. There are no sultans in Turkey any more, so I've changed the Turkish title to 'the gentleman liked it', making this dish more democratic—if not gender-neutral.

SERVES 4

4 beef cheeks (about 180 g/6⅓ oz each)
1 onion
1 green bullhorn pepper (or ½ green capsicum/pepper)
1 garlic clove
3 tomatoes
100 ml (3½ fl oz) olive oil
50 g (1¾ oz) cumin seeds
200 g (7 oz) tomato paste (to make your own, see page 24)
1 litre (35 fl oz/4 cups) beef stock
1 teaspoon salt
1 teaspoon freshly ground black pepper
250 ml (9 fl oz/1 cup) dry red wine
200 g (7 oz) green olives, pitted

EGGPLANT PURÉE
4 globe eggplants (aubergines)
juice of 2 lemons
120 g (4¼ oz) butter
300 ml (10½ fl oz) pouring (whipping) cream
1 teaspoon freshly grated nutmeg
200 g (7 oz) grated *kaşar* (or provolone)
½ teaspoon white pepper
1 teaspoon salt

Place the beef cheeks on a board and trim off any sinew or fat. Finely slice the onion. Remove the stalk and seeds from the bullhorn pepper and roughly chop. Roughly chop the garlic and tomatoes.

Heat the olive oil in a large flame-proof casserole dish over medium heat. Add the onion and cumin seeds and brown for 4 minutes. Add the chopped pepper and garlic, and fry for 2 minutes. Add the fresh tomato and tomato paste and stir to combine. Add the beef stock, salt, pepper and red wine. Add the beef cheeks, reduce the heat to low and simmer, covered, for 5 hours.

While the beef cheeks are stewing, pierce the eggplants with a fork and char the skins by placing the eggplants directly onto the flame of your cook top. Using tongs, move the eggplant around to evenly blacken and then remove from the flame.

Once the eggplants are cool enough to handle, scoop out the flesh into a large bowl. Discard the skin. Add 1 litre (35 fl oz/4 cups) of water and the lemon juice. Leave to soak for 2 minutes, then remove the eggplant, pat dry with paper towel

and place in a colander to drain for about 10 minutes. Finely chop.

Melt 100 g (3½ oz) of the butter in a frying pan over low heat. Add the eggplant pieces and whisk together to make a mash. Add the cream, freshly grated nutmeg and grated *kaşar*. Add the white pepper and salt. Simmer 5 minutes, stirring regularly. Divide the eggplant purée among four plates.

Add the olives to the casserole dish and continue to stew for 5 minutes. Remove from the heat. Put 250 ml (4 fl oz/1 cup) of the beef-cheek cooking liquid in a saucepan with the remaining butter and boil over medium heat for 5 minutes to reduce.

Place one beef cheek on each plate. Drizzle a little of the reduced sauce over each cheek, and serve.

LAMB SHOULDER PIE

The fashionable modern cooking style called sousvide, which involves cooking in a sealed bag, echoes an old Ottoman technique. We've been using pastry to seal the flavour in meat and vegetables for centuries—as evidenced by the title of this dish, which literally translates as 'enclosed lamb'.

In this case, the lamb is sealed and cooked for so long the meat falls off the bone. I've been inspired by the Australian meat pie, and made an edible dough.

SERVES 4

1 lamb shoulder (about 1.5 kg/3 lb 5 oz), bone in, shank removed
1 egg
1 tablespoon plain *yoğurt*

SPICE RUB
2 garlic cloves
1 tablespoon sea salt
1 tablespoon sweet paprika
½ tablespoon ground cinnamon
½ tablespoon freshly ground black pepper
½ tablespoon lemon pepper
1 teaspoon ground aniseed
125 ml (4 fl oz/½ cup) olive oil

POMEGRANATE GLAZE
125 ml (4 fl oz/½ cup) olive oil
1 tablespoon pomegranate molasses
(to make your own, see page 24)

PIE FILLING
2 carrots
1 onion
2 garlic cloves
1 celeriac, peeled
5 small potatoes
2 cardamom pods
1 cinnamon stick
2 bay leaves
1 star anise
125 ml (4 fl oz/½ cup) olive oil
250 ml (9 fl oz/1 cup) dry red wine
1 litre (35 fl oz/4 cups) beef stock

PASTRY
½ teaspoon dry yeast
1 teaspoon sugar
300 g (10½ oz/2 cups) plain (all-purpose) flour, plus extra for dusting
2 sprigs thyme, leaves picked and finely chopped
1 clove garlic, crushed
1 teaspoon salt
zest of 1 lemon
50 g (1¾ oz) butter

Trim any large pieces of fat from the outside of the lamb shoulder. To make the rub, crush the garlic, and mix in a bowl with the salt, spices and olive oil. Rub the mixture over the lamb, including in the cavities. Rest the lamb for 20 minutes.

Now make the glaze. Heat the olive oil and the pomegranate molasses in a wide frying pan for 2 minutes over high heat. Place the lamb in the glaze and fry for 2 minutes on each side, caramelising the glaze onto the meat.

Preheat the oven to 140°C (275°F/Gas 1).

To make the filling, roughly chop all the vegetables and place in a large pot with the cardamom pods, cinnamon stick, bay leaves and star anise. Pour in the olive oil, red wine and beef stock to cover the lamb. Cover with the lid and bake for 4½ hours until the meat is very tender. Remove the lamb from the oven and cool to room temperature.

Meanwhile, make the pastry. Mix the yeast and the sugar in 375 ml (13 fl oz/1½ cups) of lukewarm water and set aside for 5 minutes. It should start to form bubbles. Sift the flour into a mixing bowl, make a well in the middle and pour in the yeast mixture. Knead the dough for 5 minutes or until the dough is as soft as an earlobe. Mix the thyme, crushed garlic, salt, lemon zest and butter together, and then add to the dough. Knead for a further 5 minutes. Sprinkle some flour on your work surface and roll the dough into a ball. Return the dough to the bowl, cover with a damp cloth and leave to rest for at least 1 hour. The dough should double in size.

Transfer the lamb and vegetables to a casserole dish. Increase the oven heat to 200°C (400°F/Gas 6).

Roll the dough into a sheet big enough to cover the casserole dish, with an overhang of about 4 cm (1½ in) on all sides. Separate the egg and beat the egg white. Paint the egg white around the rim and outside edge of the dish. Drape the pastry sheet over the dish, and use the egg white to stick the overhang to the sides. Mix the *yoğurt* with ½ tablespoon of water. Paint that *yoğurt* mixture over the dough. Put the pie in the oven and bake for 15 minutes, or until the pastry is golden brown.

Slice the pie crust into four segments and put one on each plate, then scoop out a generous portion of meat and vegetables to put on top of the pastry, and serve.

KUYRUK MANTI

STICKY OXTAIL DUMPLINGS WITH YOĞURT BROTH

The most influential modern Middle-Eastern chef of our times is Greg Malouf, originally from Melbourne and now based in Dubai. I am lucky to have him as a friend and mentor, and this is my adaptation of his adaptation of the classic dumpling called manti *(see page 120 for the traditional version). I love the complexity of flavours and yet the simplicity of using gyoza wrappers, available in Asian supermarkets, which saves hours of rolling pastry and folding it into tiny parcels. It's a typical example of Greg's talent for blending traditional flavours with modern techniques and presentation.*

SERVES 4

2 oxtail discs (about 120 g/4¼ oz each)
100 ml (3½ fl oz) olive oil
2 celery stalks
2 carrots
1 fennel bulb
2 onions
2 garlic cloves
2 teaspoons salt
2 teaspoons freshly ground black pepper
125 ml (4 fl oz/½ cup) dry sherry
1 tablespoon capsicum (pepper) paste
    (see page 32)
2 litres (70 fl oz/8 cups chicken stock
20 parsley leaves
10 coriander (cilantro) leaves
1 teaspoon ground fenugreek
1 teaspoon ground cinnamon
½ teaspoon allspice
1 teaspoon ground cumin
1 teaspoon fennel seeds
1 packet gyoza pastry (about twenty 10 cm/
    4 in sheets), chilled
1 egg white
1 tablespoon cornflour (cornstarch)
1 tablespoon apple cider vinegar

SAUCE
½ garlic clove
250 g (9 oz/1 cup) plain *yoğurt*
pinch of salt
100 g (3½ oz) butter

1 tablespoon sweet paprika
1 tablespoon hot paprika
1 tablespoon dried mint

Preheat the oven to 180°C (350°F/Gas 4).

Put the oxtail pieces in a baking tray with the olive oil. Roughly chop the celery, carrots, fennel, onion and garlic and add them to the pan. Add half the salt and half the pepper. Cover with foil and bake for 2 hours.

Remove the tray from the oven and leave the oxtail to cool. Separate the meat from the bones. Shred the meat. Finely chop the vegetables and mix with the meat.

Heat the oxtail mixture and sherry in a large frying pan over high heat for 5 minutes to cook out the alcohol. Dilute the capsicum paste in 125 ml (4 fl oz/½ cup) of the chicken stock. Add the mixture to the pan. Mix the parsley, coriander, fenugreek, cinnamon, allspice, cumin and fennel seeds with the remaining pepper and salt in a bowl. Stir into the oxtail mixture. Reduce the heat and simmer for 3 minutes. Remove from the heat and leave to rest for 15 minutes.

Take the gyoza sheets out of the fridge 15 minutes before you want to use them. Mix the egg white,

cornflour and 250 ml (4 fl oz/1 cup) of water in a bowl. Take one gyoza sheet off the pile and lay it on a board, shiny side up. Place 2 teaspoons of the oxtail mixture in the centre of the sheet. Dip your finger in the cornflour liquid, and swipe it around the edge of the gyoza. Bring the edges together and pinch them four times so the sides stick together, to make a roughly square parcel. Place on a tray and repeat to make twenty parcels. Refrigerate the *manti* parcels, wrapped in plastic wrap, for at least 30 minutes.

When you're ready to serve, put the remaining chicken stock in a saucepan and bring to the boil over high heat. Add the apple cider vinegar, then add the *manti*. Cook for 5 minutes until the skin is translucent

For the sauce, finely crush the garlic and mix with the *yoğurt* and salt. Loosen the *yoğurt* with 2 tablespoons of the chicken stock.

Scoop the *manti* out of the pan and divide into four bowls. Liberally splash the garlic *yoğurt* over the top.

Melt the butter in a frying pan over medium heat. Add the two paprikas and sizzle for 3 minutes. Drizzle the paprika butter over each bowl, and decorate with dried mint. Serve.

KEŞKÜL
PALACE PUDDING

This gluten-free summer favourite is one of the oldest Ottoman recipes, derived from a dish called Keşkül-ü Fukara *('begging bowl'), which was generously served to the populace by the sultans to celebrate war victories, religious holidays and other significant occasions.*

The word keşkül *means a bowl made out of a coconut half shell, which the dervish monks would wear around their necks in the hope people might throw in donations (which would have been difficult if they were whirling dervishes). Nowadays, the poor don't need to go to the palace—they can find versions of* keşkül *in pudding shops across Istanbul.*

There are several traditional variations—some using only almonds, some using coconut flakes. I like crushed pistachios to give a bright green colour and a crunchy texture.

SERVES 4

40 g (1½ oz) blanched almonds
40 g (1½ oz) pistachio kernels
250 ml (9 fl oz/1 cup) milk
250 ml (9 fl oz/1 cup) pouring (whipping) cream
100 g (3½ oz) sugar
25 g (1 oz) cornflour (cornstarch)
pashmak (Persian fairy floss) and pomegranate
  seeds, to decorate (optional)

Put the almonds in a food processor and pulse finely. Pulse the pistachios separately.

Put the milk and cream in a saucepan and mix. Heat over medium heat, then add the sugar. Cook for 2 minutes, then whisk in the almond meal. Continue to whisk for 2 minutes, then scoop out 125 ml (4 fl oz/½ cup) of the mixture into a bowl. Whisk the cornflour into the bowl, and then slowly add to the cooking mixture, whisking constantly.

Continue to whisk, and bring to the boil. Add the pistachios, reduce the heat and simmer for 3 minutes, whisking. When the mixture starts to thicken, remove from the heat and leave to cool to room temperature.

Divide the *keşkül* mixture into four bowls or cups. Refrigerate for 3 hours to set. Remove from the fridge, decorate with *pashmak* and pomegranate seeds, if you like, and serve.

CRUNCHY PUMPKIN WITH TAHINI

Long before molecular gastronomy was all the rage, Turkish chefs were using chemistry to create sweets and jams. By soaking hard-shelled fruits and vegetables in quicklime, they'd soften the interior and crystallise the exterior. The most common cases for treatment were watermelon rinds and unripened figs, eggplants, walnuts and olives.

You can't use quicklime in food preparation these days, but you can get a similar effect with pickling lime or burnt lime (calcium hydroxide). You must still be careful to wash off all traces of the chemical before you start the cooking.

This dish is a speciality of Antakya in the southeast, where they use tahini as an accompaniment, under the influence of their Syrian neighbours.

SERVES 6

150 g (5½ oz/1 cup) calcium hydroxide
  (burnt lime)
½ blue pumpkin (winter squash)
1 kg (2 lb 4 oz) caster (superfine) sugar
2 cardamom pods
2 cloves
2 cinnamon sticks
135 g (4¾ oz/½ cup) tahini
115 g (4 oz/1 cup) chopped walnuts
125 ml (4 fl oz/½ cup) thick (double) cream
1 tablespoon ground cinnamon

Put the calcium hydroxide in a bucket with 10 litres (2 gal) of water. Leave to settle overnight.

Skim any skin off the surface of the bucket of water and discard. Scoop 3 litres 105 fl oz/ 12 cups) of water from the top, without disturbing the sediment at the bottom, and transfer to a large bowl. Discard the rest of the liquid. Peel the half pumpkin and cut into about thirty square pieces, roughly 4 cm (1½ in) across and 1 cm (½ in) thick. Put the pumpkin in the bowl and soak for 24 hours.

Thoroughly wash the pumpkin under cold running water for 5 minutes. Put any pumpkin offcuts in the bottom of a wide saucepan, then spread the pumpkin squares on top. Add the sugar. Close the lid and leave to rest for another 24 hours.

Crack the cardamom pods. Add all the spices to the pumpkin and sugar mixture. Put the pan over medium heat and cook for 5 minutes with the lid off. Cover with the lid, reduce the heat and simmer for 20 minutes. Remove the lid and boil for 5 more minutes on high heat. Remove from the heat and leave to cool. Discard the cloves, cardamom pods and cinnamon sticks.

To serve, stack five squares of pumpkin on each plate, in a pattern that pleases your eye. Drizzle tahini over the top. Mix the cream and cinnamon together in a bowl. Add 1 tablespoon of the cream mixture on top of each pumpkin pattern, sprinkle with walnuts and serve.

AYVA TATLISI

POACHED QUINCES WITH SOUR CHERRIES AND CLOTTED CREAM

You could have eaten this dish 2000 years ago in Anatolia. The world's first cherry growing and the world's first quince growing happened there. Writings from 72 BC discuss how the military leader Lucullus brought a cultivated cherry to Rome from a part of the empire called Pontus in northeastern Anatolia. The Romans at the time were happy to combine it with their quinces stewed in honey.

The Ottoman chefs made a habit of stewing fruits with sugar syrup and combining them with kaymak. The secret here is to cook very slowly and include the skins and the cores of the quinces while simmering, to enhance the pink colouring the Ottomans loved.

SERVES 4

100 g (3½ oz/½ cup) frozen sour cherries
4 quinces
juice of 1 lemon
1 cinnamon stick
5 cloves
660 g (1 lb 7 oz/3 cups) sugar
16 walnut kernels
125 g (4½ oz/½ cup) *kaymak* (see page 54)
 (or thick/double cream)

Take the cherries out of the freezer about 1 hour before you want to serve the dish.

Peel the skin off the quinces and reserve the skin. Halve the peeled quinces, lengthways, and remove the hard cores. Reserve the cores.

Put the lemon juice and 1 litres (35 fl oz/4 cups) of water in a bowl. This will stop the quinces from going brown.

Lay the quince skins, shiny side down, in the bottom of a wide saucepan. Place the cinnamon stick, cloves and cores on top. Put the quinces, cut side up, on top of the spices. Put 3 tablespoons of the sugar on each quince half. Pour 500 ml (17 fl oz/2 cups) of water into the pan around the quinces, being careful not to cover the quinces or wash the sugar off. Put the lid on the pan and simmer for 1 hour until the quinces are pink and soft.

Mix 110 g (3¾ oz/½ cup) of the sugar with about 25 sour cherries. Take the lid off the pot and place three cherries in each half quince. Cover again and simmer for 30 minutes. Remove from the heat and leave to cool for 30 minutes—with the lid off if the quinces are soft, lid on if the quinces are still slightly firm.

Place the quinces on a serving platter. Put two walnuts on top of each quince.

Add a dollop of *kaymak* or thick cream on top of each quince. Drizzle about 1 tablespoon of the cooking liquid over the quinces and serve.

KÜNEFE

BUFFALO MOZZARELLA AND PISTACHIO PASTRY

There is constant debate about the ownership of this dish between the neighbouring cities Antakya, Adana and Mersin. I prefer to eat the Antakya version (bigger and cheesier), but I will not take sides in the origin argument, because all three cities have many citizens of Syrian ancestry and there are versions of this dish all over the Arab world. So the Turkish ownership debate may be academic.

There are cheeses made in those towns specifically to go inside künefe. *The challenge in making the dish outside Turkey is to find the right cheese—fresh, low in salt and able to ooze when heated. I like to use buffalo mozzarella.*

SERVES 4

SYRUP

440 g (15½ oz/2 cups) sugar
1 tablespoon lemon juice

PASTRY

300 g (10½ oz) fresh buffalo mozzarella
  (or unsalted mozzarella)
500 g (1 lb 2 oz) *kadayıf* pastry
200 g (7 oz/1 cup) ghee (to make your own,
  see page 21)
125 ml (4 fl oz/½ cup) grape molasses
70 g (2½ oz/½ cup) finely ground pistachios

First make the syrup, so it has time to cool. Put the sugar and 500 ml (9 fl oz/2 cups) of cold water in a saucepan and bring to the boil over medium heat. Reduce the heat and simmer for 8 minutes. Add the lemon juice and simmer for 1 more minute. Remove from the heat and leave to cool to room temperature.

Roughly chop the mozzarella. Roughly cut the *kadayıf* pastry into chunks. Put the pastry in a bowl with half the ghee and mix with your hands until completely combined. Divide the buttered pastry into two balls.

Brush the grape molasses and a little ghee onto the base of a frying pan (or divide into smaller frying pans to make individual *künefe*). Spread half the pastry over the pan, pressing it down with the (clean) base of another pan. Spread the mozzarella evenly over the pastry, and spread the other half of the pastry over the mozzarella. Press down again on the second layer of pastry.

Place the pan over medium heat. After about 6 minutes, as the bottom is turning golden brown, turn the *künefe* out onto a plate, and then put it back into the pan with the uncooked side down. Cook the second side for a further 4 minutes. Turn off the heat and slice the *künefe* into four segments. Pour the cold syrup over the segments.

Divide the *künefe* between each plate, sprinkle with pistachios and serve.

Across Turkey, restaurants with 500 seats are not uncommon. This one is Bayazhan in Gaziantep.

İNCİR & KAYISI DOLMASI
WALNUT-STUFFED FIGS AND ALMOND-STUFFED APRICOTS

More than half the world's dried figs and dried apricots come from Turkey, so of course we have to stuff them. Turkey is the fourth-biggest producer of walnuts in the world, and the number-eight almond producer. So of course they'd be the best nuts for the stuffing.

SERVES 4

- 500 ml (9 fl oz/2 cups) milk
- 1 cinnamon stick
- 4 cloves
- 8 dried figs
- 60 g (2¼ oz/½ cup) walnuts
- 1 tablespoon vegetable oil
- 2 tablespoons grape molasses
- 2 tablespoons sugar
- 8 dried apricots
- 1 tablespoon almond meal
- 1 teaspoon icing (confectioners') sugar
- 2 tablespoons pouring (whipping) cream
- 2 tablespoons pistachio kernels

Heat the milk, cinnamon stick and cloves in a saucepan over medium heat and bring to the boil. Remove from the heat. Remove the stalks from the figs. Rest the figs in the warm milk for 30 minutes.

Preheat the oven to 180°C (350°F/Gas 4).

Roughly chop the walnuts. Remove the figs from the milk with a slotted spoon and place on a board. Open the figs with a teaspoon and stuff 1 teaspoon of chopped walnuts inside. Mix the oil and molasses together in a bowl and then brush over the figs. Place the figs on a baking tray and cook for 10 minutes until soft. Remove from the oven and leave to cool.

Meanwhile, put the sugar and 250 ml (9 fl oz/ 1 cup) of water in a saucepan and bring to the boil. Add the apricots, reduce the heat and simmer, covered, for 15 minutes. Remove from the heat and leave to cool. Remove the apricots from the syrup and leave to drain on paper towel.

Mix the almond meal, icing sugar and cream together in a bowl. Make a pocket in each apricot with a teaspoon and stuff 1 heaped teaspoon of the cream and almond mixture inside. Use the teaspoon to smooth the exposed stuffing. Finely chop the pistachios and roll the cream side of each apricot in the pistachio pieces.

Serve two figs and two apricots per person.

SEMOLINA HELVA WITH RASPBERRY ICED YOĞURT

This is not a deconstruction of a traditional dish, but a sensible reconstruction of a bastardised one. Some fashionable restaurants in Istanbul are now serving ice cream (either vanilla or sahlep) covered with a dome of warm semolina helva. Some of them even name it 'Sultan's helva' to add vintage credibility. I don't get it. For me, a good semolina helva should be warm and crumbly, so you can't make a dome out of it. And a good ice cream should be firm and cold, not half melted.

I've made the assumption that most home cooks don't have an ice cream machine, so I've explained here how to make what the Italians call a semifreddo, using raspberries and yoğurt.

SERVES 4

ICED YOĞURT
6 eggs
220 g (7¾ oz/1 cup) sugar
500 ml (9 fl oz/2 cups) whipping cream
2 tablespoons plain *yoğurt*
1 punnet (200 g/7 oz) raspberries

HELVA
200 g (7 oz) butter
2 tablespoons pine nuts
285 g (10 oz/1½ cups) fine semolina
250 ml (9 fl oz/1 cup) milk
220 g (7¾ oz/1 cup) sugar

First make the iced *yoğurt*. Separate the eggs. You are going to use all six yolks and three of the whites. Blend the egg yolks and the sugar together in a bowl. Put the cream in a kitchen mixer and blend until thick. Fold the egg yolk mixture into the cream. Whisk three egg whites until peaks form. Gently fold into the yolk mixture. Fold in the *yoğurt*. Finally, fold in the raspberries, reserving a few to serve.

Line four cups (half-filled if you want dome shapes), a rectangular tray (if you want to slice the iced *yoğurt* to serve), or any container you prefer, with plastic wrap, making sure the wrap overhangs the sides. Using a wooden spoon, push the mixture into the moulds and then place in the freezer overnight.

About 30 minutes before you want to serve this dessert, make the *helva*. Melt the butter in a frying pan over medium heat. Add the pine nuts and cook for 3 minutes, tossing constantly to evenly brown. Add the semolina and brown for 10 minutes, stirring constantly.

In a separate pan, mix the milk, sugar and 250 ml (9 fl oz/1 cup) of water, and bring to the boil over low heat. Immediately pour the boiling mixture over the semolina and continue to stir for about 10 minutes, until all the liquid is absorbed.

To serve, put one iced *yoğurt* dome (or a thick slice) on each plate and surround it with warm *helva*. Decorate with fresh raspberries and serve quickly, so the iced *yoğurt* does not melt.

GÜLLAÇ
RAMADAN RICE-PAPER BAKLAVA

Güllaç is thought to be the original form of baklava, which was turned into a more elaborate dish by the chefs in the palaces of the Ottoman sultans. For eleven months of the year in Turkey, it is almost impossible to find sheets of güllaç—a fine dried pastry made of cornflour (cornstarch). That's because it's an ingredient associated with the banquet served after sunset during the fasting month of Ramadan.

I used to serve güllaç in my restaurant for one month of the year. Then Owen, a Chinese chef who had worked with me since I opened my restaurant, showed me a round of rice paper that was readily available in all Asian supermarkets. It's smaller than the traditional güllaç sheets, but combined with milk, rosewater and nuts, it makes a desert which, to me, tastes even better than the cornflour version and is probably healthier. It's also appropriate that a Chinese person was responsible for my improved recipe. The first recorded mention of güllaç in the world was in a fourteenth century Chinese text called Yinshan Zhenyao, written by a doctor of Turkish origin in the court of the Yuan dynasty.

SERVES 4

75 g (2⅔ oz/½ cup) hazelnuts
75 g (2⅔ oz/½ cup) pistachios
500 ml (9 fl oz/2 cups) milk
110 g (3¾ oz/½ cup) sugar
½ teaspoon rosewater
½ pack (12 sheets) rice papers,
　about 20 cm (8 in) wide
25 pomegranate seeds

Using a grinder or a food processor, coarsely crush the hazelnuts. Finely crush the pistachios.

Put the milk and sugar in a saucepan over low heat and gently heat for 5 minutes to combine, being careful not to let the mixture boil. Remove from the heat and stir in the rosewater.

Put 2 tablespoons of the milk mixture in a deep round serving dish, then layer the rice papers, one at a time, shiny side up. Spread 2 tablespoons of warm milk mixture over each sheet as you go.

After the first three layers, sprinkle on half the hazelnuts. After three more layers, sprinkle on half the pistachios. After three more layers, sprinkle on the other half of the hazelnuts and, three layers after that, sprinkle on the remaining pistachios. Sprinkle the pomegranate seeds over the pistachios. Put the lid on the dish, then refrigerate for 1 hour.

Slice the milky baklava into quarters and then serve chilled.

KAHVELİ SUPANGLE

ZUPPA TURCA WITH CHOCOLATE CUSTARD

The Italians use the term zuppa inglese *(English soup) for a dessert made with custard and sponge finger biscuits (known to the English as trifle). The French use the term* crème anglaise *for what the English call custard. In Turkey, the dish called* supangle *(pronounced 'soup anglais') is made with slices of sponge and chocolate custard. Therefore I feel entitled to torture the language further by calling my mixture of chocolate custard and coffee-soaked biscuits* zuppa turca.

SERVES 4

ZUPPA TURCA
2 teaspoons Turkish coffee
50 g (1¾ oz) sugar
30 ml (1 fl oz) mastic liqueur (or white Sambuca)
30 ml (1 fl oz) Kahlua
12 sponge finger biscuits (also called ladyfingers or, in Turkey, cat's tongues)

CHOCOLATE CUSTARD
500 ml (9 fl oz/2 cups) milk
110 g (3¾ oz/½ cup) sugar
2 egg yolks
3 tablespoons cornflour (cornstarch)
1 tablespoon plain (all-purpose) flour
3 tablespoons dark cocoa
150 g (5½ oz) dark chocolate (70 per cent cocoa)

DECORATION
1 tablespoon ground pistachios
½ tablespoon shaved coconut
12 roasted coffee beans

First make a Turkish coffee in a *cezve* (see page 196) or small saucepan with 70 ml (2¼ fl oz) of water, the Turkish coffee and 1 teaspoon of the sugar. Place a piece of muslin (cheesecloth) in a tea strainer. Strain the coffee through the muslin four times, to remove all the grains.

Now make a sugar syrup. Stir the remaining sugar and 80 ml (2½ fl oz/⅓ cup) of water together in a saucepan over medium heat. Bring to the boil, then reduce the heat and simmer, uncovered, for 5 minutes. Remove from the heat and leave to cool to room temperature.

Combine the coffee with the mastic liqueur, Kahlua and sugar syrup. Spread the sponge fingers in a single layer in a baking dish. Pour over the coffee mixture and then rest in the fridge for 30 minutes.

To make the topping, warm the milk in a saucepan over low heat. Add the sugar to 125 ml (4 fl oz/½ cup) of the warm milk mixture in a bowl and whisk in the egg yolks and two flours, until smooth. Pour the egg yolk mixture into the pan, stirring constantly. Add the cocoa. Simmer for 5 minutes, stirring constantly. Shave the chocolate into the mixture and stir. As soon as the chocolate has melted in, turn off the heat.

Place a layer of soaked sponge fingers in the bottom of four pudding bowls (glass, ideally). Pour the chocolate mixture over the top.

Chill the bowls in the fridge for 1 hour. Decorate with shaved coconut, roasted coffee beans and pistachios, and serve.

The pebbly shoreline and a big high tide at the end of the day in Bodrum.

HİNDİ GÖĞSÜ
TURKEY PUDDING

This is a kind of answer to the question, 'Do they cook with turkey in Turkey?' The normal answer is 'not often', and then only on New Year's Eve in westernised families. There is, however, a traditional Ottoman desert called tavuk göğsü, *apparently with ancient Roman origins, that uses shredded chicken breast. I decided to see if turkey breast would work as well.*

But first let's talk about the bird. It originated in South America, and the first Europeans who saw it thought it was a form of guineafowl—a game bird they imagined came from Turkey. So they brought it to England under the name 'turkey fowl'. The French thought it came from India, so they called it dinde *(which translates as 'from India'). When the bird first arrived in Turkey, it was known as 'Egyptian fowl', but the Turks later followed the French and 'corrected' the name to* hindi, *which means 'Indian'. In India, the bird is called* peru, *which is the closest to its real origin.*

Anyway, the bird under any name works better than chicken in this dish, because of its bland taste, and we can safely call this a turkey pudding as well as a Turkey pudding.

SERVES 6

1 turkey breast (the fresher the better)
1 litre (35 fl oz/4 cups) milk
1 vanilla pod
220 g (7¾ oz/1 cup) sugar
2 tablespoons cornflour (cornstarch)
2 tablespoons rice flour
1 teaspoon butter
2 pieces mastic crystal
1 teaspoon ground cinnamon

Wash the breast under cold running water for 2 minutes. Pat dry with paper towel, then wrap in plastic wrap and freeze overnight.

Put the frozen turkey breast in a saucepan, cover with water and boil for 50 minutes over medium heat until fully cooked. Transfer the turkey to a bowl of iced water for 1½ hours. Change the iced water every half hour, rinsing the breast each time. Put the turkey in the freezer for 1 hour to chill. Remove and set aside for 1 hour.

Shred the rested turkey meat into hair-thin pieces, discarding any thicker, tougher shreds. (It's no problem if you have to discard half the breast.)

Put the milk in a large saucepan. Slit the vanilla pod and add to the milk. Add the sugar. Warm for 5 minutes over medium heat. Scoop 250 ml (9 fl oz/1 cup) of the milk into a bowl, add the cornflour and rice flour and whisk to combine. Pour the flour mixture into the pan, constantly whisking. Add the butter and mastic, and whisk for 2 minutes, or until the mixture thickens. Remove the pan from the heat. Remove the vanilla pod and discard. Add the turkey shreds. Whisk for 5 minutes. Pour the mixture into a 20 x 30 cm (8 x 12 in) baking tray and rest in the fridge for 3 hours to set.

Remove the tray from the fridge. You should now have a soft rectangular mat. Slice along the mat, once, and across the mat twice, to make six slabs. Transfer the slabs onto six plates. Use a spatula to fold each slab in half. Decorate with cinnamon powder and serve cold.

SOMER SUGGESTS ...

This is not a definitive list of the 'best' visiting experiences in Istanbul, but a rough guide to the places I like to visit when I return to my home town. Bear in mind that Istanbul is divided by the Bosphorus Strait, between 'the European side' and 'the Asian side'. I grew up on the Asian side (in the waterside suburb of Kadıköy). Most tourists stay on the European side, which is their loss.

FOR BREAKFAST

Van Kahvaltı Evi is the restaurant that started the big breakfast phenomenon in Istanbul. Arrive early and arrive hungry! I'm yet to see anyone yet who can clear the entire meal, but it's the best introduction to the eastern Turkish way of starting the day.
Address: Defterdar Yokuşu No. 52/A, Cihangir, Beyoğlu
Phone: 0212 293 6437

Çakmak Kahvaltı Salonu is one of the oldest breakfast houses in the Beşiktaş area, still pumping with locals and a few tourists who discovered this gem. It specialises in clotted cream with honey, local cheeses, eggs with spicy sausage and kavurma (a kind of meat stew) and it stays open for brunch and lunch.
Address: Akmaz Çeşme Sokak No. 20, Beşiktaş
Phone: 0212 227 25 65

Kale Café opened in 1982 and started the trend of breakfast on the Bosphorus—classics such as *mememen* or eggs with *sucuk*. Views are to die for.
Address: Yahya Kemal Cad. No. 2 Rumelihisarı
Phone: 0212 265 6563
Website: www.kalecafe.com

FOR LUNCH

Çiya means not one but three restaurants under the command of Musa Dağdeviren, whose research and skill put regional Anatolian food on the map long before any other chef in Turkey cared for it. The three Çiyas alone are enough reason to visit the bustling markets of Kadıköy, but I suggest you sample the many food wonders there, if you have any room left after Musa's menu.
Address: Caferağa Mh., Güneşli Bahçe Sk No. 43, Kadıköy
Phone: 0216 330 3190
Website: www.ciya.com.tr

Kantin has a beautiful room, style and service, but it's the uncompromising honesty of Şemsa Denizsel's food, based on season and freshness, that impress me most in this local bistro in the posh suburb of Nişantaşı.
Address: Akkavak Sokağı No. 30, Nişantaşı
Phone: 0212 219 3114
Website: www.kantin.biz

Hacı Abdullah is a traditional Ottoman/home-style eatery, run for 120 years by the same family. Their olive oil-braised vegetable dishes (*zeytinyağlılar*) are particularly good.
Address: Ağa Camii Atıf Yılmaz Cad. No. 9/A Beyoğlu
Phone: 0212 293 8561.
Website: www.haciabdullah.com.tr

Sultanahmet Köftecisi Selim Usta is a cheap and delicious lunch pit-stop for köfte (meatballs), in the middle of the tourist hub called Sultanahmet, the oldest part of the city.
Address: No. 12 Divanyolu, Sultanahmet. **Phone:** 0212 520 0566
Website: www.sultanahmetkoftesi.com

FOR KEBAPS

Çiya Kebap is one of Musa Dağdeviren's three restaurants in Kadıköy, offering char-grilled treats that change with the season and are authentic to their region of origin.
Address: Caferağa Mh., Güneşli Bahçe Sk No. 43, Kadıköy
Phone: 0216 330 3190
Website: www.ciya.com.tr

Antiocha is a small but very popular char-griller in the grungy and trendy area of Asmalımescit, with

no reservations, specialising in the *kebaps* of southeastern Turkey.
Address: Asmalı Mescit Mah. Minare Sokak No. 21 Beyoğlu.
Phone: 0212 292 1100
Wesite: www.antiochiaconcept.com

Zübeyir caters for people who love to sit around the grill and receive whatever the chef passes over the counter.
Address: Şht. Muhtar Mh, Beyoğlu
Phone: 0212 293 3951

FOR SEAFOOD

Poseidon offers top views of the Bosphorus, creatively grilling delicious local fish such as *lufer*, *kalkan* and *levrek*. Like anything in the affluent suburb of Bebek, it's expensive. You can also dine at the Bebek Balıkçısı next door, if Poseidon is booked out.
Address: Cevdet Paşa Cad. No. 58 D:1 Küçük Bebek
Phone: 212 287 9531
Website: www.poseidonbebek.com

Karaköy Balıkçısı—Grifin has a beautiful vista of the old city and the Bosphorus, and has served high-quality fish and *mezes* for ninety years.
Address: Tersane Cad. Kardeşim Sk No. 30
Phone: 212 243 4080
Website: www.tarihikarakoybalikcisi.com

Bebek Balıkçısı is at Cevdet Paşa Cad. No. 26 Bebek
Phone: 212 263 3447
Website: www.bebekbalikci.net

İsmet Baba, on the Asian side of the Bosphorus, has a less spectacular view but great atmosphere: wooden walls, fish nets, pictures of generations of owners and local customers who look older than the restaurant (founded in 1951).
Address: Carsi Cad. İskelesi Yanı 1A, Üsküdar, Kuzguncuk

Phone: 0216 341 3375
Website: www.ismetbaba.com.tr

PUDDINGS AND PASTRIES

Özkonak is one of the few pudding shops that still use real chicken breast in their *tavukgöğsü* pudding. The chicken-free version, called *kazandibi* (bottom of the pan), is ideal for the less adventurous.
Address: Akarsu Caddesi 46B, Cihangir
Phone: 0212 249 1307

Markiz, in the tradition of the Orient-Express era, is one of the longest surviving Parisian style patisseries in Istanbul.
Address: İstiklal Cad. No. 360-362, Beyoğlu
Phone: 0212 245 8394

Güllüoğlu Baklava Shop in Karaköy is justly famous as one of the most authentic baklava houses outside Gaziantep.
Address: Katlı Otopark Altı, Karaköy
Phone: 0212 293 0910
Website: www.gulluoglu.biz

MEZE TIME

Imroz is the most interesting *meyhane* in a district where many meyhanes have second-rate food and gypsy musicians blowing trumpets in your ear.
Address: Nevizade Sk. No. 24 Balıkpazarı/ Beyoğlu
Phone: 0212 2499073
Website: www.krependekiimroz.com

Sofyalı 9 is my local when I visit Istanbul, because the food is consistent and it's away from the bustle of the main Beyoğlu district.
Address: Asmalımescit Cad. Sofyalı Sk. No. 9 Beyoğlu
Phone: 0212 252 3810
Website: www.sofyali.com.tr/en/

Koço is a typical Greek *meyhane*, with the surprise of a small church inside the building. It was a

drinking place for my grandad and my dad. I had many *rakı*-filled nights there and probably my son will follow the family tradition when he is of age.
Address: Moda Cad. No. 171 Kadıköy
Phone: 0216 336 0795
Website: http://kocorestaurant.net

Despina was a rare breed of female *meyhane* owner, who opened her place in 1946. Madame Despina is dead now, but her place kicks on with live traditional Turkish music every night.
Address: Açıkyol Sk. No. 9, Kurtuluş
Phone: 0212 247 3357

Duble mezebar is on the terrace of the Palazzo Donizetti Hotel in the historic Pera district, famous for modern mezes (well translated on the English menu), cool crowd and wonderful views.
Address: Palazzo Donizetti Hotel, Asmalımescit Caddesi No. 55, Kat 7, Beyoğlu
Phone: 0212 2440188

WINE TASTING

Sensus Şarap & Peynir is a wine, cheese and olive oil shop in a basement under the Anemon Hotel near the Galata Tower. They claim to have 300 Turkish wines available for tasting, along with interesting snacks to line the stomach.
Address: Bereketzade Mah. Büyükhendek Cad. No. 5, Galata
Phone: 0212 245 5657

FOR DINNER

Mikla is the best known 'New Anatolian' fine diner in the city, created by Mehmet Gürs on top of the Marmara Pera Hotel. Go just before sunset and have panoramic pre-dinner drinks on the rooftop.
Address: The Marmara Pera Hotel, Meşrutiyet Cad. Tepebaşı Beyoğlu
Phone: 0212 293 5656
Website: www.miklarestaurant.com

Yeni Lokanta translates as 'new bistro', but its chef, Civan Er, ran the famous Changa restaurant before switching to a more relaxed style.
Address: İstiklal Caddesi Kumbaracı Yokuşu No. 66, Beyoğlu
Phone: 0212 292 25 50
Website: www.lokantayeni.com

Asitane is the best and most authentic of the Ottoman revival restaurants, located next door to Kariye museum.
Address: Derviş Ali Mh., Kariye Cami Sk No:6, 34240 Edirnekapı.
Phone: 0212 534 8414
Website: www.asitanerestaurant.com

neolokal is the creation of Maksut Aşkar, who is brave enough to display his team in an open kitchen, creating light adventurous dishes with a focus on regionality and sustainability.
Address: SALT Galata Bankalar Cad. No. 11, Karaköy
Phone: 0212 249 8930
Website: www.neolokal.com

STREET FOOD

The eating never stops in Istanbul. There are street sellers with queues around the block at 4 o'clock in the morning. But the best of late dining is in places called *işkembeci*—offal eateries that sell everything from tripe soup to whole roasted sheep's head.

There are *iskembeci* in every neighbourhood, generally open from dusk till dawn. The best is Apik in the suburb called Dolapdere. This is not a tourist destination, so you should go there in a cab, have your soup, and get out of there in a cab.

My favourite street-hawker dish is *kokoreç*, a kind of sausage made with sheep intestines spiced with chilli flakes, oregano and cumin..

Other stalls sell *midye dolma*—fresh mussels in their shells, stuffed with aromatic rice.

And then of course there's *simit*, sourdough pretzels dipped in molasses and sesame, which cure the munchies at any time of the day.

And these are the top three foodie things to do that don't involve eating.

The **Spice Market** is overwhelmingly touristy with hagglers and pushy storekeepers, but an oasis can be found at Area 51—Bilge Kadıoğlu's Ucuzcular shop. Bilge is the only female shop owner and speaks perfect English. She does not have higher prices for tourists and the quality of her spices is exceptional.

The **Topkapı Palace** kitchens keep closing for renovations, but they are supposed to be opened in 2015.

Kadıköy Market is not your average shopping mall. It's crammed with specialist shops selling nuts, pickles, offal, oils and pastries.

WHERE TO STAY

Expensive: If you're rich and have an interest in twentieth-century history, try the Pera Palace in Beyoğlu, where the travellers on the Orient Express, including Agatha Christie, stayed in the 1920s.
Website: www.jumeirah.com/en/hotels-resorts/istanbul/pera-palace-hotel-jumeirah.

Also at a high price, you might prefer a former prison, the Four Seasons in Sultanahmet (http://www.fourseasons.com/istanbul), or a former Ottoman palace, Ciragan Palas, on the Bosphorus
Website: www.kempinski.com/en/istanbul/ciragan-palace/welcome

Medium price (and stylish design): There are four House Hotels, in Bosphorus, Galatasaray, Nisantasi and Karakoy.
Website: www.thehousehotel.com

IN GAZIANTEP

Metanet, near the central market, is a *lokanta* where you can eat fiery lamb soup (*beyran*) for breakfast, and where they also do an excellent *lahmacun* (thin-crust pizza) closer to lunchtime.

Address: Kozluca Mahallesi, Kozluca Cad. No: 11
Phone: 0342 231 4666

Yörem, under a suburban apartment block a short cab ride from the old town centre, is where Hatice Kalan serves a variety of home-style dishes, including the legendary storyteller soup (*yuvalama*).
Address: İncilipınar Mah. 3. Cad. 15. Sk. Ali Bey Apt. No. 2/C
Phone: 0 342 230 5000.

Zekeriya Usta is where Mehmet Ozsimitci makes crisp *katmer* pancakes stuffed with pistachios and clotted cream. He closes at midday. It's in an arcade in the new part of Gaziantep, so you'll need to get a cab and show these details.
Address: Katmerci Zekeriya Usta. Çukur Mahallesi, Körükçü Sk, B. Hilmi Geçidi 16/C–D, Gaziantep
Phone: 0342 230 0971

Ali Haydar makes liver *kebaps* for breakfast. He opens at 6 am, closing before 8 am just on the outskirts of the castle.
Address: Yaprak Mh. Dere Kenarı Sk, Tabakane Mevkii

İmam Çağdaş does great *kebaps* and perfect baklava near Gaziantep's central market.
Address: Uzun Çarşı 49, Sahinbey
Phone: 0342 231 2678

IN BODRUM

Orfoz, just off the main beach, is where the Bozçağa brothers play endless variations on local seafood in convenient *meze* portions.
Address: Kumbahçe Mah. Cumhuriyet Cad. No. 177B
Phone: 0252 316 4285
Website: http://www.orfoz.net

No longer grinding flour for pide, these eighteenth century windmills are scattered over the hills behind Bodrum, on the Aegean coast.

Istanbul's Hagia Sophia and surrounding mosques at dusk.

ACKNOWLEDGEMENTS

I want to offer my thanks to ...

David Dale, for taking a chance on me and on Turkish cuisine. And to Susan Williams and Millie Dale, for allowing me to borrow David for weeks at a time.

Janni Kyritsis, the Greek chef who introduced the Turkish chef to the Italophile author.

My wonderful wife Aslı and children Deniz and Derin, for being the reason I do this.

My mother Ülkü, who taught me to fly and my father Güngör who taught me to land. My two sisters, Begüm and Çiğdem, living so far away yet so close to my heart.

Ace photographer Bree Hutchins for endangering her life and her digestive system countless times to get the best possible shots.

The team at Murdoch Books: editing whiz Emma Hutchinson; designers Hugh Ford and Sarah Odgers; stylist Michelle Noerianto; Publisher Diana Hill. And, of course, Sue Hines who had the vision to get this show on the road.

The loyal team at Efendy: my brother-in-crime Fatih Külle and our head chef Bektaş Özcan; go-to guy Utku Görmez; my kitchen assistants during the shoot Burak Yıldırım and Owen Wang and all past and current staff contributing to the success of Efendy.

Musa and Zeynep Dağdeviren, who run three Çiya restaurants in Istanbul and produce the magazine Yemek Ve Kültür (Food and Culture). Their website is http://ciya.com.tr/index_en.php.

Greg Malouf, mentor and friend, who paved the way for my generation of chefs to professionalise Middle Eastern, Turkish and Greek cuisines in Australia.

For sharing their scholarship with us: Filiz Hösükoğlu (in Gaziantep); Aylin Öney Tan (Istanbul); Nilhan Aras (Istanbul); Tuba Şatana of istanbulfood.com.

For inspiring us with their specialties: Akife Malkoç (Istanbul); Melek Boz (Bodrum); İvgen Özön (Bodrum); Bercuk Anne (Sydney); Meral Ballı (Istanbul); Fouad Kassab (Sydney); Ayşe Sencer (Istanbul); Arman Uz (Kiama); Ömer Mutlugun (Malatya).

For opening their kitchens to us: Batur Durmay of Asitane; Ezgi Güven of Ayna of Cunda Island, Ayvalik; Mehmet Gürs of Mikla, Istanbul; Şemsa Denizsel of Kantin; Maksut Aşkar of neolokal; Civan Er of Yeni; Pando Şestakof of Pando's, Istanbul; Ali Haydar, the liver master of Gaziantep; Mehmet Özsimitci, the katmer master of Gaziantep; Mustafa Hasırcı, the beyran master of Metanet; Hatice Kalan of Yörem; Çağlar and Çağrı Bozçağa of Orfoz; the ladies of Sacide, Bodrum; the Bingöl family of Miam, Bodrum; Kanat Kıral of Bodrum Lokum.

For showing us their work: Mehmet Tembel (in Oğuzeli); Aydın Kilitoğlu of Asri Bakery, Gaziantep; Telat, Burhan and Telat Jr Çağdaş of Imam Çağdaş, Gaziantep; Enis Güner of Sevilen wines.

For their hospitality: Timur Schindel of Anatolian Houses, Gaziantep; Lucio Galletto of Lucio's; Armando Percuoco of Buon Ricordo and Nour Atalla of Darling Diner.

These books informed and entertained us:
500 Years of Ottoman Cuisine, by Marianna Yerasimos (Boyut)
The Sultan's Istanbul on Five Kurush A Day, by Charles Fitzroy (Thames & Hudson)
World Food Turkey, Dani Valent (Lonely Planet)
Western Anatolia Wine Culture, by A. Nedim Atilla (Bilgi)
Osmanlı Mutfağı, by Tuğrul Şavkay (Şekerbank)
Kaz dağları'ndan bir lezzet öyküsü, by Erhan Şeker (AMK)
Osmanlı Mutfak Sözlüğü, by Priscilla Mary Işın (Kitap)
Tatlı-pasta Öğretimi, by Ekrem Muhittin Yeğen (Inkilap)

And above all, to the many peoples of many ethnicities, faiths and philosophies who enriched the food culture of Anatolia.

INDEX

Published in 2015 by Murdoch Books, an imprint of Allen & Unwin

Murdoch Books Australia
83 Alexander Street
Crows Nest NSW 2065
Phone: +61 (0)2 8425 0100
Fax: +61 (0)2 9906 2218
murdochbooks.com.au
info@murdochbooks.com.au

Murdoch Books UK
Erico House, 6th Floor
93–99 Upper Richmond Road
Putney, London SW15 2TG
Phone: +44 (0) 20 8785 5995
murdochbooks.co.uk
info@murdochbooks.co.uk

For Corporate Orders & Custom Publishing contact Noel Hammond,
National Business Development Manager, Murdoch Books Australia

Publisher: Diana Hill
Design Manager: Hugh Ford
Designer: Sarah Odgers
Photographer: Bree Hutchins
Stylist: Michelle Noerianto
Editor: Emma Hutchinson
Production Manager: Mary Bjelobrk

A cataloguing-in-publication entry is available from the catalogue of the National Library of Australia at nla.gov.au.

ISBN 978 1 74336 049 1 Australia
ISBN 978 1 74336 081 1 UK

A catalogue record for this book is available from the British Library.

Colour reproduction by Splitting Image Colour Studio Pty Ltd, Clayton, Victoria
Printed by 1010 Printing International Limited, China

Theo
& Co.

Theo
THE SEARCH FOR THE PERFECT PIZZA
& Co.
Theo Kalogeracos

UWA PUBLISHING

Theo, 1968

Prosciutto and parmesan pizza base

CONTENTS

Smoked salmon pizza

1 GETTING STARTED

IN THE BEGINNING

For as long as I can remember bread has been my favourite food – fresh crusty bread with cheese. I like butter with it as well, but it has to be really good butter. However, when I go out for breakfast with friends and everyone else is ordering toast, scrambled eggs and other breakfast food, I'll be looking around for the sweet stuff such as carrot cake. It's almost like I'm on this mission to find the perfect recipe. I suppose it's not all that surprising because at almost every stage in my life I've been making something with flour.

My parents are both Greek-born Australians who arrived in Perth around about the same time in the early 1960s, but under quite different circumstances. Dad was, and still is, a typical Athens man – a real smoothy who is always happy, even when he's in trouble. He left Athens in a bit of a hurry when he was just 15 and arrived in Fremantle as a merchant seaman a year or so later. He liked the look of the place so much he jumped ship and promptly found himself locked up, as an illegal! Mum's family was very different. They were from a small village in the north of Greece, in Macedonia, and the family had been separated during the Greek Civil War in the late 1940s. When the war was over her father – my Pop – followed his brothers to Australia to find a better life for his family. It took years of working and saving to bring his wife – my Yaya – and their children, one by one, to their new home.

My parents were married very young, and like many other wog families in the '60s we lived in the inner-city suburbs of Northbridge and North Perth. Early on Dad had lots of jobs which often took him away from home. He worked up north driving dump trucks in the Pilbara and cutting bananas in Carnarvon, but he was happiest when he was gambling. When he was at home he had this great system for

the horses, which he worked out on our big kitchen table. But his system wasn't foolproof and Mum became the family breadwinner – in every sense. After working at Brownes Dairy and Plaistowes lolly factory she ended up as a bread carter for Tolcons Bakeries. She often worked two or three jobs at a time, so I spent most of my early childhood with Yaya and Pop at their home in Monmouth Street – and I loved it.

Yaya and Pop were simple country people who knew the importance of self-sufficiency. They grew all their own vegies, and had chooks and grapevines in the backyard. It was a magical playground for me. I was their first grandchild and they spoiled me rotten.

Breakfast with them was the real deal; always beautiful home-made crusty bread, fresh feta, black olives and black tea. Pop worked for the city council cutting grass, so most of the time I was at home with Yaya on my own, and this was where my interest in cooking began. Yaya did everything with me. One of my earliest memories is standing on a kitchen chair watching her making pita, the famous Greek flat flaky pastry that has countless types of fillings. She used an old cut-down curtain rod to roll out the thin sheets of Fillo pastry on her large kitchen table. When we made spanakopita (Greek spinach pie) it was my job to brush the sheets with melted butter after she had put in the layers of spinach and feta. Making Fillo is a long, labour intensive job, but believe me it's worth taking the time for that great taste – even if you can't make it as well as my Yaya!

Spanakopita

SPINACH & FETA MIX

1	small bunch spring onions, finely chopped (white part only)
1	kg spinach, cooked (frozen spinach can be used but take care to squeeze out all excess water after defrosting)
1	cup of olive oil
1	bunch flat-leaf parsley, coarsely chopped
1	bunch fresh dill, finely chopped
450	g Greek feta, crumbled
3	free-range organic eggs, lightly whisked
	Salt and white pepper
	Fresh breadcrumbs, if needed to stiffen mix (see Method)

FILLO PASTRY

500	g plain flour
25	mL white wine vinegar
50	mL extra virgin olive oil
1	teaspoon fine salt
300	mL cold water
1	tablespoon butter
1	cup extra plain flour for dusting

1 Sauté the spring onions in a large pan until they are soft and translucent. Add spinach and cook until wilted.

2 Remove from heat and drain off excess liquid.

3 Place in a bowl and carefully stir in other ingredients with a wooden spoon. Be careful not to make a mush of green. If the mixture looks too sloppy at this stage add fresh breadcrumbs to stiffen the mix. The mixture should be pliable enough to roll into small balls.

1 Combine all the ingredients (except the dusting flour) in a bowl and mix until it comes together.

2 Knead for 10 minutes to form a smooth dough ball.

3 Roll the dough ball in extra flour, place in a clean bowl, cover with cling film and refrigerate for an hour.

4 Remove dough from the fridge and cut into six even pieces. Knead each piece into a ball.

5 Sprinkle dusting flour onto the bench and start rolling one ball at a time. (Use a rolling pin that is wider than the baking tray because this will help to make even sized sheets of Fillo) Roll the dough out one way and, when it is thin, turn it clockwise and roll it the other way.

6 Repeat rolling until the dough is as thin as paper but without any tears. The word Fillo means leaf in Greek, so that is what you are aiming for. It takes a lot of practice and it's not as simple as rolling ordinary pastry. You don't become Super Yaya overnight!

7 Place each sheet to one side to air dry, and lightly dust both sides with extra flour.

Spanakopita

PUTTING THE PIE TOGETHER

1   Preheat the oven to 180°C for
     15 minutes.

2   Melt the butter in a small saucepan.

3   Line a large baking tray with a sheet
     of greaseproof paper and place the
     first sheet of Fillo Pastry on top so it
     slightly overlaps the edge of the tray.

4   Brush the sheet lightly with
     melted butter.

5   Repeat this process with the second
     sheet of Fillo Pastry.

6   Spread half the Spinach & Feta Mix
     on to this sheet and top with the
     third sheet.

7   Spread the remaining filling on the third sheet and then place the last three sheets of Fillo
     Pastry on the pie, remembering to brush each one with melted butter, especially the top of
     the final layer.

8   Use a sharp knife to make random spike holes through the pastry to allow the pie to
     cook evenly.

9   Press the edges firmly to ensure the overhanging pastry sticks together.

10   Seal the edges of the pastry by rolling and brushing with melted butter.

11   Cook at 180°C for 30 to 40 minutes or until the top has a lovely golden colour.

12   Remove from the oven and cut into pieces while the pie is still hot. Let rest for five minutes
     before serving. This dish is just as delicious served cold the next day.

GROWING UP

My interest in bread, pastry and cakes really started when I was a teenager. I didn't like high school much, so sometimes I wagged it to help Mum on her bread delivery rounds. She had the Lockridge area, which was pretty tough in those days, but I really enjoyed the work. Back then the bakery still used the old wood-fired ovens and it made this wonderful hard crusty bread, which cracked when it was cut. I've got good memories sitting in the lunchroom with Mum at Tolcons eating that fresh bread with butter. It was delicious!

I'm quite a bit older than my brothers, Anastassios (Tasso) and Vasilli, so when Mum was working it was my job to feed them when we came home from school. I wasn't really into making omelettes and things like that, but thanks to my time with Yaya, I liked making cakes and biscuits, so that's what my brothers got.

After leaving school I didn't really know what I wanted to do, so I went to TAFE and did a pre-apprenticeship as a pastry chef. Being a food chef had some appeal, but when I did work experience at the old Boans Department Store in Wellington Street, I got chucked into the pastry section and found I was good at it. This was a bit of a surprise because I had been really bad at school, but in my pre-apprenticeship I was top of the class. I went on to become Apprentice of the Year when I was 18. Suddenly I had found something I really really liked.

BECOMING A BETTER BAKER

I did my bakery apprenticeship in two places starting with a little Scottish bakery in East Victoria Park. That was a baptism of fire because the guy who ran it might as well have been speaking Chinese. His accent was so strong I could hardly understand him and he was very demanding. We would work 12 to 14 hours a day, six and a half days a week with no breaks. It was tough work with only the two of us pumping it out. Looking back I think this is where part of my work ethic came from. Baking is hot and repetitive work, but it has to be done, so you just get on with it.

Later I moved to AMP Golden Bakeries in North Perth. This position was only five days a week, offered more money and was close to home. I thought, 'sweet, I could almost walk to work', but I found myself at the end of a machine tying knots and making horseshoe rolls, so after a while I left. I thought I'd rather work seven days a week for myself than go nuts working in a factory.

About this time my younger brother Tasso wanted to leave school and get an apprenticeship, and because Mum had worked in bakeries it seemed like a good idea to buy a bakery and run it as a family business. We found this place back in Victoria Park called Miss Cleo's Betterbake, which we shortened to Betta Bake. It had a lunch bar at the front where Mum worked; my brother and I made all the bread, pies and cakes out the back. Dad decided he would do the books! The business took off and before long we started wholesaling and had to move to premises that were three times larger. We supplied all the universities, as well as companies such as Jiffy Foods who ran lunch vans going around the industrial areas. It was all the usual things; vanilla slices, cakes, éclairs and lamingtons. Jiffy Foods used to order 800 rock cakes a day! It was huge.

Little wonder those early days taught me many life skills. I was in my early 20s and employing bakers who were often much older than me. It was difficult getting some of them to do things my way, but they usually came round. Unfortunately, there were some things I couldn't change. The Burswood Casino opened soon after we took over the bakery and Dad spent quite a bit of time there, as did the profits from Betta Bake! Sadly, I couldn't see what was going on. I even went out and got a second job to try and generate more income. By this time I had married my beautiful wife and bought a house so I had a mortgage to worry about. I was working horrendous hours and still going backwards financially. Then I realised what was happening to the business. At that time the bakery in Victoria Park sat alongside a pizza wholesale distributor. I got to know the family quite well and one day when we were comparing notes on running costs of pizza shops and bakeries I was amazed to discover the difference in profitability. Not long after, I was driving through Mundaring when I noticed some empty shops in the main street and I knew I had to make the change from baker to pizza-maker.

Rock salt & parsley dipping base

PIZZA & CAESAR

Although my heritage is Greek, and pizza is seen as an Italian speciality, I do have serious Italian connections. My wife, Liz, is Italian and the success of our pizza shop is due in no small way to my relationship with her family, in particular her wonderful uncle, my mentor and friend Caesar Saraceni.

Caesar's background was similar to that of my grandparents. They were Europeans who knew about tough times. He was the oldest male of 10 surviving children from a family of 17 (like he says – they had no television in those days!), and although he was only a young man of 24 when his father died, Caesar took on the role as the head of the household. He never married or had kids of his own, and it was taking on responsibility for his younger widowed sister and her family that kept him in Australia after coming to live in Perth during in the 1960s.

Soon after arriving here Caesar got a job working as a cook. He even worked at the famous Mama Maria's in Northbridge. Eventually he opened his own pizza and pasta place in Glendalough called, you guessed it, Caesars. He eventually ended up as a cook for Poon Brothers in Newman, one of the Pilbara towns, which had been built to house mine workers in the early days of Western Australia's iron ore boom. Lots of people think my shop takes its name from the American pizza chain, but it was actually as a mark of respect to Liz's uncle that I chose the name Little Caesars simply because he has taught me so much. I'm happy to say it's a two-way thing. Caesar loved me from the get-go because he knew how much we were alike. I don't think I'm *quite* the mega tight-arse he is, but we both hate wastage and have a firm belief that food must connect with people. Thanks to Caesar I've been able to continue with Yaya's education about traditional cooking practices. He is really big on the importance

of using seasonal ingredients, and he has been a fantastic sounding board for my new ideas. Caesar's retired now but still comes up to work with me a few days every week. The kids in the shop don't know what to make of him. He wears his pants pulled right up, socks with sandals, and shuffles everywhere – but he walks faster than everyone. He doesn't say much but he sees everything! He's a genius and has been my rock. It was no coincidence we called our son Chaz-rae which is a variation of Caesar's name pronounced in the Italian way. Even though it's a Greek tradition to name your first-born son after your father we thought this was one way to repay Caesar for the personal sacrifices he has made for his family. When Chaz was born and we told Caesar, he was over the moon.

The first pizza recipe in this book has to be the Margherita. Not only because it's the most famous name in the business, or because I have won prizes cooking it, but mostly because a good Margherita is what I think making pizza is all about. Although it's simple and uncomplicated the whole process has to be done right and that's the story of Little Caesars' success.

Saraceni family circa 1945

Margherita

2½ tablespoons Traditional Tomato Pizza
     Sauce (see page 74)
200 g Basic Pizza Dough ball
     (see page 61), rolled and ready
90   g mozzarella, grated
     Fresh tomato, sliced
3   large fresh basil leaves, roughly torn
     Extra virgin olive oil
     Cracked black pepper and sea salt

1   Preheat the oven to 250°C for 25 minutes.

2   Spread Traditional Tomato Pizza Sauce evenly over the base, leaving a crust around the edge unsauced.

3   Spread mozzarella cheese on the top, using more on the outer edges and less towards the centre.

4   Top with slices of fresh tomato, making sure that slices are not touching.

5   Cook for seven to 10 minutes at 250°C.

6   Remove from the oven, scatter the fresh basil leaves evenly across the surface and drizzle with extra virgin olive oil.

7   Season with cracked black pepper and salt, and cut into slices and serve.

2 EQUIPMENT

WOOD-FIRED PIZZA OVENS

As a baker and pastry chef I know nothing smells better than bread or cakes hot from the oven. This may be the reason why so many wood-fired pizza ovens have been built in Australian backyards in the last few years. However, as with all cooking appliances there are many traps for would-be pizza chefs. Apart from the price of ovens, which can vary from hundreds to thousands of dollars, there are other important considerations. Remember, buying an oven is like anything else: only buy something you feel comfortable using.

A good wood-fired pizza oven should have the following:

- A uniform dome shape with a smooth crack-free surface inside and outside, which will distribute heat evenly throughout the oven
- Effective insulation on the dome bricks to retain the oven's heat and assist with heat distribution
- A brick base capable of withstanding temperatures of 600°C
- Enough space inside to accommodate your largest roasting dish and a few other smaller dishes or baking trays at the same time. The floor area of the average wood-fired pizza oven should be 1m².

GET THE RIGHT FUEL

Apart from construction details the owner of a wood-fired pizza oven should also know something about its fuel requirements and how to build a good fire. The type of wood used should be well seasoned, which means it should be dry and sap-free. Timber that has been cut recently is known as green wood as it is usually full of sap. It makes a poor fuel because it creates lots of smoke, sizzles when it burns and generates far less heat than dry, seasoned wood. All green wood should be left out in the weather for at least 12 months to dry out, or season, before being used in a wood-fired pizza oven. Local Western Australian hardwoods such as jarrah and mallee roots are very good fuel sources because they burn slowly and make great coals. On the other hand, imported softwoods, such as various types of pine, burn very fast and quickly turn to powdery ash. It is important to note some fuels should *never* be used in a wood-fired pizza oven. Burning timber that has been painted, varnished or treated for white ants will release poisonous toxins and these will contaminate your food.

Suitable firewood is readily available from commercial wood suppliers; anyone who thinks they can just go and collect a pile from the any patch of bush should think

twice. Throughout Australia there are regulations on the collection of firewood from national parks, crown land and even private property, so check with the relevant authorities before heading off to the bush with your trailer and chainsaw!

Fire safety is another thing we all have to think about when cooking outdoors. The hazards of bushfires are well known in Australia and although their connection with an outdoor pizza oven may seem remote the dangers are real enough. To avoid setting fire to your own backyard, house or the entire neighbourhood, adopt the same rules you would use for an outdoor barbecue.

- Never use the oven when there is a total fire ban
- Have a cleared area of 4 m around the pizza oven
- Have a fire extinguisher available at all times.

BUILDING A FIRE

The fire is set inside the dome, at the back or to one side, and once lit it should have more wood added gradually to build up a bed of glowing coals and embers. Manufacturers often claim the oven will be ready after 30 minutes – I wish that was the case! In fact it may take between two or three hours before a fire creates a strong and even heat. Avoid cooking anything in the oven when the fire is burning like a furnace, as all good cooks know the golden rule, 'Time cooks and temperature colours'. In other words the longer a pizza is left in the oven the more it will cook, and the higher the temperature is the more it will change colour or burn.

THE COOKING PROCESS

All ovens have particular hot and cold spots and it takes time to find their locations. It's important to know where they are because pizza is cooked using a rotation process; usually involving four moves of around two minutes each. Start by placing the pizza in a cool spot to seal the base and start the cooking process. After two minutes move it to a hotter spot, closer to the coals to apply more heat to the toppings. Finish the cooking by moving the pizza onto the hottest part of the oven. Finally, just before taking the pizza from the oven, move it back to a cool spot, probably near the door, to check it is cooked. Using this sequence it's possible to have four pizzas moving through the pizza oven at any one time, but it will require clockwork precision and some clever dexterity. Working with hot food involves an element of danger, so it's best to have assistants who know what they are doing. No-one will be happy if the pizza ends up on the floor!

Unfortunately, many wood-fired pizza ovens don't have a thermometer, so some guesswork is involved. The manufacturers suggest wood-fired ovens will take three to four minutes to cook a pizza at 450°C to 500°C. In my experience this is only true if your pizza has a limited number of

ingredients on the top. With more toppings it is better to allow between seven and eight minutes of cooking time. The best way to find out about your pizza oven is to practise, practise and keep on practising.

GAS-FIRED PIZZA OVENS

Outdoor gas-fired pizza ovens, called brick ovens in the U.S. where they have been used widely for a while, are now available in Australia. The product looks exactly like its wood-fired relative but has a few features which appeal to consumers who like to be clean and green. This gas-burning alternative solves the problems of finding suitable timber and smoke. Being thermostatically controlled this new oven also takes the guesswork out of the cooking process and as a result is more energy efficient. These ovens are the way of the future and I'm sure we will see more of them popping up in backyards and restaurants in Australia.

DOMESTIC OVENS

Cooking pizza in a domestic oven may not have the same romantic appeal as the outside wood-fired experience, but can still be very effective. Like their rustic equivalents domestic ovens also have hot and cold spots, which should be used in the same way. The oven should be preheated at the maximum temperature for half an hour before cooking with the fan turned off. This creates a drier heat, which makes a crispier pizza base. As a general rule, once the oven has been preheated, it takes between seven to ten minutes at 250°C to cook a pizza in a domestic oven.

Quattro fromaggio

PIZZA STONES

Pizza stones have been around for a long time. They work on the same principle as the brick-built wood-fired pizza oven in the backyard, with the convenience of being in your kitchen where you have control over the temperature. They cook the base with a dry heat which makes the pizza nice and crispy. However, be aware that pizza stones can get dangerously hot, so here are few tips to avoid accidents:

- Preheat your oven before preheating the stone
- Clear a space on the bench top for the pizza stone before taking it out of the oven, and be sure to protect your bench top with a cutting board or tea towels; thick mittens are also essential
- Place a sheet of greaseproof paper on the stone or sprinkle semolina on its hot surface before rolling out the pizza dough
- Work quickly to assemble your pizza because the dough will start cooking straight away
- Take care both placing and removing the hot stone from the oven as it's easy to burn yourself at either stage.

PIZZA TRAYS

Pizza trays are available in various sizes and it's a good idea to have a range of small and large to suit different recipes and occasions. These days perforated trays are available and although they may be hard to find they are well worth the hunt. The small holes in the tray allow the heat to hit the pizza dough directly and therefore provide a drier heat which results in a crispier pizza base.

OTHER EQUIPMENT

To get the most out of your wood-fired pizza oven you should have a pizza poker, a pizza peel and a pizza broom. The poker will help you to build the fire and safely move wood around inside the oven while it is burning. The peel is like a spade. It has a large, flat surface attached to a long handle, and is used when building the pizza, as well as placing it in the oven and moving it around during the cooking process. The peel replaces a pizza tray when cooking in a wood-fired oven. Before placing the prepared dough on the peel a small amount of semolina must be sprinkled on the flat face of the peel. The tiny grains of semolina actually act as ball bearings and prevent the pizza from sticking to the oven floor when it is being moved around inside the oven. The pizza broom is used for removing ash and old coals from the oven once the fire has gone out.

Another essential piece of equipment no matter which oven you use is an effective pizza cutter. There are many different cutters available and choice is really a matter of personal preference. Some of the newer versions of the traditional pizza roller/cutter are quite nifty, but if it is used incorrectly there is a risk of dragging toppings from one side of the pizza to the other. A pizza rocker, which is similar to a half-moon cheese cutter, a long butcher's knife or even a cleaver can be used so long as it is sharp and able to cut cleanly and quickly. The longer it takes to cut a pizza the soggier it gets, and it will die in front of you if you don't move fast.

LESSONS OF EXPERIENCE

I learned the importance of getting the oven temperature right the hard way. In 2000 I was selected to represent Western Australia in the Dairy Farmers National Best of the Best pizza competition.

There were five competitors; one from each of the five largest states, and a simple ballot was used to determine the cooking order. I drew number two.

In those days pizzas were made in deck ovens, which opened up like regular ovens.

Number One went up first, cooked his pizza, took it out and presented it to the judges. I was up next. I had decided to make my Chicken Satay pizza, so I made it, put it in the oven and just sat back talking to the guy who was up next. Suddenly he said, 'Do you smell something?'

'Yes, something's burning…farrrccck!'

I opened the oven and there was my pizza – black underneath and raw on top. The first pizza-maker had discovered the oven wasn't cooking properly, so he had cranked the temperature up to the max. I hadn't checked the temperature when I started and it was as hot as. I tried to explain the situation to the judges but they were unsympathetic. That's competition. It was just tough luck and I had to cop it.

It wasn't all bad news though. That year I met Sidney Roberts, a chef who works for Carlton Crest Hotels. In my view Sidney is the ultimate pizza-maker, and seeing him work really opened my eyes to success in both competition and business. I learned the importance of choosing the right ingredients, as well as taking the utmost care in the process and the presentation. And the lessons paid off. In 2002 I came second in the Best of the Best competition and in 2003 I went back and won all four categories!

An important secret to successful pizza making is taking the time to work out how to get the best results from your equipment and enjoying the process on the way.

3 INGREDIENTS

For me making pizza is like life — you get out of it what you put into it. Experience has taught me the finest and freshest ingredients make the best pizzas, but as with life you can have too much of a good thing. Ideally, a good pizza should be about the combination of taste and flavour rather than being overpowered by any single ingredient.

FLOUR

The basis of any good pizza is good dough and the only way to ensure good pizza dough is to have the right kind of flour. Growing up around bakeries and becoming an apprentice baker at 17 meant I became familiar with this particular ingredient. I've learned that strong baker's flour with 12% to 15% protein level is the best kind for making pizza dough, so be sure to study the nutritional information on the side of the packet to get the best available. Organic plain flour has the advantage of giving a more earthy-tasting pizza and it may also add texture to the dough, which will surprise the taste buds. Wholemeal plain flour may be just a little too overpowering and should be used in a half-and-half combination with strong baker's flour. Some recipes for pizza dough suggest using self-raising flour, but it often has low protein levels and the added baking powder simply doesn't work for pizza dough.

THE ROLE OF YEAST

Before the invention of dry activated yeast, bakers relied on a thing called 'starter' to make their dough rise. The most common starters were made from combinations of grapes with flour, apples with oats, or potatoes, which were mixed together and allowed to ferment to create natural yeast. These microscopic natural organisms release carbon dioxide gas bubbles, which become trapped in the dough causing it to rise. Old-fashioned starters have almost disappeared since the arrival of dry or compressed fresh yeast, which is more reliable and a lot less messy.

TYPES OF DOUGH

I use different types of dough, depending on where I'm cooking. My basic pizza dough is excellent for the domestic oven, but if I'm using the wood-fired pizza oven I add other ingredients such as olive oil and semolina for added moisture and crispiness.

Just as certain ovens require certain ingredients so too do certain stomachs. Being allergic to gluten (i.e. the protein in wheat flour) doesn't mean you should miss out on pizza. Gluten-free flour is widely available and I use one made from maize which has no yeast or preservatives. However, making gluten-free pizza dough requires a particular technique to get the best results.

FLAVOURED DOUGH

The method is the same for all variations. At the stage when the pizza balls are shaped, the ball is spread flat with the heel of your hand. Half the ingredients are spread across the surface of the dough, which is then kneaded back into a ball and left to rest for five to seven minutes. When ready, the dough is rolled out like a regular pizza base then left to rise for a minimum of one hour. Finally, the pizza is brushed with olive oil and the remaining ingredients are sprinkled on the top and pressed into the dough. A 200 g ball of flavoured dough will only take four to five minutes to cook in an oven preheated to 250°C.

Dough

BASIC PIZZA DOUGH

1	kg strong baker's flour (i.e. plain flour with the highest protein level available)
10	g salt
10	g sugar
20	g dry yeast or 40 g fresh yeast
660	mL cold water

WOOD-FIRED PIZZA DOUGH

600	g strong baker's flour
400	g semolina flour
10	mL extra virgin olive oil
10	g salt
10	g sugar
20	g dry yeast
650	mL water

GLUTEN-FREE DOUGH

450	g gluten-free flour
550	mL cold water

1　To make basic or wood-fired pizza dough follow the methods detailed from page 62 onwards.

1　Place the gluten-free flour in a large bowl and slowly add cold water.

2　Mix the flour and water together until you have a firm dough which resembles shortbread. The shortness of the dough will make it hard to knead.

3　After seven to 10 minutes of kneading you should have a good pizza dough. Unfortunately, if it's rolled out and cooked immediately this pizza base will crack.

4　Roll the dough out, place it on a tray so it slightly overlaps the edges, cover it with plastic wrap and place in the fridge for a short time before cooking.

MAKING DOUGH BY HAND

Always set out the ingredients and equipment required before getting underway. The water temperature is very important. Never add warm water to the flour as it will activate the yeast too quickly and affect the end result. If it's a hot day using cold water from the refrigerator is a good idea for this very reason.

The dough can be mixed in large bowl or directly on the bench top. Start by mixing all the dry ingredients together and creating a well in the centre. Carefully pour 600 mL of water into the well and gradually incorporate the wet and dry ingredients by gently moving the water into the flour mixture. It will take three or four minutes for the dough to come together. The remaining 50 mL or 60 mL of water is only added if necessary and this depends on the nature of the flour. The gluten content of the flour affects the amount of water required, so it's always better to start with less and add more when needed than to have a dough that is too wet and sticky.

Kneading dough is a great skill and can only be learned with practice. The purpose of the process is to develop the gluten strains in the flour, so when the dough goes into the oven and rises the gluten will help the base to hold its shape. This means each slice of pizza will stay quite rigid and stop the toppings from sliding off.

The kneading process involves a consistent movement of the palms and heels of the hands, pressing down and away from the body and turning the ball of dough clockwise after every pass. If 1 kg of dough is too difficult to manage, it should be cut in half and worked in two batches. Don't be put off by the task – think of it as a good workout for your muscles!

The aim is to achieve a smooth ball of dough after 10 minutes of kneading. However, avoid watching the clock, and try to develop a feel for what is right. At

this stage it should be possible to stretch the dough quite thinly, so it is translucent when held up to the light. A well-kneaded ball of pizza dough should have a smooth skin and feel like soft plastic.

Making dough by hand is not particularly easy, but many people agree it is excellent therapy for the soul, and turning flour and water into dough seems magical.

MECHANICAL MIXERS

For people who don't like sticky fingers or messy bench tops a mechanical mixer is a better option for dough making. Nevertheless, regardless of the size and type of mixer, a dough hook is essential. Plain flat beaters will simply not make good dough. When mixing dough mechanically always add the liquids to the bowl first, followed by the dry ingredients. This technique will help distribute the dry ingredients evenly and stop them from becoming stuck on the bottom or sides of the bowl. Good dough can be made in a mechanical mixer with a dough hook in 10 to 12 minutes. Be careful to avoid over mixing the dough, as it will result in a horrible sticky mess. As with hand kneading the perfect dough should be firm and smooth. Once the dough has been prepared the rest of the process is similar to hand kneading. That is, weighing and rolling the round pizza balls followed by resting and rolling out (see Making Pizza Balls, page 69).

A bread-making machine can be used like any other mechanical mixer to make pizza dough. Add the liquid first, followed by dry ingredients, close the lid and start the machine. Once the dough is made it should be removed before it has a chance to rest and prove. As with the other methods it should be weighed, moulded and set aside to rest before being thrown or rolled.

A food processor has limited application for use in dough making as it can only be used to assist in the first stage. Add the water followed by the dry ingredients. Put the lid on and just pulsate in short bursts to bring the wet and dry ingredients together. At this stage the mix is turned out into a bowl on to the bench top and rest of the process is the same as hand kneading.

MAKING PIZZA BALLS

Dividing the dough into individual balls for pizza will vary depending on the size of pizzas required. On average a 200 g ball of dough will make a 10 inch (25 cm) pizza and the 1 kg mixture can be used to make eight 200 g pizzas.

Create round balls of dough by using the palms of your hands to cup the dough. Next, weigh and cover them with a tea towel to prevent a tough skin from forming, as this may make rolling the dough at a later stage more difficult.

Let the pizza dough balls rest under the tea towel for 10 to 15 minutes. This resting period allows the mixture to undergo chemical changes that will make it easier to roll out and help it hold its shape. Insufficient resting time usually results in serious shrinkage of the dough after it has been rolled.

PREPARING THE PIZZA BASE

There are various ways of getting regular pizza dough to the desired shape. Throwing it in the air requires skill and practice. Some people prefer to start the process by rolling the dough out with a rolling pin or with the palm of the hand. If you want to throw it, flat dough can be held in the extended fingers and thrown clockwise up in the air to a height where it can be confidently caught. Keep doing this until you get to the desired size. Throwing pizza dough allows it to stretch and relax in one continuous process, and it's a great way to impress friends and relatives! However, for the less ambitious rolling the dough is a quicker and safer option.

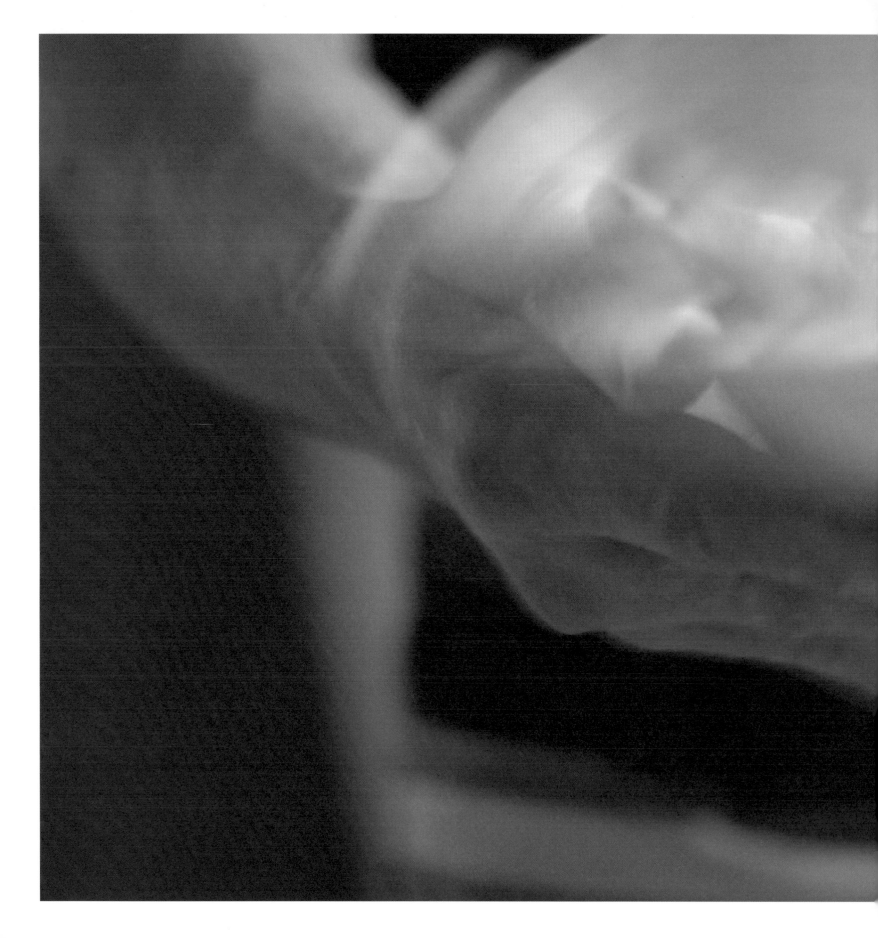

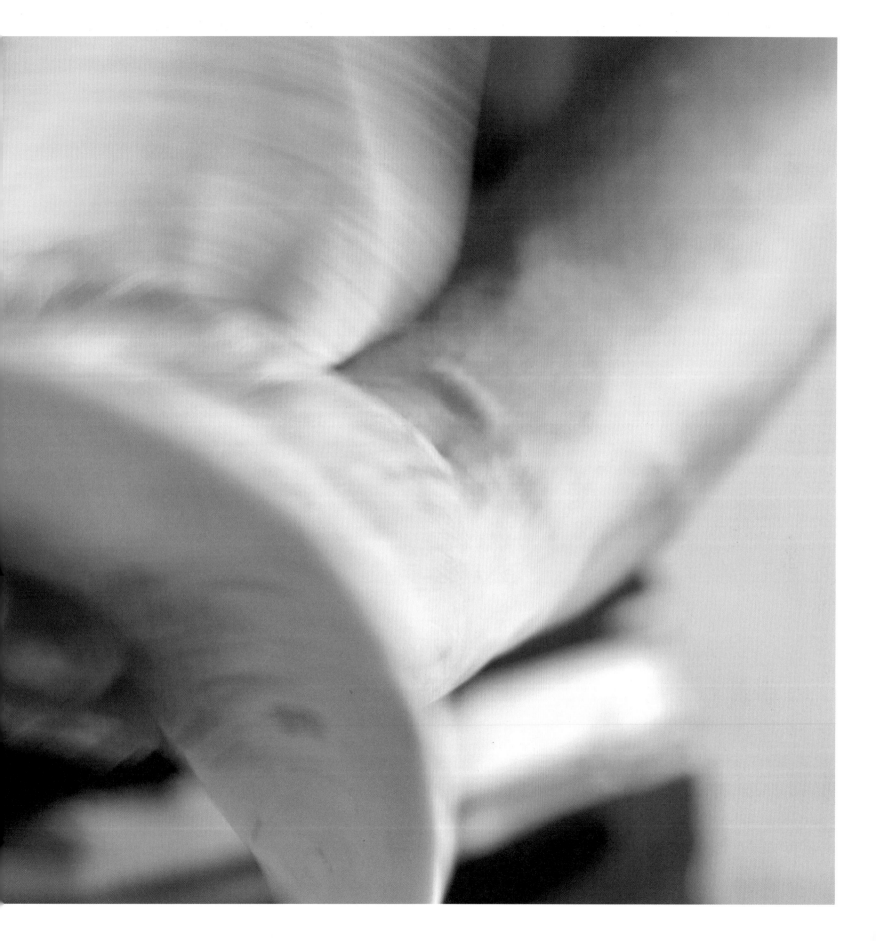

TRADITIONAL PIZZA SAUCE

Another of the key ingredients on many pizzas is tomato sauce. In Italy, birthplace of the modern pizza, the preparation of tomato sauce is a time-honoured tradition. Even though my Greek Yaya made her own tomato sauce it was not until I met Uncle Caesar that I learned the secret of making a good sauce. And the secret is simple – it's all about timing. The best tomato sauce is made once a year at the height of summer when fresh tomatoes are reddest and cheapest.

The tomatoes are boiled in copper pots and when tender put through a mechanical sieve which separates the juices from the seeds and skins. The sauce is then bottled, sealed, and used for pasta sauce. Any tomatoes that have burst or are substandard are simply placed in jars and used for lasagne or pizza. These are the equivalent of whole peeled tomatoes commercially available in cans.

In Australian supermarkets it can be difficult to find good tomatoes for sauce because they are often picked green to give a longer shelf life; fruit canned in Italy is a better choice as the tomatoes are canned when ripe. Alternatively, you can always do what Caesar does in late summer and make a trip to a market garden in your area to find the freshest and ripest tomatoes, and make your own sauce.

OTHER SAUCES

Pesto is an ingredient used at Little Caesars in sauces, dips and as a garnish. Basil is at its best in summer, so we make heaps of pesto when we can and freeze it for later use.

When a very quick recipe is called for I suggest a sun-dried tomato sauce.

It has taken many years to develop a successful white cream sauce recipe. The trick is getting the timing right. This sauce should be made the day before and can be refrigerated for up to seven days.

Home-made satay sauce is easy to make, and the end result is far superior to anything bought in a jar. This sauce can be kept for up to seven days in the fridge.

Sauces

TRADITIONAL TOMATO

400   g fresh ripe tomatoes, skins removed, or one 400 g can whole peeled tomatoes

1   garlic clove, peeled and finely chopped

1   teaspoon Basil Pesto

1   teaspoon extra virgin olive oil

    Salt and cracked black pepper

BASIL PESTO

300   mL extra virgin olive oil

2   garlic cloves

60   g pine nuts, toasted

60   g Parmesan cheese, grated

250   g fresh basil leaves, stalks removed

    Pinch of salt

SEMI-SUN-DRIED TOMATO

100   g semi-sun-dried tomatoes

3   tablespoons extra virgin olive oil or the oil the tomatoes were packaged in

1   Place all the ingredients in a food processor and pulse until they are evenly mixed. Try not to pulverise too finely as small bits of tomato flesh add to the rustic look. If the sauce is made the day before it is required it will be thicker and richer tasting.

1   Using either a pestle and mortar or a food processor, crush or process the ingredients until they form a rough paste.

2   Transfer to a small container with a lid and refrigerate until required.

1   Drain the oil away from the tomatoes.

2   Place them in a blender and blitz into a smooth paste.

3   Transfer the paste into a jar and store in the refrigerator until required.

Sauces

SATAY

2	garlic cloves
125	g roasted unsalted cashews
6	spring onions (white part only), finely chopped
2	lemon grass stalks, roughly chopped
2	red chillies, finely chopped
1½	tablespoons peanut oil
1	teaspoon coriander
375	mL coconut milk
1	teaspoon turmeric
1	teaspoon salt

1. Crush garlic, cashews, spring onions, lemon grass and chillies with a mortar and pestle or blend in a food processor until they form a fine paste.

2. Heat oil in a nonstick frying pan and add the paste.

3. After a few minutes add coriander, coconut milk and turmeric and slowly bring to the boil.

4. Add salt and simmer for another two minutes.

5. Remove from the heat and allow to cool before using on a pizza base or placing in a storage container.

WHITE CREAM

50	g butter
1	teaspoon extra virgin olive oil
¼	cup onion, very finely chopped
250	mL fresh cream
250	mL sour cream
	Salt and pepper

1. Melt butter together with oil in a nonstick saucepan.

2. Add onions and sauté until soft and translucent.

3. Add fresh and sour cream and season with pepper and salt.

4. Once the liquid reaches boiling point, turn off the heat and transfer the sauce to a bowl or a squeezie bottle.

5. When cool place in the refrigerator for 24 hours, by which time it should have formed a soft custard consistency. The sauce must always be cold when placed on a pizza, otherwise it will sink straight to the base and make the pizza soggy.

CHEESE

Mozzarella is the cheese of choice for pizza-makers and comes in various shapes and sizes. Unfortunately, the large white balls of fresh buffalo mozzarella common to Italy are not easily found in Australian supermarkets, but bocconcini, the Australian substitute, is readily available. In either case the cheese should be drained from its brine, ripped into rough pieces and placed on the pizza.

Yellow cow's milk mozzarella is the cheese most commonly used on Australian pizzas. It may not always be a stretched curd cheese like its buffalo cousin, but it still has similar characteristics. It has a mild flavour and melts easily to a lovely brown colour.

This is the reason why I always spread most of the mozzarella in a circle around the outer edge of a pizza and much less in the centre. When the cheese melts it 'flows' in towards the centre, so it's best not to have it too thick there to start with. Cow's milk mozzarella also leaves no oil spills and has a remarkable capacity to stretch. No other cheese gives the same sensational experience. After biting into a pizza, and pulling for what seems like forever as the cheese stretches to impossible lengths, the delicious mouthful is devoured. This is what pizza is all about – a bit messy, but marvellous!

Nobody should be deprived of pizza as it is just too good, so here's a tip for anyone who is lactose intolerant. Buy a good quality soya cheese, grate the whole block and freeze it in an airtight container. Unlike the fresh product frozen soya cheese doesn't dry out or go rubbery when used on pizza.

Mozzarella doesn't have to be used on its own. Here are four pizza recipes with distinctly different tastes because they combine mozzarella and other cheeses in classic combinations.

Acropolis

GREEK-STYLE VEGETARIAN PIZZA

2 ½   tablespoons Traditional Tomato Pizza
      Sauce (see page 74)

200   g Basic Pizza Dough ball
      (see page 61), rolled and ready

½   garlic clove, finely chopped

90   g mozzarella, grated

2   medium fresh tomatoes, sliced

2   tablespoons Kalamata olives, whole

1   small onion, sliced

35   g feta, crumbled

1   teaspoon oregano, chopped

      Extra virgin olive oil, for drizzling

1   Preheat the oven to 250°C for 25 minutes.

2   Spread tomato sauce evenly over the pizza base leaving the outer edge unsauced.

3   Sprinkle the finely chopped garlic over the sauce and scatter mozzarella cheese on the top.

4   Top with sliced tomatoes, Kalamata olives, onion slices and crumbled feta.

5   Cook pizza for seven to 10 minutes at 250°C. Remove from the oven and cut into slices.
    Garnish with chopped oregano and drizzle extra virgin olive oil over the pizza just before serving.

Little Birdy

2 ½ tablespoons cranberry sauce

200 g Basic Pizza Dough ball
       (see page 61), rolled and ready

90   g mozzarella, grated

90   g sliced smoked turkey

1   small onion, sliced

40   g brie, sliced

1   teaspoon flat-leaf parsley, chopped

     Salt

     Fresh parsley, extra, to garnish

1   Preheat the oven to 250°C for
     25 minutes.

2   Spread cranberry sauce evenly over
     the base.

3   Cover with mozzarella and top with
     smoked turkey and onions.

4   Add slices of brie last.

5   Cook pizza for seven to 10 minutes
     at 250°C. Remove from the oven
     and cut into slices.

6   Season with salt and garnish with
     fresh parsley before serving.

Smashing Pumpkin with Goat's Cheese

200 g Basic Pizza Dough ball
(see page 61), rolled and ready

90 g mozzarella, grated

30 g roasted and unsalted cashews, crushed

280 g roasted pumpkin, cubed and marinated
in one teaspoon of Basil Pesto
(see page 74)

25 mL White Cream Sauce (see page 76)

35 g goat's cheese, crumbled

extra Parmesan cheese, grated

1 teaspoon fresh parsley, chopped

10 g extra cashews, roughly chopped

10 g extra Parmesan cheese, grated

1 Preheat the oven to 250°C for 25 minutes.

2 Spread mozzarella evenly over the base.

3 Add crushed cashews and cubes of pumpkin.

4 Drizzle with White Cream Sauce.

5 Scatter crumbled goat's cheese and grated Parmesan evenly over the surface.

6 Cook pizza for seven to 10 minutes at 250°C. Remove from the oven and cut into slices.

7 Garnish with fresh parsley, extra cashews and Parmesan cheese before serving.

Quattro Fromaggio

2½ Traditional Tomato Pizza Sauce
    (see page 74)

200 g Basic Pizza Dough ball
    (see page 61), rolled and ready

90 g mozzarella, grated

35 g feta, crumbled

50 g ricotta

20 g Parmesan cheese, grated

1 teaspoon fresh parsley, chopped

1 teaspoon of other fresh herbs, such as
    oregano and marjoram, chopped

1 Preheat the oven to 250°C for
    25 minutes.

2 Spread sauce evenly over the base
    leaving the outer edge unsauced.

3 Cover with mozzarella, crumbled feta
    and ricotta.

4 Finish with grated Parmesan cheese.

5 Cook pizza for seven to 10 minutes
    at 250°C. Remove from the oven
    and cut into slices.

6 Garnish with fresh parsley and other
    herbs before serving.

4 PIZZA PRONTO

QUICK TIPS

Pizza is often described as fast food and this carries all the associated stigma of junk food. In my shop nothing could be further from the truth. In fact I describe pizza as good food made fast. With this idea in mind I suggest keeping your pantry or fridge stocked with a range of quality products for those times when you may be short of time or energy, as making a pizza is a quick and delicious answer to the perpetual question of 'What's for dinner?'

Although fresh is always best, most ingredients are available in jars and tins, or in the freezer section, but it pays to think before you buy.

- Grate your own mozzarella. Avoid prepackaged grated cheese as it is often a combination of mozzarella and cheddar, which will leave pools of oil on the pizza surface when it melts. Excess cheese can be frozen for later use, without reducing its quality or flavour.
- By adding a little extra virgin olive oil, salt, pepper, garlic or pesto to your tomato paste you will improve the consistency and flavour of this super pronto pizza sauce.
- If certain vegetables are out of season or you have run out, it's OK to use canned or marinated options.
- Good-quality ready-made pizza bases are hard to find. Steer clear of those that are 3 inches thick and look like a loaf of bread. If you don't have time to make your own dough consider using flat round pita or ready-made puff pastry.
- The recipes in this book have very specific quantities of ingredients. However, don't be put off if you don't have exactly the right amounts of anything. With the exception of the dessert pizzas you can be a bit free-form with most toppings.

Puff Pastry Margherita

1   sheet ready rolled puff pastry
     (should be 2 mm to 3 mm thick)

4   tablespoons Traditional Tomato Pizza
     Sauce (see page 74)

120 g mozzarella, grated

     Fresh tomato, sliced

     Salt and cracked black pepper

3   large fresh basil leaves, chopped

     Extra virgin olive oil, for drizzling

1   Preheat the oven to 250°C for 25 minutes.

2   Place the sheet of puff pastry on a sheet of baking paper or a greased oven tray.

3   Prick the surface with a fork leaving a 2 cm margin around the edge.

4   Spread sauce evenly over the surface up to the unpricked margin.

5   Top with grated mozzarella, starting from the outside of the pizza and working inwards.

6   Place slices of fresh tomato evenly on the cheese.

7   Cook pizza for seven to 10 minutes at 250°C.

8   Remove from the oven and season with salt and cracked black pepper. Garnish with torn or roughly chopped basil leaves
     and add a drizzle of extra virgin olive oil. Cut into slices and serve.

USING LEFTOVERS

Whenever you have leftovers in the refrigerator think about putting them on a pizza. For example, on Boxing Day why not use leftover Christmas turkey with slices of brie (or any other soft cheese), and spoonfuls of cranberry sauce in a variation of the Little Birdy pizza (see page 81)?

BE RESOURCEFUL

I hate throwing out good food and one of my classic pizzas developed as a result. Ever since Little Caesars opened we have offered three pastas and lasagne. In the early days nobody wanted to buy lasagne and due to a short shelf life I was eating lots of it. So I tried putting it on a pizza I made for my staff and other workers from surrounding shops who often shared dinner with us. It was a girl from the fish shop next door who got the pizza started. She came back the following day and ordered a 'Pisagne' for her family and friends. It was such a good name, and as we had plenty of leftover lasagne, I made one up. A few days later the family of her friends arrived and ordered a Pisagne. I thought, 'Let's put it on the menu.' That was five years ago and now it's huge!

And I didn't stop there. My friend Alain Fabregues who owns and runs The Loose Box Restaurant in Mundaring told me never to be afraid of mistakes because they open you up to new ideas. Although my Italian connections think the Pisagne is a huge mistake, I thought, 'Bugger it, I'm going to experiment.' In 2003 I developed the Chicken Fettuccine pizza. Even though it looks heavy, the base stays as flat as a tombstone and the layers of different texture on top make it sensational.

Pisagne

200 g Basic Pizza Dough ball
     (see page 61), rolled and ready

90   g mozzarella, grated

320 g beef lasagne, cooked
     (NB Only make this pizza when you have
     leftover lasagne made with layers of fresh
     pasta and a lovely Bolognese sauce
     between the layers.)

20   g Parmesan cheese, grated

1   teaspoon flat-leaf parsley, finely chopped

1   Preheat the oven to 250°C for
    25 minutes.

2   Carefully pull the layers of the
    lasagne apart and place them on
    the pizza base.

3   Cover evenly with grated mozzarella.

4   Finish with grated Parmesan cheese.

5   Cook pizza for seven to 10 minutes
    at 250°C. Remove from the oven
    and cut into slices.

6   Garnish with fresh parsley and
    Parmesan cheese before serving.

Chicken Fettuccine

200 g Basic Pizza Dough ball
(see page 61), rolled and ready

20 g semi-sun-dried tomatoes, chopped

170 g whole egg fettuccine, parboiled as per
instructions on the pack

90 g mozzarella, grated

45 g roasted chicken, diced and marinated in
1 teaspoon of Basil Pesto (see page 74)

80 g pancetta, diced

25 mL White Cream Sauce (see page 76)

20 g Parmesan cheese, grated

1 teaspoon flat-leaf parsley, finely chopped

1 Preheat the oven to 250°C for 25 minutes.

2 Place semi-sun-dried tomatoes on the base.

3 Cover with parboiled fettuccine and sprinkle with grated mozzarella.

4 Top with diced chicken and pancetta.

5 Drizzle cooled White Cream Sauce over other ingredients.

6 Cook pizza for seven to 10 minutes at 250°C. Remove from the oven and cut into slices.

7 Garnish with Parmesan cheese and parsley before serving.

5 WHAT'S IN A NAME?

MUSICAL INFLUENCES

Since Little Caesars opened in 1996 the business has been transformed. In the early days we only had 15 different pizzas on the menu, and now our customers can choose from 45 included on our revolving menu. Naming new pizzas is one of the fun parts of the job and customers are often surprised when they find out how it happens. In my case it's all about three important influences: my music, some very special people and the discovery of new tastes.

I've been into music ever since I was 14 when I bought my first single – *London Calling* by The Clash. There's always music playing in the shop. It's only ever my choice and it's probably too loud, but that's one of the perks of being the boss. Naturally, my love of music comes out in my pizzas.

CBGB is a good example. When I was in New York for my first big pizza competition I wasn't interested in sightseeing. I just wanted to go to CBGB (Country, Bluegrass and Blues), the famous punk rock nightclub. All the famous bands such as the Ramones and the Sex Pistols have played there, so I had to have a pizza to mark my visit.

Others names such as Mudhoney (see page 101) and Tea Party (see page 102) come from two of my favourite bands from North America, and Little Birdy (see page 81) is named after a local band that has established a reputation across Australia. The names are also closely linked to the pizza's ingredients, but it doesn't bother me if customers don't get the double meaning. I'm doing it to please myself! Eskimo Joe (see page 104) is a dessert pizza, and the name comes from the massive ball of ice cream that sits in the centre of the malt choc-chip cookie mix. I'm sure the band is happy to have such a cool dessert named after them.

CBGB

3	tablespoons Traditional Tomato Pizza Sauce (see page 74)
200	g Basic Pizza Dough ball (see page 61), rolled and ready
90	g mozzarella, grated
90	g unsalted Brazil nuts, crushed
35	g roasted chicken, diced
45	g seeded mustard
¼	cup roasted pumpkin, cubed
½	fresh green capsicum, deseeded, cleaned and sliced
1	small onion, thinly sliced
	Salt and cracked black pepper
	Extra virgin olive oil, for drizzling

1   Preheat the oven to 250°C for 25 minutes.

2   Spread sauce evenly over the base leaving a crust around the edge unsauced.

3   Cover the sauce with grated mozzarella and sprinkle with crushed Brazil nuts, reserving some for the garnish.

4   Mix the roasted chicken and the seeded mustard together in a separate bowl before placing on the pizza. Top off with roasted pumpkin, capsicum and onion.

5   Cook for seven to 10 minutes at 250°C.

6   Remove from the oven, cut into slices and season with salt and cracked black pepper. Garnish with reserved Brazil nuts and finish with a drizzle of extra virgin olive oil.

Mudhoney

BASE (MAKES TWO)

2	200 g Basic Pizza Dough balls (see page 61), rolled and ready
110	g caster sugar
110	g self-raising flour, triple sifted
½	tablespoon baking powder
40	g good-quality cocoa, sifted
110	g butter, diced and softened
2	large organic free-range eggs, room temperature
50	g milk chocolate, broken into small pieces

CHOCOLATE SAUCE

250	g plain chocolate, broken into pieces
200	mL fresh cream

TOPPING

15	g dark chocolate buttons
15	g white chocolate buttons
15	g milk chocolate buttons
1	tablespoon Chocolate Sauce
10	mL honey
	Icing sugar for dusting
	Vanilla-bean ice cream or fresh whipped cream (optional)

Base

1. Preheat oven to 250°C for 25 minutes.

2. Place all the dry ingredients to a bowl and rub in the softened butter until the mix is quite crumbly.

3. Break the eggs into a separate bowl and whisk until light and fluffy, then add chocolate pieces to whisked eggs.

4. Combine wet and dry ingredients. This will form a stiff cake mix which is then spread evenly on the pizza base. As usual leave a small margin on the edge of the pizza clean.

5. Bake for seven to 10 minutes at 250°C.

Chocolate Sauce

1. Put a pot of water on to boil. When the water starts to boil turn the heat down to a simmer and place a heat-proof bowl of chocolate pieces over the simmering water.

2. As the chocolate starts to melt, slowly add cream, stirring continuously until it is fully incorporated.

3. Remove the bowl from the water before the chocolate starts to simmer. If you do overcook the sauce you can save it by adding a small amount of oil and stirring until you have regained a runny consistency. Sometimes this isn't possible and it's best to start again! This sauce must be refrigerated and keeps for up to seven days.

Topping

1. Remove the pizza base and sauce from the oven and cut each pizza into eight slices.

2. Dust with icing sugar and scatter the three different types of chocolate buttons on the surface.

3. Drizzle with Chocolate Sauce and honey and serve with fresh whipped cream or vanilla-bean ice cream and a short black coffee. Perfecto!

Tea Party

1	large free-range organic egg
55	g butter, melted
85	g caster sugar
85	g plain flour, triple sifted
	Pinch of salt
½	teaspoon baking powder
1½	tablespoon icing sugar
2½	teaspoons cinnamon
200	g Basic Pizza Dough ball (see page 61), rolled and ready
½	fresh green apple, thinly sliced
½	fresh pear, thinly sliced
¼	cup raw brown sugar
	Icing sugar, to dust
	Canadian maple syrup
	Vanilla-bean ice cream, to serve

1   Preheat oven to 250°C for 25 minutes.

2   Place the egg and butter in a bowl and add the caster sugar, flour, salt, baking powder, icing sugar and cinnamon on top. Whisk together until the mixture has no lumps in it. Spread the batter on to the pizza base.

3   Place sliced apples and pears in a pan on a low heat and sprinkle with brown sugar. Cook slowly until all the fruit is coated with the melted sugar. Remove from the heat and cool. Using tongs carefully place the fruit evenly on the top of the batter.

4   Bake for seven to 10 minutes at 250°C.

5   Remove from the oven and cut into eight slices. Dust with icing sugar and drizzle with Canadian maple syrup, out of respect to the band. Serve with a scoop of vanilla-bean ice cream.

Eskimo Joe

BASE & TOPPING

1	large organic free-range egg
55	mL butter, melted
65	g caster sugar
65	g plain flour, triple sifted
15	g malt, powder (or 15 mL liquid if powder unavailable)
20	g small chocolate drops
½	teaspoon baking powder
	Pinch of salt
200	g Basic Pizza Dough ball (see page 61), rolled and ready
	Icing sugar, to dust
	Drizzle of Raspberry Sauce
	Vanilla-bean ice cream, to serve

RASPBERRY SAUCE

250	g raspberries (This recipe also works for most other berry fruits such as strawberries and blueberries.)
75	g caster sugar

1. Preheat oven to 250°C for 25 minutes.

2. Place the egg and butter in a bowl and add the caster sugar, flour, malt, chocolate drops, baking powder and salt on top. Whisk together until there are no lumps in the mixture.

3. Spread the batter on the pizza base.

4. Bake for seven to 10 minutes at 250°C.

5. Remove from the oven and cut into eight slices. Dust with icing sugar and drizzle with Raspberry Sauce. Serve with a scoop of vanilla-bean ice cream.

1. Wash the fruit and pat dry.

2. Cut the fruit coarsely before placing in a heavy-based saucepan over a low heat.

3. Add the sugar and stir occasionally until the sugar is dissolved and then emove from heat. The mixture will look very runny at the start, but it will thicken after cooling for 1½ to two hours. For drizzling it needs to be the consistency of honey. When it has cooled completely transfer the sauce into a squeezie bottle for drizzling over your pizza. Don't worry about having lots left over because it is great poured over ice-cream or thick Greek-style yogurt!

SPECIAL PEOPLE

Over the years I've meet some special people whose names or products have gone into the mix when I'm creating Little Caesars pizzas.

Vince Gareffa, the owner of Mondo Butchers in Perth, is a crazy character who wears T-shirts printed with FBI, which in his case stands for Full Blooded Italian. It's no surprise he calls himself the Prince of Flesh. His famous, locally produced, milk-fed veal and organically grown pork are used on White Rocks Roast and Organic Pork with Apple Sauce, two of our famous meat pizzas. The beauty of these pizzas is they can be made the day after you've had a roast dinner when you have leftovers.

Don Hancey is another local food entrepreneur, who has encouraged me to use local products on my pizzas, and so I named The Don after him. It uses Fremantle sardines marinated in locally produced extra virgin olive oil, flavoured with lemon myrtle. This is a wonderful collection of Western Australian tastes.

The person who has seriously changed my thinking about the way I make pizza is Alain Fabreques, a funny and amazing man whose restaurant, The Loose Box, has been a landmark in Mundaring since the early 1980s. He taught me to be passionate about food and to really think about the way I do

things. When Alain asked me to cook for his staff Christmas party I thought, 'No way – you must be dreaming'. But I eventually I did and I'm glad he gave me the confidence I needed. It's good to be reminded that simple food doesn't have to be unsophisticated. Thanks to Alain's encouragement Little Caesars now has the King Prawn & Pancetta pizza on the menu.

The King Prawn & Pancetta pizza is also known as Jane's Addiction after a local ABC TV host Jane Cunningham who fell in love with it when we were filming a segment for the ABC TV programme, *How the Quest was Won*. Jane isn't the only local media

Vince

personality who has helped me in some way. Others such as Todd Johnston, Natalie Locke and Nathan Morris have all played a role in promoting Little Caesars.

Nathan and Nat are presenters on Nova Radio in Perth, and I named a pizza after them simply because they decided to run a competition to let their listeners select the ingredients for a new pizza. Unfortunately, all the listeners' suggestions were disgusting, when we came off-air Nathan and Nat decided they could do better. Armed with their wish list I had one week to come up with a pizza.

The trickiest part was the taste test. I had to be at the radio station early on Friday morning. Thursday night is always really busy, so I didn't get home until 12:30am, then I was up again at 5am and off to the shop to make the pizza! To get to the radio station on time I had to drive like crazy for 50 minutes in peak-hour traffic, with the heater on full bore, hoping like hell I'd still have a good-looking pizza when I arrived.

The proof that Nathan and Nat had done me a great favour was obvious later in the day. At 4:15pm the first pizza ordered was – you guessed it – a Nathan & Nat.

DISCOVERING NEW TASTES

Other pizzas have come about after I've eaten something new and wanted to try it out on a pizza. I first tasted sweet Thai chilli sauce when I ordered some wedges and sour cream. I was confident it would work well with other ingredients, and that's how the Hot Sweet Thai Chilli Prawn pizza (see page 120) was born.

Other names come from famous combinations that work equally well such as my Greek Lamb pizza (see page 124). The traditional Greek taste of roast lamb cooked with lots of lemon and rosemary simply couldn't be called anything else. It is what it is – a straight-out punk rock star!

White Rocks Roast

90 g mozzarella, grated

200 g Basic Pizza Dough ball
(see page 61), rolled and ready

120 g roasted White Rocks veal, diced

65 g roasted potatoes, sliced

55 g onion, finely sliced

1½ tablespoons White Cream Sauce
(see page 76)

20 g Parmesan cheese, grated

1 teaspoon oregano, finely chopped

Salt

1   Preheat the oven to 250°C for 25 minutes.

2   Spread mozzarella around pizza base, with more at the outer edges than the centre.

3   Place diced veal on the cheese and top with slices of roasted potatoes and onions.
These ingredients will prevent the veal from overcooking.

4   Drizzle with White Cream Sauce and top off with half the grated Parmesan cheese
and oregano.

5   Cook for seven to 10 minutes at 250°C.

6   Remove from the oven, cut into slices and season to taste. Garnish with the remaining
oregano and grated Parmesan cheese if required.

Roast Pork

1	teaspoon salt
¼	teaspoon cracked black pepper
¼	teaspoon fennel seeds
½	teaspoon lemon thyme
1½	kg organic pork roll
3	garlic cloves, peeled
	Extra virgin olive oil

1   Place salt, pepper, fennel seeds and lemon thyme in a mortar and pestle.

2   Roughly pound the herbs and spices into a coarse powder.

3   Using a thin, long knife stab the pork roll and insert a garlic clove into the centre.
Repeat until all cloves are embedded.

4   On a bench spread the herb mix around. Rub the pork with extra virgin olive oil and then roll
it onto the herb mix, covering the entire surface, including the ends.

5   Place onto a baking tray and cover with foil and bake for about 1 hour and 30 minutes.

6   Remove roast and leave it to rest for 10 minutes before carving.

Organic Pork with Apple Sauce

BASE & TOPPING

2½ tablespoons Apple Sauce

200 g Basic Pizza Dough ball
(see page 61), rolled and ready

90 g mozzarella, grated

120 g roasted organic pork, diced
(see page 109)

55 g red Spanish onion, sliced finely

30 g potato roasted with garlic, sliced

30 g sweet potato roasted, sliced

1½ tablespoons White Cream Sauce
(see page 76)
Salt and cracked black pepper

½ tablespoon Apple Sauce, extra

20 g pork crackling
Salt and cracked black pepper

APPLE SAUCE

2 green medium-sized Granny Smith apples,
peeled, cored and diced

25 g butter

½ a lemon, juiced

3 tablespoons fresh cream
Pinch of salt and white pepper

½ teaspoon caster sugar (use only if apples
are not sweet enough)

1 Preheat oven to 250°C for 25 minutes.

2 Spread Apple Sauce around evenly over the pizza base and top with grated mozzarella.

3 Scatter the diced pork evenly over the cheese and top with slices of Spanish onion and two types of roasted potatoes.

4 Drizzle White Cream Sauce evenly over the surface.

5 Cook for 10 minutes at 250°C.

6 Remove from the oven, cut into slices and season with salt and cracked black pepper. Garnish with a dollop of Apple Sauce on each slice and place pieces of pork crackling on the side of the serving plate.

1 Place the apples in a small saucepan with a little water and cook over a medium heat, stirring occasionally. When the apples break down to a soft consistency (i.e. after about 15 minutes) add the butter, lemon juice and cream.

2 Season with salt and pepper to taste and continue stirring until a purée is formed. Take off the heat and taste before adjusting the seasoning. If the sauce is not sweet enough add caster sugar at this stage.

3 Place back on a low heat to dissolve the caster sugar, before pouring into a small bowl to cool. Always wait until the sauce is completely cool before using on a pizza. This sauce can be kept in the fridge for up to seven days so there's no need for sterilising jars and all that rubbish!

The Don

2½	tablespoons Traditional Tomato Pizza Sauce (see page 74)
200	g Basic Pizza Dough ball (see page 61), rolled and ready
90	g mozzarella, grated
80	g fresh tomatoes, sliced
60	g marinated Fremantle sardines (use sardines that have been marinated in olive oil and herbs such as native lemon myrtle)
	Salt and cracked black pepper
1	teaspoon fresh chives, finely chopped
1	lemon, cut into wedges

1 Preheat oven to 250°C for 25 minutes.

2 Spread Traditional Tomato Pizza Sauce over base and top with grated mozzarella.

3 Place a layer of sliced tomato on the cheese.

4 Remove the excess liquid from the sardines and place them at even intervals around the pizza.

5 Cook for seven to 10 minutes at 250°C.

6 Remove from the oven, cut into slices and season with salt and cracked black pepper. Garnish with chopped chives and serve with lemon wedges.

Jane's Addiction

AKA KING PRAWN & PROSCIUTTO

90	g mozzarella, grated
200	g Basic Pizza Dough ball (see page 61), rolled and ready
140	g raw peeled prawns, marinated in 9 g of Basil Pesto (see page 74) and a pinch of cracked black pepper
30	g prosciutto, sliced
1½	tablespoons White Cream Sauce (see page 76)
	Salt and cracked black pepper
1	teaspoon fresh chives, chopped
3	lemon wedges

1. Clean and marinate the prawns. To clean, hold the prawn tail in one hand and use the other to rip off its head. Peel the shell on the tail away from the flesh. Make a cut with a sharp knife down the back of the tail which will expose the prawn's 'trail' (gut), which must be removed before cooking. Wash the prawn in clean running water and pat the flesh completely dry with a paper towel before marinating.

2. Preheat oven to 250°C for 25 minutes.

3. Spread mozzarella around pizza base, with more at the outer edges than the centre.

4. Place the marinated prawns at evenly spaced intervals around the pizza. Wrap the prawns with a slice of prosciutto to protect them from overcooking.

5. Drizzle with White Cream Sauce.

6. Cook for seven to 10 minutes at 250°C.

7. Remove from the oven, cut into slices and season with salt and cracked black pepper. Garnish with freshly chopped chives and serve with lemon wedges.

Nathan & Nat

90	g mozzarella, grated
200	g Basic Pizza Dough ball (see page 61), rolled and ready
10	g pine nuts
45	g roasted chicken, diced and marinated in the juice of one lemon and a pinch of salt and pepper
30	g prosciutto, sliced
40	g roasted pumpkin, marinated in a teaspoon of Basil Pesto (see page 74)
60	g roasted red capsicum, sliced
1½	tablespoons White Cream Sauce (see page 76)
3	lemon wedges
1	teaspoon fresh flat-leaf parsley, chopped

1   Preheat oven to 250°C for 25 minutes.

2   Spread grated mozzarella around pizza base, with more at the outer edges than the centre.

3   Scatter pine nuts over the cheese and then place the rest of the ingredients in the following order: roasted chicken, prosciutto, roasted pumpkin and red capsicum.

4   Drizzle with White Cream Sauce.

5   Cook for seven to 10 minutes at 250°C.

6   Remove from the oven and cut into slices. Garnish with freshly chopped flat-leaf parsley and lemon wedges.

Hot Sweet Thai Chilli Prawn

90   g mozzarella, grated

200   g Basic Pizza Dough ball
       (see page 61), rolled and ready

100   g large uncooked prawns, peeled

80   g onion, sliced finely

1½   tablespoons sweet Thai chilli sauce
       (any *hot* commercial variety)

1   tablespoon sour cream

       Salt

½   teaspoon chilli flakes

1   teaspoon fresh parsley, finely chopped

3   lemon wedges

1. Preheat oven to 250°C for 25 minutes.

2. Spread mozzarella around pizza base, with more at the outer edges than the centre.

3. Place the prawns evenly around the pizza and cover with slices of onion. Drizzle hot sweet Thai chilli sauce all over the pizza and finish with dollops of sour cream placed randomly.

4. Cook for seven to 10 minutes at 250°C.

5. Remove from the oven, cut into slices and season with salt to taste. Garnish with dried chilli flakes and freshly chopped parsley. Serve with lemon wedges.

Roast Lamb

LAMB

1	leg of lamb (around 2 kg)
	Salt and cracked black pepper
1	lemon, juiced
1	bunch of fresh rosemary
4	garlic cloves, roughly chopped
	Extra virgin olive oil

CARAMELISED ONIONS

20	g butter
1	tablespoon olive oil
1	kg red onion, thinly sliced
500	g raw brown sugar

1. Preheat oven to 220°C for 30 minutes.

2. Take lamb out of fridge and allow to come to room temperature.

3. With a damp cloth wipe the lamb to get rid of any excess moisture, then using the tip of a sharp knife make small holes in the flesh.

4. Rub with salt and pepper pushing it into the small holes then repeat with the rosemary and garlic.

5. Drizzle the lemon juice and olive oil over the leg of lamb and massage into the flesh.

6. Place into a baking tray, cover with foil and bake for two hours. NB Cooking time is calculated by allowing an hour for each kg and an extra 15 minutes for every 250g. A slow cooking time ensures that the meat is cooked well enough that it falls off the bone.

7. Take out of the oven, remove the foil and test the meat by pushing the flesh. If it springs back quickly it is no way near ready. If it is beginning to fall off the bone turn the leg over and return to the oven for another 15 minutes. Then take it out and let it rest for 10 minutes before carving.

1. Melt butter and olive oil together in a nonstick saucepan.

2. Add onions and sauté until soft and translucent and then add the raw brown sugar.

3. Turn the heat down to very low and continue cooking, stirring occasionally, until the onions turn a lovely golden brown. This process will take about 20 minutes. The end result should be a nice thick onion mixture, a bit like a sweet jam.

123

Greek Lamb

90   g mozzarella, grated

200   g Basic Pizza Dough ball
       (see page 61), rolled and ready

110   g lamb, oven roasted with lemon and
       rosemary, and diced (see page 123)

35   g feta, diced

20   g Kalamata olives, pitted and halved

2   tablespoons Caramelised Onions
       (see page 123)

3   lemon wedges

2   tablespoons Tzatziki Dip (see page 135)

½   teaspoon rosemary

       Cracked black pepper

1   Preheat oven to 250°C for 25 minutes.

2   Spread mozzarella around pizza base, with more at the outer edges than the centre.

3   Place diced roasted lamb evenly around the pizza and follow with crumbled feta
       and Kalamata olives. Add a layer of Caramelised Onions which will protect the lamb
       from overcooking.

4   Cook for seven to 10 minutes at 250°C.

5   Remove from the oven and cut into slices.

6   Drizzle Tzatziki Dip over the pizza and garnish with chopped rosemary. Serve with lemon
       wedges and suggest that your guests squeeze a little lemon juice on each slice before they
       start munching.

GETTING IT RIGHT

Before opening Little Caesars I spent nine months checking out other pizza places in Perth. I'd looked, tasted and decided what worked and what didn't. I devised recipes and practised making them. Our opening day was incredible and I owe much to Uncle Caesar for our survival on that day. About five minutes before we opened I realised I'd forgotten about a float for the till. Caesar knew I'd forget, and had brought one with him – just in case.

By the end of the day I thought things had gone fairly well, but then a woman appeared at the door carrying three family-sized pizza boxes and demanding to know who owned the shop. As a behind-the-scenes baker I wasn't used to customer service so I simply said, 'I do.' The three pizza boxes were suddenly flying across the shop, heading straight for me.

'They're raw, they taste like shit and I want my money back,' she yelled.

I was stunned. It was impossible to believe this was happening on day one. I apologised immediately, went straight to the till, gave her the money back, locked the door, and then I cried!

It was terrible. Mostly because I knew she was right. We'd started with too little money. The oven wasn't good enough, we weren't putting on enough toppings and we just weren't doing anything right. But it didn't stay that way. Once I'd sorted the problems out I went back to the woman with a peace offering. I asked her to give the pizzas another go with no strings attached, as an act of good faith. It was a test for both of us. These days she's one of our best customers, and loves telling the story to everyone.

Luckily not all the lessons have been that difficult and these days I've got a shop that really kicks arse!

6 FAMILY FEASTS

GREEK EASTER

There's nothing quite like a Greek Orthodox Easter to celebrate the joys of eating. It's actually a whole week of eating that follows a long period of fasting.

During Lent, which is the 40 days leading up to Easter Sunday, members of the Greek Orthodox Church are supposed to stop eating a range of foods. In our house we would give up meat. Fasting didn't bother me too much, but it was a big deal for Dad. By the time Lent was over my Dad was going to make up for it! So it was not surprising that my mother started preparing early on Saturday for the breaking of the fast. She always began by making *mayiritsa,* a hearty soup, full of braised meat and vegies. She was also a champion dessert- and pastry-maker and my brothers and I waited all year for her Kourabiedes, those classic almond crescent cookies, smothered in icing sugar.

At midnight we would all go to church. When we came out every family would light a candle from the church candles and carry it home making sure it didn't go out. When we got home Dad would make a sign of the cross on the doorframe with the candle soot, then the fast was broken with Mum's special soup. Mum would then prepare the Sunday roast. At lunch time the whole extended family turned up.

MAKE YOUR OWN PIZZA FEAST

I still think feasts have a role, but why wait until Easter or Christmas? In Australia where outdoor entertaining is so popular, family feasts for small or large numbers can be easily created around the simple pizza. It's a meal to be shared, savoured and analysed by everyone. Is the Roma sauce sweet enough? Does the mozzarella stretch to just the right consistency? Is the pancetta crispy enough to eat on its own let alone be surrounded by all the other delicious ingredients? The following selection of recipes will enable you to prepare a delicious banquet for family and friends from entrée through to dessert.

Kourabiedes

200 g whole almonds, skin removed
(or 200 g almond meal)

450 g butter (at room temperature)

200 g caster sugar

3 organic free-range eggs, yolks only

1 teaspoon vanilla-bean paste or seeds
from 1 vanilla pod

900 g plain flour, triple sifted

2 teaspoons baking powder

60 mL water

Icing sugar for dusting

1 Preheat the oven to 190°C.

2 Line a flat tray with baking paper. Spread the almonds evenly across the surface and bake them for about five minutes or until they are lightly browned. Keep a close eye on them because they burn easily.

3 Remove the roasted almonds from the oven and leave them to cool before placing in a food processor. Pulse until they are chopped finely. This stage can be done by hand but the finished product must be very fine.

4 Cream the soft butter and the sugar in a medium-sized bowl. Add the egg yolks one at a time, followed by the vanilla-bean paste or vanilla bean seeds.

5 Add the sifted flour, baking powder and the finely chopped almonds to the creamed ingredients. Slowly bring the mix together to form a ball. Place the mixture on a floured bench top and knead it into a smooth dough.

6 Using a rolling pin, roll the dough out until it is 2 cm thick. Cut out half-moon-shaped cookies using a glass and place on a tray lined with baking paper. Keep bringing the leftover dough together, re-rolling it and cutting cookies until it is all used.

7 Bake for 20 minutes at 190°C.

8 Remove from the oven and cool on a wire rack, before drenching in icing sugar. These biscuits are the best!

Taramasalata

FISH ROE DIP

2	small potatoes, peeled, boiled and cooled
150	g salmon caviar
250	mL extra virgin olive oil
1½	lemons, juiced
2	tablespoons white wine vinegar
½	white onion, finely grated

OLIVE & OREGANO DIPPING BASE

200	g Basic Pizza Dough ball (see page 61)
1½	tablespoons Kalamata olives, pitted and chopped
1	teaspoon dried oregano
1	teaspoon sea salt
1	teaspoon extra virgin olive oil

1   Place cooled potatoes in a blender and process until smooth. Add the salmon caviar to potatoes and pulse to combine. If the salmon caviar is too salty it can be softened by adding a little crème fraîche (or sour cream).

2   While continuing to blend, slowly drizzle in all the extra virgin olive oil. Add the lemon juice, white wine vinegar and grated onion. Be sure to squeeze all the juice from the grated onion before adding it to the dip. Allow the dip to sit in the fridge for at least 30 minutes before serving. Taramasalata will last for up to seven days in the fridge.

1   Preheat the oven to 250°C for 25 minutes.

2   Use the ingredients above and the method for making Flavoured Pizza Dough (see page 58).

3   Cook for four to five minutes at 250°C. Remove from the oven, cut into small wedges and serve warm with the dip.

Tzatziki

DIP

500	g thick plain Greek-style yogurt
1	medium-sized continental cucumber, peeled, deseeded and finely diced
1	garlic clove, finely chopped
3	teaspoons extra virgin olive oil
1	tablespoon white wine vinegar
1	tablespoon fresh dill, finely chopped
	Salt to taste

ROCK SALT & PARSLEY DIPPING BASE

200	g Basic Pizza Dough ball (see page 61)
1	teaspoon rock salt
1	teaspoon fresh parsley, chopped finely
1	teaspoon extra virgin olive oil

1. Mix all the ingredients together in a large bowl and season with salt to taste.

2. Refrigerate for at least 20 minutes before serving.

1. Preheat the oven to 250°C for 25 minutes.

2. Use the ingredients above and the method for making Flavoured Pizza Dough (see page 58).

3. Cook for four to five minutes at 250°C. Remove from the oven, cut into small wedges and serve warm with the dip.

White Bean Dip

ITALIAN-STYLE HUMMUS

400	g canned cannelleni white beans, drained and washed
2½	tablespoons fresh flat-leaf parsley, chopped finely
2	tablespoons fresh lemon juice
1	garlic clove, finely chopped
½	teaspoon rock salt
	Pinch cracked black pepper
80	mL extra virgin olive oil

SMOKED PAPRIKA, SEA SALT & THYME DIPPING BASE

200	g Basic Pizza Dough ball (see page 61)
½	teaspoon smoked paprika
1	teaspoon sea salt
1	teaspoon fresh thyme, finely chopped
1	teaspoon extra virgin olive oil

1   Place beans, parsley, lemon juice, garlic, salt and cracked black pepper in the food processor and pulse gently until the mixture is broken down slightly.

2   Next, at a slow speed, drizzle extra virgin olive oil into the mix. The end result is a light and creamy dip.

1   Preheat the oven to 250°C for 25 minutes.

2   Use the ingredients above and the method for making Flavoured Pizza Dough (see page 58).

3   Cook for four to five minutes at 250°C. Remove from the oven, cut into small wedges or rip into pieces and serve warm with the dip.

Caprese Tricolore Salata

SALAD

200 g fresh mozzarella balls or bocconcini
balls, sliced into rounds

300 g Roma tomatoes, sliced

20 g fresh basil, coarsely chopped

300 g cherry tomatoes, sliced in half

300 g yellow pear tomatoes, sliced in half

Caprese Tricolore Salata Dressing
for drizzling

Salt and cracked black pepper

DRESSING

3 tablespoons lemon juice

Salt and cracked black pepper

3 tablespoons extra virgin olive oil

PARMESAN & PINE NUT CROUTONS

200 g rams Basic Pizza Dough ball
(see page 61)

1 teaspoon pine nuts, toasted and chopped

1 tablespoon Parmesan cheese, grated

½ teaspoon sea salt

½ teaspoon Basil Pesto (see page 74)

1 teaspoon extra virgin olive oil

1 Using a large platter arrange the slices
of Roma tomatoes and mozzarella
one after another in successive circles
evenly around platter.

2 Mix the basil with the cherry and pear
tomatoes in a separate bowl and
then pile into the centre of the dish.

3 Drizzle with Caprese Tricolore Salata
Dressing and season lightly with
salt and pepper. As my wife Liz
would say this dish is nice and light
– perfect for summer!

1 Whisk ingredients together, place in
an air tight container and store in
the fridge for at least 30 minutes.

1 Preheat the oven to 250°C for
25 minutes.

2 Use the ingredients above and the
method for making Flavoured Pizza
Dough (see page 58).

3 Cook for four to five minutes at
250°C. Remove from the oven,
cut into small wedges and serve
with salad.

Caesar Salad

DRESSING

40	g garlic, finely chopped
40	g spring onion, finely chopped
60	mL good-quality balsamic vinegar
40	g seeded mustard
20	mL lemon juice
3	anchovy fillets, very finely chopped
1	large free-range organic egg yolk
1	cup extra virgin olive oil
	Salt, as required
	Pinch of paprika
1	teaspoon flat-leaf parsley, chopped finely

SALAD

140	g romaine or cos lettuce, washed and patted dry
100	g prosciutto, grilled and crispy
40	g Parmesan cheese, shaved

CRACKED PEPPER, PROSCIUTTO & PARMESAN CROUTONS

200	g Basic Pizza Dough ball (see page 61)
	Cracked black pepper
2	slices prosciutto, grilled and very finely chopped
1	tablespoon Parmesan cheese, grated
1	teaspoon fresh rosemary, finely chopped
1	teaspoon extra virgin olive oil

1 Place the first six dressing ingredients in a food processor and process until they form a fine purée. By adding the anchovies in the dressing mix the extra flavour goes into the salad and no-one has to pick them out of the salad!

2 Add the egg yolk to the mix and pulse until dispersed evenly.

3 At a low speed drizzle in the extra virgin olive oil. Patience is important at this stage because adding the oil quickly may cause the dressing to curdle. The finished dressing should have the consistency of runny custard. Always taste the dressing before adding any salt, then fold in the paprika and parsley. This will make a serious amount of dressing and more than you will need for one salad. However, it can easily be stored in the fridge for several days.

4 Place lettuce leaves in a bowl and drizzle with prepared dressing. Carefully toss the leaves using tongs to avoid bruising. Transfer to a serving bowl.

5 Place the slices of grilled prosciutto on top of the leaves and finish the salad with shaved Parmesan cheese.

1 Preheat the oven to 250°C for 25 minutes.

2 Use the ingredients above and the method for making Flavoured Pizza Dough (see page 58).

3 Cook for four to five minutes at 250°C. Remove from the oven, cut into small wedges and serve warm with salad.

Greek Salad

SALAD

4	medium-sized truss tomatoes
1	garlic clove, finely chopped
1	green capsicum, deseeded and thinly sliced
1	yellow capsicum, deseeded and thinly sliced
1	large continental cucumber, peeled and sliced
125	g Kalamata olives
125	g feta, roughly broken (reserve 25 g for garnish)
60	mL extra virgin olive oil
15	mL balsamic vinegar
½	teaspoon flat-leaf parsley, coarsely chopped
¼	teaspoon dried oregano

OREGANO & GARLIC CROUTONS

200	g Basic Pizza Dough ball (see page 61)
½	medium-sized garlic clove, finely chopped
1	teaspoon dried oregano
1	teaspoon sea salt
1	teaspoon extra virgin olive oil

1 Combine the tomatoes, garlic, capsicums and cucumber in a large bowl and toss.

2 Add the Kalamata olives and feta and gently mix through the salad.

3 Drizzle with extra virgin olive oil and balsamic vinegar just before serving. Crumble reserved feta on top and scatter with fresh parsley and dried oregano.

1 Preheat the oven to 250°C for 25 minutes.

2 Use the ingredients above and the method for making Flavoured Pizza Dough (see page 58).

3 Cook for four to five minutes at 250°C. Remove from the oven, cut into small wedges and serve warm with salad.

Smoked Salmon

2½   tablespoons Traditional Tomato Pizza
     Sauce (see page 74)

200 g Basic Pizza Dough ball
     (see page 61), rolled and ready

90   g mozzarella, grated

40   g smoked salmon (fresh or frozen)

80   g red onion, finely sliced

20   g capers

1   tablespoon crème fraîche or sour cream

1   teaspoon fresh chives, finely chopped

     Pinch of poppy seeds

1   Preheat oven to 250°C for 25 minutes.

2   Spread Traditional Tomato Pizza Sauce evenly over the pizza base, leaving the outer
     edge unsauced.

3   Spread mozzarella around the pizza base with more at the outer edges than at the centre.

4   If the smoked salmon is frozen it can be added at this stage and topped with red onions and
     capers (if salmon is fresh it should be reserved and added as soon as the pizza is removed
     from the oven).

5   Cook for seven to 10 minutes at 250°C.

6   Remove from oven the and cut into slices. Place a dollop of crème fraîche or sour cream on
     each slice and garnish with chopped chives and poppy seeds.

Chicken Satay

3	tablespoons Satay Sauce (see page 76)
200	g Basic Pizza Dough ball (see page 61), rolled and ready
40	g button mushrooms, sliced
90	g mozzarella, grated
45	g roasted chicken, diced
40	g green capsicum, thinly sliced
55	g white onion, thinly sliced
1	teaspoon coriander leaves, finely chopped
1	tablespoon roasted unsalted cashews, crushed
½	red chilli, finely sliced

1   Preheat oven to 250°C for 25 minutes.

2   Spread satay sauce evenly over the pizza base, leaving the outer edge sauce-free.

3   Scatter button mushrooms on top of the sauce and spread grated mozzarella evenly over the mushrooms.

4   Place diced chicken evenly around the pizza and top with capsicum and onion.

5   Cook for seven to 10 minutes at 250°C.

6   Remove from the oven and cut into slices. Garnish with chilli, chopped coriander and cashews before serving.

Lemon Chicken

90	g mozzarella, grated
200	g Basic Pizza Dough ball (see page 61), rolled and ready
120	g roasted chicken, diced and marinated in the juice of one lemon
60	g red capsicum, roasted
40	g fresh green capsicum, sliced
55	g onion, thinly sliced
1½	tablespoons White Cream Sauce (see page 76)
	Salt and lemon pepper
3	lemon wedges

1   Preheat oven to 250°C for 25 minutes.

2   Spread mozzarella around the pizza base with more at the outer edges than at the centre.

3   Place chicken pieces on the cheese and top with slices of capsicum and onion. Season with salt and lemon pepper.

4   Cook for seven to 10 minutes at 250°C.

5   Remove from the oven and cut into slices. Serve with lemon wedges.

Roman Empire

2½   tablespoons Traditional Tomato Pizza
     Sauce (see page 74)

200 g Basic Pizza Dough ball
     (see page 61), rolled and ready

50   g cacciatore (or any similar hung and
     dried Italian sausage), sliced

90   g mozzarella, grated

110 g roasted eggplant, marinated in Basil
     Pesto (see page 74) and a pinch of salt

70   g ricotta

     Salt

½   teaspoon flat-leaf parsley

1   Preheat oven to 250°C for 25 minutes.

2   Spread Traditional Tomato Pizza Sauce over the pizza base, and place the slices of Italian
    sausage evenly on the sauce.

3   Spread grated mozzarella over the sausage layer, followed by the marinated eggplant and top
    with the ricotta.

4   Cook for seven to 10 minutes at 250°C.

5   Remove from the oven, cut into slices and season with salt to taste. Garnish with flat-leaf
    parsley and serve.

Greek Island Prawn

110 g large raw prawns, shelled
and deveined

½ garlic clove, chopped

Cracked black pepper

90 g mozzarella, grated

200 g Basic Pizza Dough ball
(see page 61), rolled and ready

20 g Kalamata olives, pitted

35 g feta, cubed

60 g red capsicum, roasted and
skin removed

2½ tablespoons Traditional Tomato Pizza
Sauce (see page 74)

½ teaspoon fresh flat-leaf parsley, chopped

Pinch of oregano

3 lemon wedges

1 Marinate the prawns in the chopped garlic and cracked black pepper for at least five minutes.

2 Preheat oven to 250°C for 25 minutes.

3 Spread the mozzarella around the pizza base, with more at the outer edges than the centre.

4 Place the marinated prawns evenly around the pizza, followed by Kalamata olives, cubed feta and slices of roasted capsicum.

5 Drizzle the Traditional Tomato Pizza Sauce over the top of all the ingredients. You will be amazed at the difference in the flavour of this pizza compared with those where the sauce is placed directly on the base.

6 Cook for seven to 10 minutes at 250°C.

7 Remove from the oven and cut into slices. Garnish with chopped flat-leaf parsley, oregano and lemon wedges.

Pearsciutto

2½ tablespoons Traditional Tomato Pizza
    Sauce (see page 74)

200 g Basic Pizza Dough ball
    (see page 61), rolled and ready

90 g mozzarella, grated

45 g prosciutto, thinly sliced

70 g fresh pears, thinly sliced

20 g raw brown sugar

½   teaspoon flat-leaf parsley, finely chopped

1   Preheat oven to 250°C for 25 minutes.

2   Spread the Traditional Tomato Pizza Sauce over the pizza base and top with mozzarella.
    Remember to put more cheese on the outer edges than in the centre.

3   Place slices of prosciutto evenly over the cheese and top with sliced pears.
    Sprinkle brown sugar evenly over the pears.

4   Cook for seven to 10 minutes at 250°C.

5   Remove from the oven and cut into slices. Garnish with flat-leaf parsley and serve.
    This pizza really looks and tastes great because the brown sugar semi-caramelises the pears
    and adds a nice sweetness to them.

Barbecue

3   tablespoons good-quality barbecue sauce

200 g Basic Pizza Dough ball
    (see page 61), rolled and ready

90   g leg ham, sliced

90   g mozzarella, grated

35   g Italian pepperoni, sliced

45   g roasted chicken, diced

80   g eye bacon, diced

1   Preheat oven to 250°C for 25 minutes.

2   Spread the barbecue sauce evenly over the pizza base and top with ham. Spread grated mozzarella next followed by pepperoni, roasted chicken and the bacon pieces. Drizzle a little extra barbecue sauce on top for extra flavour.

3   Cook for seven to 10 minutes at 250°C.

4   Remove from the oven, cut into slices and serve.

Apple Strudel

PIZZA

200 g Basic Pizza Dough ball
(see page 61), rolled and ready

2 tablespoons Custard

60 g sultanas

200 g apples, poached or steamed,
cooled and then sliced

Icing sugar, for dusting

Cinnamon, for dusting

½ cup fresh cream, whipped

CUSTARD

1 tablespoon custard powder

1 tablespoon caster sugar

125 mL milk

½ teaspoon vanilla bean paste

1 Preheat oven to 250°C for
25 minutes.

2 Spread custard evenly on the pizza
base and sprinkle with sultanas.
Place the slices of cooled apple
evenly all over pizza.

3 Cook for seven to 10 minutes
at 250°C.

4 Remove from the oven and cut into
slices. Dust with icing sugar and
cinnamon and place a dollop of
cream on each slice before serving.

1 Whisk the custard powder and
sugar with milk in a small bowl
and then transfer to a small heavy-
based saucepan.

2 Place on low heat and stir until the
custard starts to boil and thicken.
Remove from the heat and add the
vanilla bean paste.

3 Pour into a bowl and allow to cool
completely before spreading on
a pizza base. The custard can be
made in advance, placed in a
sealed container and stored in the
fridge for up to seven days.

Baked Upside-Down Lemon Cheesecake

PIZZA

140	g cream cheese, softened
50	mL thickened cream
½	teaspoon lemon zest
1	fresh organic free-range egg
½	tablespoon lemon juice
2½	tablespoons icing sugar
200	g Basic Pizza Dough ball (see page 61), rolled and ready
6	Granita biscuits, crushed
35	g butter, melted
125	g strawberries, washed, hulled and halved
75	g strawberry jam mixed with ½ tablespoon Strawberry Sauce
	Icing sugar, for dusting

STRAWBERRY SAUCE

50	g caster sugar
100	mL water
300	g strawberries washed and dehulled

1   Preheat oven to 250°C for 25 minutes.

2   Using a food processor or cake mixer, with a paddle or whisk, combine cream cheese, thickened cream, lemon zest, egg, lemon juice and icing sugar, and mix to a smooth, thick paste.

3   Spread this cheesecake mix evenly over pizza base.

4   Place crushed Granita biscuits in a small bowl and add the melted butter. Mix gently until combined.

5   Carefully press biscuit mix into cheesecake mix.

6   Cook for seven to 10 minutes at 250°C.

7   Remove from the oven. Place strawberry halves evenly over the surface and drizzle with Strawberry Sauce. Dust with icing sugar, cut into slices and serve.

1   Place the sugar and water into a saucepan and cook over a medium heat stirring constantly for five minutes. If it looks like it will boil over turn the heat down.

2   Place the strawberries in a food processor and puree.

3   Stir the strawberry puree into the sugar syrup and if it looks too runny continue to cook over a low heat until it thickens.

Black Forest

PIZZA

55	g butter, softened
55	g caster sugar
55	g self-raising flour, triple sifted
¼	tablespoon baking powder
20	g cocoa
1	free-range organic egg
200	g Basic Pizza Dough ball (see page 61), rolled and ready
85	g black cherries, pitted and halved (retain syrup from tin)
	Icing sugar, for dusting
	Vanilla-bean ice cream
180	g good-quality dark chocolate, chopped
	Cherry Sauce

1   Preheat the oven to 250°C for 25 minutes.

2   Place the butter and the caster sugar in a bowl and rub together to form a crumbly mix. Add the self-raising flour, baking powder and cocoa.

3   In a separate bowl lightly beat the egg before adding to the other ingredients. Using a whisk mix until the batter is smooth then spread onto pizza base.

4   Place the cherry halves evenly across the top of the cake mix.

5   Cook for seven to 10 minutes at 250°C.

6   Remove from the oven, cut into slices and dust with icing sugar. Place several scoops of vanilla ice cream in centre of the pizza and scatter the pieces of dark chocolate over the surface. Drizzle Cherry Sauce over the lot before serving.

CHERRY SAUCE

Black cherry syrup left over from tin (see Black Forest Ingredients)

Caster sugar (see Method for quantity)

1   Drain the syrup from the cherries and calculate the weight of the syrup. That is, deduct the weight of the can from the combined weight of the can and the syrup.

2   Divide the weight of the syrup by two and add that weight in caster sugar to the liquid.

3   Place sugar and cherry syrup in a small saucepan and place on a low heat to dissolve. Slowly bring to the boil and continue until the syrup has been reduced to the consistency of honey. Allow to cool before using.

Caramello Sam

PIZZA

2	tablespoons Custard (see page 159)
200	g Basic Pizza Dough ball (see page 61), rolled and ready
35	g raw brown sugar
15	g raw peanuts, crushed
10	g slivered almonds
10	g raw macadamia nuts, crushed
100	g fresh bananas, sliced
	Icing sugar for dusting
	Caramel Sauce

CARAMEL SAUCE

300	mL fresh cream
250	g caster sugar
70	g butter

1 Preheat the oven to 250°C for 25 minutes.

2 Spread the Custard evenly on the pizza base.

3 Top with raw sugar, nuts and banana slices.

4 Cook for seven to 10 minutes at 250°C.

5 Remove from the oven, dust with icing sugar and drizzle with Caramel Sauce. Cut into slices and serve.

1 Combine half the cream with all the sugar and butter in a heavy-based saucepan and place over a medium heat. Slowly bring to the boil, stirring continuously until smooth.

2 Remove from the heat and whisk in the remaining cream. If the sauce is too runny place back on a low flame and stir until you have a nice thick but still runny sauce. This sauce can be stored for up to seven days in the fridge.

7 CHANGING TABLES

THE BEST OF NEW YORK

Being a winner on the world stage is phenomenal, but the competitions are not just about testing my pizza-making skills. They are also opportunities to showcase Australian-style pizzas – which I think are the best in the world – as well as showing how we can work in teams. When the kitchen starts heating up at Little Caesars we say we're sweating like porn stars, and when it's really busy we're sweating like porn stars in a threesome! This is the kind of stamina and experience you need to take on seriously tough opposition in a new place with unfamiliar equipment and unknown ingredients.

In 2004, a year after winning the Australian 'Best of the Best' competition in Sydney, I was asked to join Team Oz – a group of pizza-makers sponsored by Dairy Farmers – and attend the America's Plate competition in New York. I met up with my cooking partner, Adelaide pizza-maker Andy Parisi, on the flight from Los Angeles to New York. This gave us some valuable time to talk about pizza. Believe it or not, for lunch the airline served us pizza – fat like a hamburger and definitely not the best in the world!

We spent the first 48 hours in New York recovering from jet lag, taking in some of the sights and, most importantly, sourcing all our ingredients. Obviously quarantine restrictions meant we were unable to bring our own, so we had a great time wandering through New York's markets and delicatessens finding the things we needed. Getting the right cheese was the biggest challenge. Most American cheeses have a high fat content and leave pools of oil on the pizza, something neither of us was happy about. We eventually settled on a low-fat skim-milk product that was most like Australian mozzarella. These shopping trips also enabled us to check out some typical New York pizza shops and convinced us we were in with a chance!

DAY 1 — FIRST COURSE

The first day of competition gave us a chance to try out all our new ingredients and to see what worked and what didn't. My role was to introduce the judges to Australian-style pizzas, with Andy as my partner. I had one hour on stage to make a suitable impression, so I decided to start with my Oysters Kilpatrick. Big mistake! The American public and judges had never heard of Oysters Kilpatrick. However, I gave a quick explanation and got on with it. Fortunately, the pizza's look and its strong flavours seemed to meet with their approval.

SECOND COURSE

For contrast I'd chosen a traditional Margherita (see page 36) as my second offering to show how a simple pizza could taste equally divine. I made a sauce with whole peeled tomatoes crushed with garlic, pesto, sea salt, cracked pepper and a little extra virgin olive oil, and topped it with low-fat skim-milk mozzarella and slices of fresh tomato. After 6½ minutes at 250°C it looked great, especially when finished with sea salt, cracked pepper, fresh basil and a generous drizzle of Western Australian extra virgin olive oil. The punters didn't have to say a word – their faces told me everything.

THIRD COURSE

Next up were my dessert pizzas. I didn't know how these would go down in New York because my research indicated very few places over there were making sweet pizza. I shouldn't have worried. I knew Americans loved Pecan Pie, so once my Mudhoney (see page 101) and New York Pecan Pie were baked and distributed the crowd went into a feeding frenzy – and were calling for more!

Theo & Andy

Oysters Kilpatrick

200 g Basic Pizza Dough ball (see page 61)

2 slices prosciutto, grilled and pulverised

1 teaspoon flat-leaf parsley, finely chopped

1 teaspoon extra virgin olive oil

2½ tablespoons Traditional Tomato Pizza Sauce

90 g mozzarella, grated

8 fresh oysters

8 slices pancetta (or diced bacon)

4 tablespoons Caramelised Onions (see page 123)

300 g smoked oysters

Worcestershire sauce, for drizzling

1 teaspoon flat-leaf parsley, finely chopped (extra)

Tabasco sauce (optional)

1 Preheat oven to 250°C for 25 minutes.

2 Prepare the pizza base using the dough, prosciutto, parsley and olive oil, and the method for making Flavoured Pizza Dough (see page 58).

3 Roll pizza dough on to a tray or pizza peel.

4 Spread Traditional Tomato Pizza Sauce evenly over the base leaving the edge sauce-free. Top with grated mozzarella.

5 Place smoked oysters and 2 tablespoons of caramelised onions evenly over the base.

6 Remove the oyster meat from the shells and wrap in pancetta. This will add flavour and protect the oysters from overcooking.

7 Put the oysters back in the shells and place them evenly around the pizza.

8 Add half a teaspoon of caramelised onions to each oyster shell. Place the other half-teaspoon of caramelised onions on the pizza in front of each oyster shell and top it with a smoked oyster.

9 Drizzle Worcestershire sauce into the oyster shells and all around the pizza.

10 Cook for seven to 10 minutes at 250°C.

11 Remove from the oven and cut into eight even slices, making sure each slice has an oyster shell.

12 Garnish with fresh chopped parsley and serve with Tabasco sauce for individual use.

New York Pecan Pie

PIZZA

125 g butter

125 g caster sugar

¼ teaspoon of vanilla bean paste or seeds
from a vanilla pod

2 large organic free-range eggs

125 g self-raising flour, triple sifted

75 g pecans, coarsely chopped

200 g Basic Pizza Dough ball
(see page 61), rolled and ready

Pecan Toffee

Caramel Sauce (see page 165)

Golden syrup

Icing sugar, to dust

Fresh cream, to serve

PECAN TOFFEE

150 g whole pecans

500 g sugar

250 mL water

1 Preheat the oven to 250°C for 25 minutes.

2 Combine the butter, sugar, vanilla bean paste or seeds and eggs in a bowl and beat until light and fluffy.

3 Sift in the flour and mix thoroughly.

4 Add the chopped pecans and fold through.

5 Spread the pecan mix evenly over the pizza base.

6 Cook seven to 10 minutes at 250°C. Check that the pizza is ready by lightly pushing the middle of the pudding with your fingertip. It's ready if it springs back slowly.

7 Remove from the oven and cut into slices. Scatter pieces of pecan toffee randomly on the top before adding a generous drizzle of caramel sauce and golden syrup. Finish with a dusting of icing sugar and serve with fresh cream.

1 Line a tray with baking paper and spread the pecans evenly across the surface.

2 In a pot or nonstick pan, dissolve the sugar in the water. Stir over a low heat until the syrup starts to boil. Keep stirring until the syrup turns a light brown.

3 Drizzle the hot toffee over the tray of pecans and leave for 20 minutes to cool and set before breaking into pieces. Pecan toffee will last for weeks — if you can resist the temptation of eating it!

END OF DAY ONE

The big queue of people waiting to taste our sweet pizza meant our time on stage on the first day of the New York competition was extended to two hours. After the demo small-time pizzeria owners from Texas to Singapore desperate to know about dessert pizzas swamped us with their questions. What a day! This bizarre experience ended with Steve Pennell, a reporter from the *West Australian*, Perth's daily newspaper, taking photos of Andy and me throwing pizza dough in Times Square!

We finished this magic day by having dinner at Les Halles, the famous New York restaurant where the head chef is Anthony

Bourdain, one of my kitchen heroes. While there I discovered copies of the Les Halles Cookbook for sale and I bought one. As we were leaving, Glen Austin, the team captain, spotted Anthony Bourdain at the bar and in typical Aussie style we went over to say G'day. Anthony was great. I told him how much I enjoyed his book *Kitchen Confidential*, especially the chapter entitled 'A day in the life…' because I thought he was writing about me. He laughed and said, 'Man – I feel your pain!' Then he signed my book with the lines, 'To Theo – good luck with the pizzas' and drew a big kitchen knife with blood dripping off the blade.

DAY TWO OF COMPETITION

The following day Andy was in front of the judges and I was helping him. He decided to make his Seafood Marinara pizza. We were invited back to do another workshop where we made his Potato & Pepperoni and Strawberry Flambé pizzas. Andy was going flat out trying to meet the demand for his Strawberry Flambés.

Finally, we all lined up on the stage for the results. Steven Green, the owner of the PMQ Pizza Exhibition Centre and presenter of America's Plate announced that the Italian team had won. He didn't even wait for the envelope with the winner's name to arrive. I was really surprised, but before we could feel any disappointment the Italian coach was on the stage with his team making his acceptance speech. Suddenly Steven Green interrupted the Italian. Talk about one of life's most embarrassing moments. Apparently Steven hadn't read the judging sheet properly and presumed Italy had won because their name was on the top of the list. But he hadn't read the actual scores and the real winner, by nine points, was Australia! We couldn't believe it! Our team was over the moon, leaping about and yelling our heads off. That night we had a wonderful celebration at New York's oldest pizzeria where, I'm happy to say, I had the best pizza I've ever had in that city.

I flew back into Perth on Saturday at 3pm, after exactly one week away. Thanks to a 36-hour flight and lost luggage in LA, I was wrecked. My whole family were at the airport to meet me, which was brilliant. All I wanted to do was go home and sleep but they took me straight to the shop. The news of our success had arrived before me, there were huge queues of people lined up at Little Caesars and the staff was struggling with the pressure! I finally finished work at 2am. I thought I would never experience a week like that in my life again, but I was wrong!

ITALIAN CHEF WARS

I returned to the US in 2006 to take part in quite a different competition – the Italian Chef Wars run by *Pizza Today* magazine. It is run along the lines of the Japanese cooking show *Iron Chef*. Four contestants, representing the USA, Italy, Canada and Australia, are given a list of 40 ingredients, which must be turned into an appetiser, main and dessert in 90 minutes. The knockout competition runs over two days with the winners from the first day going into the final on the second day. In this competition I was definitely the odd one out. I was competing against professional chefs cooking à la carte. Now that's serious pressure.

Once again I owe thanks to Alain Fabregues. When I told him I was doing this 'Black Box' thing (a selection of mystery ingredients) his advice was simple. 'Don't dick around,' he said. 'Just open the box and have a look. When you see something that you know from your shop – make that. Don't try to be too clever or you'll be lost.'

It turned out the ingredients were perfect for me. I decided to make a pizza-style Caesar salad with asparagus cooked in butter, followed by my Jane's Addiction with watermelon and basil salad. I would finish off with the Tea Party pizza, which I renamed French Cinnamon Teacake and served with poached pears, vanilla ice cream and a red merlot sugar-syrup sauce. Sweet!

By some sort of miracle I made it through the preliminary heat on the first day with a win over Chef Nick from Italy, which put me into the final against Chef Ted, the American entrant. Even though I'd made some mistakes and struggled without an assistant, I found out how things worked and knew I wouldn't make the same mistakes twice. My confidence got another boost when Pierre, the Canadian entrant, offered to be my assistant in the final.

Even though I didn't know Pierre very well we made a fantastic team and I finished with time to spare. In a weird way the result didn't really matter because I'd discovered something important. Success is all about having an efficient system and making simple things work. Mind you I'll never forget the seconds before the final announcement; 'And the winner is…[wait for it]…Chef [slowly, slowly, slowly]… Chef Theo!'

I was shocked. My dreams had come true. I thanked all the people who were there because they had been awesome, but I knew I never would have made it in Vegas if not for some very special people half a world away.

8 HOME DELIVERY

COMING HOME

Travelling overseas is great for broadening the mind, but sometimes you can get sucked in by the idea of trying something new just for the sake of being different. For example, on a recent trip to China, flying with Royal Brunei, I was offered two choices for lunch, beef curry or something I'd never heard of called 'noochee'. The person sitting next to me ordered the noochee, so I presumed it must be a local speciality. When I opened the meal I nearly pissed myself laughing. I'd ordered gnocchi, something I only ever eat if it's made by my wonderful Italian mother-in-law, Margherita.

As much as I enjoy trips away there's still nothing better than coming home. It may sound crazy, but I love the fact that Perth International Airport only has one baggage carousel; people like me can jump in the car at the airport and be home in less than 30 minutes. Being isolated from the rest of Australia and the world has its advantages. It's a bit like working in Mundaring, where being on the city's limits makes Little Caesars different from other pizza shops in Perth. Our isolation means I don't feel like I have to copy everyone 'down on the flats'. I can experiment and take the time to get my recipes right. Of course it also helps that

when people decide to make the trip up to the hills for a pizza, they are pretty hungry by the time they arrive.

As much as we love the city 'tourists', Little Caesars owes much more to the local population. When we first came to live in Mundaring and I was investigating the possibility of opening a pizza shop I discovered home delivery from the nearest outlet took two hours! Now that's not exactly fast food, so from the very beginning the local people were very happy to support a more convenient alternative.

And the locals are not just good customers. The town has also contributed to the business's success by providing a steady supply of good workers. Jobs at Little Caesars are highly sought-after because there's not that much part-time work in the town for teenagers and university students. Staff selection is quite simple. I just want my staff to be individuals. The work isn't very complicated but there are strict routines and people have to be able to fit into the production chain. Of course I'm the boss and I'm a bit of a dictator – but not the bullying type. Everyone knows where they stand in the chain and that makes Little Caesars a good place to work. It must be, because since we opened I've never sacked anyone.

Sometimes people look at me now and say, 'Gee, there must be a lot of money in pizza…' and my response is, 'No, but there is a lot of money in working 80 hours a week.' In fact, I've got much more than some money. One of the best things about my work is catching up with the kids who've left to take up professional careers and other jobs. It's great to hear them say how much they learned during their time at Little Caesars.

When I first moved to Mundaring there were very few gourmet outlets around so I developed the Mundaring Gourmet Pizza. Now this pizza remains a favourite for many customers.

MOVING ON

Little Caesars has changed massively since we opened in 1996 and it's now a time for decision making. I'm not keen to expand my business in Perth because I don't want to dilute what we do in Mundaring. It's great to be a one-of-a-kind place and not some part of a giant chain, especially now that everything is going so well. However, I know I have to keep moving forward and working on fresh ideas, but as my 'noochee' experience proved, I don't want to do something just for the sake of being different.

In recent times I've been doing some consultancy work in Indonesia. In fact, the Mundaring Gourmet Pizza has now gone

Indonesia

international, because last year I introduced it to our pizza outlet in Jakarta where it's almost as popular as it is here. When we were working on the menu for the Indonesian shop I was trying to get some distinct Asian flavours onto the menu. Green tea is a really popular Asian drink and it struck me as something that should be on the menu. This dessert pizza is now flying out the door in Jakarta, and if you're one of the many Australians who have developed a taste for green tea it might also appeal to you.

I'm not the only person in Mundaring who is thinking about the wider world. In August 2007 the town hosted Australia's inaugural Truffle Festival. This was an amazing opportunity to bring together some of Australia's finest chefs in a series of master classes where they highlighted the unique flavour of white and black truffles, which are now being cultivated in the southwest of Western Australia. The whole festival was a great success, although I suspect some of the locals are still wondering what happened to all the chocolates!

My role was to present a pizza-making demonstration and provide meals for festival workers. Everyone knows how expensive truffles are so I realised it was not realistic to use them as a pizza ingredient. However, because there are so many fantastic spin-off products I decided to use them as variations to existing pizza recipes at Little Caesars, and you can too. For example, why not try some of the following variations of ingredients:

- Truffle oil
- Truffle-flavoured seeded mustard
- Hazelnut duhka with truffle oil
- Hazelnuts soaked in Truffle flavoured honey.

Mundaring Gourmet

2½   tablespoons Traditional Tomato Pizza
      Sauce (see page 74)

200 g Basic Pizza Dough ball
      (see page 61), rolled and ready

25   g semi-sun-dried tomatoes,
      chopped roughly

90   g mozzarella, grated

6–8 slices peeled roasted eggplant, marinated
      in a tablespoon of Basil Pesto (see page
      74) and a clove of freshly chopped garlic

70   g fresh ricotta cheese, crumbled

1   teaspoon flat-leaf parsley, chopped

      Salt and cracked black pepper

1   Preheat the oven to 250°C for
      25 minutes.

2   Spread the Traditional Tomato
      Pizza Sauce evenly on the base,
      leaving the edge sauce-free.
      Place semi-sun-dried tomatoes
      evenly around the pizza and top
      with grated mozzarella.

3   Add the marinated eggplant and
      top with fresh ricotta.

4   Cook for seven to 10 minutes
      at 250°C.

5   Remove from the oven and cut into
      slices. Garnish with chopped flat-
      leaf parsley and season with
      salt and cracked black pepper
      before serving.

Green Tea

AKA GREEN DAY PIZZA

1	organic free-range egg, lightly beaten
55	g butter, melted
85	g caster sugar
85	g plain flour, triple sifted
	Pinch of salt
	Pinch of baking powder
20	g green tea powder
200	g Basic Pizza Dough ball (see page 61), rolled and ready
	Icing sugar, to dust
3	scoops vanilla-bean ice cream
	Green Tea Syrup for drizzling

GREEN TEA SYRUP

1	tablespoon green tea leaves
2	cups water
1	cup caster sugar

1 Preheat the oven to 250°C for 25 minutes.

2 Combine the lightly beaten egg and melted butter in a bowl. Add all the dry ingredients and mix well to form a smooth batter.

3 Spread this batter evenly across the pizza base.

4 Bake for seven to 10 minutes at 250°C.

5 Remove from the oven and cut into slices. Dust with icing sugar and place three scoops of ice cream in the centre of the pizza. Drizzle with Green Tea Syrup before serving.

1 Place all the ingredients in a small saucepan, and using a low heat bring to a gentle simmer. Keep on simmering until the syrup has reduced to the consistency of honey.

Peking Duck

DUCK

1	duck (about 2 kg)
2	tablespoons honey
2	tablespoons warm water
	Salt

PIZZA

200	g Basic Pizza Dough ball (see page 61), rolled and ready
120	g Peking Duck, sliced
90	g Mozzarella cheese, grated
2	Spring onions, sliced
½	Cucumber, sliced lengthways
2	Red chillies, finely sliced
	Hoisin sauce

1 Mix the honey and warm water together.

2 Cut the wing tips off the duck as they will burn during the cooking process. Rinse the duck under running water and then pat dry. Remove any excess fat from the cavity and if you don't like the look of the beak and nose chop that off as well.

3 Boil water in a pot big enough to hold the whole duck. When the water has boiled place the duck into the water and cook for three to four minutes as this will tighten the skin. Remove from the water, drain and pat dry.

4 While the skin is warm rub the salt all over and brush with the honey and water mixture. Place on a plate and store in the fridge overnight.

5 Preheat the oven at 200°C for 30 minutes.

6 Place the duck into a roasting tray breast side up and cook for 90 minutes, but check after 60 minutes to make sure the meat is not getting too dark.

7 Remove from the oven and carve. Cut up small pieces for the pizza, retaining the skin for serving with the pizza.

1 Preheat the oven to 250°C for 25 minutes.

2 Spread the mozzarella cheese evenly over the pizza base.

3 Place the Peking Duck pieces on the base, making sure there are no bones.

4 Cover with spring onions and place in the oven for seven to 10 minutes.

5 Remove from the oven and slice. Top with cucumber and red chillies, Drizzle hoisin sauce and finish with crispy Peking duck skin before serving.

THE ROAD TO CHINA

Some time before the Truffle Festival I had been thinking about the wider world. In late 2006 I travelled to China with two friends, Paul Zisopoulos and Raffaelle Brutzo, to conduct pizza demonstrations on behalf of PMQ *Pizza Magazine* at the Shanghai Food Expo. It was the most amazing experience and nothing could have prepared us for it. It wasn't just our tasty pizzas the Chinese chewed up. They soaked up every bit of information we could give them on weights, ingredients and techniques, and this signalled a great business opportunity.

Opening a number of pizza shops in Shanghai represents an interesting reversal of the usual pattern of Australia's trade with China. In this new and exciting venture several staff members from Little Caesars will be given the opportunity to work with us as managers in China. They've all finished their studies, so it will be a wonderful adventure. For me it's something else as well. The night I won the Italian Chef Wars in Las Vegas I found myself in a hotel room on my own. I had won a great prize but it didn't make me feel as good as I thought it would. I don't want to do things that way anymore. This time when I take on a new challenge I want all of us – family, friends and staff – to cross the finishing line together.

UWAP is an imprint of UWA Publishing
a division of The University of Western Australia.

THE UNIVERSITY OF
WESTERN AUSTRALIA
Achieve International Excellence

UWA Publishing
Crawley, Western Australia 6009
www.uwap.uwa.edu.au

This paperback edition reprinted in 2009.
Reprinted in 2009, 2011.
Copyright © Theo Kalogeracos 2008.

The moral right of the author has been asserted.

ISBN 978 1 921401 40 4 (pbk.)
A full CIP record for this book is available from
the National Library of Australia.

Consultant Writer: Lea Redding
Edited by Kate Evans
Designed & Typeset by Anna Maley-Fadgyas
Photography by Craig Kinder at f22 Photography
Assistant Photographer: Alana Blowfield
Styling by Ursula Nairn
Printed in Thailand by Imago

THANKS

Mia Famiglia. Elisabetta and Chaz-rae.

Liz, I spend more time working than at home and I'm sorry about that. One day it will change. Everything we have done we have done together – we started with nothing and we're trying to build something great. We will always have each other and our special boy and that's all we need.

Together forever. Xo

Chaz, you are growing up too fast and I miss you always. You are the first thing on my mind when I wake up and the last when I go to sleep. All I want to do is watch you grow into the man you will become. You can do anything and I will be there for you always, I love you.

From little things big things grow.

My biggest thanks are to UWA Publishing for the huge effort on this book. Without you all it would not have seen the light of day. As I have learnt on this journey, a book is not just one person's work but a group of talented people all working together. So, starting with Janice, thanks for taking scraps of paper and presenting them to Terri-ann, who took a punt on me – the minute I heard your 'Radiohead' ring tone I felt comfortable. Thank you for taking a risk on this book and I hope I don't let you down. To Lea, you poor thing having to tape my conversations and then go home and listen to me talk all over again. I doubt that you got anything out of it but I got a free therapist to listen to me talk about my life. Thanks a bunch to Kate for being there for every stage of the book. I think the best part of this book is the photos so thank you to the talented Craig Kinder and the hard arse Ursula Nairn – you took pizza to another level. To Anna, how do you know what images to use and where to put them? That's a tough job! Our helper on the shoot Alana, Emma for letting us use your house. Fiddy, Millar and Kate big love, and to Dexter from Arcla, thanks for the oven. For permitting photos to be taken at their work (as if they weren't busy enough) Kailis Bros. Seafood, Milkd Cafe and Mondo Butchers.

To all my Greek family, especially Mum your strength after what you have been through shines like the brightest star; Tas the fix-it brother (it must be duck time!), I can call you anytime and you are there for me; and thanks to the Aussie family you brought into our family, Trin and the kids – Greek/Aussies Evan and Yana lots of love. To all my Macedonian family, especially Yaya and Papou, I was lucky to grow up with you, everything I like about myself comes from you and you will never be far from my thoughts. To my Italian side, thank you all, especially Mamma for teaching me unconditional love – how can I repay you for that? And Zio, you bally, you have always been there and always will be there, you are my safety net. 'Grazie Tanto Zio'. Sandra and Louie for helping out at the very beginning, much thanks and the Anglo/Indian/Italian side, Milton, Flavia and Bianca.

To all the people who have worked at Little Caesars, some of you have been good but some of you have been great. I thank you for allowing me into your lives. As sad as it has been to see you go, I am happy to watch you grow and leave the nest of our little pizzeria to follow your own careers. To the loyal Mundaring pizza eaters and to the ones that travel from afar, you keep us all busy, make work enjoyable and we hope we never let you down. To Joe and Dion Panossion, who have kept Liz and I on the right track from the get go, many thanks. To my Mundaring brother Alain, together we have built a friendship out of our own madness of hard work and stubbornness. One day we will be old sitting on your farm in Toodyay wishing we where strong enough to get back in the kitchen, but that day is far away. Clifton family, friends for life. David and Florin thank you and congratulations on your newest family member – you took me out of Perth to Indonesia and you opened my eyes. To the Prince of Flesh, Mr Don, Olivier; standouts in Perth's foodie world. I've ended up with what I wanted – the face and hands of a worker and from looking at Craig's photos, too much coffee and not enough sleep! I got what I wished for. Cooking like rock and roll is a state of mind not an area code. To the Mundaring area, a very special place. Zop...this is only the beginning for us.

To Dairy Farmers who started all this with a competition that did not seem significant at the time but has turned my world up-side down. It has been a long journey with many stand-out people from within a big company, big thanks to you all for looking out for me along the way.

To the one person who told me 'don't be stupid of course you can write a book just write it down and I will fix it for you', little did she know that I don't use things like capital letters, full stops, commas or any other form of normal writing. Julie and your loving husband David, thank you both for starting this process and believing in me, I owe you dinner at the Loose Box as promised.

To Ryan Adams, Jeff Buckley, Nick Cave, The Eskys, J Mascis, Dom Mariani, Michael Miller, Mark Lanegan, The Jebs, Isaac Brock, Noel Gallagher, Thom Yorke, Kelly Jones, Todd Pickett, James Mercer, Billy Corgan, Led Zeppelin for the Presence album all killer no filler, Matthew Sweet, Elliott Smith, Bono, Jack White, Paul Weller, Josh Rouse, Tom Waits, Tim Rogers, Paul Kelly, Bon Scott, Paul Stanley, Gene Simmons, Lennon & McCartney, Alex Turner, J Cantrell, L Stanley, Henry Rollins, David McComb, Iggy Pop etc. etc. etc.

To the music from the radio, my CD's or fantastic vinyl LP's you have the ability to trigger a memory like nothing else. One song can remind me of a place, a food or a time and I thank you for that as I try and put a little of it into my pizzas. It's all about memories, you don't need photos or videos for those memories, the sound, taste and smell will take you back to your favourite pizzeria or to a place where you ate some amazing food.

La dolce vita!

UWA Publishing would also like to thank the following photographers for the use of their images: Robert Pickard; Market day, page 8; Vegetable patch, page 72; Cheese shop, page 77 and Vince Gareffa, page 107. Daniele Vinaccia, Firewood, page 42. Andrew W M Beierle, Tomato Sauce, page 73. Steven Pennells, Times Square, page 169. Peter Crumpton, Las Vegas, page 177. Nitesh Bhundia, Downtown Shanghai, page 189.